Time Series Analysis with Python Cookbook

Practical recipes for exploratory data analysis,
data preparation, forecasting, and model evaluation

Tarek A. Atwan

BIRMINGHAM—MUMBAI

Time Series Analysis with Python Cookbook

Copyright © 2022 Packt Publishing

Publishing Product Manager: Reshma Raman

Senior Editors: Roshan Ravikumar, Tazeen Shaikh

Content Development Editor: Shreya Moharir

Technical Editor: Rahul Limbachiya

Copy Editor: Safis Editing

Project Coordinator: Aparna Nair

Proofreader: Safis Editing

Indexer: Manju Arasan

Production Designer: Vijay Kamble

Marketing Coordinator: Priyanka Mhatre

First published: June 2022

Production reference: 1100622

Published by Packt Publishing Ltd.

Livery Place

35 Livery Street

Birmingham

B3 2PB, UK.

ISBN 978-1-80107-554-1

www.packt.com

To my mother, who never gets tired of providing unconditional love and support; everything I am, and the person I will become, I owe it to you.

Contributors

About the author

Tarek A. Atwan is a data analytics expert with over 16 years of international consulting experience, providing subject matter expertise in data science, machine learning operations, data engineering, and business intelligence. He has taught multiple hands-on coding boot camps, courses, and workshops on various topics, including data science, data visualization, Python programming, time series forecasting, and blockchain at different universities in the United States. He is regarded as an industry mentor and advisor, working with executive leaders in various industries to solve complex problems using a data-driven approach.

I owe a big thank you to Packt's fantastic editorial team for this project. Thank you for your dedication and persistence throughout this long journey to ensure this project is a success. I could not have done this without the love and support from my family, my mother, Hanan, Mohammad, Mai, and Ebtissam. I am grateful for the company of very talented and inspirational friends around me; thank you, Anish Sana and Ajit Sonawane, for being there. To my beautiful kids, this journey is for you to realize nothing in life comes easy; work hard, keep your heads up, and be the best you can be.

About the reviewers

Emil Bogomolov is a **machine learning** (**ML**) lead at Youpi Inc. He is engaged in creating new ways of collaboration using video. Previously, he was a research engineer in the computer vision group at the Skolkovo Institute of Science and Technology. He is the co-author of papers published at international conferences, such as VISAPP, WACV, and CVPR, and an educational courses author on data analysis at online schools. Emil is also a frequent speaker at technology conferences and author of tech articles on ML and AI.

Jeevanshu Dua has been working in the data science industry since 2019. When he completed a small ML course, he was offered work as an assistant teacher of Python, as he has a degree in engineering. He has recently joined Rangam as a data scientist to start a new journey in his career. He loves teaching and talking about data science.

I had immense pleasure reading and being a part of this book.

Prajjwal Nijhara is an electrical engineering student at Aligarh Muslim University and a member of the AUV-ZHCET club, where he works on computer vision. He is a mentor at AMU-OSS and has worked with DeepSource as a developer-relation intern for 6 months.

Catherine Azam is the lead architect at GoBubble, where she helps make the internet a safer, kinder place for everybody with a social media page by developing emotional AI that shields users from hateful posts. She started her career as a statistician and has had exposure to industries as varied as financial services, telecommunications, automotive, and blockchain, including working for companies such as Sky and IBM. She has held various job titles, from researcher to data scientist, data engineer to cloud engineer, and enjoys exploring random subjects by looking at datasets – anything that can be quantified, ranging from the hard sciences to humanities.

Table of Contents

3

Reading Time Series Data from Databases

4

Persisting Time Series Data to Files

5

Persisting Time Series Data to Databases

6

Working with Date and Time in Python

7

Handling Missing Data

8

Outlier Detection Using Statistical Methods

9

Exploratory Data Analysis and Diagnosis

10

Building Univariate Time Series Models Using Statistical Methods

13

Deep Learning for Time Series Forecasting

Index

Other Books You May Enjoy

Preface

A familiar association people make is between forecasting and financial data. In reality, forecasting is used in many industries, leveraging historical data to make future predictions. More specifically, this book is about time series analysis, a process to gain better insight from historical data, capture trends and cyclical patterns, and build a suitable forecasting model.

When working with data that contains observations that change over time and is recorded at specific intervals, you are dealing with time series data. You will find time series data in many domains, and the discipline of time series analysis covers various use cases. For example, time series analysis is used in science (forecasting weather, earthquakes, air quality, or species growth), finance (forecasting stock return, budget, sales, or volatility), government (forecasting inflation, unemployment rates, GDP, or population birth rate), medical (tracking infectious disease transmission, monitoring electrocardiogram or blood glucose, or forecasting healthcare costs), engineering (predictive maintenance, production decline analysis, or traffic volume forecasting), business (inventory management, product demand planning, resource planning), and much more. Pretty much, time series data is all around us, and you will most definitely be encountering such data.

By picking this book, you are looking for practical recipes that you can apply and use – less on theory and more on the practical. The book will take you through the complete journey of time series analysis, covering the end-to-end process, including acquiring and ingesting various types of time series data, exploring the data, transforming and manipulating the data, and training models to use in forecasting.

The book covers concepts, techniques, and algorithms commonly used and more advanced and recent approaches with practical use. For example, you will learn to train and validate different models covering statistical methods, machine learning algorithms, and various deep learning architectures for forecasting and outlier (or anomaly) detection. Most importantly, the variety of datasets used in this book will give you a better insight into how these different models work and how you can pick the most appropriate approach to solve your specific problem.

Who this book is for

This book is for data analysts, business analysts, data scientists, data engineers, or Python developers who want practical Python recipes for time series analysis and forecasting techniques. Fundamental knowledge of Python programming is required. Although having a basic math and statistics background will be beneficial, it is not necessary. Prior experience working with time series data to solve business problems will also help you to better utilize and apply the different recipes in this book.

What this book covers

Chapter 1, Getting Started with Time Series Analysis, is a general introduction to Python development best practices. You will learn different techniques to create and manage virtual environments, install and manage Python packages, manage dependencies, and finally, how to install and manage Jupyter extensions.

Chapter 2, Reading Time Series Data from Files, is an introduction to time series data. This chapter shows you how to read data from various and commonly used file types, whether stored locally or on the cloud. The recipes will highlight advanced options for ingesting, preparing, and transforming data into a time series DataFrame for later analysis.

Chapter 3, Reading Time Series Data from Databases, picks up from *Chapter 2, Reading Time Series Data from Files*, and focuses on reading data from various database systems, including relational (PostgreSQL and MySQL) and non-relational (MongoDB and InfluxDB), whether on-premises or a cloud service (Amazon Redshift and Snowflake). The recipes will highlight different methods and techniques to offer flexibility on how data can be ingested, prepared, and transformed into a time series DataFrame for later analysis.

Chapter 4, Persisting Time Series Data to Files, covers different options and use cases to store time series data for later retrieval. The techniques will cover various methods and file types, whether on-premises or in the cloud. In addition, this chapter covers serialization, compression, overwriting, or appending to files.

Chapter 5, Persisting Time Series Data to Databases, builds on *Chapter 4, Persisting Time Series Data to Files*, focusing on writing data for scale. This covers different techniques for writing data to relational and non-relational database systems like those discussed in *Chapter 2, Reading Time Series Data from Files*, including on-premises and cloud services.

Chapter 6, Working with Date and Time in Python, takes a practical and intuitive approach to an intimidating topic. You will learn how to deal with the complexity of dates and time in your time series data. The chapter illustrates practical use cases for handling time zones, custom holidays, and business days, working with Unix epoch and UTC. Typically, this intimidating topic is presented in a fun and practical way that you will find helpful to apply right away.

Chapter 7, Handling Missing Data, explores different methods for identifying and handling missing data. You will learn different imputation and interpolation techniques. The chapter starts with simple statistical methods for univariate imputation and then explores various univariate interpolation algorithms for more advanced multivariate imputation.

Chapter 8, Outlier Detection Using Statistical Methods, covers statistical methods for outlier and anomaly detection. These practical yet straightforward techniques are easy to interpret and implement. The chapter uses data from the **Numenta Anomaly Benchmark (NAB)** to evaluate different anomaly detection algorithms.

Chapter 9, Exploratory Data Analysis and Diagnosis, dives into visualization techniques for effective **Exploratory Data Analysis (EDA)** with interactive visualizations. You will learn how to investigate and diagnose your time series data to test for specific assumptions such as stationarity and autocorrelation. Finally, the chapter covers practical recipes for transforming your time series data using a family of power transforms, decomposition, and differencing methods.

Chapter 10, Building Univariate Time Series Models Using Statistical Methods, kick offs the journey into modeling and forecasting time series. The chapter intuitively explains what **autocorrelation function (ACF)** and **partial autocorrelation function (PACF)** plots are and how they are used, and then moves in to training, diagnosing, and comparing different models, including exponential smoothing, **autoregressive integrated moving average (ARIMA)**, and **seasonal ARIMA (SARIMA)**. Additionally, this chapter introduces grid search and hyperparameter tuning.

Chapter 11, Additional Statistical Modeling Techniques for Time Series, picks up from *Chapter 10, Building Univariate Time Series Models Using Statistical Methods*, diving into more advanced and practical models, such as **vector autoregressive (VAR)** for multivariate time series, **generalized autoregressive conditional heteroskedasticity (GARCH)** for forecasting volatility, and an introduction to the Prophet algorithm and library.

Chapter 12, Forecasting Using Supervised Machine Learning, will take you from classical time series forecasting techniques to more advanced machine learning algorithms. The chapter shows how time series data can be transformed appropriately to be suitable for supervised machine learning. In addition, you will explore a variety of machine learning algorithms and implement multi-step forecasting, using both scikit-learn and sktime.

Chapter 13, Deep Learning for Time Series Forecasting, covers more advanced deep learning architectures using TensorFlow/Keras and PyTorch. The chapter starts with a high-level API (Keras) and then dives into more complex implementations, using a lower-level API (PyTorch).

Chapter 14, Outlier Detection Using Unsupervised Machine Learning, continues from *Chapter 8, Outlier Detection Using Statistical Methods*, but focuses on more advanced unsupervised machine learning methods. You will use the same datasets from the NAB to allow you to compare statistical and machine learning techniques using the same benchmark data. The techniques cover a variety of machine learning algorithms.

Chapter 15, Advanced Techniques for Complex Time Series, will introduce more complex time series data that contains multiple seasonal patterns. The chapter includes how such time series data can be decomposed and explores different modeling techniques, including state-space models.

To get the most out of this book

You should be comfortable coding in Python, with some familiarity with Matplotlib, NumPy, and pandas. The book covers a wide variety of libraries, and the first chapter will show you how to create different virtual environments for Python development. Working knowledge of the Python programming language will assist with understanding the key concepts covered in this book; however, a Python crash-course tutorial is provided in the code bundle for anyone who needs a refresher. It is recommended, but not required, to install either **Anaconda**, **Miniconda**, or **Miniforge**. Throughout the chapters, you will see instructions using either pip or Conda.

Alternatively, you can use *Colab*, and all you need is a browser.

Software/hardware covered in the book	Operating system requirements
Python 3.7+	Windows, macOS, or Linux
JupyterLab or the Jupyter Notebook	Windows, macOS, or Linux

In *Chapter 3, Reading Time Series Data from Databases,* and *Chapter 5, Persisting Time Series Data to Databases,* you will be working with different databases, including PostgreSQL, MySQL, InfluxDB, and MongoDB. If you do not have access to such databases, you can install them locally on your machine or use Docker and download the appropriate image using `docker pull` to download images from Docker Hub `https://hub.docker.com` – for example, `docker pull influxdb` to download InfluxDB. You can download Docker from the official page here: `https://docs.docker.com/get-docker/`.

Alternatively, you can explore hosted services such as *Aiven* `https://aiven.io`, which offers a 30-day trial and supports PostgreSQL, MySQL, and InfluxDB. For the recipes using *AWS Redshift* and *Snowflake,* you will need to have a subscription. You can subscribe to the AWS free tier here: `https://aws.amazon.com/free`. You can subscribe for a 30-day Snowflake trial here: `https://signup.snowflake.com`.

Similarly, in *Chapter 2, Reading Time Series Data from Files,* and *Chapter 4, Persisting Time Series Data to Files,* you will learn how to read and write data to *AWS* S3 buckets. This will require an AWS service subscription and should be covered under the free tier. For a list of all services covered under the free tier, you can visit the official page here: `https://aws.amazon.com/free`.

If you are using the digital version of this book, we advise you to type the code yourself or access the code from the book's GitHub repository (a link is available in the next section). Doing so will help you avoid any potential errors related to the copying and pasting of code.

To get the most value out of this book, it is important that you continue to experiment with the recipes further using different time series data. Throughout the recipes, you will see a recurring theme in which multiple time series datasets are used. This is done deliberately so that you can observe how the results vary on different data. You are encouraged to continue with that theme on your own.

If you are looking for additional datasets, in addition to those provided in the GitHub repository, you can check out some of the following links:

- `https://ourworldindata.org`
- `https://www.kaggle.com/datasets?search=time+series`
- `https://github.com/numenta/NAB` (specific to anomaly and outlier detection)
- `https://fred.stlouisfed.org`
- `https://datasetsearch.research.google.com`

Download the example code files

You can download the example code files for this book from GitHub at `https://github.com/PacktPublishing/Time-Series-Analysis-with-Python-Cookbook`. If there's an update to code, it will be updated in the GitHub repository.

We also have other code bundles from our rich catalog of books and videos available at `https://github.com/PacktPublishing/`. Check them out!

Code in Action

The *Code in Action* videos for this book can be viewed at `https://bit.ly/3xDwOG1`.

Download the color images

We also provide a PDF file that has color images of the screenshots and diagrams used in this book. You can download it here: `https://static.packt-cdn.com/downloads/9781801075541_ColorImages.pdf`.

Conventions used

There are a number of text conventions used throughout this book.

`Code in text`: Indicates code words in text, database table names, folder names, filenames, file extensions, pathnames, dummy URLs, user input, and Twitter handles. Here is an example: "Mount the downloaded `WebStorm-10*.dmg` disk image file as another disk in your system."

A block of code is set as follows:

```
file = Path("../../datasets/Ch8/nyc_taxi.csv")
nyc_taxi = pd.read_csv(folder / file,
                       index_col='timestamp',
                       parse_dates=True)
nyc_taxi.index.freq = '30T'
```

Any command-line input or output is written as follows:

```
conda install -c conda-forge pyod
```

Bold: Indicates a new term, an important word, or words that you see on screen. For instance, words in menus or dialog boxes appear in **bold**. Here is an example: "Select **System info** from the **Administration** panel."

> **Tips or Important Notes**
> Appear like this.

Sections

In this book, you will find several headings that appear frequently (*Getting ready*, *How to do it...*, *How it works...*, *There's more...*, and *See also*).

To give clear instructions on how to complete a recipe, use these sections as follows.

Getting ready

This section tells you what to expect in the recipe and describes how to set up any software or any preliminary settings required for the recipe.

How to do it...

This section contains the steps required to follow the recipe.

How it works...

This section usually consists of a detailed explanation of what happened in the previous section.

There's more...

This section consists of additional information about the recipe in order to make you more knowledgeable about the recipe.

See also

This section provides helpful links to other useful information for the recipe.

Get in touch

Feedback from our readers is always welcome.

General feedback: If you have questions about any aspect of this book, email us at customercare@packtpub.com and mention the book title in the subject of your message.

Errata: Although we have taken every care to ensure the accuracy of our content, mistakes do happen. If you have found a mistake in this book, we would be grateful if you would report this to us. Please visit www.packtpub.com/support/errata and fill in the form.

Piracy: If you come across any illegal copies of our works in any form on the internet, we would be grateful if you would provide us with the location address or website name. Please contact us at copyright@packt.com with a link to the material.

If you are interested in becoming an author: If there is a topic that you have expertise in and you are interested in either writing or contributing to a book, please visit authors.packtpub.com.

Share Your Thoughts

Once you've read *Time Series Analysis with Python Cookbook*, we'd love to hear your thoughts! Scan the QR code below to go straight to the Amazon review page for this book and share your feedback.

https://packt.link/r/1-801-07554-9

Your review is important to us and the tech community and will help us make sure we're delivering excellent quality content.

1

Getting Started with Time Series Analysis

When embarking on a journey to learn coding in **Python**, you will often find yourself following instructions to install packages and import libraries, followed by a flow of a code-along stream. Yet an often-neglected part of any data analysis or data science process is ensure that the right development environment is in place. Therefore, it is critical to have the proper foundation from the beginning to avoid any future hassles, such as an overcluttered implementation or package conflicts and dependency crisis. Having the right environment setup will serve you in the long run when you complete your project, ensuring you are ready to package your deliverable in a reproducible and production-ready manner.

Such a topic may not be as fun and may feel administratively heavy as opposed to diving into the core topic or the project at hand. But it is this foundation that differentiates a seasoned developer from the pack. Like any project, whether it is a **machine learning** project, a **data visualization** project, or a **data integration** project, it all starts with planning and ensuring all the required pieces are in place before you even **begin** with the core development.

In this chapter, you will learn how to set up a **Python virtual environment**, and we will introduce you to two common approaches for doing so. These steps will cover commonly used environment management and package management tools. This chapter is designed to be hands-on so that you avoid too much jargon and can dive into creating your virtual environments in an iterative and fun way.

As we progress throughout this book, there will be several new Python libraries that you will need to install specific to **time series analysis**, **time series visualization**, **machine learning**, and **deep learning** on time series data. It is advised that you don't skip this chapter, regardless of the temptation to do so, as it will help you establish the proper foundation for any code development that follows. By the end of this chapter, you will have mastered the necessary skills to create and manage your Python virtual environments using either **conda** or **venv**.

The following recipes will be covered in this chapter:

- Development environment setup
- Installing Python libraries
- Installing JupyterLab and JupyterLab extensions

Technical requirements

In this chapter, you will be primarily using the command line. For macOS and Linux, this will be the default Terminal (`bash` or `zsh`), while on a Windows OS, you will use the **Anaconda Prompt**, which comes as part of the Anaconda installation. Installing Anaconda will be discussed in the following *Getting ready* section.

We will use **Visual Studio Code** for the IDE, which is available for free at `https://code.visualstudio.com`. It supports Linux, Windows, and macOS.

Other valid alternative options that will allow you to follow along include the following:

- **Sublime Text 3** at `https://www.sublimetext.com/3`
- **Atom** at `https://atom.io/`
- **PyCharm Community Edition** at `https://www.jetbrains.com/pycharm/download/`

The source code for this chapter is available at `https://github.com/PacktPublishing/Time-Series-Analysis-with-Python-Cookbook`.

Development environment setup

As we dive into the various recipes provided in this book, you will be creating different Python virtual environments to install all your dependencies without impacting other Python projects.

You can think of a virtual environment as isolated buckets or folders, each with a Python interpreter and associated libraries. The following diagram illustrates the concept behind isolated, self-contained virtual environments, each with a different Python interpreter and different versions of packages and libraries installed:

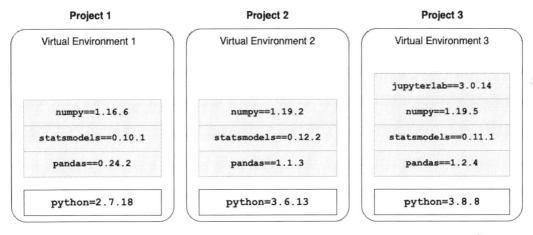

Figure 1.1 – An example of three different Python virtual environments, one for each Python project

These environments are typically stored and contained in separate folders inside the `envs` subfolder within the main Anaconda folder installation. For example, on macOS, you can find the `envs` folder under `Users/<yourusername>/opt/anaconda3/envs/`. On Windows OS, it may look more like `C:\Users\<yourusername>\anaconda3\envs`.

Each environment (folder) contains a **Python interpreter**, as specified during the creation of the environment, such as a Python 2.7.18 or Python 3.9 interpreter.

Generally speaking, upgrading your Python version or packages can lead to many undesired side effects if testing is not part of your strategy. A common practice is to replicate your current Python environment to perform the desired upgrades for testing purposes before deciding whether to move forward with the upgrades. This is the value that environment managers (`conda` or `venv`) and package managers (`conda` or `pip`) bring to your development and production deployment process.

Getting ready

In this section, it is assumed that you have the latest Python version installed by doing one of the following:

- The recommended approach is to install through a Python distribution such as **Anaconda** (`https://www.anaconda.com/products/distribution`), which comes preloaded with all the essential packages and supports Windows, Linux, and macOS (including M1 support as of version 2022.05). Alternatively, you can install **Miniconda** (`https://docs.conda.io/en/latest/miniconda.html`) or **Miniforge** (`https://github.com/conda-forge/miniforge`).

- Download an installer directly from the official Python site `https://www.python.org/downloads/`.

- If you are familiar with **Docker**, you can download the official Python image. You can visit Docker Hub to determine the desired image to pull `https://hub.docker.com/_/python`. Similarly, **Anaconda** and **Miniconda** can be used with Docker by following the official instructions here : `https://docs.anaconda.com/anaconda/user-guide/tasks/docker/`

At the time of writing, the latest Python version that's available is Python 3.10.4.

> **Latest Python Version Supported in Anaconda**
>
> The latest version of Anaconda, 2022.05, released on May 6, 2022, supports the latest version of Python 3.10.4. By default, Anaconda will implement Python 3.9.12 as the base interpreter. In addition, you can create a Python virtual environment with Python version 3.10.4 using `conda create`, which you will see later in this recipe.

The simplest and most efficient way to get you up and running quickly and smoothly is to go with a Python distribution such as *Anaconda* or *Miniconda*. I would even go further and recommend that you go with Anaconda.

If you are a macOS or Linux user, once you have Anaconda installed, you are pretty much all set for using your default Terminal. To verify the installation, open your Terminal and type the following:

```
$ conda info
```

The following screenshot shows the standard output when running `conda info`, which outlines information regarding the installed `conda` environment. You should be interested in the listed versions for both `conda` and Python:

```
> conda info

         active environment : base
        active env location : /Users/tarekatwan/opt/anaconda3
                shell level : 1
           user config file : /Users/tarekatwan/.condarc
     populated config files : /Users/tarekatwan/.condarc
              conda version : 4.13.0
        conda-build version : 3.21.8
             python version : 3.9.12.final.0
           virtual packages : __osx=10.16=0
                             __unix=0=0
                             __archspec=1=x86_64
           base environment : /Users/tarekatwan/opt/anaconda3  (writable)
          conda av data dir : /Users/tarekatwan/opt/anaconda3/etc/conda
      conda av metadata url : None
               channel URLs : https://repo.anaconda.com/pkgs/main/osx-64
                             https://repo.anaconda.com/pkgs/main/noarch
                             https://repo.anaconda.com/pkgs/r/osx-64
                             https://repo.anaconda.com/pkgs/r/noarch
              package cache : /Users/tarekatwan/opt/anaconda3/pkgs
                             /Users/tarekatwan/.conda/pkgs
           envs directories : /Users/tarekatwan/opt/anaconda3/envs
                             /Users/tarekatwan/.conda/envs
                   platform : osx-64
                 user-agent : conda/4.13.0 requests/2.27.1 CPython/3.9.12 Darwin/21.5.0 OSX/10.16
                    UID:GID : 501:20
                 netrc file : None
               offline mode : False
```

Figure 1.2 – Verifying Conda's installation on macOS using the Terminal

If you installed Anaconda on a Windows OS, you need to use Anaconda Prompt. To launch it, you can type Anaconda in the Windows search bar and select one of the Anaconda Prompts listed (**Anaconda Prompt** or **Anaconda PowerShell Prompt**). Once **Anaconda Prompt** has been launched, you can run the `conda info` command.

How to do it...

In this recipe, I will cover two popular environment management tools. If you have Anaconda, Miniconda, or Miniforge installed, then conda should be your preferred choice since it provides both *package dependency management* and *environment management* for Python (and supports many other languages). On the other hand, the other option is using venv, which is a Python module that provides *environment management*, comes as part of the standard library in Python 3, and requires no additional installation.

Both conda and venv allow you to create multiple virtual environments for your Python projects that may require different Python interpreters (for example, 2.7, 3.8, or 3.9) or different Python packages. In addition, you can create a sandbox virtual environment to experiment with new packages to understand how they work without affecting your base Python installation.

Creating a separate virtual environment for each project is a best practice taken by many developers and data science practitioners. Following this recommendation will serve you well in the long run, helping you avoid common issues when installing packages, such as package dependency conflicts.

Using Conda

Start by opening your terminal (Anaconda Prompt for Windows):

1. First, let's ensure that you have the latest conda version. This can be done by using the following command:

    ```
    conda update conda
    ```

    The preceding code will update the conda package manager. This is helpful if you are using an existing installation. This way, you make sure you have the latest version.

2. If you have Anaconda installed, then you can update to the latest version using the following command:

    ```
    conda update anaconda
    ```

3. You will now create a new virtual environment named py39 with a specific Python version, which in this case, is Python 3.9:

    ```
    $ conda create -n py39 python=3.9
    ```

    Here, -n is a shortcut for --name.

4. `conda` may identify additional packages that need to be downloaded and installed. You may be prompted on whether you want to proceed or not. Type y and then hit *Enter* to proceed.

5. You could have skipped the confirmation message in the preceding step by adding the -y option. Use this if you are confident in what you are doing and do not require the confirmation message, allowing `conda` to proceed immediately without prompting you for a response. You can update your command by adding the -y or --yes option, as shown in the following code:

```
$ conda create -n py39 python=3.9 -y
```

6. Once the setup is complete, you will be ready to *activate* the new environment. Activating a Python environment means that our $PATH environment variable will be updated to point to the specified Python interpreter from the virtual environment (folder). You can confirm this using the `echo` command:

```
$ echo $PATH
> /Users/tarekatwan/opt/anaconda3/bin:/Users/tarekatwan/
opt/anaconda3/condabin:/usr/local/bin:/usr/bin:/bin:/usr/
sbin:/sbin
```

The preceding code works on Linux and macOS. If you are using the Windows Anaconda Prompt you can use `echo %path%`. On the Anaconda PowerShell Prompt you can use `echo $env:path`.

Here, we can see that our $PATH variable is pointing to our base `conda` environment and not our newly created virtual environment.

7. Now, activate your new py39 environment and test the $PATH environment variable again. You will notice that it is now pointing to the envs folder – more specifically, the py39/bin subfolder:

```
$ conda activate py39
$ echo $PATH
> /Users/tarekatwan/opt/anaconda3/envs/py39/bin:/Users/
tarekatwan/opt/anaconda3/condabin:/usr/local/bin:/usr/
bin:/bin:/usr/sbin:/sbin
```

8. Another way to confirm that our new virtual environment is the active environment is by running the following command:

```
$ conda info --envs
```

The preceding command will list all the `conda` environments that have been created. Notice that `py39` is listed with an `*`, indicating it is the active environment. The following screenshot shows that we have four virtual environments and that `py39` is currently the active one:

```
> conda info --envs
# conda environments:
#
base                     /Users/tarekatwan/opt/anaconda3
fintech                  /Users/tarekatwan/opt/anaconda3/envs/fintech
py39                  *  /Users/tarekatwan/opt/anaconda3/envs/py39
timeseries               /Users/tarekatwan/opt/anaconda3/envs/timeseries
```

Figure 1.3 – List of all Python virtual environments that have been created using conda

9. Once you activate a specific environment, any package you install will only be available in that isolated environment. For example, let's install the pandas library and specify which version to install in the `py39` environment. At the time of writing, pandas 1.4.2 is the latest version:

```
$ conda install pandas=1.4.2
```

Notice that `conda` will prompt you again for confirmation to let you know what additional package will be downloaded and installed. Here, conda is checking for all the dependencies that pandas 1.4.2 needs and is installing them for you. You can also skip this confirmation step by adding the `-y` or `--yes` option at the end of the statement.

The message will also point out the environment location where the installation will occur. The following is an example of a prompted message for installing pandas 1.4.2:

```
> conda activate py39
> conda install pandas=1.4.2
Collecting package metadata (current_repodata.json): done
Solving environment: done

## Package Plan ##

  environment location: /Users/tarekatwan/opt/anaconda3/envs/py39

  added / updated specs:
    - pandas=1.4.2


The following packages will be downloaded:

    package                    |            build
    ---------------------------|-----------------------------
    numpy-1.22.3               |   py39h2e5f0a9_0          11 KB
    numpy-base-1.22.3          |   py39h3b1a694_0         5.1 MB
    ---------------------------------------------------------------
                                          Total:          5.1 MB

The following NEW packages will be INSTALLED:

    blas               pkgs/main/osx-64::blas-1.0-mkl
    bottleneck         pkgs/main/osx-64::bottleneck-1.3.4-py39h67323c0_0
    intel-openmp       pkgs/main/osx-64::intel-openmp-2021.4.0-hecd8cb5_3538
    mkl                pkgs/main/osx-64::mkl-2021.4.0-hecd8cb5_637
    mkl-service        pkgs/main/osx-64::mkl-service-2.4.0-py39h9ed2024_0
    mkl_fft            pkgs/main/osx-64::mkl_fft-1.3.1-py39h4ab4a9b_0
    mkl_random         pkgs/main/osx-64::mkl_random-1.2.2-py39hb2f4e1b_0
    numexpr            pkgs/main/osx-64::numexpr-2.8.1-py39h2e5f0a9_0
    numpy              pkgs/main/osx-64::numpy-1.22.3-py39h2e5f0a9_0
    numpy-base         pkgs/main/osx-64::numpy-base-1.22.3-py39h3b1a694_0
    packaging          pkgs/main/noarch::packaging-21.3-pyhd3eb1b0_0
    pandas             pkgs/main/osx-64::pandas-1.4.2-py39he9d5cce_0
    pyparsing          pkgs/main/noarch::pyparsing-3.0.4-pyhd3eb1b0_0
    python-dateutil    pkgs/main/noarch::python-dateutil-2.8.2-pyhd3eb1b0_0
    pytz               pkgs/main/noarch::pytz-2021.3-pyhd3eb1b0_0
    six                pkgs/main/noarch::six-1.16.0-pyhd3eb1b0_1


Proceed ([y]/n)? y
```

Figure 1.4 – Conda's confirmation prompt listing all the packages

10. Once you press *y* and hit *Enter*, conda will begin downloading and installing these packages.

11. Once you are done working in the current py39 environment, you can deactivate and return to the base Python as shown in the following command:

```
$ conda deactivate
```

12. If you no longer need the py39 environment and wish to delete it, you can do so with the env remove command. The command will completely delete the environment and all the installed libraries. In other words, it will delete (remove) the entire folder for that environment:

```
$ conda env remove -n py39
```

Using venv

Once Python 3x has been installed, you get access to the built-in venv module, which allows you to create virtual environments (similar to conda). Notice that when using venv, you will need to provide a *path* to where you want the virtual environment (folder) to be created. If one isn't provided, it will be created in the current directory where you are running the command from. In the following code, we will create the virtual environment in the Desktop directory.

Follow these steps to create a new environment, install a package, and then delete the environment using venv:

1. First, decide where you want to place the new virtual environment and specify the path. In this example, I have navigated to Desktop and ran the following command:

```
$ cd Desktop
$ python -m venv py3
```

The preceding code will create a new py3 folder in the Desktop directory. The py3 folder contains several subdirectories, the Python interpreter, standard libraries, and other supporting files. The folder structure is similar to how conda creates its environment folders in the envs directory.

2. Let's activate the py3 environment and examine the $PATH environment variable to verify that it is active. The following script is for Linux and macOS (bash or zsh) and assumes you are running the command from the Desktop directory:

```
$ source py3/bin/activate
$ echo $ PATH
> /Users/tarekatwan/Desktop/py3/bin:/Users/tarekatwan/
opt/anaconda3/bin:/Users/tarekatwan/opt/anaconda3/
condabin:/usr/local/bin:/usr/bin:/bin:/usr/sbin:/sbin
```

Here, we can see that the py3 environment has been activated.

On Windows, there is no bin subfolder, so you will need to run the command using the following syntax, again assuming you are running the command from the Desktop directory:

```
$ py3/Scripts/activate.bat
```

If you are running the command in PowerShell, you will need to specify Activate.ps1, as shown in the following:

```
py3\Scripts\Activate.ps1
```

3. Now, let's check which version has been installed by using the following command:

```
$ python --version
> Python 3.9.12
```

4. Once you are done developing using the py3 environment, you can deactivate it to return to the base Python environment using the deactivate command:

```
$ deactivate
```

5. If you no longer need the py3 environment and wish to remove it, just delete the entire py3 folder and that's it.

How it works...

Once a virtual environment is activated, you can validate the location of the active Python interpreter to confirm that you are using the right one. Earlier, you saw how the $PATH environment variable changes once you activate a virtual environment. You can achieve similar results using the which command in Linux and macOS, the Get-Command in Windows PowerShell, or the where command in Windows Command Prompt.

The following is an example on macOS:

```
$ which python
> /Users/tarekatwan/opt/anaconda3/envs/py39/bin/python
```

This will show the path to the Python interpreter. The output of the preceding statement will show a different path, depending on whether the environment was created with conda or venv. When activating a conda virtual environment, it will be inside the envs folder, as shown in the following:

```
/Users/tarekatwan/opt/anaconda3/envs/py39/bin/python
```

When activating a venv virtual environment, the path will be the same path that you provided when it was created, as shown here:

```
/Users/tarekatwan/Desktop/py3/bin/python
```

Any additional packages or libraries that you install after you have *activated* a virtual environment will be isolated from other environments and reside in the environment's folder structure.

If we compare the folder structures of both venv and conda, you can see similarities, as shown in the following screenshot:

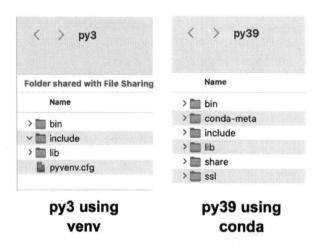

Figure 1.5 – Comparing folder structures using conda and venv

Recall that when using `conda`, all environments will default to the `/envs/` location inside the `anaconda3/` directory. When using `venv`, you need to provide a path to specify where to create the directory or project; otherwise, it will default to the current directory that you used to run the command. Similarly, you can specify a different path using `conda` with the option `-p` or `--prefix`. Note that when using `venv`, you cannot specify the Python version since it relies on the active or base Python version being used to run the command. This is in contrast to `conda`, which allows you to specify a different Python version regardless of the base Python version installed. For example, the current Python version for the base environment is 3.9.12, and you can create a 3.10.4 environment using the following:

```
conda create -n py310 python=3.10 -y
```

The preceding code will create a new `py310` environment with Python 3.10.4.

Another advantage of `conda`, is that it provides two features: a *package and dependency manager* and a *virtual environment manager*. This means we can use the same `conda` environment to create additional environments using `conda create`, and also install packages using `conda install <package name>`, which you will use in the next recipe, *Installing Python libraries*.

Keep in mind that when using `venv`, it is *only* a virtual environment manager, and you will still need to rely on `pip` as a package manager to install packages; for example, `pip install <package name>`.

Additionally, when using `conda` to install packages, it will check for any conflicts and will prompt you for any recommendations, including the need to upgrade, downgrade, or install additional package dependencies.

Lastly, an added benefit of using `conda` is that you can create environments for other languages and not just Python. This includes Julia, R, Lua, Scala, Java, and more.

There's more...

In the preceding examples, you were able to create Python virtual environments from scratch using `conda`. The virtual environments you created do not contain any packages yet, so you will need to install the required packages for your project.

There are other ways to create your virtual environment in `conda` that we will discuss here.

Creating a virtual environment using a YAML file

You can create a virtual environment from a **YAML** file. This option gives greater control in defining many aspects of the environment, including all the packages that should be installed all in one step.

You can create a YAML file in VSCode. Here is an example of a YAML file (`env.yml`) that creates a `conda` environment labeled `tscookbook` using Python 3.9:

```
#env.yml
name: tscookbook
channels:
  - conda-forge
  - defaults
dependencies:
  - python=3.9
  - pip
  # Data Analysis
  - statsmodels
  - scipy
  - pandas
  - numpy
  - tqdm
  # Plotting
  - matplotlib
  - seaborn
  # Machine learning
  - scikit-learn
  # Jupyter Environment
  - jupyter
```

To create your virtual environment using the `env.yml` file, you can use `conda env create -f`, like so:

```
$ conda env create -f env.yml
```

Once this process is completed, you can activate the environment:

```
$ conda activate tscookbook
```

You can also bootstrap your YAML file from an existing environment. This is very useful if you want to share your environment configurations with others or create a backup for later use. This can be done with the following command from the activated environment:

```
$ conda env export > environment.yml
```

This will generate the environment.yml file for you.

Cloning a virtual environment from another environment

This is a great feature if you want to experiment with new packages or upgrade existing packages, but you do not want to risk breaking the existing code in your current project. Here, you can opt to create a copy of your environment so that you can do your experiments there before you decide whether to proceed with the changes. Cloning can be done in conda with the following command:

```
$ conda create --name newpy39 --clone py39
```

See also

It is worth mentioning that Anaconda comes with another tool called **anaconda-project** to package your conda project artifacts and create a YAML file for reproducibility. Think of this as an alternative approach to developing your YAML manually. For more information, please reference the official GitHub repository here: https://github. com/Anaconda-Platform/anaconda-project.

For a list of arguments, you can type the following in your terminal:

```
$ anaconda-project --help
```

If you are using a machine that does not allow you to install any software or you are using an older machine with limited capacity or performance, then do not worry. There are other options so that you can follow the recipes in this book.

Some alternative options that you can explore are as follows:

- **Google Colab** comprises hosted Python notebooks that already have some of the most popular data science packages preinstalled, including pandas, statsmodels, scikit-learn, and TensorFlow. Colab allows you to install additional packages from within the notebook using pip install. A great feature of Colab is that you get the option to configure your notebook so that you can use a CPU, GPU, or TPU for free. You can explore Colab by going to https://colab.research. google.com/.

- **Kaggle Notebooks**, similar to Colab, comprises hosted Jupyter notebooks with many of the most popular data science packages already preinstalled. It also allows you to `pip install` any additional packages that are required. For more information, please refer to `https://www.kaggle.com/docs/notebooks`.

- **Replit** offers a free, in-browser IDE that supports more than 50+ languages, including Python. All you need to do is create an account and create your new `replit` space (`https://replit.com/`).

Installing Python libraries

In the preceding recipe, you were introduced to the YAML environment configuration file, which allows you to create a Python virtual environment and all the necessary packages in one step using one line of code:

```
$ conda env create -f environment.yml
```

Throughout this book, you will need to install several Python libraries to follow the recipes. There are several methods for installing Python libraries, which you will explore in this recipe.

Getting ready

You will create and use different files in this recipe, including a `requirements.txt`, `environment_history.yml`, and other files. These files are available to download from the GitHub repository for this book: `https://github.com/PacktPublishing/Time-Series-Analysis-with-Python-Cookbook./tree/main/code/Ch1`.

In this chapter, you will become familiar with how to generate your `requirements.txt` file, as well as installing libraries in general.

How to do it...

The easiest way to install a collection of libraries at once is by using a `requirements.txt` file.

In a nutshell, the `requirements.txt` file lists the Python libraries and their associated versions that you want to install. You can create your `requirements.txt` file manually or export it from an existing Python environment.

Using conda

With `conda`, you have different options for installing our packages in bulk. You can either create a new environment and install all the packages listed in a `requirements.txt` file at once (using the `conda create` statement), or you can install the Python packages to an existing environment using the `requirements.txt` file (using the `conda install` statement):

- *Option 1*: Create a new `conda` environment and install the libraries in one step. For example, you can create a new environment for each chapter and use the associated `requirements.txt` file:

```
$ conda create --name ch1 -f requirements.txt
```

- *Option 2*: Install the necessary libraries to an existing `conda` environment. In this example, you have an existing `timeseries` environment, which you will need to activate first and then install the libraries from the `requirements.txt` file:

```
$ conda activate timeseries
$ conda install -f requirements.txt
```

Using venv and pip

Since `venv` is just an environment manager, you will need to use `pip` as your package manager tool. You will start by using `venv` to create a new environment, and then use `pip` to install the packages:

- On *Mac/Linux*: Create and then activate the `venv` environment before you install the packages:

```
$ python -m venv Desktopn/timeseries
$ source Desktopn/timeseries/bin/activate
$ pip install -r requirements.txt
```

- On *Windows*: Create and activate the `venv` environment and then install the packages:

```
$ python -m venv .\Desktop\timeseries
$ .\Desktop\timeseries\Scripts\activate
$ pip install -r requirements.txt
```

Notice that in the preceding code for Windows, the `activate` file extension was not specified (either `.bat` or `.ps1`). This is valid and will work on either Windows Prompt or PowerShell.

How it works...

In the preceding code, the `requirements.txt` file was provided so that you can install the necessary libraries.

But how can you generate your `requirements.txt` file?

There are two approaches to creating the `requirements.txt` file. Let's take a look at both.

Creating the file manually

Since it is a simple file format, you can create the file using any text editor, such as VSCode, and list the packages you want to install. If you do not specify the package version, then the latest version that's available will be considered for installation. See the following example for the `simple.txt` file (*hint: the file does not need to be named* `requirements.txt`):

```
pandas==1.4.2
matplotlib
```

First, let's test out `venv` and `pip`. Run the following script (I am running this on a Mac):

```
$ python -m venv ch1
$ source ch1/bin/activate
$ pip install -r simple.txt
$ pip list
Package           Version
---------------   -------
cycler            0.11.0
fonttools         4.33.3
kiwisolver        1.4.2
matplotlib        3.5.2
numpy             1.22.4
packaging         21.3
pandas            1.4.2
Pillow            9.1.1
pip               22.0.4
pyparsing         3.0.9
python-dateutil   2.8.2
pytz              2022.1
setuptools        58.1.0
```

```
six                    1.16.0

$ deactivate
```

What are those additional packages? These are based on the dependencies in `pandas` and `matplotlib` that `pip` identified and installed for us.

Now, let's use the same `simple.txt` file but using `conda` this time:

```
$ conda create -n ch1  --file simple.txt python=3.9
```

Once the installation is completed, you can activate the environment and list the packages that were installed:

```
$ conda activate ch1
$ conda list
```

You may notice that the list is pretty large. More packages are installed compared to the `pip` approach. You can get a count of the libraries that have been installed using the following command:

```
$ conda list | wc -l
> 54
```

There are a few things to keep in mind here:

- `conda` installs packages from the Anaconda repository, as well as from the Anaconda cloud.

- `pip` installs packages from **Python Package Index (PyPI)** repository.

- `conda` does a very thorough analysis of all the packages it plans to download and does a better job when it comes to version conflicts than `pip`.

Bootstrapping a file

The second option is to generate the `requirements.txt` file from an existing environment. This is very useful when you are recreating environments for future use or when sharing your list of packages and dependencies with others, to ensure reproducibility and consistency. Say you worked on a project and installed specific libraries and you want to ensure that when you share your code, other users can install the same libraries. This is where generating the `requirements.txt` file comes in handy. Similarly, the option to export the YAML environment configuration file was demonstrated earlier.

Let's see how this can be done in both `pip` and `conda`. Keep in mind that both methods will export the list of packages that are already installed and their current versions.

venv and pip freeze

`pip freeze` allows you to export all pip-installed libraries in your environment. First, activate the `ch1` environment you created earlier with `venv`, then export the list of packages to a `requirements.txt` file. The following example is on a macOS using the Terminal:

```
$ source ch1/bin/activate
$ pip freeze > requirements.txt
$ cat requirements.txt
>>>
cycler==0.11.0
fonttools==4.33.3
kiwisolver==1.4.2
matplotlib==3.5.2
numpy==1.22.4
...
```

Once done, you can run the `deactivate` command.

Conda

Let's activate the environment we created earlier with `conda` (the `ch1` environment) and export the list of packages:

```
$ conda activate ch1
$ conda list -e > conda_requirements.txt
$ cat conda_requirements.txt
>>>
# This file may be used to create an environment using:
# $ conda create --name <env> --file <this file>
# platform: osx-64
blas=1.0=mkl
bottleneck=1.3.4=py39h67323c0_0
brotli=1.0.9=hb1e8313_2
ca-certificates=2022.4.26=hecd8cb5_0
certifi=2022.5.18.1=py39hecd8cb5_0
```

```
cycler=0.11.0=pyhd3eb1b0_0
...
```

There's more...

When you exported the list of packages installed with conda, the conda_
requirements.txt file contained a large list of packages. If you want to export only the
packages that you explicitly installed (without the additional packages that conda added),
then you can use conda env export command with the --from-history flag:

```
$ conda activate ch1
$ conda env export --from-history > env.yml
$ cat env.yml
>>>
name: ch1
channels:
  - defaults
dependencies:
  - matplotlib
  - pandas==1.2.0
prefix: /Users/tarek.atwan/opt/anaconda3/envs/ch1
```

Note that you do not have to activate that environment first, as we have been doing so far.
Instead, you can add the -n or --name option to specify the name of the environment.
Otherwise, it will default to the currently active environment. This is what the modified
script would look like:

```
conda env export -n ch1 --from-history > env.yml
```

See also

- To find a list of all the available packages from Anaconda, you can visit https://
  docs.anaconda.com/anaconda/packages/pkg-docs/.
- To search for package in the PyPI repository, you can visit https://pypi.org/.

Installing JupyterLab and JupyterLab extensions

Throughout this book, you can follow along using your favorite Python IDE (for example, PyCharm or Spyder) or text editor (for example, Visual Studio Code, Atom, or Sublime). There is another option based on the concept of notebooks that allows interactive learning through a web interface. More specifically, Jupyter Notebook or JupyterLab are the preferred methods for learning, experimenting, and following along with the recipes in this book. Interestingly, the name Jupyter is derived from the three programming languages: Julia, Python, and R. Alternatively, you can use Google's Colab or Kaggle Notebooks. For more information, refer to the *See also* section from the *Development environment setup* recipe of this chapter. If you are not familiar with Jupyter Notebooks, you can get more information here: `https://jupyter.org/`.

In this recipe, you will install Jupyter Notebook, JupyterLab, and additional JupyterLab extensions.

Additionally, you will learn how to install individual packages as opposed to the bulk approach we tackled in earlier recipes.

> **Using Conda in Future Examples**
>
> Moving forward, when a new environment is created or additional packages are installed, the code will be written using `conda`. The previous recipes already covered the two different approaches to creating virtual environments (`venv` versus `conda`) and installing packages (`pip` versus `conda`), which should allow you to proceed with whichever choice you prefer.

Getting ready

We will create a new environment and install the main packages needed for this chapter, primarily pandas:

```
$ conda create -n timeseries python=3.9 pandas -y
```

This code creates a new Python 3.9 environment named `timeseries`. The last portion of the statement lists the individual packages that you will be installing. If the list of packages is large, you should use a `requirements.txt` file instead. If there is a handful of packages, then they can be listed individually separated by spaces, as follows:

```
$ conda create -n timeseries python=3.9 pandas matplotlib
statsmodels -y
```

Once the environment has been created and the packages have been installed, go ahead and activate it:

```
$ conda activate timeseries
```

How to do it...

Now that we have created our environment and activated it, let's install Jupyter:

1. Now that we have activated our environment, we can simply use `conda install` to install any additional packages that were not included in `conda create`:

    ```
    $ conda install jupyter -y
    ```

2. You can launch your JupyterLab instance by typing the following command:

    ```
    $ jupyter lab
    ```

    Notice that this runs a local web server and launches the JupyterLab interface on your default browser, pointing to `localhost:8888/lab`. The following screenshot shows a similar screen that you would see in your terminal once you've typed in the preceding code:

Figure 1.6 – Launching JupyterLab will run a local web server

3. To terminate the web server, press *Ctrl* + *C* twice on your terminal or click **Shut Down** from the **File** menu in the Jupyter GUI, as shown in the following screenshot:

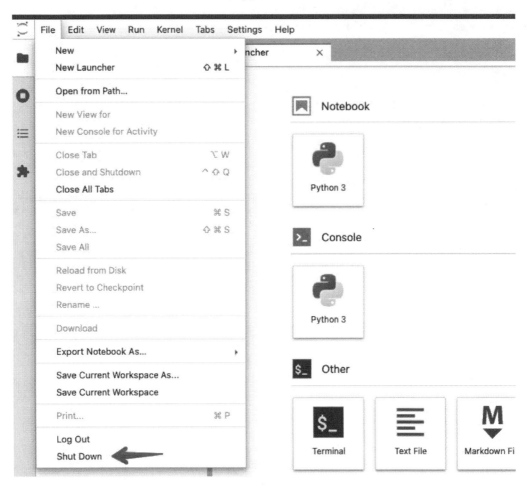

Figure 1.7 – Shutting down the JupyterLab web server

4. Now, you can safely close your browser.

5. Notice that in the preceding example, when JupyterLab was initiated, it launched on your default browser. If you wish to use a different browser, you can update the code like so:

```
$ jupyter lab --browser=chrome
```

In this example, I am specifying that I want it to launch on Chrome as opposed to Safari, which is the default on my machine. You can change the value to your preferred browser, such as Firefox, Opera, Chrome, and so on.

6. If you do not want the system to launch the browser automatically, you can do this with the following code:

```
$ jupyter lab --no-browser
```

The web server will start, and you can open any of your preferred browsers manually and just point it to `http://localhost:8888`.

If you are asked for a token, you can copy and paste the URL with the token as displayed in the Terminal, which looks like this:

```
To access the server, open this file in a browser:
        file:///Users/tarek.atwan/Library/Jupyter/
runtime/jpserver-44086-open.html
    Or copy and paste one of these URLs:
        http://localhost:8888/lab?token=5c3857b9612aecd3
c34e9a40e5eac4509a6ccdbc8a765576
    or http://127.0.0.1:8888/lab?token=5c3857b9612aecd3
c34e9a40e5eac4509a6ccdbc8a765576
```

7. Lastly, if the default `port 8888` is in use or you wish to change the port, then you can add `-p` and specify the port number you desire, as shown in the following example. Here, I am instructing the web server to use `port 8890`:

```
$ jupyter lab --browser=chrome --port 8890
```

This will launch Chrome at `localhost:8890/lab`.

8. Notice that when JupyterLab launches, you only see one kernel in the **Notebooks/Console** sections. This is the base Python kernel. The expectation was to see two kernels reflecting the two environments we have: the base and the `timeseries` virtual environment. Let's check how many virtual environments we have with this command:

A. The following screenshot shows the JupyterLab interface, with only one kernel. This belongs to the base environment:

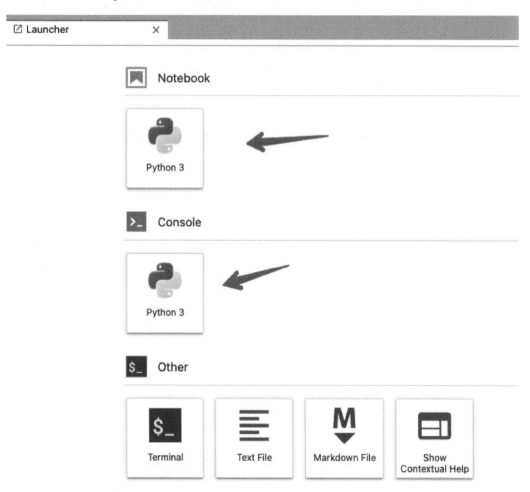

Figure 1.8 – JupyterLab interface showing only one kernel, which belongs to the base environment

B. The following screenshot shows the two Python environments:

```
> conda info --envs
# conda environments:
#
base                     /Users/tarek.atwan/opt/anaconda3
timeseries            *  /Users/tarek.atwan/opt/anaconda3/envs/timeseries
```

Figure 1.9 – Showing two Python environments

We can see that the timeseries virtual environment is the active one.

9. You will need to install a Jupyter kernel for the new `timeseries` environment. First, shut down the web server (though it will still work even if you did not). Assuming you are still in the active `timeseries` Python environment, just type the following command:

```
$ python -m ipykernel install --user  --name timeseries
--display-name "Time Series"
> Installed kernelspec timeseries in /Users/tarek.atwan/
Library/Jupyter/kernels/timeseries
```

10. We can check the number of kernels available for Jupyter using the following command:

```
$ jupyter kernelspec list
```

The following screenshot shows the `kernelspec` files that were created and their location:

```
> jupyter kernelspec list
Available kernels:
  timeseries     /Users/tarek.atwan/Library/Jupyter/kernels/timeseries
  python3        /Users/tarek.atwan/opt/anaconda3/envs/timeseries/share/jupyter/kernels/python3
```

Figure 1.10 – List of kernels available for Jupyter

These act as pointers that connect the GUI to the appropriate environment to execute our Python code.

11. Now, you can launch your JupyterLab again and notice the changes:

```
$ jupyter lab
```

The following screen will appear once it has been launched:

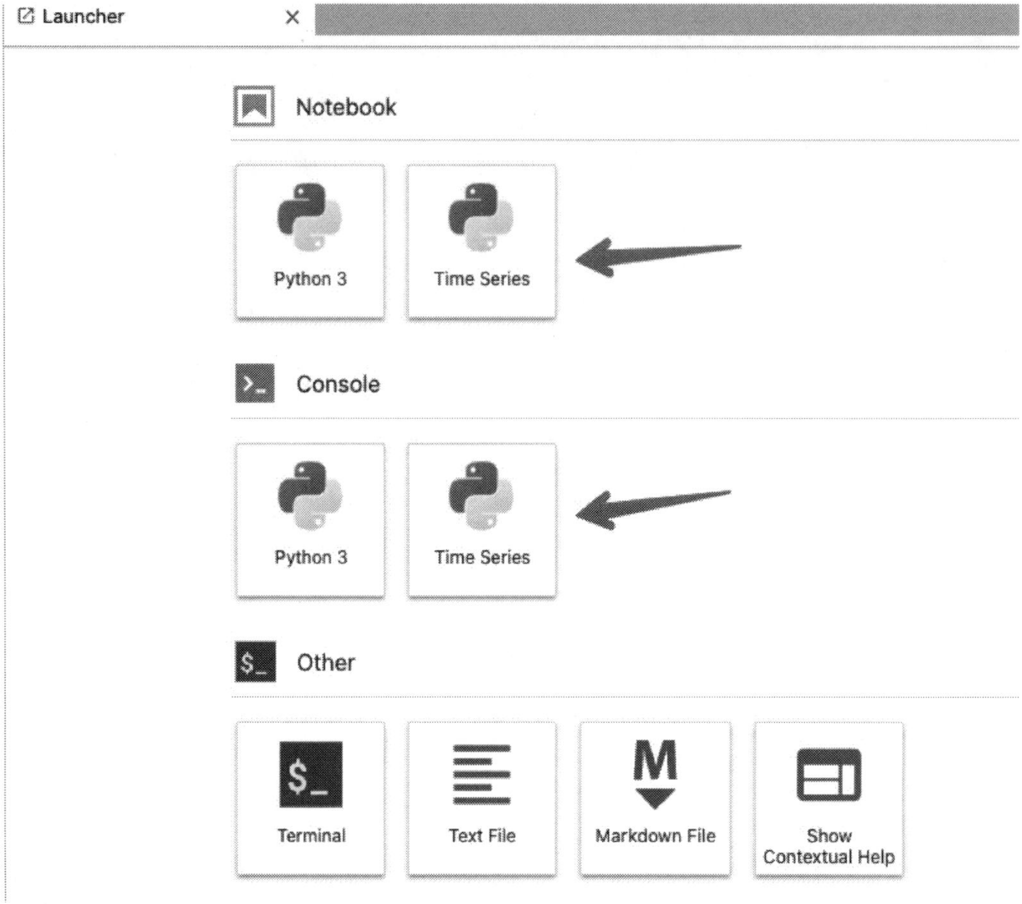

Figure 1.11 – Notice now our Time Series kernel is available in JupyterLab

How it works...

When you created the new `timeseries` environment and installed our desired packages using `conda install`, it created a new subfolder inside the `envs` folder to isolate the environment and packages installed from other environments, including the base environment. When executing the `jupyter notebook` or `jupyter lab` command from the base environment, it will need to read from a `kernelspec` file (JSON) to map to the available kernels in order to make them available. The `kernelspec` file can be created using `ipykernel`, like so:

```
python -m ipykernel install --user  --name timeseries
--display-name "Time Series"
```

Here, `--name` refers to the environment name and `--display-name` refers to the display name in the Jupyter GUI, which can be anything you want. Now, any libraries that you install inside the `timeseries` environment can be accessed from Jupyter through the kernel (again, think of it as a mapping between the Jupyter GUI and the backend Python environment).

There's more...

JupyterLab allows you to install several useful extensions. Some of these extensions are created and managed by Jupyter, while others are created by the community.

You can manage JupyterLab extensions in two ways: through the command line using `jupyter labextension install <someExtension>` or through the GUI using **Extension Manager**. The following screenshot shows what the Jupyter Extension Manager UI looks like:

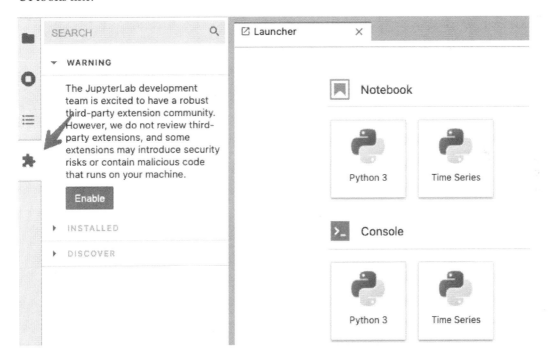

Figure 1.12 – Clicking the extension manager icon in JupyterLab

Once you click **Enable**, you will see a list of available Jupyter extensions. To install an extension, just click on the **Install** button.

Some packages will require Node.js and npm to be installed first and you will see a warning similar to the following:

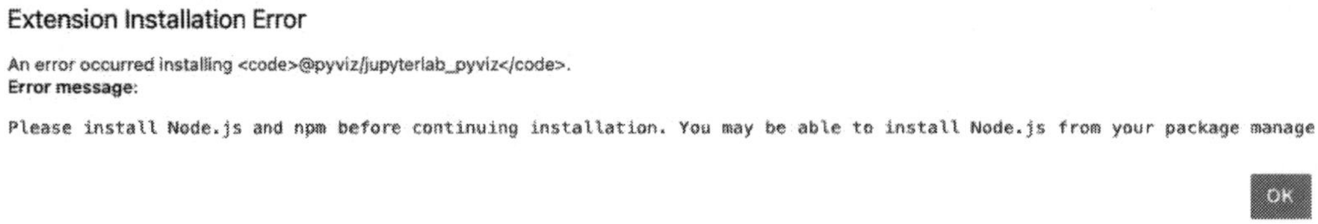

Extension Installation Error

An error occurred installing <code>@pyviz/jupyterlab_pyviz</code>.
Error message:

Please install Node.js and npm before continuing installation. You may be able to install Node.js from your package manage

OK

Figure 1.13 – Extension Installation Error when Node.js is required

You can download and install Node.js directly from `https://nodejs.org/en/`.

Alternatively, you can use `conda` to install Node.js by using the following command:

```
$ conda install -c conda-forge nodejs
```

See also

- To learn more about JupyterLab extensions, please refer to the official documentation here: `https://jupyterlab.readthedocs.io/en/stable/user/extensions.html`.

- If you want to learn more about how JupyterLab extensions are created with example demos, please refer to the official GitHub repository here: `https://github.com/jupyterlab/extension-examples`.

- In *step 9*, we manually installed the `kernelspec` files, which created the mapping between Jupyter and our `conda` environment. This process can be automated using nb_conda. For more information on the nb_conda project, please refer to the official GitHub repository here: `https://github.com/Anaconda-Platform/nb_conda`.

2

Reading Time Series Data from Files

In this chapter, we will use **pandas**, a popular **Python** library with a rich set of I/O tools, data wrangling, and date/time functionality to streamline working with **time series data**. In addition, you will explore several reader functions available in pandas to ingest data from different file types, such as **Comma-Separated Value (CSV)**, Excel, and SAS. You will explore reading from files, whether they are stored locally on your drive or remotely on the cloud, such as an **AWS S3 bucket**.

Time series data is complex and can be in different shapes and formats. Conveniently, the pandas reader functions offer a vast number of arguments (parameters) to help handle such variety in the data.

The pandas library provides two fundamental data structures, Series and DataFrame, implemented as classes. The DataFrame class is a distinct data structure for working with tabular data (think rows and columns in a spreadsheet). The main difference between the two data structures is that a Series is one-dimensional (single column), and a DataFrame is two-dimensional (multiple columns). The relationship between the two is that you get a Series when you slice out a column from a DataFrame. You can think of a DataFrame as a side-by-side concatenation of two or more Series objects.

A particular feature of the Series and DataFrames data structures is that they both have a labeled axis called index. A specific type of index that you will often see with time series data is the `DatetimeIndex` which you will explore further in this chapter. Generally, the index makes slicing and dicing operations very intuitive. For example, to make a DataFrame ready for time series analysis, you will learn how to create DataFrames with an index of type `DatetimeIndex`.

We will cover the following recipes on how to ingest data into a pandas DataFrame:

- Reading data from CSVs and other delimited files
- Reading data from an Excel file
- Reading data from URLs
- Reading data from a SAS dataset

> **Why DatetimeIndex?**
>
> A pandas DataFrame with an index of type `DatetimeIndex` unlocks a large set of features and useful functions needed when working with time series data. You can think of it as adding a layer of intelligence or awareness to pandas to treat the DataFrame as a time series DataFrame.

Technical requirements

In this chapter and forward, we will be using pandas 1.4.2 (released April 2, 2022) extensively.

Throughout our journey, you will be installing additional Python libraries to use in conjunction with pandas. You can download the Jupyter notebooks from the GitHub repository (`https://github.com/PacktPublishing/Time-Series-Analysis-with-Python-Cookbook./blob/main/code/Ch2/Chapter%202.ipynb`) to follow along.

You can download the datasets used in this chapter from the GitHub repository using this link: `https://github.com/PacktPublishing/Time-Series-Analysis-with-Python-Cookbook./tree/main/datasets/Ch2`.

Reading data from CSVs and other delimited files

In this recipe, you will use the `pandas.read_csv()` function, which offers a large set of parameters that you will explore to ensure the data is properly read into a time series DataFrame. In addition, you will learn how to specify an index column, parse the index to be of the type `DatetimeIndex,` and parse string columns that contain dates into `datetime` objects.

Generally, using Python, data read from a CSV file will be in string format (text). When using the `read_csv` method in pandas, it will try and infer the appropriate data types (dtype), and, in most cases, it does a great job at that. However, there are situations where you will need to explicitly indicate which columns to cast to a specific data type. For example, you will specify which column(s) to parse as dates using the `parse_dates` parameter in this recipe.

Getting ready

You will be reading a CSV file that contains hypothetical box office numbers for a movie. The file is provided in the GitHub repository for this book. The data file is in `datasets/Ch2/movieboxoffice.csv`.

How to do it...

You will ingest our CSV file using pandas and leverage some of the available parameters in `read_csv`:

1. First, let's load the libraries:

    ```
    import pandas as pd
    from pathlib import Path
    ```

2. Create a `Path` object for the file location:

    ```
    filepath =\
     Path('../../datasets/Ch2/movieboxoffice.csv')
    ```

3. Read the CSV file into a DataFrame using the `read_csv` function and passing the `filepath` with additional parameters.

The first column in the CSV file contains movie release dates, and it needs to be set as an index of type `DatetimeIndex` (`index_col=0` and `parse_dates=['Date']`). Specify which columns you want to include by providing a list of column names to `usecols`. The default behavior is that the first row includes the header (`header=0`):

```
ts = pd.read_csv(filepath,
                 header=0,
                 parse_dates=['Date'],
                 index_col=0,
                 infer_datetime_format=True,
                 usecols=['Date',
                          'DOW',
                          'Daily',
                          'Forecast',
                          'Percent Diff'])
ts.head(5)
```

This will output the following first five rows:

Date	DOW	Daily	Forecast	Percent Diff
2021-04-26	Friday	$125,789.89	$235,036.46	-46.48%
2021-04-27	Saturday	$99,374.01	$197,622.55	-49.72%
2021-04-28	Sunday	$82,203.16	$116,991.26	-29.74%
2021-04-29	Monday	$33,530.26	$66,652.65	-49.69%
2021-04-30	Tuesday	$30,105.24	$34,828.19	-13.56%

Figure 2.1 – The first five rows of the ts DataFrame using JupyterLab

4. Print a summary of the DataFrame to check the index and column data types:

```
ts.info()
>> <class 'pandas.core.frame.DataFrame'>
DatetimeIndex: 128 entries, 2021-04-26 to 2021-08-31
Data columns (total 4 columns):
 #   Column          Non-Null Count   Dtype
---  ------          --------------   -----
 0   DOW             128 non-null     object
```

```
1    Daily          128 non-null    object
2    Forecast       128 non-null    object
3    Percent Diff   128 non-null    object
dtypes: object(4)
memory usage: 5.0+ KB
```

5. Notice that the Date column is now an index (not a column) of type
    DatetimeIndex. Additionally, both Daily and Forecast columns have the
    wrong dtype inference. You would expect them to be of type float. The issue is
    due to the source CSV file containing dollar signs ($) and thousand separators (,)
    in both columns. The presence of non-numeric characters will cause the columns to
    be interpreted as strings. A column with the dtype object indicates either a string
    column or a column with mixed dtypes (not homogeneous).

    To fix this, you need to remove both the dollar sign ($) and thousand separators (,)
    or any non-numeric character. You can accomplish this using str.replace(),
    which can take a regular expression to remove all non-numeric characters but
    exclude the period (.) for the decimal place. Removing these characters does not
    convert the dtype, so you will need to cast those two columns as a float dtype
    using .astype(float):

    ```
    clean = lambda x: x.str.replace('[^\d]','', regex=True)
    c_df = ts[['Daily', 'Forecast']].apply(clean, axis=1)
    ts[['Daily', 'Forecast']] = c_df.astype(float)
    ```

    Print a summary of the updated DataFrame:

    ```
    ts.info()
    >> <class 'pandas.core.frame.DataFrame'>
    DatetimeIndex: 128 entries, 2021-04-26 to 2021-08-31
    Data columns (total 4 columns):
     #   Column         Non-Null Count   Dtype
    ---  ------         --------------   -----
     0   DOW            128 non-null     object
     1   Daily          128 non-null     float64
     2   Forecast       128 non-null     float64
     3   Percent Diff   128 non-null     object
    dtypes: float64(2), object(2)
    memory usage: 5.0+ KB
    ```

Now, you have a DataFrame with `DatetimeIndex` and both `Daily` and `Forecast` columns are of dtype `float64` (numeric fields).

How it works...

Using pandas for data transformation is fast since it loads the data into memory. For example, the `read_csv` method reads and loads the entire data into a DataFrame in memory. When requesting a DataFrame summary with the `info()` method, in addition to column and index data types, the output will display memory usage for the entire DataFrame. To get the exact memory usage for each column, including the index, you can use the `memory_usage()` method:

```
ts.memory_usage()
>>
Index           1024
DOW             1024
Daily           1024
Forecast        1024
Percent Diff    1024
dtype: int64
```

The total will match what was provided in the DataFrame summary:

```
ts.memory_usage().sum()

>> 5120
```

So far, you have used a few of the available parameters when reading a CSV file using `read_csv`. The more familiar you become with the different options available in any of the pandas reader functions, the more upfront preprocessing you can do during data ingestion (reading).

You leveraged the built-in `parse_dates` argument, which takes in a list of columns (either specified by name or position). The combination of `index_col=0` and `parse_dates=[0]` produced a DataFrame with an index of type `DatetimeIndex`.

Let's inspect the parameters used in this recipe as defined in the official `pandas.read_csv()` documentation (`https://pandas.pydata.org/pandas-docs/stable/reference/api/pandas.read_csv.html`):

- `filepath_or_buffer`: This is the first positional argument and the only required field needed (at a minimum) to read a CSV file. Here, you passed the Python path object named `filepath`. This can also be a string that represents a valid file path such as `'../../datasets/Ch2/movieboxoffice.csv'` or a URL that points to a remote file location, such as an AWS S3 bucket (we will examine this later in the *Reading data from URLs* recipe in this chapter).

- `sep`: This takes a string to specify which delimiter to use. The default is a comma delimiter (`,`) which assumes a CSV file. If the file is separated by another delimiter, such as a pipe (`|`) or semicolon (`;`), then the argument can be updated, such as `sep="|"` or `sep=";"`.

  Another alias to `sep` is `delimiter`, which can be used as well as a parameter name.

- `header`: In this case, you specified that the first `row` (`0`) value contains the header information. The default value is `infer`, which usually works as-is in most cases. If the CSV does not contain a header, then you specify `header=None`. If the CSV has a header but you prefer to supply custom column names, then you need to specify `header=0` and overwrite it by providing a list of new column names to the `names` argument.

  Recall that you specified which columns to include by passing a list of column names to the `usecols` parameter. These names are based on the file header (the first row of the CSV file).

  If you decide to provide custom header names, you cannot reference the original names in the `use_cols` parameter; this will produce the following error: `ValueError: Usecols do not match columns`.

- `parse_dates`: In the recipe, you provided a list of column positions using `[0]`, which specified only the first column (by position) should be parsed. The `parse_dates` argument can take a list of column names, such as `["Date"]`, or a list of column positions, such as `[0, 3]`, indicating the first and the fourth columns. If you only intend to parse the index column(s) specified in the `index_col` parameter, you only need to pass `True` (Boolean).

- **index_cols**: Here, you specified that the first column by position (`index_col=0`) will be used as the DataFrame index. Alternatively, you could provide the column name as a string (`index_col='Date'`). The parameter also takes in a list of integers (positional indices) or strings (column names), which would create a `MultiIndex` object.

- **usecols**: The default value is `None`, which includes all the columns in the dataset. Limiting the number of columns to only those that are required results in faster parsing and overall lower memory usage, since you only bring in what is needed. The `usecols` arguments can take a list of *column names*, such as `['Date', 'DOW', 'Daily', 'Percent Diff', 'Forecast']` or a list of *positional indices*, such as `[0, 1, 3, 7, 6]`, which would produce the same result.

There's more...

There are situations where `parse_dates` may not work (it just cannot parse the date). In such cases, the column(s) will be returned unchanged, and no error will be thrown. This is where the `date_parser` parameter can be useful.

For example, you can pass a `lambda` function that uses the `to_datetime` function in pandas to `date_parser`. You can specify the string representation for the date format inside `to_datetime()`, as demonstrated in the following code:

```
date_parser =lambda x: pd.to_datetime(x, format="%d-%b-%y")
ts = pd.read_csv(filepath,
                 parse_dates=[0],
                 index_col=0,
                 date_parser=date_parser,
                 usecols=[0,1,3, 7, 6])
ts.head()
```

The preceding code will print out the first five rows of the `ts` DataFrame displaying a properly parsed `Date` index.

	DOW	Daily	Forecast	Percent Diff
Date				
2021-04-26	Friday	$125,789.89	$235,036.46	-46.48%
2021-04-27	Saturday	$99,374.01	$197,622.55	-49.72%
2021-04-28	Sunday	$82,203.16	$116,991.26	-29.74%
2021-04-29	Monday	$33,530.26	$66,652.65	-49.69%
2021-04-30	Tuesday	$30,105.24	$34,828.19	-13.56%

Figure 2.2 – The first five rows of the ts DataFrame using JupyterLab

Let's break it down. In the preceding code, you passed two arguments to the `to_datetime` function: the object to convert to datetime and an explicit format string. Since the date is stored as a string in the form *26-Apr-21*, you passed `"%d-%b-%y"` to reflect that:

- `%d` represents the day of the month, such as `01` or `02`.

- `%b` represents the abbreviated month name, such as `Apr` or `May`.

- `%y` represents a two-digit year, such as `19` or `20`.

Other common string codes include the following:

- `%Y` represents the year as a four-digit number, such as `2020` or `2021`.

- `%B` represents the month's full name, such as `January` or `February`.

- `%m` represents the month as a two-digit number, such as `01` or `02`.

For more information on Python's string formats for representing dates, visit `https://strftime.org`.

See also

According to the pandas documentation, the `infer_datetime_format` parameter in `read_csv()` function can speed up the parsing by 5–10x. This is how you can add this to our original script:

```
ts = pd.read_csv(filepath,
                 header=0,
                 parse_dates=[0],
                 index_col=0,
                 infer_datetime_format= True,
```

```
usecols=['Date',
         'DOW',
         'Daily',
         'Forecast',
         'Percent Diff'])
```

Note that given the dataset is small, the speed improvement may be insignificant.

For more information, please refer to the *pandas.read_csv* documentation: `https://pandas.pydata.org/docs/reference/api/pandas.read_csv.html`.

Reading data from an Excel file

To read data from an Excel file, you will need to use a different reader function from pandas. Generally, working with Excel files can be a challenge since the file can contain formatted multi-line headers, merged header cells, and images. They may also contain multiple worksheets with custom names (labels). Therefore, it is vital that you always inspect the Excel file first. The most common scenario is reading from an Excel file that contains data partitioned into multiple sheets, which is the focus of this recipe.

In this recipe, you will be using the `pandas.read_excel()` function and examining the various parameters available to ensure the data is read properly as a DataFrame with a `DatetimeIndex` for time series analysis. In addition, you will explore different options to read Excel files with multiple sheets.

Getting ready

To use `pandas.read_excel()`, you will need to install an additional library for reading and writing Excel files. In the `read_excel()` function, you will use the engine parameter to specify which library (engine) to use for processing an Excel file. Depending on the Excel file extension you are working with (for example, `.xls` or `.xlsx`), you may need to specify a different engine that may require installing an additional library.

The supported libraries (engines) for reading and writing Excel include `xlrd`, `openpyxl`, `odf`, and `pyxlsb`. When working with Excel files, the two most common libraries are usually `xlrd` and `openpyxl`.

The `xlrd` library only supports `.xls` files. So, if you are working with an older Excel format, such as `.xls`, then `xlrd` will do just fine. For newer Excel formats, such as `.xlsx`, we will need a different engine, and in this case, `openpyxl` would be the recommendation to go with.

To install `openpyxl` using `conda`, run the following command in the terminal:

```
>>> conda install openpyxl
```

To install using `pip`, run the following command:

```
>>> pip install openpyxl
```

We will be using the `sales_trx_data.xlsx` file, which you can download from the book's GitHub repository. See the *Technical requirements* section of this chapter. The file contains sales data split by year into two sheets (`2017` and `2018`), respectively.

How to do it...

You will ingest the Excel file (`.xlsx`) using pandas and `openpyxl`, and leverage some of the available parameters in `read_excel()`:

1. Import the libraries for this recipe:

    ```
    import pandas as pd
    from pathlib import Path
    filepath = \
    Path('../../datasets/Ch2/sales_trx_data.xlsx')
    ```

2. Read the Excel (`.xlxs`) file using the `read_excel()` function. By default, pandas will only read from the first sheet. This is specified under the `sheet_name` parameter, which is set to `0` as the default value. Before passing a new argument, you can use `pandas.ExcelFile` first to inspect the file and determine the number of sheets available. The `ExcelFile` class will provide additional methods and properties, such as `sheet_name`, which returns a list of sheet names:

    ```
    excelfile = pd.ExcelFile(filepath)
    excelfile.sheet_name


    >> ['2017', '2018']
    ```

    If you have multiple sheets, you can specify which sheets you want to ingest by passing a list to the `sheet_name` parameter in `read_excel`. The list can either be positional arguments, such as first, second, and fifth sheets with `[0, 1, 4]`, sheet names with `["Sheet1", "Sheet2", "Sheet5"]`, or a combination of both, such as first sheet, second sheet, and a sheet named `"Revenue"` `[0, 1, "Revenue"]`.

In the following code, you will use sheet positions to read both the first and second sheets (0 and 1 indexes). This will return a Python `dictionary` object with two DataFrames. Notet hat the returned dictionary (key-value pair) has numeric keys (0 and 1) representing the first and second sheets (positional index), respectively:

```
ts = pd.read_excel(filepath,
                   engine='openpyxl',
                   index_col=1,
                   sheet_name=[0,1],
                   parse_dates=True)


ts.keys()
>> dict_keys([0, 1])
```

3. Alternatively, you can pass a list of sheet names. Notice that the returned dictionary keys are now strings and represent the sheet names as shown in the following code:

```
ts = pd.read_excel(filepath,
                   engine='openpyxl',
                   index_col=1,
                   sheet_name=['2017','2018'],
                   parse_dates=True)


ts.keys()
>> dict_keys(['2017', '2018'])
```

4. If you want to read from all the available sheets, you will pass None instead. The keys for the dictionary, in this case, will represent sheet names:

```
ts = pd.read_excel(filepath,
                   engine='openpyxl',
                   index_col=1,
                   sheet_name=None,
                   parse_dates=True)


ts.keys()
>> dict_keys(['2017', '2018'])
```

The two DataFrames within the dictionary are identical (homogeneous-typed) in terms of their schema (column names and data types). You can inspect each DataFrame with `ts['2017'].info()` and `ts['2018'].info()`.

They both have a `DatetimeIndex` object, which you specified in the `index_col` parameter. The 2017 DataFrame consists of 36,764 rows and the 2018 DataFrame consists of 37,360. In this scenario, you want to stack (combine) the two (think `UNION` in SQL) into a single DataFrame that contains all 74,124 rows and a `DatetimeIndex` that spans from `2017-01-01` to `2018-12-31`.

To combine the two DataFrames along the index axis (stacked one on top of the other), you will use the `pandas.concat()` function. The default behavior of the `concat()` function is to concatenate along the index axis (`axis=0`). In the following code, you will explicitly specify which DataFrames to concatenate:

```
ts_combined = pd.concat([ts['2017'],ts['2018']])


ts_combined.info()
>> <class 'pandas.core.frame.DataFrame'>
DatetimeIndex: 74124 entries, 2017-01-01 to 2018-12-31
Data columns (total 4 columns):
 #    Column                  Non-Null Count    Dtype
---   ------                  --------------    -----
 0    Line_Item_ID            74124 non-null    int64
 1    Credit_Card_Number      74124 non-null    int64
 2    Quantity                74124 non-null    int64
 3    Menu_Item               74124 non-null    object
dtypes: int64(3), object(1)
memory usage: 2.8+ MB
```

5. When you have multiple DataFrames returned (think multiple sheets), you can use the `concat()` function on the returned dictionary. In other words, you can combine the `concat()` and `read_excel()` functions in one statement. In this case, you will end up with a `MultiIndex` DataFrame where the first level is the sheet name (or number) and the second level is the `DatetimeIndex`. For example, using the `ts` dictionary, you will get a two-level index: `MultiIndex([('2017', '2017-01-01'), ..., ('2018', '2018-12-31')], names=[None, 'Date'], length=74124)`.

To reduce the number of levels, you can use the `droplevel(level=0)` method to drop the first level after pandas `.concat()` shown as follows:

```
ts_combined = pd.concat(ts).droplevel(level=0)
```

6.   If you are only reading one sheet, the behavior is slightly different. By default, `sheet_name` is set to 0, which means it reads the first sheet. You can modify this and pass a different value (single value), either the sheet name (string) or sheet position (integer). When passing a single value, the returned object will be a pandas DataFrame and not a dictionary:

```
ts = pd.read_excel(filepath,
                   index_col=1,
                   sheet_name='2018',
                   parse_dates=True)


type(ts)
>> pandas.core.frame.DataFrame
```

Do note though that if you pass a single value inside two brackets (`[1]`), then pandas will interpret this differently and the returned object will be a dictionary that contains one DataFrame.

Lastly, note that you did not need to specify the engine in the last example. The `read_csv` function will determine which engine to use based on the file extension. So, for example, suppose the library for that engine is not installed. In that case, it will throw an `ImportError` message, indicating that the library (dependency) is missing.

How it works...

The `pandas.read_excel()` function has many common parameters with the `pandas.read_csv()` function that you used earlier. The `read_excel` function can either return a DataFrame object or a dictionary of DataFrames. The dependency here is whether you are passing a single value (scalar) or a list to `sheet_name`.

In the `sales_trx_data.xlsx` file, both sheets had the same schema (homogeneous-typed). The sales data was partitioned (split) by year, where each sheet contained sales for a particular year. In this case, concatenating the two DataFrames was a natural choice. The `pandas.concat()` function is like the `DataFrame.append()` function, in which the second DataFrame was added (appended) to the end of the first DataFrame. This should be similar in behavior to the `UNION` clause for those coming from a SQL background.

There's more...

An alternative method to reading an Excel file is with the `pandas.ExcelFile()` class, which returns a pandas `ExcelFile` object. Earlier in this recipe, you used `ExcelFile()` to inspect the number of sheets in the Excel file through the `sheet_name` property.

The `ExcelFile` class has several useful methods, including the `parse()` method to parse the Excel file into a DataFrame, similar to the `pandas.read_excel()` function.

In the following example, you will use the `ExcelFile` class to parse the first sheet, assign the first column as an index, and print the first five rows:

```
excelfile = pd.ExcelFile(filepath)
excelfile.parse(sheet_name='2017',
                index_col=1,
                parse_dates=True) head()
```

You should see similar results for the first five rows of the DataFrame:

Date	Line_Item_ID	Credit_Card_Number	Quantity	Menu_Item
2017-01-01	1	7437926611570790	1	spicy miso ramen
2017-01-01	2	7437926611570790	1	spicy miso ramen
2017-01-01	3	8421920068932810	3	tori paitan ramen
2017-01-01	4	8421920068932810	3	tori paitan ramen
2017-01-01	5	4787310681569640	1	truffle butter ramen

Figure 2.3 – The first five rows of the ts DataFrame using JupyterLab

From *Figure 2.3*, it should become clear that `ExcelFile.parse()` is equivalent to `pandas.read_excel()`.

See also

For more information on `pandas.read_excel()` and `pandas.ExcelFile()`, please refer to the official documentation:

- *pandas.read_excel()*: `https://pandas.pydata.org/docs/reference/api/pandas.read_excel.html`

- *pandas.ExcelFile.parse()*: `https://pandas.pydata.org/docs/reference/api/pandas.ExcelFile.parse.html`

Reading data from URLs

Files can be downloaded and stored locally on your machine, or stored on a remote server or cloud location. In the earlier two recipes, *Reading from CSVs and other delimited files*, and *Reading data from an Excel file*, both files were stored locally.

Many of the pandas reader functions can read data from remote locations by passing a URL path. For example, both `read_csv()` and `read_excel()` can take a URL to read a file that is accessible via the internet. In this recipe, you will read a CSV file using `pandas.read_csv()` and Excel files using `pandas.read_excel()` from remote locations, such as GitHub and AWS S3 (private and public buckets). You will also read data directly from an HTML page into a pandas DataFrame.

Getting ready

You will need to install the **AWS SDK for Python (Boto3)** for reading files from S3 buckets. Additionally, you will learn how to use the `storage_options` parameter available in many of the reader functions in pandas to read from S3 without the Boto3 library.

To use an S3 URL (for example, `s3://bucket_name/path-to-file`) in pandas, you will need to install the `s3fs` library. You will also need to install an HTML parser for when we use `read_html()`. For example, for the parsing engine (the HTML parser), you can install either `lxml` or `html5lib`; pandas will pick whichever is installed (it will first look for `lxml`, and if that fails, then for `html5lib`). If you plan to use `html5lib` you will need to install Beautiful Soup (`beautifulsoup4`).

To install using pip, you can use the following command:

```
>>> pip install boto3 s3fs lxml
```

To install using Conda, you can use:

```
>>> conda install boto3 s3fs lxml -y
```

How to do it...

This recipe will present you with different scenarios when reading data from online (remote) sources. Let's import pandas upfront since you will be using it throughout this recipe:

```
import pandas as pd
```

Reading data from GitHub

Sometimes, you may find useful public data on GitHub that you want to use and read directly (without downloading). One of the most common file formats on GitHub are CSV files. Let's start with the following steps:

1. To read a CSV file from GitHub, you will need the URL to the raw content. If you copy the file's GitHub URL from the browser and use it as the file path, you will get a URL that looks like this: `https://github.com/PacktPublishing/Time-Series-Analysis-with-Python-Cookbook./blob/main/datasets/Ch2/AirQualityUCI.csv`. This URL is a pointer to the web page in GitHub and not the data itself; hence when using `pd.read_csv()`, it will throw an error:

```
url = 'https://github.com/PacktPublishing/Time-Series-
Analysis-with-Python-Cookbook./blob/main/datasets/Ch2/
AirQualityUCI.csv'
pd.read_csv(url)


ParserError: Error tokenizing data. C error: Expected 1
fields in line 62, saw 2
```

2. Instead, you will need the raw content, which will give you a URL that looks like this: `https://media.githubusercontent.com/media/PacktPublishing/Time-Series-Analysis-with-Python-Cookbook./main/datasets/Ch2/AirQualityUCI.csv`:

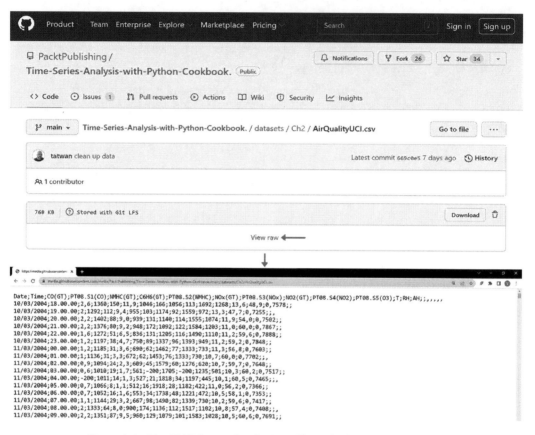

Figure 2.4 – The GitHub page for the CSV file. Note the View raw button

3. In *Figure 2.4*, notice that the values are not comma-separated (not a comma-delimited file); instead, the file uses semicolon (;) to separate the values.

The first column in the file is the `Date` column. You will need to parse (`parse_date` parameter) and convert it to `DatetimeIndex` (`index_col` parameter).

Pass the new URL to `pandas.read_csv()`:

```
url = 'https://media.githubusercontent.com/media/
PacktPublishing/Time-Series-Analysis-with-Python-
Cookbook./main/datasets/Ch2/AirQualityUCI.csv'
date_parser = lambda x: pd.to_datetime(x,
```

```
       format="%d/%m/%Y")

df = pd.read_csv(url,
                 delimiter=';',
                 index_col='Date',
                 date_parser=date_parser)
df.iloc[:3,1:4]
>>
           CO(GT)   PT08.S1(CO)   NMHC(GT)
Date
2004-03-10    2.6      1360.00        150
2004-03-10    2.0      1292.25        112
2004-03-10    2.2      1402.00         88
```

We successfully ingested the data from the CSV file in GitHub into a DataFrame and
printed the first three rows of select columns.

Reading data from a public S3 bucket

AWS supports **virtual-hosted-style** URLs such as `https://bucket-name.`
`s3.Region.amazonaws.com/keyname`, **path-style** URLs such as `https://`
`s3.Region.amazonaws.com/bucket-name/keyname`, and using `S3://bucket/`
`keyname`. Here are examples of how these different URLs may look for our file:

- A virtual hosted-style URL or an object URL: `https://tscookbook.s3.us-`
  `east-1.amazonaws.com/AirQualityUCI.xlsx`

- A path-style URL: `https://s3.us-east-1.amazonaws.com/`
  `tscookbook/AirQualityUCI.xlsx`

- An S3 protocol: `s3://tscookbook/AirQualityUCI.csv`

In this example, you will be reading the `AirQualityUCI.xlsx` file, which has only
one sheet. It contains the same data as `AirQualityUCI.csv`, which we read earlier
from GitHub.

Note that in the URL, you do not need to specify the region as `us-east-1`. `us-east-`
`1`, which represents US East (North Virginia), is an exception and will not be the case for
other regions:

```
url = 'https://tscookbook.s3.amazonaws.com/AirQualityUCI.xlsx'
df = pd.read_excel(url,
```

```
                        index_col='Date',
                        parse_dates=True)
```

Read the same file using the S3:// URL:

```
s3uri = 's3://tscookbook/AirQualityUCI.xlsx'
df = pd.read_excel(s3uri,
                        index_col='Date',
                        parse_dates=True)
```

You may get an error such as the following:

```
ImportError: Install s3fs to access S3
```

This indicates that either you do not have the s3fs library installed or possibly you are not using the right Python/Conda environment.

Reading data from a private S3 bucket

When reading files from a private S3 bucket, you will need to pass your credentials to authenticate. A convenient parameter in many of the I/O functions in pandas is storage_options, which allows you to send additional content with the request, such as a custom header or required credentials to a cloud service.

You will need to pass a dictionary (key-value pair) to provide the additional information along with the request, such as username, password, access keys, and secret keys to storage_options as in {"username": username, "password": password}.

Now, you will read the AirQualityUCI.csv file, located in a private S3 bucket:

1. You will start by storing your AWS credentials in a config .cfg file outside your Python script. Then, use configparser to read the values and store them in Python variables. You do not want your credentials exposed or hardcoded in your code:

    ```
    # Example aws.cfg file
    [AWS]
    aws_access_key=your_access_key
    aws_secret_key=you_secret_key
    ```

    You can load the aws.cfg file using config.read():

    ```
    import configparser
    config = configparser.ConfigParser()
    ```

```
config.read('aws.cfg')


AWS_ACCESS_KEY = config['AWS']['aws_access_key']
AWS_SECRET_KEY = config['AWS']['aws_secret_key']
```

2. The *AWS Access Key ID* and *Secret Access Key* are now stored in AWS_ACCESS_KEY and AWS_SECRET_KEY. Use pandas.read_csv() to read the CSV file and update the storage_options parameter by passing your credentials, as shown in the following code:

```
s3uri = "s3://tscookbook-private/AirQuality.csv"
df = pd.read_csv(s3uri,
                    index_col='Date',
                    parse_dates=True,
                    storage_options= {
                            'key': AWS_ACCESS_KEY,
                            'secret': AWS_SECRET_KEY
                        })
df.iloc[:3, 1:4]
>>
            CO(GT)   PT08.S1(CO)   NMHC(GT)
Date
2004-10-03    2,6       1360.0       150.0
2004-10-03      2       1292.0       112.0
    2,2     1402.0       88.0
```

3. Alternatively, you can use the AWS SDK for Python (Boto3) to achieve similar results. The boto3 Python library gives you more control and additional capabilities (beyond just reading and writing to S3). You will pass the same credentials stored earlier in AWS_ACCESS_KEY and AWS_SECRET_KEY and pass them to AWS, using boto3 to authenticate:

```
import boto3
bucket = "tscookbook-private"
client = boto3.client("s3",
                    aws_access_key_id =AWS_ACCESS_KEY,
                    aws_secret_access_key = AWS_SECRET_KEY)
```

Now, the `client` object has access to many methods specific to the AWS S3 service for creating, deleting, and retrieving bucket information, and more. In addition, Boto3 offers two levels of APIs: client and resource. In the preceding example, you used the client API.

The client is a low-level service access interface that gives you more granular control, for example, `boto3.client("s3")`. The resource is a higher-level object-oriented interface (an abstraction layer), for example, `boto3.resource("s3")`.

In *Chapter 4, Persisting Time Series Data to Files*, you will explore the resource API interface when writing to S3. For now, you will use the client interface.

4. You will use the `get_object` method to retrieve the data. Just provide the bucket name and a key. The key here is the actual filename:

```
data = client.get_object(Bucket=bucket, Key='AirQuality.
csv')
df = pd.read_csv(data['Body'],
                index_col='Date',
                parse_dates=True)


df.iloc[:3, 1:4]
>>
            CO(GT)    PT08.S1(CO)    NMHC(GT)
Date
2004-10-03    2,6        1360.0        150.0
2004-10-03     2         1292.0        112.0
2004-10-03    2,2        1402.0         88.0
```

5. When calling the `client.get_object()` method, a dictionary (key-value pair) is returned, as shown in the following example:

```
{'ResponseMetadata': {
'RequestId':'MM0CR3XX5QFBQTSG',
'HostId':'vq8iRCJfuA4eWPgHBGhdjir1x52Tdp80ADaSxWrL4Xzsr
VpebSZ6SnskPeYNKCOd/RZfIRT4xIM=',
'HTTPStatusCode':200,
'HTTPHeaders': {'x-amz-id-2': 'vq8iRCJfuA4eWPgHBGhdjir1x52
Tdp80ADaSxWrL4XzsrVpebSZ6SnskPeYNKCOd/RZfIRT4xIM=',
    'x-amz-request-id': 'MM0CR3XX5QFBQTSG',
    'date': 'Tue, 06 Jul 2021 01:08:36 GMT',
```

```
    'last-modified': 'Mon, 14 Jun 2021 01:13:05 GMT',
    'etag': '"2ce337accfeb2dbbc6b76833bc6f84b8"',
    'accept-ranges': 'bytes',
    'content-type': 'binary/octet-stream',
    'server': 'AmazonS3',
    'content-length': '1012427'},
    'RetryAttempts': 0},
    'AcceptRanges': 'bytes',
  'LastModified': datetime.datetime(2021, 6, 14, 1, 13, 5,
tzinfo=tzutc()),
  'ContentLength': 1012427,
  'ETag': '"2ce337accfeb2dbbc6b76833bc6f84b8"',
  'ContentType': 'binary/octet-stream',
  'Metadata': {},
  'Body': <botocore.response.StreamingBody at
0x7fe9c16b55b0>}
```

The content you are interested in is in the response body under the Body key. You passed data['Body'] to the read_csv() function, which loads the response stream (StreamingBody) into a DataFrame.

Reading data from HTML

pandas offers an elegant way to read HTML tables and convert the content into a pandas DataFrame using the pandas.read_html() function:

1. In the following recipe, we will extract HTML tables from Wikipedia for COVID-19 pandemic tracking cases by country and by territory (https://en.wikipedia. org/wiki/COVID-19_pandemic_by_country_and_territory):

    ```
    url = "https://en.wikipedia.org/wiki/COVID-19_pandemic_
    by_country_and_territory"
    results = pd.read_html(url)
    print(len(results))
    >> 71
    ```

2. `pandas.read_html()` returned a list of DataFrames, one for each HTML table found in the URL. Keep in mind that the website's content is dynamic and gets updated regularly, and the results may vary. In our case, it returned 71 DataFrames. The DataFrame at index `15` contains summary on COVID-19 cases and deaths by region. Grab the DataFrame (at index `15`) and assign it to the `df` variable, and print the returned columns:

```
df = results[15]
df.columns
>> Index(['Region[28]', 'Total cases', 'Total deaths',
'Cases per million',
       'Deaths per million', 'Current weekly cases',
'Current weekly deaths',
       'Population millions', 'Vaccinated %[29]'],
    dtype='object')
```

3. Display the first five rows for `Total cases`, `Total deaths`, and the `Cases per million` columns.

```
df[['Total cases', 'Total deaths', 'Cases per million']].
head()

>>
```

	Total cases	Total deaths	Cases per million
0	139300788	1083815	311412
1	85476396	1035884	231765
2	51507114	477420	220454
3	56804073	1270477	132141
4	21971862	417507	92789

How it works...

Most of the pandas reader functions accept a URL as a path. Examples include the following:

*   `pandas.read_csv()`
*   `pandas.read_excel()`

- `pandas.read_parquet()`
- `pandas.read_table()`
- `pandas.read_pickle()`
- `pandas.read_orc()`
- `pandas.read_stata()`
- `pandas.read_sas()`
- `pandas.read_json()`

The URL needs to be one of the valid URL schemes that pandas supports, which includes `http` and `https`, `ftp`, `s3`, `gs`, or the `file` protocol.

The `read_html()` function is great for scraping websites that contain data in HTML tables. It inspects the HTML and searches for all the `<table>` elements within the HTML. In HTML, table rows are defined with the `<tr> </tr>` tags and headers with the `<th></th>` tags. The actual data (cell) is contained within the `<td> </td>` tags. The `read_html()` function looks for `<table>`, `<tr>`, `<th>`, and `<td>` tags and converts the content into a DataFrame, and assigns the columns and rows as they were defined in the HTML. If an HTML page contains more than one `<table></table>` tag, `read_html` will return them all and you will get a list of DataFrames.

The following code demonstrates how `pandas.read_html()` works:

```
import pandas as pd
html = """
 <table>
   <tr>
     <th>Ticker</th>
     <th>Price</th>
   </tr>
   <tr>
     <td>MSFT</td>
     <td>230</td>
   </tr>
   <tr>
     <td>APPL</td>
     <td>300</td>
   </tr>
     <tr>
```

```
        <td>MSTR</td>
        <td>120</td>
    </tr>
  </table>

  </body>
  </html>
  """

df = pd.read_html(html)
df[0]
>>
   Ticker   Price
0    MSFT    230
1    APPL    300
2    MSTR    120
```

In the preceding code, the read_html() function parsed the HTML code and converted the HTML table into a pandas DataFrame. The headers between the <th> and </th> tags represent the column names of the DataFrame, and the content between the <tr></td> and </td></tr> tags represent the row data of the DataFrame. Note that if you go ahead and delete the <table> and </table> table tags, you will get the ValueError: No tables found error.

There's more...

The read_html() function has an optional attr argument, which takes a dictionary of valid HTML <table> attributes, such as id or class. For example, you can use the attr parameter to narrow down the tables returned to those that match the class attribute sortable as in <table class="sortable">. The read_html function will inspect the entire HTML page to ensure you target the right set of attributes.

In the previous exercise, you used the `read_html` function on the COVID-19 Wikipedia page, and it returned 71 tables (DataFrames). The number of tables will probably increase as time goes by as Wikipedia gets updated. You can narrow down the result set and guarantee some consistency by using the `attr` option. First, start by inspecting the HTML code using your browser. You will see that several of the `<table>` elements have multiple classes listed, such as `sortable`. You can look for other unique identifiers.

```
<table class="wikitable sortable mw-datatable covid19-
countrynames jquery-tablesorter" id="thetable" style="text-
align:right;">
```

Note, if you get the error `html5lib not found`, please install it you will need to install both `html5lib` and `beautifulSoup4`.

To install using `conda`, use the following:

```
conda install html5lib beautifulSoup4
```

To install using `pip`, use the following:

```
pip install html5lib beautifulSoup4
```

Now, let's use the `sortable` class and request the data again:

```
url = "https://en.wikipedia.org/wiki/COVID-19_pandemic_by_
country_and_territory"
df = pd.read_html(url, attrs={'class': 'sortable'})
len(df)
>>  7
df[3].columns
>>
Index(['Region[28]', 'Total cases', 'Total deaths', 'Cases per
million',
        'Deaths per million', 'Current weekly cases', 'Current
weekly deaths',
        'Population millions', 'Vaccinated %[29]'],
      dtype='object')
```

The list returned a smaller subset of tables (from 71 down to 7).

See also

For more information, please refer to the official `pandas.read_html` documentation: `https://pandas.pydata.org/docs/reference/api/pandas.read_html.html`.

Reading data from a SAS dataset

In this recipe, you will read a SAS data file and, more specifically, a file with the `SAS7BDAT` extension. SAS is commercial statistical software that provides data mining, business intelligence, and advanced analytics capabilities. Many large organizations in various industries rely on SAS, so it is very common to encounter the need to read from a SAS dataset.

Getting ready

In this recipe, you will be using pandas to read a `.sas7bdat` file. These files can be extremely large, and you will be introduced to different ways to read such files more efficiently.

To get ready, you can download the SAS sample dataset from `http://support.sas.com/kb/61/960.html`. You will be reading the `DCSKINPRODUCT.sas7bdat` file.

The SAS data file is also provided in the GitHub repository for this book.

How to do it...

You will use the `pandas.read_sas()` function, which can be used to read both SAS XPORT (`.xpt`) and `SAS7BDAT` file formats. However, there is no SAS writer function in pandas:

1. Start by importing pandas and creating the path variable to the file. This file is not large (14.7 MB) compared to a typical SAS file, which can be 100+ GB:

    ```
    import pandas as pd
    path = '../../datasets/Ch2/DCSKINPRODUCT.sas7bdat'
    ```

2. One of the advantages of using pandas is that it provides data structures for in-memory analysis, hence the performance advantage when analyzing data. On the other hand, this can also be a constraint when loading large datasets into memory. Generally, the amount of data you can load is limited by the amount of memory available. However, this can be an issue if the dataset is too large and exceeds the amount of memory.

One way to tackle this issue is by using the chunksize parameter. The chunksize parameter is available in many reader and writer functions, including read_sas. The DCSKINPRODUCT.sas7bdat file contains 152130 records, so you will use a chunksize parameter to read 10000 records at a time:

```
df = pd.read_sas(path, chunksize=10000)
type(df)
>> pandas.io.sas.sas7bdat.SAS7BDATReader
```

3. The returned object is not a DataFrame but a SAS7BDATReader object. You can think of this as an iterator object that you can iterate through. At each iteration or chunk, you get a DataFrame of 10,000 rows at a time. You can retrieve the first chunk using the next() method that is, df.next(). Every time you use the next() method, it will retrieve the next batch or chunk (the next 10,000 rows). You can also loop through the chunks, for example, to do some computations. This can be helpful when the dataset is too large to fit in memory, allowing you to iterate through manageable chunks to do some heavy aggregations. The following code demonstrates this concept:

```
results = []
for chunk in df:
    results.append(
        chunk)
len(results)
>> 16


df = pd.concat(results)
df.shape
>> (152130, 5)
```

There were 16 chunks (DataFrames) in total; each chunk or DataFrame contained 10000 records. Using the concat function, you can combine all 16 DataDrames into a large DataFrame of 152130 records.

4. Reread the data in chunks, and this time group by DATE and aggregate using sum and count, as shown in the following:

```
df = pd.read_sas(path, chunksize=10000)
results = []
for chunk in df:
    results.append(
```

```
           chunk.groupby('DATE')['Revenue']
               .agg(['sum', 'count']))
```

5. The `results` object is now a list of DataFrames. Now, let's examine the result set:

```
results[0].loc['2013-02-10']
>>
sum        923903.0
count          91.0
Name: 2013-02-10 00:00:00, dtype: float64


results[1].loc['2013-02-10']
>>
sum       8186392.0
count          91.0
Name: 2013-02-10 00:00:00, dtype: float64


results[2].loc['2013-02-10']
>>
sum       5881396.0
count          91.0
Name: 2013-02-10 00:00:00, dtype: float64
```

6. From the preceding output, you can observe that we have another issue to solve. Notice that the observations for 2013-02-10 got split. This is a common issue when chunking since it splits the data disregarding their order or sequence.

    You can resolve this by combining the results in a meaningful way. For example, you can use the `reduce` function in Python. The `reduce` function allows you to perform a rolling computation (also known as *folding* or *reducing)* based on some function you provide. The following code demonstrates how this can be implemented:

```
from functools import reduce
final = reduce(lambda x1, x2: x1.add(x2, fill_value=0),
results)
type(final)
```

```
>> pandas.core.frame.DataFrame

final.loc['2013-02-10']
>>
sum        43104420.0
count          1383.0
Name: 2013-02-10 00:00:00, dtype: float64
final.shape
>> (110, 2)
```

From the preceding output, the 16 chunks or DataFrames were reduced to a single value per row (index). We leveraged the pandas.DataFrame.add() function to add the values and use zero (0) as a fill value when the data is missing.

How it works...

Using the chunksize parameter in the read_sas() function will not return a DataFrame but rather an iterator (a SAS7BDATReader object). The chunksize parameter is available in most reader functions in pandas, such as read_csv, read_hdf, and read_sql, to name a few. Similarly, using the chunkize parameter with those functions will also return an iterator.

If chunksize is not specified, the returned object would be a DataFrame of the entire dataset. This is because the default value is None in all the reader functions.

Chunking is great when the operation or workflow is simple and not sequential. An operation such as groupby can be complex and tricky when chunking, which is why we added two extra steps:

- Stored the resulting DataFrame to a list.
- Used Python's reduce() function, which takes two arguments, a function and an iterator. It then applies the function element-wise and does it cumulatively from left to right to reduce down to a one result set. We also leveraged the DataFrame's add() method, which matches DataFrame indices to perform an element-wise addition.

There's more...

There are better options when working with large files than using pandas, especially if you have memory constraints and cannot fit the entire data into the memory. **Chunking** is a great option, but it still has an overhead and relies on memory. The pandas library is a single-core framework and does not offer parallel computing capabilities. Instead, there are specialized libraries and frameworks for parallel processing designed to work with big data. Such frameworks do not rely on loading everything into memory and instead can utilize multiple CPU cores, disk usage, or expand into multiple worker nodes (think multiple machines). For example, **Dask** chunks your data, creates a computation graph, and parallelizes the smaller tasks (chunks) behind the scenes, thus speeding the overall processing time and reducing memory overhead.

These frameworks are great but will require you to spend time learning the framework and rewriting your code to leverage these capabilities. So, there is a steep learning curve initially. Luckily, this is where the **Modin** project comes into play. For example, the Modin library acts as a wrapper or, more specifically, an abstraction on top of Dask or Ray that uses a similar API to pandas. Modin makes optimizing your pandas' code much more straightforward without learning another framework, and all it takes is a single line of code.

Before installing any library, it is highly advised that you create a separate virtual environment, for example, using conda. The concept and purpose behind creating virtual environments were discussed in detail in *Chapter 1, Getting Started with Time Series Analysis*, with multiple examples.

To install Modin using Conda (with a Dask backend), run the following:

```
>> conda install -c conda-forge modin-dask
```

To install with Pip, use the following:

```
>> pip install modin[dask]
```

You will measure the time and memory usage using pandas and again using Modin. To measure memory usage, you will need to install the memory_profiler library.

```
>> pip install memory_profiler
```

The memory_profiler library provides IPython and Jupyter magics such as %memit and %mprun, similar to known magics such as %timeit and %time.

Start by loading the required libraries:

```
import memory_profiler
import pandas as pd


path = '../../datasets/Ch2/large_file.csv'
```

You will start by using pandas to read the file `large_file.csv`:

```
%%time
%memit pd.read_csv(path).groupby('label_source').count()
```

The preceding code should output something similar to the following:

```
peak memory: 161.35 MiB, increment: 67.34 MiB
CPU times: user 364 ms, sys: 95.2 ms, total: 459 ms
Wall time: 1.03 s
```

Now, you will load Modin and specify Dask as the engine:

```
from modin.config import Engine
Engine.put("dask")   # Modin will use Dask
import modin.pandas as pd
from distributed import Client
client = Client()
```

Notice that in the preceding code that Modin has a pandas implementation. This way, you can leverage your existing code without modification. You will now rerun the same code:

```
%%time
%memit pd.read_csv(path).groupby('label_source').count()
```

The preceding code should produce an output similar to the following:

```
peak memory: 137.12 MiB, increment: 9.34 MiB
CPU times: user 899 ms, sys: 214 ms, total: 1.11 s
Wall time: 1.91 s
```

Observe how the peak memory was reduced from `160 MiB` to `137.12 MiB` using Modin (Dask). Most importantly, notice how the memory increment went down from `67 MiB` to `9 MiB` with Modin. Overall, with Modin, you got lower memory usage. However, Modin (Dask) will show more significant advantages with more extensive operations on larger datasets.

See also

- For more information on `pandas.read_sas()`, you can refer to the official documentation: `https://pandas.pydata.org/docs/reference/api/pandas.read_sas.html`.

- There are other Python projects dedicated to making working with large datasets more scalable and performant and, in some cases, better options than pandas.

  - Dask: `https://dask.org/`

  - Ray: `https://ray.io/`

  - Modin: `https://modin.readthedocs.io/en/latest/`

  - Vaex: `https://vaex.io/`

3
Reading Time Series Data from Databases

Databases extend what you can store to include text, images, and media files and are designed for efficient read and write operations at a massive scale. Databases can store terabytes and petabytes of data with efficient and optimized data retrieval capabilities, such as when we are performing analytical operations on **data warehouses** and **data lakes**. A data warehouse is a database designed to store large amounts of structured data, mostly integrated from multiple source systems, built specifically to support business intelligence reporting, dashboards, and advanced analytics. A data lake, on the other hand, stores a large amount of data that is structured, semi-structured, or unstructured in its raw format. In this chapter, we will continue to use the **pandas** library to read data from databases. We will create time series DataFrames by reading data from **relational** (SQL) databases and **non-relational** (NoSQL) databases.

Additionally, you will explore working with third-party data providers to pull financial data from their database systems.

In this chapter, you will create time series DataFrames with a `DatetimeIndex` data type by covering the following recipes:

- Reading data from a relational database
- Reading data from Snowflake
- Reading data from a document database (MongoDB)
- Reading third-party financial data using APIs
- Reading data from a time series database (InfluxDB)

Technical requirements

In this chapter, we will be using pandas 1.4.2 (released April 2, 2022) extensively.

You will be working with different types of databases, such as PostgreSQL, Amazon Redshift, MongoDB, InfluxDB, and Snowflake. You will need to install additional Python libraries to connect to these databases.

You can also download the Jupyter notebooks from this book's GitHub repository (`https://github.com/PacktPublishing/Time-Series-Analysis-with-Python-Cookbook`) to follow along.

Reading data from a relational database

In this recipe, you will read data from PostgreSQL, a popular open source relational database.

You will explore two methods for connecting to and interacting with PostgreSQL. First, you will start by using `psycopg2`, a PostgreSQL Python connector, to connect and query the database, then parse the results into a pandas DataFrame. In the second approach, you will query the same database again but this time using **SQLAlchemy**, an **object-relational mapper** (**ORM**) that is well integrated with pandas.

Getting ready

In this recipe, it is assumed that you have the latest PostgreSQL installed. At the time of writing, version 14 is the latest stable version (version 15 is still in beta).

To connect to and query the database in Python, you will need to install `psycopg2`, a popular PostgreSQL database adapter for Python. You will also need to install *SQLAlchemy*, which provides flexibility regarding how you want to manage the database, whether it is for writing or reading data.

To install the libraries using `conda`, run the following command:

```
>>> conda install sqlalchemy psycopg2 -y
```

To install the libraries using `pip`, run the following command:

```
>>> pip install sqlalchemy psycopg2
```

How to do it...

We will start by connecting to the PostgreSQL instance, querying the database, loading the result set into memory, and finally parsing the data into a time series DataFrame.

In this recipe, I will be connecting to a PostgreSQL instance that is running locally, so my connection would be to `localhost` (`127.0.0.1`). You will need to adjust this for your own PostgreSQL database setting.

Using the psycopg2 PostgreSQL adapter for Python

`psycopg2` is a Python library (and a database driver) that provides additional functionality and features when you are working with a PostgreSQL database. Follow these steps:

1. Start by importing the necessary libraries. Define a Python dictionary where you will store all the parameter values required to establish a connection to the database, such as `host`, `database` name, `user` name, and `password`:

    ```
    import psycopg2
    import pandas as pd
    params = {
        "host": "127.0.0.1",
        "database": "postgres",
        "user": "postgres",
        "password": "password"
    }
    ```

2. You can establish a connection by passing the parameters to the `.connect()` method. Once connected, you can create a cursor object that can be used to execute SQL queries:

    ```
    conn = psycopg2.connect(**params)
    cursor = conn.cursor()
    ```

3. The cursor object provides several attributes and methods, including `execute()` and `fetchall()`. The following code uses the cursor object to pass a SQL query and then checks the number of records that have been produced by that query using the `.rowcount` attribute:

```
cursor.execute("""
SELECT date, last, volume
FROM yen_tbl
ORDER BY date;
""")
cursor.rowcount
>> 10902
```

4. The returned result set after executing the query will not include a header (no columns names). Alternatively, you can grab the column names from the cursor object using the `description` attribute, as shown in the following code:

```
cursor.description
>>
(Column(name='date', type_code=1082),
 Column(name='last', type_code=1700),
 Column(name='volume', type_code=1700))
```

5. You can use a list comprehension to extract the column names from `cursor.description` to use as column headers when creating the DataFrame:

```
columns = [col[0] for col in cursor.description]
columns
>> ['date', 'last', 'volume']
```

6. Now, fetch the results that were produced by the executed query and store them in a pandas DataFrame. Make sure that you pass the column names that you just captured:

```
data = cursor.fetchall()
df = pd.DataFrame(data, columns=columns)
df.info()
>>
<class 'pandas.core.frame.DataFrame'>
RangeIndex: 10902 entries, 0 to 10901
```

```
Data columns (total 3 columns):
 #    Column   Non-Null Count    Dtype
---   ------   --------------    -----
 0    date      10902 non-null   object
 1    last      10902 non-null   object
 2    volume    10902 non-null   object
dtypes: object(3)
memory usage: 255.6+ KB
```

Notice that the date column is returned as an object type, not a datetime type.

7. Parse the date column using pd.to_datetime() and set it as the index for the DataFrame:

```
df = df.set_index('date')
df.index = pd.to_datetime(df.index)
df.tail(3)
>>
                last      volume
date
2019-10-11    9267.0    158810.0
2019-10-14    9261.0     69457.0
2019-10-15    9220.0    108342.0
```

In the preceding code, the cursor returned a list of tuples without a header. You can instruct the cursor to return a RealDictRow type, which will include the column name information. This is more convenient when converting into a DataFrame. This can be done by passing the RealDictCursor class to the cursor_factory parameter:

```
from psycopg2.extras import RealDictCursor
cursor = conn.cursor(cursor_factory=RealDictCursor)
cursor.execute("SELECT * FROM yen_tbl;")
data = cursor.fetchall()
df = pd.DataFrame(data)
```

8. Close the cursor and the connection to the database:

```
In [12]: cursor.close()
In [13]: conn.close()
```

Starting from version 2.5, `psycopg2` connections and cursors can be used in Python's `with` statement for exception handling when committing a transaction. The cursor object provides three different fetching functions; that is, `fetchall()`, `fetchmany()`, and `fetchone()`. The `fetchone()` method returns a single tuple. The following example shows this concept:

```
import psycopg2
url = 'postgresql://postgres:password@localhost:5432'
with psycopg2.connect(url) as conn:
    with conn.cursor() as cursor:
        cursor.execute('SELECT * FROM yen_tbl')
        data = cursor.fetchall()
```

Using SQLAlchemy and psycopg2

SQLAlchemy is a very popular open source library for working with relational databases in Python. SQLAlchemy can be referred to as an **object-relational mapper (ORM)**, which provides an abstraction layer (think of an interface) so that you can use object-oriented programming to interact with a relational database.

You will be using SQLAlchemy because it integrates very well with pandas, and several of the pandas SQL reader and writer functions depend on SQLAlchemy as the abstraction layer. SQLAlchemy does the translation behind the scenes for any pandas SQL read or write requests. This translation ensures that the SQL statement from pandas is represented in the right syntax/format for the underlying database type (MySQL, Oracle, SQL Server, or PostgreSQL, to name a few).

Some of the pandas SQL reader functions that rely on SQLAlchemy include `pandas.read_sql()`, `pandas.read_sql_query()`, and `pandas.read_sql_table()`. Let's perform the following steps:

1. Start by importing the necessary libraries. Note that, behind the scenes, SQLAlchemy will use `psycopg2` (or any other database driver that is installed and supported by SQLAlchemy):

```
import pandas as pd
from sqlalchemy import create_engine
engine = create_engine("postgresql+psycopg2://
postgres:password@localhost:5432")
query = "SELECT * FROM yen_tbl"
df = pd.read_sql(query,
```

```
                engine,
                index_col='date',
                parse_dates={'date': '%Y-%m-%d'})

df['last'].tail(3)
>>
date
2019-10-11    9267.0
2019-10-14    9261.0
2019-10-15    9220.0
Name: last, dtype: float64
```

In the preceding example, for `parse_dates`, you passed a dictionary in the
format of {key: value}, where `key` is the column name and `value` is a string
representation of the date format. Unlike the previous `psycopg2` approach,
`pandas.read_sql()` did a better job of getting the data types correct. Notice
that our index is of the `DatetimeIndex` type:

```
df.info()
>>
<class 'pandas.core.frame.DataFrame'>
DatetimeIndex: 10902 entries, 1976-08-02 to 2019-10-15
Data columns (total 8 columns):
 #   Column                    Non-Null Count   Dtype
---  ------                    --------------   -----
 0   open                      10902 non-null   float64
 1   high                      10902 non-null   float64
 2   low                       10902 non-null   float64
 3   last                      10902 non-null   float64
 4   change                    1415 non-null    float64
 5   settle                    10902 non-null   float64
 6   volume                    10902 non-null   float64
 7   Previous Day Open Interest 10902 non-null  float64
dtypes: float64(8)
memory usage: 766.5 KB
```

2. You could also accomplish the same results using the `pandas.read_sql_query()` function. This will also return an index of the O type:

```
df = pd.read_sql_query(query,
                       engine,
                       index_col='date',
                       parse_dates={'date':'%Y-%m-%d'})
```

3. pandas provides another SQL reader function called `pandas.read_sql_table()` that does not take a SQL query, instead taking a table name. Think of this as a `SELECT * FROM sometable` query:

```
df = pd.read_sql_table('yen_tbl',
                       engine,
                       index_col='date')
```

How it works...

Let's examine the engine connection string for SQLAlchemy:

```
create_engine("dialect+driver://username:password@host:port/
dbname")
```

Creating the engine is the first step when working with SQLAlchemy as it provides instructions on the database that is being considered. This is known as a **dialect**.

Earlier, you used `psycopg2` as the database driver for PostgreSQL. `psycopg2` is referred to as a **database API (DBAPI)** and SQLAlchemy supports many DBAPI wrappers based on Python's DBAPI specifications to connect to and interface with various types of relational databases. It also comes with built-in dialects to work with different flavors of RDBMS, such as the following:

-   SQL Server
-   SQLite
-   PostgreSQL
-   MySQL
-   Oracle
-   Snowflake

When connecting to a database using SQLAlchemy, we need to specify the dialect and the driver (DBAPI) to be used. This is what the format looks like for PostgreSQL:

```
create_engine("postgresql+psycopg2://username:password@
localhost:5432")
```

In the previous code examples, we did not need to specify the psycopg2 driver since it is the default DBAPI that is used by SQLAlchemy. This example would work just fine, assuming that psycopg2 is installed:

```
create_engine("postgresql://username:password@localhost:5432")
```

There are other PostgreSQL drivers (DBAPI) that are supported by SQLAlchemy, including the following:

- psycopg2
- pg8000
- asyncpg
- pygresql

For a more comprehensive list of supported dialects and drivers, you can visit the official documentation page at https://docs.sqlalchemy.org/en/14/dialects/.

The advantage of using SQLAlchemy is that it is well integrated with pandas. If you read the official pandas documentation for read_sql(), read_sql_query(), and read_sql_table(), you will notice that the conn argument is expecting a SQLAlchemy connection object (engine).

There's more...

When you executed the query against yen_tbl, it returned 10,902 records. Imagine working with a larger database that returned millions of records, if not more. This is where **chunking** helps.

The chunksize parameter allows you to break down a large dataset into smaller and more manageable chunks of data that can fit into your local memory. When executing the read_sql() function, just pass the number of rows to be retrieved (per chunk) to the chunksize parameter, which then returns a generator object. You can then loop through that object or use next(), one chunksize at a time, and perform whatever calculations or processing needed. Let's look at an example of how chunking works. You will request 5 records (rows) at a time:

```
df = pd.read_sql(query,
                 engine,
                 index_col='date',
                 parse_dates=True,
                 chunksize=5)
# example using next
next(df)['last']
>>
date
1976-08-02     3401.0
1976-08-03     3401.0
1976-08-04     3401.0
1976-08-05     3401.0
1976-08-06     3401.0
Name: last, dtype: float64


# example using a for loop
df = pd.read_sql(query,
                 engine,
                 index_col='date',
                 parse_dates=True,
                 chunksize=5000)


for idx, data in enumerate(df):
    print(idx, data.shape)
>>
0 (5000, 8)
1 (5000, 8)
2 (902, 8)
```

The preceding code demonstrated how chunking works. Using the chunksize parameter should reduce memory usage since the code loads 5,000 rows at a time. The PostgreSQL database being used contains 10,902 rows, so it took three rounds to retrieve the entire dataset: 5,000 on the first, 5,000 on the second, and the last 902 records on the third.

See also

Since you just explored connecting to and querying PostgreSQL, it is worth mentioning that **Amazon Redshift**, a cloud data warehouse, is based on PostgreSQL at its core. This means you can use the same connection information (the same dialect and DBAPI) to connect to AWS Redshift. Here is an example:

```
import pandas as pd
from sqlalchemy import create_engine
host = 'redshift-cluster.somecluster.us-east-1.redshift.
amazonaws.com'
port = 5439
database = 'dev'
username = 'awsuser'
password = 'yourpassword'
query = "SELECT * FROM yen_tbl"
chunksize = 1000

aws_engine = create_engine(f"postgresql+psycopg2://
{username}:{password}@{host}:\
                {port}/{database}")

df = pd.read_sql(query,
                aws_engine,
                index_col='date',
                parse_dates=True,
                chunksize=chunksize)
```

The preceding example worked by using the postgresql dialect to connect to Amazon Redshift. There is also a specific SQLAlchemy Redshift dialect that still relies on the psycopg2 driver. To learn more about sqlalchemy-redshift, you can refer to the project's repository here: https://github.com/sqlalchemy-redshift/sqlalchemy-redshift.

The following example shows how the RedShift dialect can be used:

```
create_engine(f"redshift+psycopg2://{username}:{password}@
{host}:\
                                {port}/{database}")
```

For additional information regarding these topics, take a look at the following links:

- For *SQLAlchemy*, you can visit `https://www.sqlalchemy.org/`.
- For the `pandas.read_sql()` function, you can visit `https://pandas.pydata.org/docs/reference/api/pandas.read_sql.html`.

Even though you used `psycopg2` in this recipe, keep in mind that `psycopg3` is in the works. If you are interested in keeping track of when the library will be officially released, you can visit `https://www.psycopg.org/psycopg3/`.

Reading data from Snowflake

A very common place to extract data for analytics is usually a company's *data warehouse*. Data warehouses host a massive amount of data that, in most cases, contains integrated data to support various reporting and analytics needs, in addition to historical data from various source systems.

The evolution of the cloud brought us cloud data warehouses such as **Amazon Redshift**, **Google BigQuery**, **Azure SQL Data Warehouse**, and **Snowflake**.

In this recipe, you will work with *Snowflake*, a powerful **Software as a Service (SaaS)** cloud-based data warehousing platform that can be hosted on different cloud platforms, such as **Amazon Web Services (AWS)**, **Google Cloud Platform (GCP)**, and **Microsoft Azure**. You will learn how to connect to Snowflake using Python to extract time series data and load it into a pandas DataFrame.

Getting ready

This recipe assumes you have access to Snowflake. To connect to Snowflake, you will need to install the Snowflake Python connector.

To install Snowflake using `conda`, run the following command:

```
conda install -c conda-forge snowflake-sqlalchemy snowflake-
connector-python
```

To install Snowflake using `pip`, run the following command:

```
pip install "snowflake-connector-python[pandas]"
pip install --upgrade snowflake-sqlalchemy
```

How to do it...

We will explore two ways to connect to the Snowflake database. In the first method, you will be using the Snowflake Python connector to establish our connection, as well as to create our cursor to query and fetch the data. In the second method, you will explore *SQLAlchemy* and how it integrates with the pandas library. Let's get started:

1. We will start by importing the necessary libraries:

   ```
   import pandas as pd
   from snowflake import connector
   from configparser import ConfigParser
   ```

2. The Snowflake connector has a set of input parameters that need to be supplied to establish a connector. You can create a `.cfg` file, such as `snow.cfg`, to store all the necessary information in the following format:

   ```
   [SNOWFLAKE]
   USER=<your_username>
   PASSWORD=<your_password>
   ACCOUNT=<your_account>
   WAREHOUSE=<your_warehouse_name>
   DATABASE=<your_database_name>
   SCHEMA=<you_schema_name>
   ROLE=<your_role_name>
   ```

3. Using `ConfigParser`, you can extract the content under the `[SNOWFLAKE]` section to avoid exposing or hardcoding your credentials. You can read the entire content of the `[SNOWFLAKE]` section and convert it into a dictionary object, as shown here:

   ```
   connector.paramstyle='qmark'
   config = ConfigParser()
   config.read('snow.cfg')
   config.sections()
   params = dict(config['SNOWFLAKE'])
   ```

4. You will need to pass the parameters to `connector.connect()` to establish a connection with Snowflake. We can easily unpack the dictionary's content since the dictionary keys match the parameter names, as per Snowflake's documentation. Once the connection has been established, we can create our cursor:

```
con = connector.connect(**params)
cursor = con.cursor()
```

5. The cursor object has many methods, including `execute`, to pass a SQL statement to the database, as well as several fetch methods to retrieve the data. In the following example, we will query the `ORDERS` table and leverage the `fetch_pandas_all` method to get a pandas DataFrame:

```
query = "select * from ORDERS;"
cursor.execute(query)
df = cursor.fetch_pandas_all()
```

6. Inspect the DataFrame using `df.info()`:

```
df.info()
>>
<class 'pandas.core.frame.DataFrame'>
Int64Index: 15000 entries, 0 to 4588
Data columns (total 9 columns):
 #   Column           Non-Null Count   Dtype
---  ------           --------------   -----
 0   O_ORDERKEY       15000 non-null   int32
 1   O_CUSTKEY        15000 non-null   int16
 2   O_ORDERSTATUS    15000 non-null   object
 3   O_TOTALPRICE     15000 non-null   float64
 4   O_ORDERDATE      15000 non-null   object
 5   O_ORDERPRIORITY  15000 non-null   object
 6   O_CLERK          15000 non-null   object
 7   O_SHIPPRIORITY   15000 non-null   int8
 8   O_COMMENT        15000 non-null   object
dtypes: float64(1), int16(1), int32(1), int8(1),
object(5)
memory usage: 922.9+ KB
```

7. From the preceding output, you can see that the DataFrame's Index is just a sequence of numbers and that the O_ORDERDATE column is not a Date field. This can be fixed by parsing the O_ORDERDATE column with a DatetimeIndex and setting it as an index for the DataFrame:

```
df_ts = (df.set_index(pd.to_datetime(df['O_ORDERDATE'])))
        .drop(columns='O_ORDERDATE'))
df_ts.iloc[0:3, 1:5]
```

Now, you should have a time series DataFrame with a DatetimeIndex (O_ORDERDATE):

O_ORDERDATE	O_CUSTKEY	O_ORDERSTATUS	O_TOTALPRICE	O_ORDERPRIORITY
1994-08-07	781	F	134013.09	2-HIGH
1996-10-20	824	O	117400.53	2-HIGH
1995-09-29	760	O	117234.60	5-LOW

Figure 3.1 – The first three rows of the time series df_ts DataFrame

8. You can inspect the index of the DataFrame and print the first two indexes:

```
df_ts.index[0:2]
>> DatetimeIndex(['1994-08-07', '1996-10-20'],
dtype='datetime64[ns]', name='O_ORDERDATE', freq=None)
```

The DataFrame now has O_ORDERDATE as the index and the proper data type; that is, DatetimeIndex.

9. You can repeat the same process but without the additional effort of manually parsing the O_ORDERDATE column and setting it as an index. Here, you can use SQLAlchemy and leverage the pandas.read_sql() reader function to perform these operations:

```
from sqlalchemy import create_engine
from snowflake.sqlalchemy import URL
url = URL(**params)
engine = create_engine(url)
connection = engine.connect()

df = pd.read_sql(query,
                connection,
```

```
                    index_col='o_orderdate',
                    parse_dates='o_orderdate')
df.info()
>>
<class 'pandas.core.frame.DataFrame'>
DatetimeIndex: 15000 entries, 1994-08-07 to 1994-06-13
Data columns (total 8 columns):
 #   Column          Non-Null Count   Dtype
---  ------          --------------   -----
 0   o_orderkey      15000 non-null   int64
 1   o_custkey       15000 non-null   int64
 2   o_orderstatus   15000 non-null   object
 3   o_totalprice    15000 non-null   float64
 4   o_orderpriority 15000 non-null   object
 5   o_clerk         15000 non-null   object
 6   o_shippriority  15000 non-null   int64
 7   o_comment       15000 non-null   object
dtypes: float64(1), int64(3), object(4)
memory usage: 1.0+ MB
```

Notice that O_ORDERDATE is now an index and of the DatetimeIndex type.

How it works...

The Snowflake Python connector requires several input variables to connect to the database. These include the following:

Parameter	Required	Description
account	Yes	This can be obtained from https://<account>. snowflakecomputing.com/.
user	Yes	Login name for the user.
password	Yes	Password for the user.
database		Specifies the default database to use.
schema		Specifies the default schema to use.
role		Specifies the default role to use.
warehouse		Specifies the default warehouse to use.

Table 3.1 – Input variables for the Snowflake Python connector

For a complete list of parameters that are available for the `connect()` function, you can refer to the official documentation at `https://docs.snowflake.com/en/user-guide/python-connector-api.html#module-snowflake-connector`.

Once the connection is accepted, you could create your cursor object. The cursor provides several useful attributes and methods, including `description`, `rowcount`, `rownumber`, `execute()`, `execute_async()`, `fetchone()`, `fetchall()`, `fetch_pandas_all()`, and `fetch_pandas_batches()`, to name few.

For a complete list of attributes and methods, you can refer to the official documentation at `https://docs.snowflake.com/en/user-guide/python-connector-api.html#object-cursor`.

Using SQLAlchemy, you were able to leverage the `pandas.read_sql()` reader function and use the many parameters available to transform and process the data at read time. The Snowflake `fetch_pandas_all()` function, on the other hand, does not take in any parameters, and you will need to parse and adjust the DataFrame afterward.

The Snowflake SQLAlchemy library provides a convenience method, URL, to help construct the connection string to connect to the Snowflake database. Typically, SQLAlchemy expects a URL to be provided in the following format:

```
'snowflake://<user>:<password>@<account>/<database>/<schema>
?warehouse=<warehouse>&role=<role>'
```

Using the URL method, we passed our parameters and the method took care of constructing the connection string that is expected:

```
engine = create_engine(URL(
    account = '<your_account>',
    user = '<your_username>',
    password = '<your_password>',
    database = '<your_database>',
    schema = '<your_schema>',
    warehouse = '<your_warehouse>',
    role='<your_role>',
))
```

There's more...

You may have noticed that the columns in the returned DataFrame, when using the Snowflake Python connector, all came back in uppercase, while they were lowercased when using Snowflake SQLAlchemy.

The reason for this is because Snowflake, by default, stores unquoted object names in uppercase when these objects are created. In the previous code, for example, our Order Date column was returned as O_ORDERDATE.

To explicitly indicate the name is case-sensitive, you will need to use quotes when creating the object in Snowflake (for example, `'o_orderdate'` or `'OrderDate'`). In contrast, using Snowflake SQLAlchemy converts the names into lowercase by default.

See also

- For more information on the Snowflake Connector for Python, you can visit the official documentation at `https://docs.snowflake.com/en/user-guide/python-connector.html`.

- For more information regarding Snowflake SQLAlchemy Toolkit, you can visit the official documentation at `https://docs.snowflake.com/en/user-guide/sqlalchemy.html`.

Reading data from a document database (MongoDB)

MongoDB, a **NoSQL** database, stores data in documents and uses BSON (a JSON-like structure) to store schema-less data. Unlike relational databases, where data is stored in tables that consist of rows and columns, document-oriented databases store data in collections and documents.

A document represents the lowest granular level of data being stored, as rows do in relational databases. A collection, like a table in relational databases, stores documents. Unlike relational databases, a collection can store documents of different schemas and structures.

Getting ready

In this recipe, it is assumed that you have a running instance of MongoDB. To get ready for this recipe, you will need to install the PyMongo Python library to connect to MongoDB.

To install MongoDB using `conda`, run the following command:

```
$ conda install -c anaconda pymongo -y
```

To install MongoDB using `pip`, run the following command:

```
$ python -m pip install pymongo
```

> **Note about Using MongoDB Atlas**
>
> If you are connecting to MongoDB Atlas (Cloud) Free Tier or their M2/M5 shared tier cluster, then you will be using the *mongodb+srv* protocol. In this case, you can either specify this during the pip install with `python -m pip install pymongo[srv]` or you can just install **dnspython** with `pip install dnspython`.

How to do it...

In this recipe, you will connect to the MongoDB instance that you have set up. If you are using an on-premises install (local install or Docker container), then your connection string will be `mongodb://localhost:27017`. If you are using Atlas, then your connection may look more like `mongodb+srv://<username>:<password>@<clusterName>.yqcgb.mongodb.net/<DatabaseName>?retryWrites=true&w=majority"`.

Perform the following steps:

1. First, let's import the necessary libraries:

```
import pandas as pd
from pymongo import MongoClient
```

2. Establish a connection to MongoDB. For a local instance (on-premises), this would look something like this:

```
# connecting to on-premise instance
url = "mongodb://localhost:27017"
client = MongoClient(url)
MongoClient(host=['localhost:27017'],
                document_class=dict,
                    tz_aware=False,
                        connect=True)
>> MongoClient(host=['localhost:27017'], document_
class=dict, tz_aware=False, connect=True)
```

If you are connecting to Atlas, the connection string will look more like this:

```
# connecting to Atlas cloud Cluster
cluster = 'cluster0'
username = 'user'
password = 'password'
database = 'stock_data'
url = \
f"mongodb+srv://{username}:{password}@{cluster}.3rncb.
mongodb.net/{database}"
client =  MongoClient(url)
client

>> MongoClient(host=['cluster0-shard-00-00.3rncb.
mongodb.net:27017', 'cluster0-shard-00-01.3rncb.
mongodb.net:27017', 'cluster0-shard-00-02.3rncb.
mongodb.net:27017'], document_class=dict, tz_
aware=False, connect=True, authsource='somesource',
replicaset='Cluster0-shard-0', ssl=True)
```

3. You can list all the databases available. In this example, I named the database stock_data and the collection microsoft:

```
client.list_database_names()
>> ['admin', 'config', 'local', 'stock_data']
```

4. You can list the collections that are available under the stock_data database using list_collection_names:

```
db = client['stock_data']
db.list_collection_names()
>> ['microsoft']
```

5. Now, you can specify which collection to query. In this case, there is one collection called microsoft:

```
collection = db['microsoft']
```

6. Now, query the database into a pandas DataFrame using .find():

```
results = collection.find({})
msft_df = \
```

```
pd.DataFrame(results).set_index('Date').drop(columns='_
id')
msft_df.head()
>>

                      MSFT
Date
2020-05-18    183.049850
2020-05-19    181.782730
2020-05-20    184.304169
2020-05-21    182.090454
2020-05-22    182.169861
```

How it works...

The first step is to create a MongoDB client object (**MongoClient**) for the database instance. This will give you access to a set of functions, such as `list_databases_names()`, and additional attributes, such as `address`.

`MongoClient()` accepts a connection string that should follow MongoDB's URI format, as follows:

```
client = MongoClient("mongodb://localhost:27017")
```

Alternatively, the same can be accomplished by explicitly providing *host* (string) and *port* (numeric) positional arguments, as follows:

```
client = MongoClient('localhost', 27017)
```

The host string can either be the hostname or the IP address, as shown here:

```
client = MongoClient('127.0.0.1', 27017)
```

Note that to connect to your localhost that uses the default port (`27017`), you can establish a connection without providing any arguments, as shown in the following code:

```
# using default values for host and port
client = MongoClient()
```

Once the connection has been established, you can connect to the database, list its collections, and query any document available. The flow in terms of navigation before we can query our documents is to specify our database, then select the collection we are interested in, and then submit the query.

In the preceding example, our database was called `stock_data`, which contained a collection called `msft`. You can have multiple collections in a database, and multiple documents in a collection. To think of this in terms of relational databases, recall that a collection is like a table and that documents represent rows in that table.

In Python, we can specify our database using different syntax, as shown in the following code. Keep in mind that all these statements will produce a `pymongo.database.Database` object:

```
# Specifying the database
db = client['stock_data']
db = client.stock_data
db = client.get_database('stock_data')
```

In the preceding code, `get_database()` can take in additional arguments for the `codec_options`, `read_preference`, `write_concern`, and `read_concern` parameters, where the latter two are focused more on operations across nodes and how to determine if the operation was successful or not.

Similarly, once you have the `PyMongo` database object, you can specify a collection using different syntax, as shown in the following example:

```
# Specifying the collection
collection = db.microsoft
collection = db['microsoft']
collection = db.get_collection('microsoft')
```

The `get_collection()` method provides additional parameters, similar to `get_database()`.

The three syntax variations in the preceding example return a `pymongo.database.Collection` object, which comes with additional built-in methods and attributes such as `find`, `find_one`, `update`, `update_one`, `update_many`, `remove`, `delete_one`, and `delete_many`, to name a few.

Once you are at the collection level (a PyMongo collection object), you can start querying the data. In our recipe, we used `find()`, which you can think of as doing something similar to using a `SELECT` statement in SQL.

In the *How to do it…* section, in *step 6*, we queried the entire collection to retrieve all the documents using this line of code:

```
collection.find({})
```

The empty dictionary, {}, in find() represents our filtering criteria. When you pass an empty filter criterion with {}, you are retrieving everything. This resembles SELECT * in a SQL database. The filter takes a key-value pair to return a select number of documents where the keys match the values specified. The following is an example:

```
results = collection.find({'MSFT': {'$gt':260}}, {'_id':0})
list(results)
>>
[{'Date': datetime.datetime(2021, 4, 16, 0, 0), 'MSFT':
260.739990234375},
 {'Date': datetime.datetime(2021, 4, 21, 0, 0), 'MSFT':
260.5799865722656},
 {'Date': datetime.datetime(2021, 4, 23, 0, 0), 'MSFT':
261.1499938964844},
 {'Date': datetime.datetime(2021, 4, 26, 0, 0), 'MSFT':
261.54998779296875},
 {'Date': datetime.datetime(2021, 4, 27, 0, 0), 'MSFT':
261.9700012207031}]
```

In the preceding code, we added a filter to only retrieve data where MSFT values are greater than 260. We also specified that we do not want to return the _id field. This way, there is no need to drop it when creating our DataFrame.

Generally, when collection.find() is executed, it returns a **cursor** (more specifically, a pymongo.cursor.Cursor object). This cursor object is just a pointer to the result set of the query, which allows us to iterate over the results. You can then use a for loop or next() (think of a Python iterator). However, in our recipe, instead of looping through our cursor object, we conveniently converted the entire result set into a pandas DataFrame.

There's more...

There are different ways to retrieve data from MongoDB using PyMongo. In the previous section, we used db.collection.find(), which always returns a cursor. As we discussed earlier, find() returns all the matching documents that are available in the specified collection. If you want to return the first occurrence of matching documents, then db.collection.find_one() would be the best choice and would return a dictionary object, not a cursor. Keep in mind that this only returns one document, as shown in the following example:

```
db.microsoft.find_one()
>>>
```

```
{'_id': ObjectId('60a1274c5d9f26bfcd55ba06'),
 'Date': datetime.datetime(2020, 5, 18, 0, 0),
 'MSFT': 183.0498504638672}
```

When it comes to working with cursors, there are several ways you can traverse through the data:

- Converting into a **pandas DataFrame** using pd.DataFrame(cursor), as shown in the following code:

  ```
  cursor = db.microsoft.find()
  df = pd.DataFrame(cursor)
  ```

- Converting into a Python **list** or **tuple**:

  ```
  data = list(db.microsoft.find())
  ```

  You can also convert the Cursor object into a Python list and then convert that into a pandas DataFrame, like this:

  ```
  data = list(db.microsoft.find())
  df = pd.DataFrame(data)
  ```

- Using next() to get move the pointer to the next item in the result set:

  ```
  cursor = db.microsoft.find()
  cursor.next()
  ```

- **Looping** through the object, for example, with a for loop:

  ```
  cursor = db.microsoft.find()
  for doc in cursor:
      print(doc)
  ```

- Specifying an **index**. Here, we are printing the first value:

  ```
  cursor = db.microsoft.find()
  cursor[0]
  ```

Note that if you provided a slice, such as cursor[0:1], which is a range, then it will return an error.

See also

For more information on the PyMongo API, please refer to the official documentation, which you can find here: `https://pymongo.readthedocs.io/en/stable/index.html`.

Reading third-party financial data using APIs

In this recipe, you will use a very useful library, `pandas-datareader`, which provides remote data access so that you can extract data from multiple data sources, including **Yahoo Finance**, **Quandl**, and **Alpha Vantage**, to name a few. The library not only fetches the data but also returns the data as a *pandas DataFrame* and the index as a `DatetimeIndex`.

Getting ready

For this recipe, you will need to install `pandas-datareader`.

To install it using `conda`, run the following command:

```
>>> conda install -c anaconda pandas-datareader -y
```

To install it using `pip`, run the following command:

```
>>> pip install pandas-datareader
```

How to do it...

In this recipe, you will use the *Yahoo API* to pull stock data for **Microsoft** and **Apple**. Let's get started:

1. Let's start by importing the necessary libraries:

    ```
    import pandas as pd
    import datetime
    import matplotlib.pyplot as plt
    import pandas_datareader.data as web
    ```

2. Create the `start_date`, `end_date`, and `tickers` variables. `end_date` is today's date, while `start_date` is 10 years back from today's date:

```
start_date = (datetime.datetime.today() -
        datetime.timedelta(weeks=52*10)).strftime('%Y-
%m-%d')

end_date = datetime.datetime.today().strftime('%Y-%m-%d')
tickers = ['MSFT','AAPL']
```

3. Pass these variables to `web.DataReader()` and specify `yahoo` as `data_source`. The returned dataset will have a `Date` index of the `DatetimeIndex` type:

```
dt = web.DataReader(name=tickers,
                    data_source='yahoo',
                    start=start_date,
                    end=end_date)['Adj Close']
dt.tail(2)
>>
Symbols           MSFT          AAPL
Date
2021-09-14   299.790009   148.119995
2021-09-15   304.820007   149.029999
```

In the preceding example, `pandas-datareader` took care of all data processing and returned a pandas DataFrame and a `DatetimeIndex` index, which was already implemented.

How it works...

The `DataReader()` function requires four positional arguments:

- `name`, which takes a list of symbols.
- `data_source`, which indicates which API/data source to use. For example, `yahoo` indicates Yahoo Finance data. If you are using Quandl, we just need to change the value to `quandl` or `av-daily` to indicate Alpha Vantage Daily stock.
- `start_date` sets the left boundary for the date range. If no value is given, then it will default to `1/1/2010`.

- `end_date` sets the right boundary for the date range. If no value is given, then it will default to today's date. We could have omitted the end date in the preceding example and gotten the same results.

There's more…

The library also provides high-level functions specific to each data provider, as opposed to the generic `web.DataReader()` class.

The following is an example of using the `get_data_yahoo()` function:

```
dt = web.get_data_yahoo(tickers)['Adj Close']
dt.tail(2)
>>
Symbols            MSFT            AAPL
Date
2021-09-14   299.790009   148.119995
2021-09-15   304.820007   149.029999
```

The preceding code will retrieve 5 years' worth of data from today's date. Notice that we did not specify start and end dates and relied on the default behavior. The three positional arguments this function takes are `symbols` and the `start` and `end` dates.

Additionally, the library provides other high-level functions for many of the data sources, as follows:

- `get_data_quandl`
- `get_data_tiingo`
- `get_data_alphavantage`
- `get_data_fred`
- `get_data_stooq`
- `get_data_moex`

See also

For more information on `pandas-datareader`, you can refer to the official documentation at `https://pandas-datareader.readthedocs.io/en/latest/`.

Reading data from a time series database (InfluxDB)

A time series database, a type of **NoSQL** database, is optimized for time-stamped or time series data and provides improved performance, especially when working with large datasets containing IoT data or sensor data. In the past, common use cases for time series databases were mostly associated with financial stock data, but their use cases have expanded into other disciplines and domains. InfluxDB is a popular open source time series database with a large community base. In this recipe, we will be using InfluxDB's latest release; that is, v2.2. The most recent InfluxDB releases introduced the Flux data scripting language, which you will use with the Python API to query our time series data.

For this recipe, we will be using the **National Oceanic and Atmospheric Administration** (**NOAA**) water sample data provided by InfluxDB. For instructions on how to load the sample data, please refer to the InfluxDB official documentation at `https://docs.influxdata.com/influxdb/v2.2/reference/sample-data/`

Getting ready

This recipe assumes that you have a running instance of InfluxDB since we will be demonstrating how to query the database and convert the output into a pandas DataFrame for further analysis.

Before you can interact with InfluxDB using Python, you will need to install the InfluxDB Python SDK. We will be working with InfluxDB 2.x, so you will need to install `influxdb-client` v1.29.1 (not `influxdb-python`).

You can install this using `pip`, as follows:

```
$ pip install influxdb-client
```

To install using conda use the following:

```
conda install -c conda-forge influxdb-client
```

How to do it...

We will be leveraging the `Influxdb_client` Python SDK for InfluxDB 2.x, which provides support for pandas DataFrames in terms of both read and write functionality. Let's get started:

1. First, let's import the necessary libraries:

    ```
    from influxdb_client import InfluxDBClient
    import pandas as pd
    ```

2. To establish your connection using `InfluxDBClient(url="http://localhost:8086", token=token)`, you will need to define the `token`, `org`, and `bucket` variables:

```
token = "c5c0JUoz-\
joisPCttI6hy8aLccEyaflyfNj1S_
Kff34N_4moiCQacH8BLbLzFu4qWTP8ibSk3JNYtv9zlUwxeA=="
org = "my-org"
bucket = "noaa"
```

3. Now, you are ready to establish your connection by passing the URL, `token`, and `org` parameters to `InlfuxDBClient()`:

```
client = InfluxDBClient(url="http://localhost:8086",
                        token=token,
                        org=org)
```

4. Next, you will instantiate `query_api`:

```
query_api = client.query_api()
```

5. Then, you must pass your Flux query and request the results to be in pandas DataFrame format using the `query_data_frame()` method:

```
query = '''
        from(bucket: "noaa")
            |> range(start: 2019-09-01T00:00:00Z)
            |> filter(fn: (r) => r._measurement == "h2o_
temperature")
            |> filter(fn: (r) => r.location == "coyote_
creek")
            |> filter(fn: (r) => r._field == "degrees")
            |> movingAverage(n: 120)
        '''
result = client.query_api().query_data_frame(org=org,
query=query)
```

6. In the preceding Flux script, we filtered the data to include h2o_temparature for the coyote_creek location. Let's inspect the DataFrame. Pay attention to the data types in the following output:

```
result.info()
<class 'pandas.core.frame.DataFrame'>
Int64Index: 15087 entries, 0 to 15086
Data columns (total 9 columns):
 #    Column          Non-Null Count   Dtype
---   ------          --------------   -----
 0    result          15087 non-null   object
 1    table           15087 non-null   object
 2    _start          15087 non-null   datetime64[ns,
tzutc()]
 3    _stop           15087 non-null   datetime64[ns,
tzutc()]
 4    _time           15087 non-null   datetime64[ns,
tzutc()]
 5    _value          15087 non-null   float64
 6    _field          15087 non-null   object
 7    _measurement    15087 non-null   object
 8    location        15087 non-null   object
dtypes: datetime64[ns, tzutc()](3), float64(1), object(5)
```

7. Let's inspect the first 5 rows of our dataset result. Notice that InfluxDB stores time in nanosecond [ns] precision and that the datetime is in the UTC time zone [tzutc]:

```
result.loc[0:5, '_time':'_value']
>>
                             _time       _value
0 2021-04-01 01:45:02.350669+00:00   64.983333
1 2021-04-01 01:51:02.350669+00:00   64.975000
2 2021-04-01 01:57:02.350669+00:00   64.916667
3 2021-04-01 02:03:02.350669+00:00   64.933333
4 2021-04-01 02:09:02.350669+00:00   64.958333
5 2021-04-01 02:15:02.350669+00:00   64.933333
```

How it works...

InfluxDB 1.8x introduced the **Flux** query language as an alternative query language to **InfluxQL**, with the latter having a closer resemblance to SQL. InfluxDB 2.0 introduced the concept of **buckets**, which is where data is stored, whereas Influx 1.x stored data in databases.

Given the major changes in InfluxDB 2.x, there is a dedicated Python library for InfluxDB called `influxdb-client`. On the other hand, the previous `influxdb` library works only with InfluxDB 1.x and is not compatible with InfluxDB 2.x. Unfortunately, the `influxdb-client` Python API does not support **InfluxQL**, so you can only use **Flux** queries.

In this recipe, we started by creating an instance of `InfluxDbClient`, which later gave us access to `query_api()`. We used this to pass our Flux query to our `noaa` bucket.

`query_api` gives us additional methods to interact with our bucket:

- `query()` returns the result as a **FluxTable**.
- `query_csv()` returns the result as a CSV iterator (CSV reader).
- `query_data_frame()` returns the result as a pandas DataFrame.
- `query_data_frame_stream()` returns a stream of pandas DataFrames as a generator.
- `query_raw()` returns the result as raw unprocessed data in s string format.
- `query_stream()` is similar to `query_data_frame_stream` but returns a stream of `FluxRecord` as a generator.

In the preceding code, you used `client.query_api()` to fetch the data, as shown here:

```
result = client.query_api().query_data_frame(org=org,
query=query)
```

You used `query_data_frame`, which executes a synchronous Flux query and returns a pandas DataFrame with which you are familiar.

There's more...

There is an additional argument that you can use to create the DataFrame index.
In `query_data_frame()`, you can pass a list as an argument to the `data_frame_index` parameter, as shown in the following example:

```
result =\
query_api.query_data_frame(query=query,
                                        data_frame_index=['_time'])


result['_value'].head()
>>
_time
2021-04-01 01:45:02.350669+00:00      64.983333
2021-04-01 01:51:02.350669+00:00      64.975000
2021-04-01 01:57:02.350669+00:00      64.916667
2021-04-01 02:03:02.350669+00:00      64.933333
2021-04-01 02:09:02.350669+00:00      64.958333
Name: _value, dtype: float64
```

This returns a time series DataFrame with a `DatetimeIndex` (`_time`).

See also

- If you are new to Flux, then check out the *Get Started with Flux* official
  documentation at `https://docs.influxdata.com/influxdb/v2.0/query-data/get-started/`.

- Please refer to the official InfluxDB-Client Python library documentation on GitHub
  at `https://github.com/influxdata/influxdb-client-python`.

4

Persisting Time Series Data to Files

In this chapter, you will be using the **pandas** library to persist your **time series DataFrames** to a different file format, such as **CSV**, **Excel**, and **pickle** files. When performing analysis or data transformations on DataFrames, you are essentially leveraging pandas' in-memory analytics capabilities, which offer great performance. But being in-memory means that the data can easily be lost since it is not persisting on disk.

When working with DataFrames, there will be a need to persist your data for future retrieval, creating backups, or for sharing your data with others. The `pandas` library is bundled with a rich set of writer functions to persist your in-memory DataFrames (or series) to disk in various file formats. These writer functions allow you to store data to a local drive or to a remote server location such as a cloud storage filesystem, including **Google Drive**, **AWS S3**, and **Dropbox**.

In this chapter, you will explore writing to different file formats locally as well as cloud storage locations, such as AWS S3.

Here are the recipes that will be covered in this chapter:

- Time series data serialization with `pickle`
- Writing to CSV and other delimited files
- Writing data to an Excel file
- Storing data to a private S3 bucket

Technical requirements

In this chapter and beyond, we will be using pandas 1.4.2 (released April 2, 2022) extensively.

Throughout our journey, you will be installing several Python libraries to work in conjunction with pandas. These are highlighted in the *Getting ready* section for each recipe. You can also download Jupyter notebooks from the GitHub repository (`https://github.com/PacktPublishing/Time-Series-Analysis-with-Python-Cookbook`) to follow along. You can download the datasets used in this chapter here `https://github.com/PacktPublishing/Time-Series-Analysis-with-Python-Cookbook./tree/main/datasets/Ch4`

Serializing time series data with pickle

Often when working with data in Python, you may want to persist Python data structures or objects, such as a pandas DataFrame, to disk as opposed to keeping it in memory. One technique is to serialize your data into a byte stream to store to a file. In Python, the **pickle** module is a popular approach to object serialization and de-serialization (the reverse of serialization), also known as **pickling** and **unpickling**, respectively.

Getting ready

The `pickle` module comes with Python and no additional installation is needed.

In this recipe, we will use two different methods for serializing the data, commonly referred to as pickling.

You will be using the COVID-19 dataset provided by the *COVID-19 Data Repository by the Center for Systems Science and Engineering (CSSE) at Johns Hopkins University*, which you can download from the official GitHub repository here: `https://github.com/CSSEGISandData/COVID-19`.

How to do it...

You will write to a `pickle` file using pandas' `DataFrame.to_pickle()` function, and then explore an alternative option by using the `pickle` library directly.

Writing to a pickle file using pandas

You will start by reading the COVID-19 time series data into a DataFrame, making some transformations, and then persisting the results to a `pickle` file for future analysis. This should resemble a typical scenario for persisting data that is still a work-in-progress (in terms of analysis):

1. To start, let's load the CSV data into a pandas DataFrame:

```
import pandas as pd
from pathlib import Path
file = \
Path('../../datasets/Ch4/time_series_covid19_confirmed_
global.csv')
df = pd.read_csv(file)
df.head()
```

The preceding code will display the first five rows of the DataFrame:

	Province/State	Country/Region	Lat	Long	1/22/20	1/23/20	1/24/20	1/25/20	1/26/20	1/27/20	...	9/19/21	9/20/21	9/21/21	9/22/21	9/23/21	9/24/21	9/25/21	9/26/21	9/27/21	9/28/21
0	NaN	Afghanistan	33.93911	67.709953	0	0	0	0	0	0	...	154487	154585	154712	154757	154800	154960	154960	154960	155072	155093
1	NaN	Albania	41.15330	20.168300	0	0	0	0	0	0	...	162953	163404	164276	165096	165864	166690	167354	167893	168188	168782
2	NaN	Algeria	28.03390	1.659600	0	0	0	0	0	0	...	201600	201766	201948	202122	202283	202449	202574	202722	202877	203045
3	NaN	Andorra	42.50630	1.521800	0	0	0	0	0	0	...	15124	15140	15140	15153	15156	15167	15167	15167	15189	15192
4	NaN	Angola	-11.20270	17.873900	0	0	0	0	0	0	...	52307	52644	52968	53387	53840	54280	54795	55121	55583	56040

5 rows × 620 columns

Figure 4.1 – The first five rows of the COVID-19 confirmed global cases

You can observe from the output that this is a wide DataFrame with 620 columns where each column represents the data's collection date, starting from **1/22/20** to **9/28/21**.

2. Let's assume that part of the analysis is to focus on United States and data collected in the summer of 2021 (June, July, August, and September). You will transform the DataFrame by applying the necessary filters, and then unpivot the data so that the dates are in rows as opposed to columns (converting from a wide to a long format):

```
# filter data where Country is United States
df_usa = df[df['Country/Region'] == 'US']
# filter columns from June to end of September
df_usa_summer = df_usa.loc[:, '6/1/20':'9/30/20']
```

```
# unpivot using pd.melt()
df_usa_summer_unpivoted = pd.melt(
        df_usa_summer,
        value_vars = df_usa_summer.columns,
        value_name ='cases',
        var_name='date').set_index('date')

df_usa_summer_unpivoted.index = \
pd.to_datetime(df_usa_summer_unpivoted.index)
```

3. Inspect the df_usa_summer_unpivoted DataFrame and print the first five records:

```
df_usa_summer_unpivoted.info()
>> <class 'pandas.core.frame.DataFrame'>
DatetimeIndex: 122 entries, 2020-06-01 to 2020-09-30
Data columns (total 1 columns):
 #    Column   Non-Null Count    Dtype
---   ------   --------------    -----
 0    cases    122 non-null      int64
dtypes: int64(1)
memory usage: 1.9 KB

df_usa_summer_unpivoted.head()
>>
            cases
date
2020-06-01  1816679
2020-06-02  1837948
2020-06-03  1857728
2020-06-04  1879463
2020-06-05  1904375
```

You narrowed our dataset and transformed it from a wide DataFrame to a long time series DataFrame.

4. You are now satisfied with the dataset and ready to pickle (serialize) the dataset to the `covid_usa_summer_2020.pkl` file using the `DataFrame.to_pickle()` function:

```
output = \
Path('../../datasets/Ch4/covid_usa_summer_2020.pkl')
df_usa_summer_unpivoted.to_pickle(output)
```

Pickling preserves the schema of the DataFrame. When you ingest the pickled data again (de-serialization), you will get back the DataFrame in its original construct, for example, with a `DatetimeIndex` type.

5. Read the `pickle` file using the `pandas.read_pickle()` reader function and inspect the DataFrame:

```
unpickled_df = pd.read_pickle(output)
unpickled_df.info()
>>
<class 'pandas.core.frame.DataFrame'>
DatetimeIndex: 122 entries, 2020-06-01 to 2020-09-30
Data columns (total 1 columns):
 #   Column  Non-Null Count  Dtype
---  ------  --------------  -----
 0   cases   122 non-null    int64
dtypes: int64(1)
memory usage: 1.9 KB
```

From the preceding example, you were able to de-serialize the data using `pandas.read_pickle()` into a DataFrame, with all the transformations and datatypes preserved.

Writing a pickle file using the pickle library

Python comes shipped with the `pickle` library, which you can import and use to serialized (pickle) objects using dump (to write) and load (to read). In the following steps, you will use `pickle.dump()` and `pickle.load()` to serialize and then de-serialize the df_usa_summer_unpivoted DataFrame.

1. Import the `pickle` library:

```
import pickle
```

2. You then persist the `df_usa_summer_unpivoted` DataFrame using the `dump()` method:

```
output = \
Path('../../datasets/Ch4/covid_usa_summer_2020_v2.pkl')
pickle.dump(df_usa_summer_unpivoted,
            open(output, "wb"))
```

3. Read and inspect the file using the `load()` method. Notice in the following code that the ingested object is a pandas DataFrame, even though you used `pickle.load()` as opposed to `Pandas.read_pickle()`. Pickling preserved the schema and data structure as you would expect:

```
df = pickle.load(open(output, "rb"))
type(df)
>> pandas.core.frame.DataFrame
```

4. For better write and read management, you can use a `with open()` clause. All you need to do is specify the mode as either wb for writing in binary mode or rb for reading in binary mode, as in the following example:

```
with open(output, "wb") as file:
    pickle.dump(df_usa_summer_unpivoted, file)

with open(output, "rb") as file:
    df = pickle.load(file)
```

How it works...

In Python, pickling is the process of serializing any Python object. More concretely, it uses a binary serialization protocol to convert objects into binary information, which is not a human-readable format. The protocol used allows us to reconstruct (de-serialize) the pickled information into its original format without losing any valuable information. As in the preceding examples, we confirmed that a time series DataFrame when reconstructed (de-serialization) returned to its exact form (schema).

The pandas `DataFrame.to_pickle()` function has two additional parameters that are important to know. The first is the **compression** parameter, which is also available in other writer functions such as `to_csv()`, `to_json()`, and `to_paraquet()`, to name a few.

In the case of the `DataFrame.to_pickle()` function, the default compression value is set to *infer*, which lets pandas determine which compression mode to use based on the file extension provided. In the previous example, we used `DataFrame.to_pickle(output)` where `output` was defined with a `.pkl` file extension, as in `covid_usa_summer_2020.pkl`. If you change it to `covid_usa_summer_2020.zip`, then the output will be a compressed binary serialized file stored in ZIP format. Other supported compression modes include `gzip`, `bz2`, and `xz`.

The second parameter is **protocol**. By default, the `DataFrame.to_pickle()` writer function uses the highest protocol, which as of this writing is set to 5. According to the Pickle documentation, there are 6 different protocols to choose from when pickling, starting from protocol version 0 to the latest protocol version, 5.

Outside of pandas, you can check what is the highest protocol configuration by using the following command:

```
pickle.HIGHEST_PROTOCOL
>> 5
```

Similarly, by default, `pickle.dump()` uses the `HIGHEST_PROTOCOL` value if no other value was provided. The construct looks like the following code:

```
with open(output, "wb") as file:
    pickle.dump(df_usa_summer_unpivoted,
                file,
                pickle.HIGHEST_PROTOCOL)

with open(output, "wb") as file:
    pickle.dump(df_usa_summer_unpivoted,
                file,
                5)
```

The preceding two code snippets are equivalent.

There's more...

One of the advantages of pickling a binary serialization method is that we can pretty much pickle most Python objects, whether they are a dictionary, a machine learning model, a Python function, or a more complex data structure, such as a pandas DataFrame. There are some limitations though on certain objects, such as lambda functions.

Let's examine how you can pickle a function and its output. You will create a `covid_by_country` function that takes three arguments: *CSV file to read, number of days back*, and *country*. The function will return a time series DataFrame. You will then pickle both the function and the function's output as well:

```
def covid_by_country(file, days, country):
    ts = pd.read_csv(file)
    ts = ts[ts['Country/Region'] == country]
    final = ts.iloc[:, -days:].sum()
    final.index = pd.to_datetime(final.index)
    return final


file = \
Path('../../datasets/Ch4/time_series_covid19_confirmed_global.
csv')


us_past_120_days = covid_by_country(file, 200, 'US')
us_past_120_days(title=f'COVID confirmed case for US',
            xlabel='Date',
            ylabel='Number of Confirmed Cases')
```

The function would output the following plot:

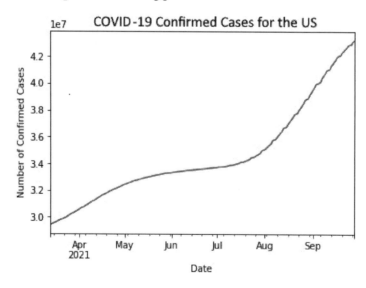

Figure 4.2 – Output of the covid_by_country function

Before pickling your objects, you can further enhance the content by adding additional information to remind you what the content is all about. In the following code, you will serialize the function and the returned DataFrame with additional content (think metadata) using a Python dictionary:

```
from datetime import datetime
metadata = {
    'date': datetime.now(),
    'data': '''
        COVID-19 Data Repository by the
        Center for Systems Science and Engineering (CSSE)
        at Johns Hopkins University'
        ''',
    'author': 'Tarek Atwan',
    'version': 1.0,
    'function': covid_by_country,
    'example' : us_120_plot
}

output = Path('../../datasets/Ch4/covid.pkl')
with open(output, 'wb') as file:
    pickle.dump(metadata, file)
```

To gain a better intuition on how this works, you can load the content and de-serialize using `pickle.load()`:

```
with open(output, 'rb') as file:
    content = pickle.load(file)
content.keys()
>> dict_keys(['date', 'data', 'author', 'version', 'function',
'example'])
```

You can retrieve and use the function, as shown in the following code:

```
file = \
Path('../../datasets/Ch4/time_series_covid19_confirmed_global.
csv')
new_func = content['function']
new_func(file, 120, 'China').tail()
>>
2021-09-24     108227
2021-09-25     108266
2021-09-26     108309
2021-09-27     108344
2021-09-28     108386
dtype: int64
```

You can also retrieve the previous DataFrame stored for the US:

```
content['example'].tail()
>>
2021-09-24     42852871
2021-09-25     42900402
2021-09-26     42931354
2021-09-27     43116442
2021-09-28     43227604
dtype: int64
```

The preceding examples demonstrate how pickling can be useful to store objects as well as additional metadata information. This can be helpful when you are storing a work-in-progress or if you are performing multiple experiments and want to keep track of them and their outcomes.

See also

- For more information about `Pandas.DataFrame.to_pickle`, please visit this page: `https://pandas.pydata.org/pandas-docs/stable/reference/api/pandas.DataFrame.to_pickle.html`.

- For more information about the Python Pickle module, please visit this page: `https://docs.python.org/3/library/pickle.html`.

Writing to CSV and other delimited files

In this recipe, you will export a DataFrame to a CSV file and leverage the different parameters available to use in the `DataFrame.to_csv()` writer function.

Getting ready

The file is provided in the GitHub repository for this book, which you can find here: `https://github.com/PacktPublishing/Time-Series-Analysis-with-Python-Cookbook`. The file is named `movieboxoffice.csv`.

To prepare, let's first read the file into a DataFrame with the following code:

```python
import pandas as pd
from pathlib import Path
filepath = Path('../../datasets/Ch4/movieboxoffice.csv')
movies = pd.read_csv(filepath,
                header=0,
                parse_dates=[0],
                index_col=0,
                infer_datetime_format=True,
                usecols=['Date',
                        'Daily'])
movies.info()
>>
<class 'pandas.core.frame.DataFrame'>
DatetimeIndex: 128 entries, 2021-04-26 to 2021-08-31
Data columns (total 1 columns):
 #   Column  Non-Null Count  Dtype
---  ------  --------------  -----
 0   Daily   128 non-null    object
dtypes: object(1)
memory usage: 2.0+ KB
```

You now have a time series DataFrame with an index of type `DatetimeIndex`

How to do it...

Writing a DataFrame to a CSV file is pretty straightforward with pandas. The DataFrame object has access to many writer methods such as `.to_csv`, which is what you will be using in the following steps:

1. You will use the pandas DataFrame writer method to persist the DataFrame as a CSV file. The method has several parameters, but at a minimum, all you need is pass a file path and filename:

```
output = Path('../../datasets/Ch4/my_movies.csv')
movies.to_csv(output)
```

The CSV file created is comma-delimited by default.

2. To change the delimiter, use the `sep` parameter and pass in a different argument. In the following code, you are creating a pipe (|)-delimited file:

```
output = Path('../../datasets/Ch4/piped_movies.csv')
movies.to_csv(output, sep='|')
```

3. Read the pipe-delimited file and inspect the resulting DataFrame object:

```
movies_df = pd.read_csv(output, sep='|')
movies_df.info()
<class 'pandas.core.frame.DataFrame'>
RangeIndex: 128 entries, 0 to 127
Data columns (total 2 columns):
 #   Column  Non-Null Count  Dtype
---  ------  --------------  -----
 0   Date    128 non-null    object
 1   Daily   128 non-null    object
dtypes: object(2)
memory usage: 2.1+ KB
```

Note from the preceding output that when reading the CSV file, some information was lost. For example, the Date datatype that was originally a DatetimeIndex type is now a string type. The DataFrame does not have an index of type DatetimeIndex (the index is now a RangeIndex type, which is just a range for the row numbers). This means you will need to configure the read_csv() function and pass the necessary arguments to parse the file properly (this is in contrast to when reading a pickled file, as in the preceding recipe, *Serializing time series data with pickle*). Generally, CSV file formats do not preserve index type or column datatype information.

How it works...

The default behavior for `DataFrame.to_csv()` is to write a comma-delimited CSV file based on the default `sep` parameter, which is set to `","`. You can overwrite this by passing a different delimiter, such as tab (`"\t"`), pipe (`"|"`), or semicolon (`";"`).

The following code shows examples of different delimiters and their representations:

```
# tab "\t"
Date      DOW Daily     Avg To Date Day Estimated
2019-04-26  Friday  157461641    33775    157461641    1    False
2019-04-27  Saturday    109264122    23437    266725763    2
False
2019-04-28  Sunday  90389244    19388    357115007    3    False


# comma ","
Date,DOW,Daily,Avg,To Date,Day,Estimated
2019-04-26,Friday,157461641,33775,157461641,1,False
2019-04-27,Saturday,109264122,23437,266725763,2,False
2019-04-28,Sunday,90389244,19388,357115007,3,False


# semicolon ";"
Date;DOW;Daily;Avg;To Date;Day;Estimated
2019-04-26;Friday;157461641;33775;157461641;1;False
2019-04-27;Saturday;109264122;23437;266725763;2;False
2019-04-28;Sunday;90389244;19388;357115007;3;False


# pipe "|"
Date|DOW|Daily|Avg|To Date|Day|Estimated
2019-04-26|Friday|157461641|33775|157461641|1|False
2019-04-27|Saturday|109264122|23437|266725763|2|False
2019-04-28|Sunday|90389244|19388|357115007|3|False
```

There's more...

Notice in the preceding example that the comma-separated string values are not encapsulated within double quotes (`""`). What will happen if our string object contains commas (`,`) and we write it to a comma-separated CSV file? Let's see how pandas handles this scenario.

In the following code, we will create a `person` DataFrame:

```python
import pandas as pd
person = pd.DataFrame({
    'name': ['Bond, James', 'Smith, James', 'Bacon, Kevin'],
    'location': ['Los Angeles, CA', 'Phoenix, AZ', 'New York, NY'],
    'net_worth': [10000, 9000, 8000]
    })

person
>>

         name           location   net_worth
0   Bond, James    Los Angeles, CA      10000
1   Smith, James        Phoenix, AZ       9000
2   Bacon, Kevin       New York, NY       8000
```

Now, export the DataFrame to a CSV file. You will specify `index=False` to ignore the index (row names) when exporting:

```python
person.to_csv('person_a.csv', index=False)
```

If you inspect a `person_a.csv` file, you will see the following representation (notice the double quotes added by pandas):

```
name,location,net_worth
"Bond, James","Los Angeles, CA",10000
"Smith, James","Phoenix, AZ",9000
"Bacon, Kevin","New York, NY",8000
```

The `.to_csv()` function has a `quoting` parameter with a default value set to `csv.QUOTE_MINIMAL`. This comes from the Python **csv** module, which is part of the Python installation. The `QUOTE_MINIMAL` argument only quotes fields that contain special characters, such as a comma (`","`).

The csv module provides us with four such constants that we can pass as arguments to the `quoting` parameter within the `.to_csv()` function. These include the following:

- `csv.QUOTE_ALL`: Quotes all the fields whether numeric or non-numeric
- `csv.QUOTE_MINIMAL`: The default option in the `.to_csv()` function, which quotes values that contain special characters
- `csv.QUOTE_NONNUMERIC`: Quotes all non-numeric fields
- `csv.QUOTE_NONE`: To not quote any field

To better understand how these values can impact the output CSV, in the following example you will test passing different quoting arguments. This is done using the `person` DataFrame:

```python
import csv
person.to_csv('person_b.csv',
              index=False,
              quoting=csv.QUOTE_ALL)

person.to_csv('person_c.csv',
              index=False,
              quoting=csv.QUOTE_MINIMAL)

person.to_csv('person_d.csv',
              index=False,
              quoting= csv.QUOTE_NONNUMERIC)

person.to_csv('person_e.csv',
              index=False,
              quoting= csv.QUOTE_NONE, escapechar='\t')
```

Now, if you open and inspect these files, you should see the following representations:

```
person_b.csv
"name","location","net_worth"
"Bond, James","Los Angeles, CA","10000"
"Smith, James","Phoenix, AZ","9000"
"Bacon, Kevin","New York, NY","8000"
```

person_c.csv

```
name,location,net_worth
"Bond, James","Los Angeles, CA",10000
"Smith, James","Phoenix, AZ",9000
"Bacon, Kevin","New York, NY",8000
```

person_d.csv

```
"name","location","net_worth"
"Bond, James","Los Angeles, CA",10000
"Smith, James","Phoenix, AZ",9000
"Bacon, Kevin","New York, NY",8000
```

person_e.csv

```
name,location,net_worth
Bond, James,Los Angeles , CA,10000
Smith, James,Phoenix , AZ,9000
Bacon, Kevin,New York, NY,8000
```

Note that in the preceding example, when using CSV.QUOTE_NONE, you will need to provide an additional argument for the escapechar parameter; otherwise, it will throw an error.

See also

- For more information on the Pandas.DataFrame.to_csv() function, please refer to this page: https://pandas.pydata.org/docs/reference/api/pandas.DataFrame.to_csv.html.

- For more information on the CSV module, please refer to this page: https://docs.python.org/3/library/csv.html.

Writing data to an Excel file

In this recipe, you will export a DataFrame as an Excel file format and leverage the different parameters available to use in the DataFrame.to_excel() writer function.

Getting ready

In the *Reading data from an Excel file* recipe in *Chapter 2, Reading Time Series Data from Files*, you were instructed to install openpyxl for the read engine. For this recipe, you will be using the same openpyxl for the write engine.

The file is provided in the GitHub repository for this book, which you can find here: https://github.com/PacktPublishing/Time-Series-Analysis-with-Python-Cookbook. The file is named movieboxoffice.csv.

To install openpyxl using conda, run the following:

```
>>> conda install openpyxl
```

You can also use pip:

```
>>> pip install openpyxl
```

How to do it...

To write the DataFrame to an Excel file, you need to provide the writer function with filename and sheet_name parameters. The file name contains the file path and name. Make sure the file extension is .xlsx since you are using openpyxl. The DataFrame. to_excel() method will determine which engine to use based on the file extension, for example, .xlsx or .xls. You can also specify which engine to use with the engine parameter, as shown in the following code:

1. Determine the location of file output, and create the file path, desired sheet name, and engine to the DataFrame.to_excel() writer function:

```
output = \
Path('../../datasets/Ch4/daily_boxoffice.xlsx')
movies.to_excel(output,
            sheet_name='movies',
            engine='openpyxl') # default engine for
xlsx
```

The preceding code will create a new Excel file in the specified location. You can open and inspect the file, as shown in the following figure:

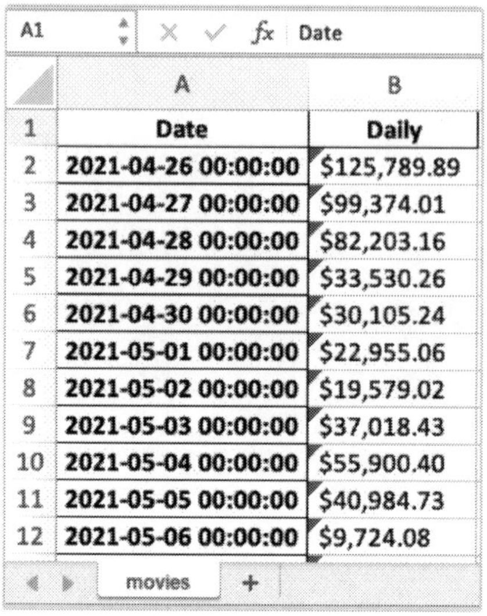

	A	B
1	Date	Daily
2	2021-04-26 00:00:00	$125,789.89
3	2021-04-27 00:00:00	$99,374.01
4	2021-04-28 00:00:00	$82,203.16
5	2021-04-29 00:00:00	$33,530.26
6	2021-04-30 00:00:00	$30,105.24
7	2021-05-01 00:00:00	$22,955.06
8	2021-05-02 00:00:00	$19,579.02
9	2021-05-03 00:00:00	$37,018.43
10	2021-05-04 00:00:00	$55,900.40
11	2021-05-05 00:00:00	$40,984.73
12	2021-05-06 00:00:00	$9,724.08

Figure 4.3 – Example output from the daily_boxoffice.xlsx file

Note that the sheet name is `movies`. In the Excel file, you will notice that `Date` is not in the format you would expect. Let's say the expectation was for the `Date` column to be in a specific format, such as `MM-DD-YYYY`.

2. To achieve this, you will use another pandas-provided class, the `pandas.ExcelWriter` class, which gives us access to two properties for date formatting, `datetime_format` and `date_format`. The following code shows how this can be achieved:

```
date_format = 'MM-DD-YYYY'
with pd.ExcelWriter(output,
                    engine='openpyxl',
                    mode='a',
                   if_sheet_exists='replace') as writer:
    writer.datetime_format = date_format
    movies.to_excel(writer, sheet_name='movies_fixed_
dates')
```

The following is a representation of what the new output would look like. This was accomplished by passing `MM-DD-YYYY` to the `datetime_format` property of the `writer` object:

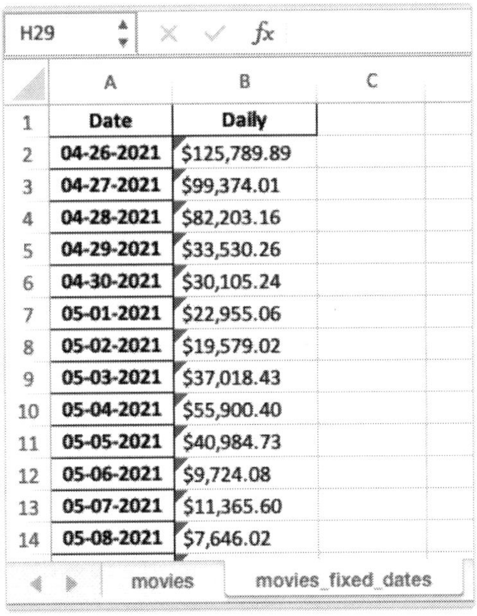

	A	B	C
1	Date	Daily	
2	04-26-2021	$125,789.89	
3	04-27-2021	$99,374.01	
4	04-28-2021	$82,203.16	
5	04-29-2021	$33,530.26	
6	04-30-2021	$30,105.24	
7	05-01-2021	$22,955.06	
8	05-02-2021	$19,579.02	
9	05-03-2021	$37,018.43	
10	05-04-2021	$55,900.40	
11	05-05-2021	$40,984.73	
12	05-06-2021	$9,724.08	
13	05-07-2021	$11,365.60	
14	05-08-2021	$7,646.02	

Figure 4.4 – pd.ExcelWriter helped change the Date string format to MM-DD-YYYY

How it works...

The `pandas.DataFrame.to_excel()` method by default creates a new Excel file if it doesn't exist or overwrites the file if it exists. To append to an existing Excel file or write to multiple sheets, you will need to use the `Pandas.ExcelWriter` class. The `ExcelWriter()` class has a `mode` parameter that can accept either `"w"` for write or `"a"` for append. Similarly, `ExcelWriter` by default is set to `"w"` (write mode) and, thus, if `"a"` (append mode) is not specified, it will result in overwriting the Excel file (any existing content will be erased).

Additionally, when using append mode (`mode="a"`) you will need to specify the `if_sheet_exists` parameter within `ExcelWriter`, which accepts one of three values:

- `error`, which raises a `ValueError` exception.
- `replace`, which overwrites the existing worksheet.
- `new`, which creates a new worksheet with a new name. If you re-execute the preceding code and update `if_sheet_exists='new'`, then a new sheet will be created and named `movies_fixed_dates1`.

Finally, even though `ExcelWriter` takes `datetime_format` and `date_format` parameters, sometimes you may not get the expected outcome. Instead, you can overwrite these properties against the writer object, as shown in the following code (which is similar to what you did in the preceding example):

```
with pd.ExcelWriter(output) as writer:
    writer.datetime_format = 'MM-DD-YYYY'
    writer.date_format = 'MM-DD-YYYY'
```

There's more...

If you need to create multiple worksheets in the same Excel file, then `ExcelWriter` can be used to achieve this. For example, assume the goal is to split each month's data into its own sheet and name the sheet accordingly. In the following code, you will add a `Month` column and use that to split that DataFrame by month, using `groupby` to write each group into a new sheet:

```
output = Path('../../datasets/Ch4/boxoffice_by_month.xlsx')
with pd.ExcelWriter(output,
                    engine='openpyxl') as writer:
    for month, data in movies.groupby('Month'):
        writer.datetime_format = 'YYYY-MM-DD'
        data.to_excel(writer, sheet_name=month)
```

The preceding code will create a new Excel file called `boxoffice_by_month.xlsx` with five sheets for each month, as shown in the following figure:

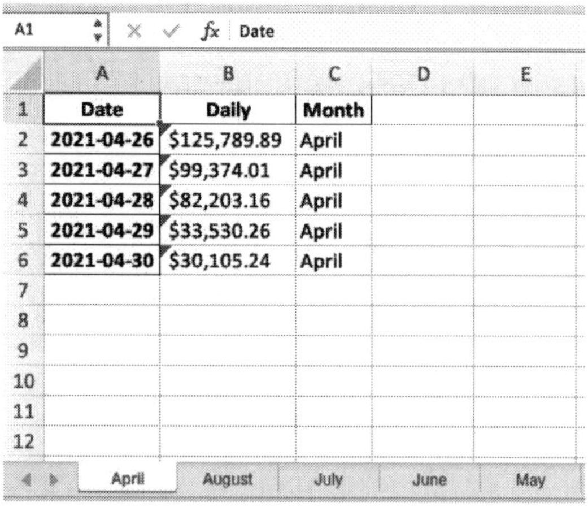

	A	B	C	D	E
1	Date	Daily	Month		
2	2021-04-26	$125,789.89	April		
3	2021-04-27	$99,374.01	April		
4	2021-04-28	$82,203.16	April		
5	2021-04-29	$33,530.26	April		
6	2021-04-30	$30,105.24	April		
7					
8					
9					
10					
11					
12					

April | August | July | June | May

Figure 4.5 – Each month in the movies DataFrame was written to its own sheet in Excel

See also

The pandas `to_excel()` method and `ExcelWriter` class make it very convenient to write DataFrames to an Excel file. If you want a more granular control, outside of pandas DataFrames, then you should consider exploring the `openpyxl` library that you installed as the reader/writer engine. As an example, the `openpyxl` library provides some support to pandas DataFrames with the `dataframe_to_rows()` function:

- To learn more about `Pandas.DataFrame.to_excel()`, please refer to `https://pandas.pydata.org/pandas-docs/stable/reference/api/pandas.DataFrame.to_excel.html`.

- To learn more about `Pandas.ExcelWriter()`, please refer to `https://pandas.pydata.org/pandas-docs/stable/reference/api/pandas.ExcelWriter.html#pandas.ExcelWriter`.

- To learn more about `openpyxl`, please refer to `https://openpyxl.readthedocs.io/en/stable/index.html`.

- To learn more about `openpyxl.utils.dataframe`, please refer to `https://openpyxl.readthedocs.io/en/stable/pandas.html`.

Storing data to S3

In this recipe, you will explore writing to AWS S3 using pandas and another approach using the AWS Python SDK. The pandas approach can be used to write files to other cloud storage locations, such as Azure or Google Cloud.

Getting ready

In the *Reading data from a URL* recipe in *Chapter 2, Reading Time Series Data from Files*, you were instructed to install `boto3` and `s3fs` in order to read from AWS S3 buckets. In this recipe, you will be leveraging the same libraries.

To install using `pip`, you can use this:

```
>>> pip install boto3 s3fs
```

To install using `conda`, you can use this:

```
>>> conda install boto3 s3fs -y
```

You will be working with the `boxoffice_by_month.xlsx` file that we created in the previous recipe, *Writing data to an Excel file*. The file is provided in the GitHub repository for this book, which you can find here: `https://github.com/PacktPublishing/Time-Series-Analysis-with-Python-Cookbook`.

How to do it...

Several of the pandas writer functions provide support to writing directly to a remote or cloud storage filesystem using, for example, AWS's `s3://` or Google's `gcs://` protocols. These writer functions provide the `storage_options` parameter to support working with remote file storage systems. It takes in a Python dictionary to provide additional information such as credentials, or any information required by the remote server or cloud provider as a key-value pair.

In this recipe, you will write your DataFrame to an S3 bucket. You will explore writing to a private and non-private bucket:

1. You will start by storing your AWS credentials in a config `.cfg` file outside your Python script. Then, use `configparser` to read the values and store them in Python variables. You do not want your credentials exposed or hardcoded in your code:

```
Example aws.cfg file
[AWS]
aws_access_key=your_access_key
aws_secret_key=you_secret_key
```

We can then load an `aws.cfg` file using `config.read()`:

```
import configparser
config = configparser.ConfigParser()
config.read('aws.cfg')

AWS_ACCESS_KEY = config['AWS']['aws_access_key']
AWS_SECRET_KEY = config['AWS']['aws_secret_key']
```

2. Import the remaining required libraries and read the data that you will be writing to AWS S3:

```
import pandas as pd
from pathlib import Path
source = "../../datasets/Ch4/boxoffice_by_month.xlsx"
```

```
movies = pd.concat(pd.read_excel(source,
                sheet_name=None,
                index_col='Date',
                parse_dates=True)).droplevel(0)
```

3. Write the `movies` DataFrame to two different buckets: a CSV format to the bucket marked as private (which blocks all public access) and in Excel format to the public bucket (disabled blocking). The code is very similar whether it is a public or private bucket, assuming you have the right privileges (Amazon Identity and Access Management permissions):

```
movies.to_excel('s3://tscookbook/movies.xlsx',
                sheet_name='Sheet1',
                storage_options={'key': AWS_ACCESS_KEY,
                                'secret': AWS_SECRET_
KEY})


movies.to_csv('s3://tscookbook-private/updateAirQuality.
csv',
                storage_options={'key': AWS_ACCESS_KEY,
                                'secret': AWS_SECRET_
KEY})
```

Upon inspecting S3, you will see the two files in each of the buckets. It may take a few seconds before the file is shown through the AWS Management Console. The following figure shows the content of the `tscookbook-private` bucket:

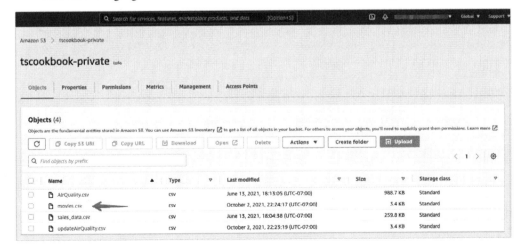

Figure 4.6 – movies.csv successfully written to AWS S3 using the DataFrame.to_csv() writer function

How it works...

In the preceding code section, we used both the `DataFrame.to_csv()` and `DataFrame.to_excel()` methods to write to AWS S3. Similarly, you could use other writer functions to write different file formats to any cloud storage, such as **Google Cloud Storage (GCS)** or S3. The `storage_options` parameter makes it possible to pass a key-value pair containing information required for the storage connection; for example, AWS S3 requires passing a *key* and a *secret*.

Examples of pandas DataFrame writer functions that support `storage_options` include the following:

- `Pandas.DataFrame.to_excel()`
- `Pandas.DataFrame.to_json()`
- `Pandas.DataFrame.to_parquet()`
- `Pandas.DataFrame.to_pickle()`

There's more...

For more granular control, you can use the Boto3 Python API to write data to S3. Like the *Reading data from a URL* recipe in *Chapter 2, Reading Time Series Data from Files*, you will use Boto3 but this time to write the file.

You will use the *resource* API, which is a higher-level abstraction from Boto3. Notice the use of `StringIO()`, an in-memory Unicode placeholder, which is used for an in-memory text stream of the DataFrame content.

You will use `StringIO` and pass it as an argument to the file path parameter in `DataFrame.to_csv()`. Pretty much, you are instructing `.to_csv()` to not output the content into a file but rather as an in-memory text stream for text I/O:

```
import boto3
from io import StringIO
bucket = "tscookbook-private"
s3_client = boto3.resource("s3",
            aws_access_key_id = AWS_ACCESS_KEY,
            aws_secret_access_key = AWS_SECRET_KEY)


with StringIO() as in_memory_buffer:
    movies.to_csv(in_memory_buffer)
```

```
    response = s3_client.Object(bucket, 'new_df.csv').
put(Body=in_memory_buffer.getvalue())
    status = response['ResponseMetadata']['HTTPStatusCode']
    if status == 200:
        print('Successful Write')
    else:
        print('Unsuccessful Write - ', status)


>> Successful Write
```

In the preceding code, you converted the pandas DataFrame into a CSV format with
.to_csv, and then stored the output as an in-memory text buffer, which later was passed
as Body (content) in the put (write) request. The following figure shows the file being
placed in CSV format:

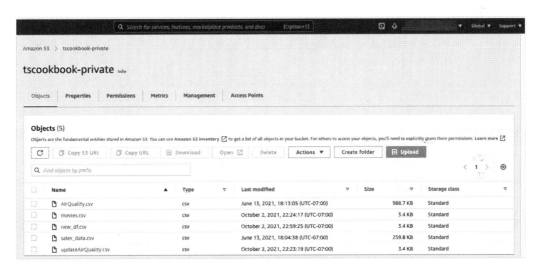

Figure 4.7 – new_df.csv successfully written to AWS S3 using the boto3 library

See also

For more information on the Boto3 S3 API, please refer to the documentation here:

```
https://boto3.amazonaws.com/v1/documentation/api/latest/
reference/services/s3.html
```

5
Persisting Time Series Data to Databases

It is very common that, after completing a **data analysis** task, in which data is extracted from a source system, processed, transformed, and possibly modeled, the output is stored in a database for persistence. You can always store the data in a flat file or export to a CSV, but when dealing with a large amount of corporate data (including proprietary data), you will need a more robust and secure way to store it. **Databases** offer several advantages, including security (encryption at rest), concurrency (allowing many users to query the database without impacting performance), fault tolerance, **ACID** compliance, optimized read-write mechanisms, distributed computing, and distributed storage.

In a corporate context, once data is stored in a database, it can be shared across different departments; for example, finance, marketing, sales, and product development can now access the data stored for their own needs. Furthermore, the data can now be democratized and applied to numerous use cases by different roles within an organization, such as business analysts, data scientists, data engineers, marketing analysts, and business intelligence developers.

In this chapter, you will be writing your time series data to a database system for persistence. You will explore different types of databases (relational and non-relational) and use **Python** to push your data.

More specifically, you will be using the **pandas** library, since you will be doing much of your analysis using pandas **DataFrames**. You will learn how to use the pandas library to persist your time series DataFrame to a database storage system. Many databases offer Python APIs and connectors, and recently many of them support pandas DataFrames (for reading and writing) given their popularity and mainstream adoption. In this chapter, you will be working with a relational database, a document database, a cloud data warehouse, and a specialized time series database.

The goal of this chapter is to give you first-hand experience working with different methods to connect to these database systems to persist your time series DataFrame.

Here is the list of the recipes that we will cover in this chapter:

- Writing time series data to a relational database (PostgreSQL and MySQL)
- Writing time series data to MongoDB
- Writing time series data to InfluxDB
- Writing time series data to Snowflake

> **Writing to a database and permissions**
>
> Keep in mind that when you install your own database instance, or use your own cloud service, writing your data is straightforward, since you are in the owner/admin role.
>
> This will not be the case in any corporation when it's their database system. You will need to align and work with the database owners and maintainers, and possibly IT, database admins, or cloud admins. In most cases, they can grant you the proper permissions to write your data to a sandbox or a development environment. Then, once you are done, possibly the same or another team (such as a DevOps team) may want to inspect the code and evaluate performance before they migrate the code to a Quality Assurance (QA) / User Acceptance Testing (UAT) environment. Once there, the business may get involved to test and validate the data for approval, and then finally it may get promoted to the production environment so that everyone can start using the data.

Technical requirements

In this chapter and beyond, we will be using the pandas 1.4.2 library (released on April 2, 2022) extensively.

Throughout our journey, you will be installing several Python libraries to work in conjunction with pandas. These are highlighted in the *Getting ready* section for each recipe. You can also download the Jupyter notebooks from the GitHub repository at `https://github.com/PacktPublishing/Time-Series-Analysis-with-Python-Cookbook` to follow along.

Writing time series data to a relational database (PostgreSQL and MySQL)

In this recipe, you will write your DataFrame to a relational database (**PostgreSQL**). The approach is the same for any relational database system that is supported by the **SQLAlchemy** Python library. You will experience how SQLAlchemy makes it simple to switch the backend database (called dialect) without the need to alter the code. The abstraction layer provided by the SQLAlchemy library makes it feasible to switch to any supported database, such as from PostgreSQL to MySQL, using the same code.

The sample list of supported relational databases (dialects) in SQLAlchemy includes the following:

- Microsoft SQL Server
- MySQL/MariaDB
- PostgreSQL
- Oracle
- SQLite

Additionally, there are external dialects available to install and use with SQLAlchemy to support other databases (dialects), such as **Snowflake**, **AWS RedShift**, and **Google BigQuery**. Please visit the official page of SQLAlchemy for a list of available dialects: `https://docs.sqlalchemy.org/en/14/dialects/`.

Getting ready

In the *Reading data from relational database* recipe in *Chapter 3, Reading Time Series Data from Databases,* you installed `sqlalchemy` and `psycopg2` for the read engine. For this recipe, you will be using these two libraries again.

You will also use the `pandas-datareader` library to pull stock data.

To install the libraries using `Conda`, run the following:

```
>>> conda install sqlalchemy psycopg2 pandas-datareader -y
```

To install the libraries using `pip`, run the following:

```
>>> pip install sqlalchemy psycopg2 pandas-datareader
```

The file is provided in the GitHub repository for this book, which you can find here: `https://github.com/PacktPublishing/Time-Series-Analysis-with-Python-Cookbook`.

How to do it...

In this recipe, you will be pulling Amazon's stock data for 2020 using the `pandas-datareader` library into a pandas DataFrame, and then writing the DataFrame to a PostgreSQL database:

1. Start by importing the libraries and creating a SQLAlchemy engine. The engine informs SQLAlchemy and pandas which dialect (database) we are planning to interact with, as well as connection details to that instance:

    ```
    import pandas as pd
    from sqlalchemy import create_engine
    import pandas-datareader.data as web


    engine = create_engine("postgresql://postgres:password@
    localhost:5433/postgres")
    ```

2. Use `pandas-datareader` to request 2020 Amazon stock data. You will use the AMZN ticker:

    ```
    amzn_df_2020 = web.get_data_yahoo('AMZN',
                                      start='2020-01-01',
                                      end='2020-12-31')
    ```

```
amzn_df_2020.shape
>> (253, 6)
amzn_df_2020.head()
```

The output is as follows:

	High	Low	Open	Close	Volume	Adj Close
Date						
2020-01-02	1898.010010	1864.150024	1875.000000	1898.010010	4029000	1898.010010
2020-01-03	1886.199951	1864.500000	1864.500000	1874.969971	3764400	1874.969971
2020-01-06	1903.689941	1860.000000	1860.000000	1902.880005	4061800	1902.880005
2020-01-07	1913.890015	1892.040039	1904.500000	1906.859985	4044900	1906.859985
2020-01-08	1911.000000	1886.439941	1898.040039	1891.969971	3508000	1891.969971

Figure 5.1 – The first five rows of AMZN ticker stock data for 2020

3. Write the DataFrame to the PostgreSQL database as a new Amazon table. This is achieved using the `DataFrame.to_sql()` writer function, which leverages SQLAlchemy's capabilities to convert the DataFrame into the appropriate table schema and translate the data into the appropriate `CREATE TABLE` and `INSERT` SQL statements specific to PostgreSQL (dialect):

```
amzn_df_2020.to_sql('amazon',
                    engine,
                    if_exists='replace')
```

Once the preceding code is executed, a new `amazon` table is created in the `postgres` database (default).

4. Confirm the data was written to the database by querying the `amazon` table and counting the number of records:

```
query = '''
select count(*) from amazon;
'''
engine.execute(query).fetchone()
>> (253,)
```

5. Now, pull additional Amazon stock data (the first 6 months of 2021) and append it to the same Amazon table. Here, you will take advantage of the `if_exists` parameter in the `.to_sql()` writer function.

    Request additional data from the `pandas-datareader` API and append it to the database table. Make sure to pass `append` to the `if_exists` parameter, as shown in the following code:

    ```
    amzn_df_2021 = web.get_data_yahoo('AMZN',
                                        start='2021-01-01',
                                        end='2021-06-01')
    amzn_df_2021.shape
    >> (103, 6)
    amzn_df_2020.to_sql('amazon',
                    engine,
                    if_exists='append')
    ```

6. Count the total number of records to ensure we have appended 103 records to the original 253 records. You will run the same query that was executed earlier, as shown in the following code:

    ```
    query = '''
    select count(*) from amazon;
    '''

    engine.execute(query).fetchone()
    >> (356,)
    ```

    Indeed, you can observe that all of the 353 records were written to the Amazon table.

How it works...

By using the `Pandas.to_sql()` writer function, SQLAlchemy handles many details under the hood, such as creating the table schema, inserting our records, and committing to the database.

Working with pandas and SQLAlchemy to write and read to a relational database is very similar. We discussed using SQLAlchemy for reading data in the *Reading data from a relational database* recipe in *Chapter 3, Reading Time Series Data from Databases*. Many of the concepts discussed apply here as well.

We always start with `create_engine` and specify the database dialect. Using the `DataFrame.to_sql()` function will map the DataFrame data types to the appropriate PostgreSQL data types. The advantage of using an **Object Relational Mapper (ORM)** such as SQLAlchemy is that it gives you an abstraction layer, so you do not have to worry about *how to* convert the DataFrame schema into a specific database schema.

In the preceding example, you used the `if_exists` parameter in the `DataFrame.to_sql()` function with two different arguments:

1. Initially, you set the value to `replace`, which would overwrite the table if it existed. If we translate this overwrite operation into SQL commands, it will execute a DROP TABLE followed by CREATE TABLE. This can be dangerous if you already have a table with data and you intended to append to it. Because of this concern, the default value is set to `fail` if you did not pass any argument. This default behavior would throw an error if the table existed.

2. In the second portion of your code, the plan was to insert additional records into the existing table, and you updated the argument from `replace` to `append`.

Note that when you pulled the stock data using `pandas-datareader`, it automatically assigned the date as `DatetimeIndex`. In other words, the date was not a column but an index. The default behavior in `to_sql()` is to write the DataFrame index as a column in the database, which is controlled by the `index` parameter. This is a Boolean parameter, and the default is set to `True`, which writes the DataFrame index as a column.

Another interesting parameter that can be extremely useful is `chunksize`. The default value is `None`, which writes all the rows in the DataFrame at once. If your dataset is extremely large, you can use the `chunksize` parameter to write to the database in batches; for example, a `chunksize` of 500 would write to the database in batches of 500 rows at a time.

There's more...

When using the `pandas read_sql`, `read_sql_table`, `read_sql_query`, and `to_sql` I/O functions, they expect a SQLAlchemy connection object (SQLAlchemy engine). To use SQLAlchemy to connect to a database of choice, you need to install the appropriate Python DBAPI (driver) for that specific database (for example, MySQL, PostgreSQL, or Oracle). This gives you the advantage of writing your script once and still having it work with other backend databases (dialects) that are supported by SQLAlchemy. To demonstrate this, let's extend the last example.

You will use the same code, but this time write to a MySQL database. The only requirement, aside from a running MySQL instance, is installing a Python DBAPI (driver) for MySQL. There are different choices that are listed on the SQLAlchemy page (`https://docs.sqlalchemy.org/en/14/dialects/mysql.html`) and, for this example, you will install `PyMySQL`.

To install using `Conda`, run the following command:

```
conda install -c anaconda pymysql
```

To install using `pip`, run the following command:

```
pip install pymysql
```

You will use the same code for PostgreSQL; the only difference is the SQLAlchemy engine, which uses MySQL DBAPI:

```
engine = create_engine("mysql+pymysql://root:password@
localhost:3306/stocks")
amzn_df_2020.to_sql('amazon',
                    engine,
                    if_exists='replace')


query = '''
select count(*) from amazon;
'''
engine.execute(query).fetchone()
>> (253,)
```

Notice in the preceding code, the `create_engine` is pointing to a database called `stocks` in MySQL database. Again, as you did before with PostgreSQL, you will append the second DataFrame to the same table:

```
amzn_df_2021.to_sql('amazon',
                    engine,
                    if_exists='append')


query = '''
select count(*) from amazon;
'''
```

```
engine.execute(query).fetchone()
>> (356,)
```

Note that all you needed was to create an engine that specified the *MySQL* dialect. In this example, `pymysql` was used. SQLAlchemy takes care of the translation behind the scenes to convert the DataFrame schema into a MySQL schema.

See also

Here are some additional resources:

- To learn more about the `pandas.to_sql()` function, you can visit `https://pandas.pydata.org/docs/reference/api/pandas.DataFrame.to_sql.html`.
- To learn more about SQLAlchemy features, you can start by reading their features page: `https://www.sqlalchemy.org/features.html`.

Writing time series data to MongoDB

MongoDB is a document database system that stores data in **BSON** format. When you query data from MongoDB, the data will be represented in JSON format. BSON is similar to JSON; it is the binary encoding of JSON. Unlike JSON though, it is not in a human-readable format. JSON is great for transmitting data and is system-agnostic. BSON is designed for storing data and is associated with MongoDB.

In this recipe, you will explore writing a `pandas` DataFrame to MongoDB.

Getting ready

In the *Reading data from a document database* recipe in *Chapter 3, Reading Time Series Data from Databases*, we installed `pymongo`. For this recipe, you will be using that same library again.

To install using `Conda`, run the following:

```
$ conda install -c anaconda pymongo -y
```

To install using `pip`, run the following:

```
$ python -m pip install pymongo
```

The file is provided in the GitHub repository for this book, which you can find here: `https://github.com/PacktPublishing/Time-Series-Analysis-with-Python-Cookbook`.

How to do it...

To store data in MongoDB, you will create a **database** and a **collection**. A database contains one or more collections, which are like tables in relational databases. Once a collection is created, you will write your data as documents. A collection contains documents, which are equivalent to rows in relational databases.

1. Start by importing the necessary libraries:

    ```
    import pandas as pd
    from pymongo import MongoClient
    ```

2. Create a `MongoClient` instance to create a connection to the database:

    ```
    client = MongoClient('mongodb://localhost:27017')
    ```

3. Create a new database named `stocks` and a new collection named `amazon`:

    ```
    db = client['stocks']
    collection = db['amazon']
    ```

    So far, nothing has been written in the database (there is no database or collection created yet). They will be created once we insert your records (write to the database).

4. Prepare the DataFrame by converting to a Python dictionary using the `DataFrame.to_dict()` method. You will need to pass the argument `orient='records'` to `to_dict()` to produce a list that follows the `[{'column_name': value}]` format. The following code demonstrates how to transform the DataFrame:

    ```
    amzn_records = amzn_df_2020.reset_index().to_
    dict(orient='records')
    amzn_records[0:1]
    >>
    [{'Date': Timestamp('2020-01-02 00:00:00'),
      'High': 1898.010009765625,
      'Low': 1864.1500244140625,
      'Open': 1875.0,
      'Close': 1898.010009765625,
    ```

```
    'Volume': 4029000,
    'Adj Close': 1898.010009765625}]
```

Note the format – each record (row) from the DataFrame is now a dictionary inside a list. You now have a list of length 253 for each record:

```
len(amzn_records)
>> 253
```

On the other hand, the `to_dict()` default orient value is `dict`, which produces a dictionary that follows the `{column -> {index -> value}}` pattern.

5. Now, you are ready to write to the `amazon` collection using the `insert_many()` function. This will create both the `stocks` database and the `amazon` collection along with the documents inside the collection:

```
collection.insert_many(amzn_records)
```

6. You can validate that the database and collection are created with the following code:

```
client.list_database_names()
>> ['admin', 'config', 'local', 'stocks']
db.list_collection_names()
>> ['amazon']
```

7. You can check the total number of documents written and query the database, as shown in the following code:

```
collection.count_documents({})
>> 253
# filter documents that are greater than August 1, 2020
# and retrieve the first record
import datetime
collection.find_one({'Date': {'$gt': datetime.
datetime(2020, 8,1)}})
>>
{'_id': ObjectId('615bfec679449e4481a5fcf8'),
 'Date': datetime.datetime(2020, 8, 3, 0, 0),
 'High': 3184.0,
 'Low': 3104.0,
 'Open': 3180.510009765625,
 'Close': 3111.889892578125,
```

```
            'Volume': 5074700,
        'Adj Close': 3111.889892578125}
```

How it works...

`PyMongo` provides us with two insert functions to write our records as documents into a collection. These functions are as follows:

- `.insert_one()` inserts one document into a collection.
- `.insert_many()` inserts multiple documents into a collection.

There is also `.insert()`, which inserts one or more documents into a collection that is supported by older MongoDB engines.

In the preceding example, you used `insert_many()` and passed the data to be written into documents all at once. You had to convert the DataFrame to a list-like format using `orient='records'`.

When documents are created in the database, they get assigned a unique `_id` value. When inserting documents when the document does not exist, one will be created and a new `_id` value generated. You can capture the `_id` value since the insert functions do return a result object (`InsertOneResult` or `InsertManyResult`). The following code shows how this is accomplished with `.insert_one` and `InsertOneResult`:

```
one_record = (amzn_df_2021.reset_index()
                          .iloc[0]
                          .to_dict())
one_record
>>
{'Date': Timestamp('2021-01-04 00:00:00'),
 'High': 3272.0,
 'Low': 3144.02001953125,
 'Open': 3270.0,
 'Close': 3186.6298828125,
 'Volume': 4411400,
 'Adj Close': 3186.6298828125}

result_id = collection.insert_one(one_record)
result_id
>> <pymongo.results.InsertOneResult at 0x7fc155ecf780>
```

The returned object is an instance of `InsertOneResult`; to see the actual value, you can use the `.insert_id` property:

```
result_id.inserted_id
>> ObjectId('615c093479449e4481a5fd64')
```

There's more...

In the preceding example, we did not think about our document strategy and stored each DataFrame row as a document. If we have hourly or minute data, as an example, what is a better strategy to store the data in MongoDB? Should each row be a separate record?

One strategy we can implement is **bucketing** our data. For example, if we have hourly stock data, we can bucket it into a time range (such as 24 hours) and store all the data for that time range into one document.

Similarly, if we have sensor data from multiple devices, we can also use the bucket pattern to group the data as we please (for example, by device ID and by time range) and insert them into documents. This will reduce the number of documents in the database, improve overall performance, and simplify our querying as well.

In the following example, we will create a new collection to write to and bucket the daily stock data by month:

```
bucket = db['stocks_bucket']
amzn_df_2020['month'] = amzn_df_2020.index.month
```

In the preceding code, you added a `month` column to the DataFrame and initiated a new collection as `stocks_bucket`. Remember that this will not create the collection until we insert the data. In the next code segment, you will loop through the data and write your monthly buckets:

```
for month in amzn_df_2020.index.month.unique():
    record = {}
    record['month'] = month
    record['symbol'] = 'AMZN'
    record['price'] = list(amzn_df_2020[amzn_df_2020['month']
== month]['Close'].values)
    bucket.insert_many([record])
bucket.count_documents({})
>> 12
```

Indeed, there are 12 documents in the `stocks_bucket` collection, one for each month, as opposed to the stocks collection, which had 253 documents, one for each trading day.

Query the database for June to see how the document is represented:

```
bucket.find_one({'month': 6})
>>
{'_id': ObjectId('615d4e67ad102432df7ea691'),
 'month': 6,
 'symbol': 'AMZN',
 'price': [2471.0400390625,
  2472.409912109375,
  2478.39990234375,
  2460.60009765625,
  2483.0,
  2524.06005859375,
  2600.860107421875,
  2647.449951171875,
  2557.9599609375,
  2545.02001953125,
  2572.679931640625,
  2615.27001953125,
  2640.97998046875,
  2653.97998046875,
  2675.010009765625,
  2713.820068359375,
  2764.409912109375,
  2734.39990234375,
  2754.580078125,
  2692.8701171875,
  2680.3798828125,
  2758.820068359375]}
```

As of **MongoDB 5.0**, the database natively supports time series data by creating a special collection type called **time series collection**. Once defined as a time series collection, MongoDB uses more efficient writing and reading, supporting complex aggregations that are specific to working with time series data.

In the following example, you will store the same DataFrame, but this time, you will define the collection using `create_collection()` and specify the time series parameter to indicate that it is a time series collection. Additional options that are available include `timeField`, `metaField`, and `granularity`:

```
ts = db.create_collection(name = "stocks_ts",
                           capped =  False,
                           timeseries = {"timeField": "Date",
                                          "metaField":
"metadata"})
[i for i in db.list_collections() if i['name'] =='stocks_ts']
>>
[{'name': 'stocks_ts',
  'type': 'timeseries',
  'options': {'timeseries': {'timeField': 'Date',
    'metaField': 'metadata',
    'granularity': 'seconds',
    'bucketMaxSpanSeconds': 3600}},
  'info': {'readOnly': False}}]
```

From the result set, you can see that the collection is the `timeseries` type.

Next, create the records that will be written as documents into the time series collection:

```
cols = ['Close']
records = []
for month in amzn_df_2020[cols].iterrows():
    records.append(
        {'metadata':
                {'ticker': 'AMZN', 'type': 'close'},
            'date': month[0],
            'price': month[1]['Close']})
records[0:1]
>>
[{'metadata': {'ticker': 'AMZN', 'type': 'close'},
  'date': Timestamp('2020-01-02 00:00:00'),
  'price': 1898.010009765625}]
```

Now, write your records using `.insert_many()`:

```
ts.insert_many(records)
ts.find_one({})
>>
{'date': datetime.datetime(2020, 1, 2, 0, 0),
 'metadata': {'ticker': 'AMZN', 'type': 'close'},
 'price': 1898.010009765625,
 '_id': ObjectId('615d5badad102432df7eb371')}
```

If you have ticker data in minutes, you can take advantage of the `granularity` attribute, which can be `seconds`, `minutes`, or `hours`.

See also

For more information on storing time series data and bucketing in MongoDB, you can refer to this MongoDB blog post:

`https://www.mongodb.com/blog/post/time-series-data-and-mongodb-part-2-schema-design-best-practices`

Writing time series data to InfluxDB

When working with large time series data, such as a sensor or **Internet of Things** (**IoT**) data, you will need a more efficient way to store and query such data for further analytics. This is where **time series databases** shine, as they are built exclusively to work with complex and very large time series datasets.

In this recipe, we will work with **InfluxDB** as an example of how to write to a time series database.

Getting ready

You will be using the `ExtraSensory` dataset, a mobile sensory dataset made available by the University of California, San Diego, which you can download here: `http://extrasensory.ucsd.edu/`.

There are 278 columns in the dataset. You will be using two of these columns to demonstrate how to write to InfluxDB. You will be using the timestamp (date ranges from `2015-07-23` to `2016-06-02`, covering 152 days) and the watch accelerometer reading (measured in milli G-forces or milli-G).

Before you can interact with InfluxDB using Python, you will need to install the InfluxDB Python library. We will be working with InfluxDB 2.X, so make sure you are installing `influxdb-client` 1.21.0 (and not `influxdb-python`, which supports InfluxDB up to 1.8x).

You can install the library with `pip` by running the following command:

```
$ pip install 'influxdb-client[extra]'
```

How to do it...

You will start this recipe by reading the mobile sensor data – specifically, the watch accelerometer – and performing some data transformations to prepare the data before writing the time series DataFrame to InfluxDB:

1. Let's start by loading the required libraries:

    ```
    from influxdb_client import InfluxDBClient, WriteOptions
    from influxdb_client.client.write_api import SYNCHRONOUS
    import pandas as pd
    from  pathlib import Path
    ```

2. The data consists of 60 compressed CSV files (`csv.gz`), which you read using `pandas.read_csv()`, since it has a compression parameter that is set to `infer` by default. What this means is that based on the file extension, `pandas` will determine which compression or decompression protocol to use. The files have a (`gz`) extension, which will be used to infer which decompression protocol to use. Alternatively, you can specifically indicate which compression protocol to use with `compression='gzip'`.

    In the following code, you will read one of these files, select both `timestamp` and `watch_acceleration:magnitude_stats:mean` columns, and, finally, perform a backfill operation for all na (missing) values:

    ```
    path = Path('../../datasets/Ch5/ExtraSensory/')
    file = '0A986513-7828-4D53-AA1F-E02D6DF9561B.features_
    labels.csv.gz'

    columns = ['timestamp',
                'watch_acceleration:magnitude_stats:mean']
    df = pd.read_csv(path.joinpath(file),
    ```

```
                usecols=columns)
df = df.fillna(method='backfill')
df.columns = ['timestamp','acc']
df.shape
>> (3960, 2)
```

From the preceding output, you have 3960 sensor readings in that one file.

3. To write the data to InfluxDB, you need at least a measurement column and a timestamp column. Our timestamp is currently a Unix timestamp (**epoch**) in seconds, which is an acceptable format for writing out data to InfluxDB. For example, 2015-12-08 7:06:37 PM shows as 1449601597 in our dataset.

InfluxDB stores timestamps in epoch nanoseconds on disk, but when querying data, InfluxDB will display the data in **RFC3339 UTC format** to make it more human-readable. So, 1449601597 in RFC3339 would be represented as 2015-12-08T19:06:37+00:00.000Z. Note the precision in InfluxDB is in nanoseconds.

In the following step, you will convert the Unix timestamp to a format that is more human readable for our analysis in pandas, which is also an acceptable format with InfluxDB:

```
df['timestamp'] = pd.to_datetime(df['timestamp'],
                                 origin='unix',
                                 unit='s',
                                 utc=True)
df.set_index('timestamp', inplace=True)
df.head()
```

The output is as follows:

timestamp	acc
2015-12-08 19:06:37+00:00	995.369977
2015-12-08 19:07:37+00:00	995.369977
2015-12-08 19:08:37+00:00	995.369977
2015-12-08 19:09:37+00:00	996.406005
2015-12-08 19:10:55+00:00	1034.180063

Figure 5.2 – Sensor DataFrame with timestamp as index and acceleration column

In the preceding code, we used the `unit` parameter and set it to `'s'` for `seconds`. This instructs `pandas` to calculate the number of seconds based on the origin. The `origin` parameter is set to `unix` by default, so the conversion will calculate the number of seconds to the Unix epoch start provided. The `utc` parameter is set to `True`, which will return a UTC `DatetimeIndex` type. The `dtype` data type of our DataFrame index is now `'datetime64[ns, UTC]`.

4. Establish a connection to the InfluxDB database. All you need is to pass your API read/write token. When writing to the database, you will need to specify the bucket and organization name as well:

```
bucket = "sensor"
org = "my-org"
token = "<yourtoken>"
client = InfluxDBClient(url="http://localhost:8086",
token=token)
```

5. Initialize `write_api` and configure `WriterOptions`. This includes specifying `writer_type` as `SYNCHRONOUS`, `batch_size`, and `max_retries` before it fails:

```
writer = client.write_api(WriteOptions(SYNCHRONOUS,
                          batch_size=500,
                          max_retries=5_000))

writer.write(bucket=bucket,
             org=org,
             record=df,
             write_precision='ns',
             data_frame_measurement_name='acc',
             data_frame_tag_columns=[])
```

6. You can verify that our data is written properly by passing a simple query using the `query_data_frame` method, as shown in the following code:

```
query = '''
        from(bucket: "sensor")
        |> range(start: 2015-12-08)
        '''
result = client.query_api()
```

```
influx_df = result.query_data_frame(
                            org=org,
                            query=query,
                            data_frame_index='_time')
```

7. Inspect the returned DataFrame:

```
Influx_df.info()
>>
<class 'pandas.core.frame.DataFrame'>
DatetimeIndex: 3960 entries, 2015-12-08 19:06:37+00:00 to
2015-12-11 18:48:27+00:00
Data columns (total 7 columns):
 #    Column       Non-Null Count   Dtype
---   ------       --------------   -----
 0    result       3960 non-null    object
 1    table        3960 non-null    object
 2    _start       3960 non-null    datetime64[ns, UTC]
 3    _stop        3960 non-null    datetime64[ns, UTC]
 4    _value       3960 non-null    float64
 5    _field       3960 non-null    object
 6    _measurement 3960 non-null    object
dtypes: datetime64[ns, UTC](2), float64(1), object(4)
memory usage: 247.5+ KB
```

Note that the DataFrame has two columns of the datetime64[ns, UTC] type.

Now that you are done, you need to close your writer object using writer.close() and shut down the client using client.close().

How it works...

When writing a DataFrame to InfluxDB, we need to define a few things that are required by InfluxDB, which includes the following:

- **Measurement**: These are the values we are tracking. InfluxDB accepts one measurement per data point.

- **Field**: We do not need to specify fields per se, since any columns not in the tag definition will be marked as fields. Fields are metadata objects stored as key-value pairs. Fields are not indexed, unlike tags.

- **Tag** (optional): A metadata object in which we specify columns that get indexed for improved query performance. This is stored as a key-value pair as well.

`WriteAPI` supports *synchronous* and *asynchronous* writes. `WriteAPI` also provides several options when writing to InfluxDB (such as line protocol strings, line protocol bytes, data point structure, dictionary style, as well as support for `pandas` DataFrames). In the *Reading data from time series database (InfluxDB)* recipe in *Chapter 3, Reading Time Series Data from Databases*, we used the `query_data_frame()` method to specify that the results of the query should be returned as a `pandas` DataFrame. Similarly, `write_api` provides us with specific DataFrame parameters when writing DataFrames directly to InfluxDB:

- `data_frame_measurement_name`: The name of the measurement for writing `pandas` DataFrames

- `data_frame_tag_columns`: The list of DataFrame columns that are tags; the rest of the columns will be fields

There's more...

In the previous example, we had to manually flush the data using `writer.close()` and terminate the connection using `client.close()`. For better resource management (for example, automatically closing the connection) and exception handling, you can benefit from using the `with` statement. The following example shows how you can rewrite the same code in a cleaner format:

```
with InfluxDBClient(url="http://localhost:8086", token=token)
as client:
    with client.write_api(WriteOptions(SYNCHRONOUS,
                    batch_size=500,
                    max_retries=5_000)) as writer:

        writer.write(bucket=bucket,
                    org=org,
                    record=df,
                    write_precision='ns',
                    data_frame_measurement_name='acc',
                    data_frame_tag_columns=[])
```

See also

- To learn more about the InfluxDB line protocol, please refer to their documentation here: `https://docs.influxdata.com/influxdb/v2.0/reference/syntax/line-protocol/`.

- To learn more about the Python API for InfluxDB 2.x, please refer to the official documentation here: `https://docs.influxdata.com/influxdb/cloud/tools/client-libraries/python/`.

Writing time series data to Snowflake

Snowflake has become a very popular cloud database option for building big data analytics, due to its scalability, performance, and being SQL-oriented (a columnar-stored relational database).

Snowflake's connector for Python simplifies the interaction with the database whether it's for reading or writing data, or, more specifically, the built-in support for `pandas` DataFrames. In this recipe, you will use the sensor IoT dataset prepared in the *Writing time series data to InfluxDB* recipe. The technique applies to any `pandas` DataFrame that you plan to write to Snowflake.

Getting ready

To connect to Snowflake, you will need to install the Snowflake Python connector.

To install using `Conda`, run the following:

```
conda install -c conda-forge snowflake-sqlalchemy snowflake-connector-python
```

To install using `pip`, run the following:

```
pip install "snowflake-connector-python[pandas]"
pip install --upgrade snowflake-sqlalchemy
```

How to do it...

You will write the `df` DataFrame from the previous recipe, to Snowflake by leveraging SQLAlchemy and the `DataFrame.to_sql()` writer function. You will create a new Snowflake table and then see how you can append to it as well:

1. Let's start by importing the libraries needed for this recipe:

    ```
    import pandas as pd
    from snowflake.connector.pandas_tools import pd_writer
    from sqlalchemy import create_engine
    from snowflake.sqlalchemy import URL
    from configparser import ConfigParser
    ```

2. The Snowflake connector has a set of input parameters that need to be supplied to establish a connector. You can create a `.cfg` file, for example, `snow.cfg`, to store all the necessary information, using the following format:

    ```
    [SNOWFLAKE]
    USER=<your_username>
    PASSWORD=<your_password>
    ACCOUNT=<your_account>
    WAREHOUSE=<your_warehouse_name>
    DATABASE=<your_database_name>
    SCHEMA=<you_schema_name>
    ROLE=<your_role_name>
    ```

3. Using `ConfigParser`, you can extract the content under the `[SNOWFLAKE]` section to avoid exposing or hardcoding your credentials. You can read the entire content of the `[SNOWFLAKE]` section and convert it into a dictionary object, as follows:

    ```
    config = ConfigParser()
    config.read('snow.cfg')
    config.sections()
    params = dict(config['SNOWFLAKE'])
    ```

4. You will use the `snowflake.sqlalchemy.URL` method to construct the connection string to the Snowflake database that you will later pass to SQLAlchemy's `create_engine` function:

```
url = URL(**params)
engine = create_engine(url)
```

5. Let's examine the DataFrame that we plan to write to Snowflake:

```
df.head()
```

Here is the output:

timestamp	acc
2015-12-08 19:06:37+00:00	995.369977
2015-12-08 19:07:37+00:00	995.369977
2015-12-08 19:08:37+00:00	995.369977
2015-12-08 19:09:37+00:00	996.406005
2015-12-08 19:10:55+00:00	1034.180063

Figure 5.3 – The first five rows with a lowercase column name and an index

6. Note that the DataFrame has a timestamp as an index of the `DatetimeIndex` type. First, you will need to convert the index to a DataFrame column since the API does not support writing an index object, and because you do not want to lose that information, you will need to make it a column. Secondly, note that the column names are lowercase, which will generate an error when writing to Snowflake. You will need to at least have one uppercase letter in the name. To make it easier, just uppercase the column names:

```
df = df.reset_index()
df.columns = df.columns.str.upper()
df.head()
```

The output is as follows:

	TIMESTAMP	ACC
0	2015-12-08 19:06:37+00:00	995.369977
1	2015-12-08 19:07:37+00:00	995.369977
2	2015-12-08 19:08:37+00:00	995.369977
3	2015-12-08 19:09:37+00:00	996.406005
4	2015-12-08 19:10:55+00:00	1034.180063

Figure 5.4 – The first five rows of the updated DataFrame with two uppercase columns

7. Write the DataFrame to Snowflake using the `.to_sql()` writer function. You will need to pass an insertion method; in this case, you will pass the `pd_writer` object:

```
df.to_sql('sensor',
            engine,
            index=False,
             method=pd_writer,
            if_exists='replace')
```

8. To read and verify that the data was written, you can use `pandas.read_sql()` to query the table:

```
query = 'SELECT * FROM SENSOR;'
snow_df = pd.read_sql(query, engine, index_
col='timestamp')
snow_df.info()
>>
<class 'pandas.core.frame.DataFrame'>
DatetimeIndex: 3960 entries, 2015-12-08 19:06:37 to 2015-
12-11 18:48:27
Data columns (total 1 columns):
 #   Column  Non-Null Count  Dtype
---  ------  --------------  -----
 0   acc     3960 non-null   float64
dtypes: float64(1)
memory usage: 61.9 KB
```

Note that the timestamp is returned as a `DatetimeIndex` type.

How it works...

The Snowflake Python API provides two mechanisms for writing pandas DataFrames to Snowflake, which are provided to you from `pandas_tools`:

```
from snowflake.connector.pandas_tools import pd_writer, write_
pandas
```

In the recipe, you used `pd_writer` and passed it as an insertion method to the `DataFrame.to_sql()` writer function. When using `pd_writer` within `to_sql()`, you can change the insertion behavior through the `if_exists` parameter, which takes three arguments:

- `fail`, which raises `ValueError` if the table exists
- `replace`, which drops the table before inserting new values
- `append`, which inserts the data into the existing table

If the table doesn't exist, SQLAlchemy takes care of creating the table for you and maps the data types from `pandas` DataFrames to the appropriate data types in the Snowflake database. This is also true when reading the data from Snowflake using the SQLAlchemy engine through `pandas.read_sql()`.

Note that `pd_writer` uses the `write_pandas` function behind the scenes. They both work by dumping the DataFrame into Parquet files, uploading them to a temporary stage, and, finally, copying the data into the table via `COPY INTO`.

In the *Reading data from Snowflake* recipe in *Chapter 3, Reading Time Series Data from Databases*, we discussed how Snowflake, by default, stores unquoted object names in uppercase when these objects were created. Due to this, when using SQLAlchemy to write the DataFrame, you will need to either make the column names all uppercase or at least uppercase one character; otherwise, it will throw an error on the insert.

For example, if you did not uppercase the column names and used `to_sql()` to write to Snowflake, assuming the table did not exist, the table will be created along with the columns, all with uppercase letters, as shown in the following screenshot:

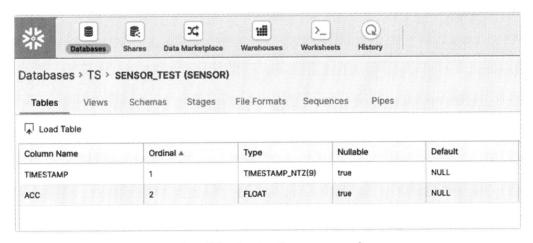

Figure 5.5 – Snowflake showing the uppercase column names

But when it comes to inserting the record, you will get a match error, as follows:

```
ProgrammingError: SQL compilation error: error line 1 at
position 86
invalid identifier '"timestamp"'
```

From the preceding error, the culprit is the quoted column name, which does not match what is in Snowflake since, by default, Snowflake has them all uppercase. Here is an experiment you can do in Snowflake (**Snowflake worksheets**) to see the issue firsthand:

```
insert into sensor_test ("timestamp", "acc") values ('2015-12-
08 19:06:37.000', '995.369977')
>> SQL compilation error: error line 1 at position 25 invalid
identifier '"timestamp"'

insert into sensor_test ("TIMESTAMP", "ACC") values ('2015-12-
08 19:06:37.000', '995.369977')
```

The first query will return the same error we received when using .to_sql(), while the second query is successfully executed. *Figure 5.5* shows Snowflake's classic web interface. If you create a new Snowflake account, you will probably use the new **Snowsight** web interface by default. Of course, you can always switch to the classic console as well.

There's more...

The `write_pandas` function can be used to write (insert) data into a table similar to `pd_write`, but in addition, it does return a tuple of (`success`, `num_chunks`, `num_rows`, `output`).

Using `write_pandas` does not leverage SQLAlchemy, so it assumes a table already exists to write the data into. Here is an example using `write_pandas` to write to the same sensor table:

```python
from snowflake import connector
from snowflake.connector.pandas_tools import pd_writer, write_pandas

con = connector.connect(**params)
cursor = con.cursor()

# delete records from the previous write
cursor.execute('DELETE FROM sensor;')

success, nchunks, nrows, copy_into = write_pandas(con, df,
table_name='SENSOR')
```

Print the returned values after the query has executed:

```python
print('success: ', success)
print('number of chunks: ', nchunks)
print('number of rows: ', nrows)
print('COPY INTO output', copy_into)
>>
success:  True
number of chunks:  1
number of rows:  3960
COPY INTO output [('raeqh/file0.txt', 'LOADED', 3960, 3960, 1,
0, None, None, None, None)]
```

The information presented confirms the number of records written and the number of chunks, as well as output from the `COPY INTO sensor` statement.

In this recipe, you learned about two options for writing pandas DataFrames directly to Snowflake. The first was using the `DataFrame.to_sql()` writer function using SQLAlchemy, and the second was using Snowflake's connector and `pd_writer()` function.

See also

- For more information on `write_pandas` and `pd_write`, please visit the Snowflake documentation here: `https://docs.snowflake.com/en/user-guide/python-connector-api.html#write_pandas`.

- For more information on the pandas `DataFrame.to_sql()` function, please visit the pandas documentation here: `https://pandas.pydata.org/docs/reference/api/pandas.DataFrame.to_sql.html`.

6
Working with Date and Time in Python

At the core of time-series data is **time**. **Time-series data** is a sequence of observations or data points captured in successive order. In the context of a DataFrame, time-series data has an ordered index type `DatetimeIndex` as you have seen in earlier chapters.

Being familiar with manipulating date and time in time-series data is an essential component of time series analysis and modeling. In this chapter, you will find recipes for common scenarios when working with date and time in time-series data.

Python has several built-in modules for working with date and time, such as the `datetime`, `time`, `calendar`, and `zoneinfo` modules. Additionally, there are other popular libraries in Python that further extend the capability to work with and manipulate date and time, such as `dateutil`, `pytz`, and `arrow`, to name a few.

You will be introduced to the `datetime` module in this chapter but then transition to use **pandas** for enhanced and more complex date and time manipulation, and generate time-series DataFrames with a sequence of `DatetimeIndex`. In addition, the `pandas` library contains several date-specific and time-specific classes that inherit from the aforementioned Python modules. In other words, you will not need to import additional date/time Python libraries.

You will be introduced to pandas classes such as `Timestamp`, `Timedelta`, `Period`, and `DateOffset`. You will notice similarities between the functionality – for example, the pandas `Timestamp` class is equivalent to Python's `Datetime` class and can be interchangeable in most scenarios. Similarly, `pandas.Timedelta` is equivalent to Python's `datetime.timedelta` object. The `pandas` library offers a more straightforward, intuitive, and powerful interface to handle most of your date and time manipulation needs without importing additional modules. When using pandas, you will appreciate having a library that contains everything you need to work with time-series data and can easily handle many challenging tasks.

Here is the list of the recipes that we will cover in this chapter:

- Working with `DatetimeIndex`
- Providing a format argument to `DateTime`
- Working with Unix epoch timestamps
- Working with time deltas
- Converting `DateTime` with time zone information
- Working with date offsets
- Working with custom business days

In a real-world scenario, you may not use all or any of these techniques. Still, it is critical to be aware of the options when facing a particular scenario that requires certain adjustments or formatting of dates.

Technical requirements

In this chapter and going forward, we will extensively use pandas 1.4.2 (released on April 2, 2022. This applies to all the recipes in this chapter.

Load these libraries in advance, since you will be using them throughout the chapter:

```
import pandas as pd
import numpy as np
import datetime as dt
```

You will use dt, np, and pd aliases going forward.

You can download the Jupyter notebooks from the GitHub repository at `https://github.com/PacktPublishing/Time-Series-Analysis-with-Python-Cookbook./tree/main/code/Ch6` to follow along.

Working with DatetimeIndex

The `pandas` library has many options and features to simplify tedious tasks when working with time-series data, dates, and time.

When working with time-series data in Python, it is common to load into a pandas DataFrame with an index of type `DatetimeIndex`. As an index, the `DatetimeIndex` class extends pandas DataFrame capabilities to work more efficiently and intelligently with time-series data. This was demonstrated numerous times in *Chapter 2, Reading Time Series Data from Files*, and *Chapter 3, Reading Time Series Data from Databases*.

By the end of this recipe, you will appreciate pandas' rich set of date functionality to handle almost any representation of date/time in your data. Additionally, you will learn how to use different functions in pandas to convert date-like objects to a DatetimeIndex.

How to do it...

In this recipe, you will explore Python's `datetime` module and learn about the `Timestamp` and `DatetimeIndex` classes and the relationship between them.

1. To understand the relationship between Python's `datetime.datetime` class and pandas' `Timestamp` and `DatetimeIndex` classes, you will create three different `datetime` objects representing the date `2021, 1, 1`. You will then compare these objects to gain a better understanding:

```
dt1 = dt.datetime(2021,1,1)
dt2 = pd.Timestamp(2021-1-1)
dt3 = pd.to_datetime('2021-1-1')
```

Inspect the datetime representation:

```
print(dt1)
print(dt2)
print(dt3)
>>
2021-01-01 00:00:00
2021-01-01 00:00:00
2021-01-01 00:00:00
```

Inspect their data types:

```
print(type(dt1))
print(type(dt2))
print(type(dt3))
>>
<class 'datetime.datetime'>
<class 'pandas._libs.tslibs.timestamps.Timestamp'>
<class 'pandas._libs.tslibs.timestamps.Timestamp'>
```

And finally, let's see how they compare:

```
dt1 == dt2 == dt3
>> True
isinstance(dt2, dt.datetime)
>> True
isinstance(dt2, pd.Timestamp)
>> True
isinstance(dt1, pd.Timestamp)
>> False
```

You can see from the preceding code that pandas' `Timestamp` object is equivalent to Python's `Datetime` object:

```
issubclass(pd.Timestamp, dt.datetime)
>> True
```

Note that `dt2` is an instance of `pandas.Timestamp` class, and the `Timestamp` class is a subclass of Python's `dt.datetime` class (but not vice versa).

2. When you used the `pandas.to_datetime()` function, it returned a `Timestamp` object. Now, use `pandas.to_datetime()` on a list and examine the outcome:

```
dates = ['2021-1-1', '2021-1-2']
pd_dates = pd.to_datetime(dates)
print(pd_dates)
print(type(pd_dates))
>>
DatetimeIndex(['2021-01-01', '2021-01-02'],
dtype='datetime64[ns]', freq=None)
<class 'pandas.core.indexes.datetimes.DatetimeIndex'>
```

Interestingly, the output is now of type `DatetimeIndex` created using the same `pandas.to_datetime()` function that you used earlier. Previously, when using the same function on an individual object, the result was of type `Timestamp`, but when applied on a list, it produced a sequence of type `DatetimeIndex`. You will perform one more task to make things clearer.

Print out the first item (slice) from the `pd_dates` variable:

```
print(pd_dates[0])
print(type(pd_dates[0]))
>>
2021-01-01 00:00:00
<class 'pandas._libs.tslibs.timestamps.Timestamp'>
```

From the preceding output, you can infer a relationship between the two classes: `DatetimeIndex` and `Timestamp`. A DatetimeIndex is a sequence (list) of `Timestamp` objects.

3. Now that you know how to create a `DatetimeIndex` using the `pandas.to_datetime()` function, let's further expand on this and see what else you can do with the function. For example, you will see how simple it is to convert different `datetime` representations, including strings, integers, lists, pandas series, or other `datetime` objects, into a `DatetimeIndex`.

Let's create a `dates` list:

```
dates = ['2021-01-01',
         '2/1/2021',
         '03-01-2021',
         'April 1, 2021',
         '20210501',
         np.datetime64('2021-07-01'), # numpy datetime64
         datetime.datetime(2021, 8, 1), # python
datetime
         pd.Timestamp(2021,9,1) # pandas Timestamp
         ]
```

Parse the list using `pandas.to_datetime()`:

```
parsed_dates = pd.to_datetime(
                dates,
                infer_datetime_format=True,
                errors='coerce'
```

```
                        )
print(parsed_dates)

>>

DatetimeIndex(['2021-01-01', '2021-02-01', '2021-03-01',
    '2021-04-01', '2021-05-01', '2021-07-01', '2021-08-01',
    '2021-09-01'],
                    dtype='datetime64[ns]', freq=None)
```

Notice how the that the `to_datetime()` function properly parsed the entire list of different string representations and date types such as Python's `Datetime` and NumPy's `datetime64`. Similarly, you could have used the `DatetimeIndex` constructor directly, as follows:

```
pd.DatetimeIndex(dates)
```

This would produce similar results.

4. The `DatetimeIndex` object gives access to many useful properties and methods to extract additional date and time properties. As an example, you can extract `day_name`, `month`, `year`, `days_in_month`, `quarter`, `is_quarter_start`, `is_leap_year`, `is_month_start`, `is_month_end`, and `is_year_start`. The following code shows how this can be done:

```
print(f'Name of Day : {parsed_dates.day_name()}')
print(f'Month : {parsed_dates.month}')
print(f'Year : {parsed_dates.year}')
print(f'Days in Month : {parsed_dates.days_in_month}')
print(f'Quarter {parsed_dates.quarter}')
print(f'Quarter Start : {parsed_dates.is_quarter_start}')
print(f'Leap Year : {parsed_dates.is_leap_year}')
print(f'Month Start : {parsed_dates.is_month_start}')
print(f'Month End : {parsed_dates.is_month_end}')
print(f'Year Start : {parsed_dates.is_year_start}')
```

The preceding code produces the following results:

```
Name of Day : Index(['Friday', 'Monday', 'Monday',
'Thursday',

                    'Saturday', 'Thursday', Sunday',
'Wednesday'],
```

```
                    dtype='object')
Month : Int64Index([1, 2, 3, 4, 5, 7, 8, 9],
dtype='int64')
Year : Int64Index([2021, 2021, 2021, 2021, 2021, 2021,
2021, 2021], dtype='int64')
Days in Month : Int64Index([31, 28, 31, 30, 31, 31, 31,
30], dtype='int64')
Quarter Int64Index([1, 1, 1, 2, 2, 3, 3, 3],
dtype='int64')
Quarter Start : [ True False False  True False  True
False False]
Leap Year : [False False False False False False False
False]
Month Start : [
True  True  True  True  True  True  True  True]
Month End : [False False False False False False False
False]
Year Start : [ True False False False False False False
False]
```

These properties and methods will be very useful when transforming your time-series datasets for analysis.

How it works...

The, `pandas.to_datetime()` is a powerful function that can intelligently parse different date representations from strings. As you saw in *step 4* in the previous *How to do it...* section, the string examples, such as `'2021-01-01'`, `'2/1/2021'`, `'03-01-2021'`, `'April 1, 2021'`, and `'20210501'`, were parsed correctly. Other date representations such as `'April 1, 2021'` and `'1 April 2021'`, can be parsed using the `to_datetime()` function as well, and I'll leave it to you to explore additional examples that come to mind.

The `to_datetime` function contains the `errors` parameter. In the following example, you specify `errors='coerce'` which instructs pandas to set any value it could not parse as NaT indicating a missing value. You will learn more about NaT in the Performing data quality checks recipe in *Chapter 7, Handling Missing Data*.

```
pd.to_datetime(
                dates,
                infer_datetime_format=True,
```

```
                            errors='coerce'
    )
```

In pandas, there are different representations to indicate missing values – np.NaN represents missing numeric values (**Not a Number**), while pd.NaT represents missing datetime values (**Not a Time**). Finally, pandas' pd.NA is used to represent missing scalar values (**Not Available**).

The errors parameter in to_datetime can take one of the three valid string options:

- raise, which means it will raise an exception (error out).

- coerce will not cause it to raise an exception. Instead, it will just replace pd.NaT, indicating a missing datetime value.

- ignore will also not cause it to raise an exception. Instead, it will just pass in the original value.

Here is an example using the ignore value:

```
pd.to_datetime(['something 2021', 'Jan 1, 2021'],
                errors='ignore')
>> Index(['something 2021', 'Jan 1, 2021'], dtype='object')
```

When the errors parameter is set to 'ignore', pandas will not raise an error if it stumbles upon a date representation it cannot parse. Instead, the input value is passed as-is. For example, notice from the preceding output that the to_datetime function returned an Index type and not a DatetimeIndex. Further, the items in the Index sequence are of dtype object (and not datetime64). In pandas, the object dtype represents strings or mixed types.

There's more...

An alternate way to generate a of DatetimeIndex is with the pandas.date_range() function. The following code provides a starting date and the number of periods to generate and specifies a daily frequency with D:

```
pd.date_range(start='2021-01-01', periods=3, freq='D')
>>
DatetimeIndex(['2021-01-01', '2021-01-02', '2021-01-03'],
dtype='datetime64[ns]', freq='D')
```

`pandas.date_range()` requires at least three of the four parameters to be provided – `start`, `end`, `periods`, and `freq`. If you do not provide enough information, you will get a `ValueError` exception with the following message:

```
ValueError: Of the four parameters: start, end, periods, and
freq, exactly three must be specified
```

Let's explore the different parameter combinations required to use the `date_range` function. In the first example, provide a start date, end date, and specify a daily frequency. The function will always return a range of equally spaced time points:

```
pd.date_range(start='2021-01-01',
              end='2021-01-03',
              freq='D')
>>
DatetimeIndex(['2021-01-01', '2021-01-02', '2021-01-03'],
dtype='datetime64[ns]', freq='D')
```

In the second example, provide a start date and an end date, but instead of frequency, provide a number of periods. Remember that the function will always return a range of equally spaced time points:

```
pd.date_range(start='2021-01-01',
              end='2021-01-03',
              periods=2)
>>
DatetimeIndex(['2021-01-01', '2021-01-03'],
dtype='datetime64[ns]', freq=None)
pd.date_range(start='2021-01-01',
              end='2021-01-03',
              periods=4)
>>
DatetimeIndex(['2021-01-01 00:00:00', '2021-01-01 16:00:00',
               '2021-01-02 08:00:00', '2021-01-03 00:00:00'],
              dtype='datetime64[ns]', freq=None)
```

In the following example, provide an end date and the number of periods returned, and indicate a daily frequency:

```
pd.date_range(end='2021-01-01', periods=3, freq='D')
DatetimeIndex(['2020-12-30', '2020-12-31', '2021-01-01'],
dtype='datetime64[ns]', freq='D')
```

Note, the `pd.date_range()` function can work with a minimum of two parameters if the information is sufficient to generate equally spaced time points and infer the missing parameters. Here is an example of providing start and end dates only:

```
pd.date_range(start='2021-01-01',
              end='2021-01-03')
>>
DatetimeIndex(['2021-01-01', '2021-01-02', '2021-01-03'],
dtype='datetime64[ns]', freq='D')
```

Notice that pandas was able to construct the date sequence using the start and end dates and default to daily frequency. Here is another example:

```
pd.date_range(start='2021-01-01',
              periods=3)
>>
DatetimeIndex(['2021-01-01', '2021-01-02', '2021-01-03'],
dtype='datetime64[ns]', freq='D')
```

With `start` and `periods`, pandas has enough information to construct the date sequence and default to daily frequency.

Now, here is an example that lacks enough information on how to generate the sequence and will cause pandas to throw an error:

```
pd.date_range(start='2021-01-01',
              freq='D')
>>
ValueError: Of the four parameters: start, end, periods, and
freq, exactly three must be specified
```

Note that with just a start date and frequency, pandas does not have enough information to construct the date sequence. Therefore, adding either `periods` or the end date will be sufficient.

See also

To learn more about pandas' `to_datetime()` function and the `DatetimeIndex` class, please check out these resources:

- *pandas.DatetimeIndex* documentation: `https://pandas.pydata.org/docs/reference/api/pandas.DatetimeIndex.html`

- *pandas.to_datetime* documentation: `https://pandas.pydata.org/docs/reference/api/pandas.to_datetime.html`

Providing a format argument to DateTime

When working with datasets extracted from different data sources, you may encounter date columns stored in string format, whether from files or databases. In the previous recipe, *Working with DatetimeIndex*, you explored the `pandas.to_datetime()` function that can parse various date formats with minimal input. However, you will want more granular control to ensure that the date is parsed correctly. For example, you will now be introduced to the `strptime` and `strftime` methods and see how you can specify formatting in `pandas.to_datetime()` to handle different date formats.

In this recipe, you will learn how to parse strings that represent dates to a `datetime` or **date** object (an instance of the class `datetime.datetime` or `datetime.date`).

How to do it...

Python's `datetime` module contains the `strptime()` method to create `datetime` or `date` from a string that contains a date. You will first explore how you can do this in Python and then extend this to pandas:

1. Let's explore a few examples, parsing strings to `datetime` objects using `datetime.strptime`. You will parse four different representations of January 1, 2022 that will produce the same output – `datetime.datetime(2022, 1, 1, 0, 0)`:

```
dt.datetime.strptime('1/1/2022', '%m/%d/%Y')
dt.datetime.strptime('1 January, 2022', '%d %B, %Y')
dt.datetime.strptime('1-Jan-2022', '%d-%b-%Y')
dt.datetime.strptime('Saturday, January 1, 2022', '%A, %B
%d, %Y')
>>
datetime.datetime(2022, 1, 1, 0, 0)
```

Note that the output is a `datetime` object, representing the year, month, day, hour, and minute. You can specify only the date representation, as follows:

```
dt.datetime.strptime('1/1/2022', '%m/%d/%Y').date()
>>
datetime.date(2022, 1, 1)
```

Now, you will have a `date` object instead of `datetime`. You can get the readable version of `datetime` using the `print()` function:

```
dt_1 = dt.datetime.strptime('1/1/2022', '%m/%d/%Y')
print(dt_1)
>>
2022-01-01 00:00:00
```

2. Now, let's compare what you did using the `datetime.strptime` method using `pandas.to_datetime` method:

```
pd.to_datetime('1/1/2022', format='%m/%d/%Y')
pd.to_datetime('1 January, 2022', format='%d %B, %Y')
pd.to_datetime('1-Jan-2022', format='%d-%b-%Y')
pd.to_datetime('Saturday, January 1, 2022', format='%A,
%B %d, %Y')
>>
Timestamp('2022-01-01 00:00:00')
```

Similarly, you can get the string (readable) representation of the `Timestamp` object using the `print()` function:

```
dt_2 = pd.to_datetime('1/1/2022', format='%m/%d/%Y')
print(dt_2)
>>
2022-01-01 00:00:00
```

3. There is an advantage in using `pandas.to_datetime()` over Python's `datetime` module. The `to_datetime()` function can parse a variety of date representations, including string date formats with minimal input or specifications. The following code explains this concept; note that the `format` is omitted:

```
pd.to_datetime('Saturday, January 1, 2022')
pd.to_datetime('1-Jan-2022')
>>
Timestamp('2022-01-01 00:00:00')
```

Note that unlike `datetime`, which requires integer values or to use the `strptime` method for parsing strings, the `pandas.to_datetime()` function can intelligently parse different date representations without specifying a format (this is true in most cases).

How it works...

In this recipe, you used Python's `datetime.datetime` and `pandas.to_datetime` methods to parse dates in string formats. When using `datetime`, you had to use the `dt.datetime.strptime()` function to specify the date format representation in the string using format codes (example `%d`, `%B`, and `%Y`).

For example, in `datetime.strptime('1 January, 2022', '%d %B, %Y')`, you provided the `%d`, `%B`, and `%Y` format codes in the exact order and spacing to represent the formatting provided in the string. Let's break this down:

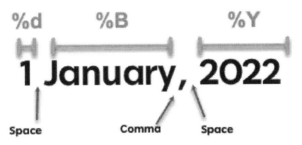

Figure 6.1 – Understanding the format

- `%d` indicates that the first value is a zero-padded digit representing the day of the month, followed by a space to display spacing between the digit and the next object.

- `%B` is used to indicate that the second value represents the month's full name. Note that this was followed by a comma (`,`) to describe the exact format in the string, for example `"January,"`. Therefore, it is crucial to match the format in the strings you are parsing to include any commas, hyphens, backslashes, spaces, or whichever separator characters are used.

- To adhere to the string format, there is a space after the comma (`,`), followed by `%Y` to reflect the last value represents a four-digit year.

> **Format Directives**
>
> Remember that you always use the percent sign (%) followed by the format code (a letter with or without a negative sign). This is called a formatting directive. For example, lower case y, as in `%y`, represents the year 22 without the century, while uppercase y, as in `%Y`, represents the year 2022 with the century. Here is a list of common Python directives that can be used in the `strptime()` function: `https://docs.python.org/3/library/datetime.html#strftime-and-strptime-format-codes`.

Recall that you used `pandas.to_datetime()` to parse the same string objects as with `dt.datetime.strptime()`. The biggest difference is that the pandas function can accurately parse the strings without explicitly providing an argument to the format parameter. That is one of many advantages of using pandas for time-series analysis, especially when handling complex date and `datetime` scenarios.

There's more...

Now you know how to use `pandas.to_datetime()` to parse string objects to `datetime`. So, let's see how you can apply this knowledge to transform a DataFrame column that contains date information in string format to a `datetime` data type.

In the following code, you will create a small DataFrame:

```
df = pd.DataFrame(
        {'Date': ['January 1, 2022', 'January 2, 2022',
'January 3, 2022'],
        'Sales': [23000, 19020, 21000]}
            )
df
>>
Date   Sales
0      January 1, 2022    23000
1      January 2, 2022    19020
2      January 3, 2022    21000

df.info()
>>
<class 'pandas.core.frame.DataFrame'>
```

```
RangeIndex: 3 entries, 0 to 2
Data columns (total 2 columns):
 #    Column   Non-Null Count   Dtype
---   ------   --------------   -----
 0    Date     3 non-null       object
 1    Sales    3 non-null       int64
dtypes: int64(1), object(1)
memory usage: 176.0+ bytes
```

To update the DataFrame to include a DatetimeIndex, you will parse the Date column to datetime and then assign it as an index to the DataFrame:

```
df['Date'] = pd.to_datetime(df['Date'])
df.set_index('Date', inplace=True)
df.info()
>>
<class 'pandas.core.frame.DataFrame'>
DatetimeIndex: 3 entries, 2022-01-01 to 2022-01-03
Data columns (total 1 columns):
 #    Column   Non-Null Count   Dtype
---   ------   --------------   -----
 0    Sales    3 non-null       int64
dtypes: int64(1)
memory usage: 48.0 bytes
```

Note how the index is now of the DatetimeIndex type, and there is only one column in the DataFrame (Sales), since Date is now an index.

See also

To learn more about pandas.to_datetime, please visit the official documentation page here: https://pandas.pydata.org/docs/reference/api/pandas.to_datetime.html.

Working with Unix epoch timestamps

Epoch timestamps, sometimes referred to as **Unix time** or **POSIX time**, are a common way to store datetime in an integer format. This integer represents the number of seconds elapsed from a reference point, and in the case of a Unix-based timestamp, the reference point is January 1, 1970, at midnight (00:00:00 UTC). This arbitrary date and time represent the baseline, starting at 0. So, we just increment in seconds for every second beyond that time.

Many databases, applications, and systems store dates and time in numeric format, making it mathematically easier to work with, convert, increment, decrement, and so on. Note that in the case of the **Unix epoch**, it is based on **UTC**, which stands for **Universal Time Coordinated**. Using UTC is a clear choice when building applications used globally, making it easier to store dates and timestamps in a standardized format. This makes it easier to work with dates and time without worrying about daylight saving or different time zones around the globe. UTC is the standard international time used in aviation systems, weather forecast systems, the International Space Station, and so on.

You will, at some point, encounter Unix epoch timestamps, and to make more sense of the data, you will need to convert it to a human-readable format. This is what will be covered in this recipe. Again, you will explore the ease of using pandas' built-in functions to work with Unix epoch timestamps.

How to do it...

Before we start converting the Unix time to a human-readable datetime object, which is the easy part, let's first gain some intuition about the idea of storing dates and time as a numeric object (a floating-point number):

1. You will use time from the time module (part of Python) to request the current time in seconds. This will be the time in seconds since the epoch, which for Unix systems starts from January 1, 1970, at 00:00:00 UTC:

```
import time
epoch_time = time.time()
print(epoch_time)
print(type(epoch_time))
>>
1635220133.855169
<class 'float'>
```

2. Now, copy the numeric value you have and visit `https://www.epoch101.com`. The website should display your current epoch time. If you scroll down, you can paste the number and convert it to a human-readable format. Make sure that you click on **seconds**, as shown in the following figure:

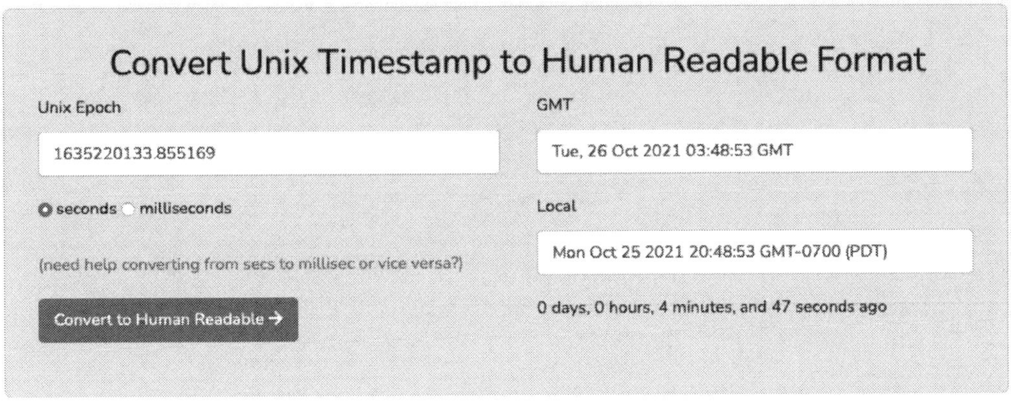

Convert Unix Timestamp to Human Readable Format

Unix Epoch	GMT
1635220133.855169	Tue, 26 Oct 2021 03:48:53 GMT

○ seconds ○ milliseconds

(need help converting from secs to millisec or vice versa?)

Local

Mon Oct 25 2021 20:48:53 GMT-0700 (PDT)

Convert to Human Readable →

0 days, 0 hours, 4 minutes, and 47 seconds ago

Figure 6.2 – Converting a Unix timestamp to a human-readable format in both GMT and local time

Note, the GMT format was given as `Tue, 26 Oct 2021 03:48:53 GMT` and my local format as `Mon Oct 25, 2021, 20:48:53 GMT-0700 (PDT)`.

3. Let's see how pandas converts the epoch timestamp. The convenience here is that you will be using the same `pandas.to_datetime()` function that you should be familiar with by now, as you have used it in the previous two recipes from this chapter. This is one of the many conveniences you get when using pandas. For example, in the following code, you will use `pandas.to_datetime()` to parse the Unix epoch `1635220133.855169`:

```
import pandas as pd
t = pd.to_datetime(1635220133.855169, unit='s')
print(t)
>>
2021-10-26 03:48:53.855169024
```

Note the need to specify units as seconds. The output is similar to that in *Figure 6.1* for the GMT format.

4. If you want `datetime` to be time-zone aware – for example, the US/Pacific time zone – you can use `tz_localize('US/Pacific')`. To get a more accurate conversion though, it is better to do it in two steps:

    I.   Convert the time zone-naive object to UTC using `tz_localize('UTC')`.

    II. Then, convert it to the desired time zone using `tz_convert()`.

    The following code shows how this is done to convert to the Pacific time zone:

    ```
    t.tz_localize('UTC').tz_convert('US/Pacific')
    >>
    Timestamp('2021-10-25 20:48:53.855169024-0700', tz='US/
    Pacific')
    ```

    Compare this to *Figure 6.1* for the local **Pacific Daylight Time (PDT)** format, and it will be the same.

5. Let's put all of this together. You will convert a DataFrame that contains a `datetime` column in Unix epoch format to a human-readable format. You will start by creating a new DataFrame with Unix epoch timestamps:

    ```
    df = pd.DataFrame(
            {'unix_epoch': [1641110340,  1641196740,
    1641283140, 1641369540],
                    'Sales': [23000, 19020, 21000, 17030]}
                    )
    df
    >>
            unix_epoch  Sales
    0       1641110340  23000
    1       1641196740  19020
    2       1641283140  21000
    3       1641369540  17030
    ```

6. Create a new column, call it `Date` by parsing the `unix_epoch` column into a `datetime` (which defaults to GMT), then localize the output to UTC, and convert to a local time zone. Finally, set the `Date` column as the index:

    ```
    df['Date'] = pd.to_datetime(df['unix_epoch'], unit='s')
    df['Date'] = df['Date'].dt.tz_localize('UTC').dt.tz_
    convert('US/Pacific')
    df.set_index('Date', inplace=True)
    ```

```
df

>>                                 unix_epoch   Sales

Date

2022-01-01 23:59:00-08:00          1641110340   23000

2022-01-02 23:59:00-08:00          1641196740   19020

2022-01-03 23:59:00-08:00          1641283140   21000

2022-01-04 23:59:00-08:00          1641369540   17030
```

Note that since the Date column was of the datetime type (not DatetimeIndex), you had to use the Series.dt accessor to tap into the built-in methods and attributes for the datetime objects. In the last step, you converted datetime to a DatetimeIndex object (a DataFrame index). If you recall from the *Working with DatetimeIndex* recipe of this chapter, a DatetimeIndex object can access any of the datetime methods and attributes without using the dt accessor.

7. If you do not need the time in your index (DatetimeIndex), given your data is daily and there is no use case for using time, then you can request just the date, as shown in the following code:

```
df.index.date

>>
array([datetime.date(2022, 1, 1), datetime.date(2022, 1,
2), datetime.date(2022, 1, 3), datetime.date(2022, 1,
4)], dtype=object)
```

Note that the output displays the date without time.

How it works...

So far, you have used pandas.to_datetime() to parse dates in string format to a datetime object by leveraging the format attribute (see the *Providing a format argument to DateTime* recipe). In this recipe, you used the same function, but instead of providing a value to format, you passed a value to the unit parameter, as in unit="s.".

The unit parameter tells pandas which unit to use when calculating the difference from the epoch start. In this case, the request was in seconds. However, there is another critical parameter that you do not need to adjust (in most cases), which is the origin parameter. For example, the default value is origin='unix', which indicates that the calculation should be based on the Unix (or POSIX) time set to 01-01-1970 00:00:00 UTC.

This is what the actual code looks like:

```
pd.to_datetime(1635220133.855169, unit='s', origin='unix')
>>
Timestamp('2021-10-26 03:48:53.855169024')
```

There's more...

If you would like to store your `datetime` value in Unix epoch, you can do this by subtracting `1970-01-01` and then floor-divide by a unit of `1` second. Python uses / as the division operator, // as the floor division operator to return the floored quotient, and % as the modulus operator to return the remainder from a division.

Start by creating a new pandas DataFrame:

```
df = pd.DataFrame(
        {'Date': pd.date_range('01-01-2022', periods=5),
        'order' : range(5)}
                )
df
>>
       Date         order
0    2022-01-01     0
1    2022-01-02     1
2    2022-01-03     2
3    2022-01-04     3
4    2022-01-05     4
```

You can then perform the transformation, as follows:

```
(df['Date'] -  pd.Timestamp("1970-01-01")) //
pd.Timedelta("1s")
>>
0    1640995200
1    1641081600
2    1641168000
3    1641254400
4    1641340800
```

You have now generated your Unix epochs. There are different ways to achieve similar results. The preceding example is the recommended approach from pandas, which you can read more about here: `https://pandas.pydata.org/pandas-docs/stable/user_guide/timeseries.html#from-timestamps-to-epoch`.

See also

To learn more about `pandas.to_datetime`, please visit the official documentation page here: `https://pandas.pydata.org/docs/reference/api/pandas.to_datetime.html`.

Working with time deltas

When working with time-series data, you may need to perform some calculations on your `datetime` columns, such as adding or subtracting. Examples can include adding 30 days to purchase `datetime` to determine when the return policy expires for a product or when a warranty ends. For example, the `Timedelta` class makes it possible to derive new `datetime` objects by adding or subtracting at different ranges or increments, such as seconds, daily, and weekly. This includes time zone-aware calculations.

In this recipe, you will explore two practical approaches in pandas to capture date/time differences – the `pandas.Timedelta` class and the `pandas.to_timedelta` function.

How to do it...

In this recipe, you will work with hypothetical sales data for a retail store. You will generate the sales DataFrame, which will contain items purchased from the store and the purchase date. You will then explore different scenarios using the `Timedelta` class and the `to_timedelta()` function:

1. Start by importing the `pandas` library and creating a DataFrame with two columns, `item` and `purchase_dt`, which will be standardized to UTC:

    ```
    df = pd.DataFrame(
            {
            'item': ['item1', 'item2', 'item3', 'item4',
    'item5', 'item6'],
            'purchase_dt': pd.date_range('2021-01-01',
    periods=6, freq='D', tz='UTC')
    ```

```
            }
  )
  df
```

The preceding code should output a DataFrame with six rows (items) and two columns (item and purchase_dt):

	item	purchase_dt
0	item1	2021-01-01 00:00:00+00:00
1	item2	2021-01-02 00:00:00+00:00
2	item3	2021-01-03 00:00:00+00:00
3	item4	2021-01-04 00:00:00+00:00
4	item5	2021-01-05 00:00:00+00:00
5	item6	2021-01-06 00:00:00+00:00

Figure 6.3 – The DataFrame with the item purchased and purchase datetime (UTC) data

2. Add another datetime column to represent the expiration date, which is 30 days from the purchase date:

```
df['expiration_dt'] = df['purchase_dt'] +
pd.Timedelta(days=30)
df
```

The preceding code should add a third column (expiration_dt) to the DataFrame, which is set at 30 days from the date of purchase:

	item	purchase_dt	expiration_dt
0	item1	2021-01-01 00:00:00+00:00	2021-01-31 00:00:00+00:00
1	item2	2021-01-02 00:00:00+00:00	2021-02-01 00:00:00+00:00
2	item3	2021-01-03 00:00:00+00:00	2021-02-02 00:00:00+00:00
3	item4	2021-01-04 00:00:00+00:00	2021-02-03 00:00:00+00:00
4	item5	2021-01-05 00:00:00+00:00	2021-02-04 00:00:00+00:00
5	item6	2021-01-06 00:00:00+00:00	2021-02-05 00:00:00+00:00

Figure 6.4 – The updated DataFrame with a third column reflecting the expiration date

3. Now, assume you are asked to create a special extended date for return, and this one is set at 35 days, 12 hours, and 30 minutes from the purchase date:

```
df['extended_dt'] = df['purchase_dt'] +\
                pd.Timedelta('35 days 12 hours 30
minutes')
df
```

The preceding code should add a fourth column (extended_dt) to the DataFrame, reflecting the new datetime, based on the additional 35 days, 12 hours, and 30 minutes:

	item	purchase_dt	expiration_dt	extended_dt
0	item1	2021-01-01 00:00:00+00:00	2021-01-31 00:00:00+00:00	2021-02-05 12:30:00+00:00
1	item2	2021-01-02 00:00:00+00:00	2021-02-01 00:00:00+00:00	2021-02-06 12:30:00+00:00
2	item3	2021-01-03 00:00:00+00:00	2021-02-02 00:00:00+00:00	2021-02-07 12:30:00+00:00
3	item4	2021-01-04 00:00:00+00:00	2021-02-03 00:00:00+00:00	2021-02-08 12:30:00+00:00
4	item5	2021-01-05 00:00:00+00:00	2021-02-04 00:00:00+00:00	2021-02-09 12:30:00+00:00
5	item6	2021-01-06 00:00:00+00:00	2021-02-05 00:00:00+00:00	2021-02-10 12:30:00+00:00

Figure 6.5 – The updated DataFrame with a fourth datetime column reflecting the extended date

4. Assume that you are asked to convert the time zone from UTC to the local time zone of the retailer store's headquarters, which is set in Los Angeles:

```
df.iloc[:,1:] = df.iloc[: ,1:].apply(
            lambda x: x.dt.tz_convert('US/Pacific')
            )
df
```

After converting from UTC to the US/Pacific time zone (Los Angeles), you are overwriting the datetime columns (purchased_dt, expiration_dt, and extended_dt). The DataFrame structure should remain the same – six rows and four columns – but now the data looks different, as shown in the following screenshot:

	item	purchase_dt	expiration_dt	extended_dt
0	item1	2020-12-31 16:00:00-08:00	2021-01-30 16:00:00-08:00	2021-02-05 04:30:00-08:00
1	item2	2021-01-01 16:00:00-08:00	2021-01-31 16:00:00-08:00	2021-02-06 04:30:00-08:00
2	item3	2021-01-02 16:00:00-08:00	2021-02-01 16:00:00-08:00	2021-02-07 04:30:00-08:00
3	item4	2021-01-03 16:00:00-08:00	2021-02-02 16:00:00-08:00	2021-02-08 04:30:00-08:00
4	item5	2021-01-04 16:00:00-08:00	2021-02-03 16:00:00-08:00	2021-02-09 04:30:00-08:00
5	item6	2021-01-05 16:00:00-08:00	2021-02-04 16:00:00-08:00	2021-02-10 04:30:00-08:00

Figure 6.6 – The updated DataFrame where all datetime columns are not in Los Angeles (US/Pacific)

5. Finally, you can calculate the delta between the extended and original expiration dates. Since they are both datetime data types, you can achieve this with a simple subtraction between the two columns:

```
df['exp_ext_diff'] = (
        df['extended_dt'] - df['expiration_dt']
        )
df
```

Your final DataFrame should now have a fifth column that captures the difference between the extended date and the expiration date:

	item	purchase_dt	expiration_dt	extended_dt	exp_ext_diff
0	item1	2020-12-31 16:00:00-08:00	2021-01-30 16:00:00-08:00	2021-02-05 04:30:00-08:00	5 days 12:30:00
1	item2	2021-01-01 16:00:00-08:00	2021-01-31 16:00:00-08:00	2021-02-06 04:30:00-08:00	5 days 12:30:00
2	item3	2021-01-02 16:00:00-08:00	2021-02-01 16:00:00-08:00	2021-02-07 04:30:00-08:00	5 days 12:30:00
3	item4	2021-01-03 16:00:00-08:00	2021-02-02 16:00:00-08:00	2021-02-08 04:30:00-08:00	5 days 12:30:00
4	item5	2021-01-04 16:00:00-08:00	2021-02-03 16:00:00-08:00	2021-02-09 04:30:00-08:00	5 days 12:30:00
5	item6	2021-01-05 16:00:00-08:00	2021-02-04 16:00:00-08:00	2021-02-10 04:30:00-08:00	5 days 12:30:00

Figure 6.7 – The updated DataFrame with a fifth column

These types of transformations and calculations are simplified without needing any additional libraries, thanks to pandas' built-in capabilities to work with time-series data and datetime overall.

How it works...

Time deltas can be handy for capturing the difference between two date or time objects. In pandas, the `pandas.Timedelta` class is equivalent to Python's `datetime.timedelta` class and behaves very similarly. However, the advantage of pandas is that it includes a wide range of classes and functions for working with time-series data. These built-in functions within pandas, in general, are simpler and more efficient when working with DataFrames. Let's try this quick experiment to demonstrate how pandas' `Timedelta` class is a subclass of Python's `timedelta` class:

```
import datetime as dt
import pandas as pd


pd.Timedelta(days=1) == dt.timedelta(days=1)
>> True
```

Let's validate that `pandas.Timedelta` is an instance of `datetime.timedelta`:

```
issubclass(pd.Timedelta, dt.timedelta)
>>
True
dt_1 = pd.Timedelta(days=1)
dt_2 = dt.timedelta(days=1)
isinstance(dt_1, dt.timedelta)
>> True
isinstance(dt_1, pd.Timedelta)
>> True
```

Python's `datetime.timedelta` class accepts integer values for these parameters – `days`, `seconds`, `microseconds`, `milliseconds`, `minutes`, `hours`, and `weeks`. On the other hand, `pandas.Timedelta` takes both integers and strings, as demonstrated in the following snippet:

```
pd.Timedelta(days=1, hours=12, minutes=55)
>> Timedelta('1 days 12:55:00')


pd.Timedelta('1 day 12 hours 55 minutes')
>> Timedelta('1 days 12:55:00')
```

```
pd.Timedelta('1D 12H 55T')
>> Timedelta('1 days 12:55:00')
```

Once you have defined your `Timedelta` object, you can use it to make calculations on `date`, `time`, or `datetime` objects:

```
week_td = pd.Timedelta('1W')
pd.to_datetime('1 JAN 2022') + week_td
>> Timestamp('2022-01-08 00:00:00')
```

In the preceding example, `week_td` represents a 1-week `Timedelta` object, which can be added (or subtracted) from `datetime` to get the difference. By adding `week_td`, you are incrementing by 1 week. What if you want to add 2 weeks? You can use multiplication as well:

```
pd.to_datetime('1 JAN 2022') + 2*week_td
>> Timestamp('2022-01-15 00:00:00')
```

There's more...

Using `pd.Timedelta` is straightforward and makes working with large time-series DataFrames efficient without importing additional libraries, as it is built into pandas.

In the previous *How to do it...* section, you created a DataFrame and added additional columns based on the `timedelta` calculations. You can also add the `timedelta` object into a DataFrame and reference it by its column. Finally, let's see how this works.

First, let's construct the same DataFrame used earlier:

```
import pandas as pd

df = pd.DataFrame(
        {
        'item': ['item1', 'item2', 'item3', 'item4', 'item5',
'item6'],
        'purchase_dt': pd.date_range('2021-01-01', periods=6,
 freq='D', tz='UTC')
        }
)
```

This should print out the DataFrame shown in *Figure 6.2*. Now, you will add a new column that contains the Timedelta object (1 week) and then use that column to add and subtract from the purchased_dt column:

```
df['1 week'] = pd.Timedelta('1W')
df['1_week_more'] = df['purchase_dt'] + df['1 week']
df['1_week_less'] = df['purchase_dt'] - df['1 week']
df
```

The preceding code should produce a DataFrame with three additional columns. The 1 week column holds the Timedelta, object and because of that, you can reference the column to calculate any time differences you need:

	item	purchase_dt	1 week	1_week_more	1_week_less
0	item1	2021-01-01 00:00:00+00:00	7 days	2021-01-08 00:00:00+00:00	2020-12-25 00:00:00+00:00
1	item2	2021-01-02 00:00:00+00:00	7 days	2021-01-09 00:00:00+00:00	2020-12-26 00:00:00+00:00
2	item3	2021-01-03 00:00:00+00:00	7 days	2021-01-10 00:00:00+00:00	2020-12-27 00:00:00+00:00
3	item4	2021-01-04 00:00:00+00:00	7 days	2021-01-11 00:00:00+00:00	2020-12-28 00:00:00+00:00
4	item5	2021-01-05 00:00:00+00:00	7 days	2021-01-12 00:00:00+00:00	2020-12-29 00:00:00+00:00
5	item6	2021-01-06 00:00:00+00:00	7 days	2021-01-13 00:00:00+00:00	2020-12-30 00:00:00+00:00

Figure 6.8 – The updated DataFrame with three additional columns

Let's check the data types for each column in the DataFrame:

```
df.info()
>>
<class 'pandas.core.frame.DataFrame'>
RangeIndex: 6 entries, 0 to 5
Data columns (total 5 columns):
 #   Column        Non-Null Count    Dtype
---  ------        --------------    -----
 0   item          6 non-null        object
 1   purchase_dt   6 non-null        datetime64[ns, UTC]
 2   1 week        6 non-null        timedelta64[ns]
 3   1_week_more   6 non-null        datetime64[ns, UTC]
 4   1_week_less   6 non-null        datetime64[ns, UTC]
```

```
dtypes: datetime64[ns, UTC](3), object(1), timedelta64[ns](1)
memory usage: 368.0+ bytes
```

Note that the 1 week column is a particular data type, timedelta64 (our Timedelta object), which allows you to make arithmetic operations on the date, time, and datetime columns in your DataFrame.

In the *Working with DatetimeIndex* recipe, you explored the pandas.date_range() function to generate a DataFrame with DatetimeIndex. The function returns a range of equally spaced time points based on the start, end, period and frequency parameters.

Similarly, you have an option to generate TimdedeltaIndex with a fixed frequency using the pandas.timedelta_range() function, which takes similar parameters as the pandas.date_range() function. Here is a quick example:

```
df = pd.DataFrame(
        {
        'item': ['item1', 'item2', 'item3', 'item4', 'item5'],
        'purchase_dt': pd.date_range('2021-01-01', periods=5,
freq='D', tz='UTC'),
        'time_deltas': pd.timedelta_range('1W 2 days 6 hours',
periods=5)
        }


)
df
```

The output is as follows:

	item	purchase_dt	time_deltas
0	item1	2021-01-01 00:00:00+00:00	9 days 06:00:00
1	item2	2021-01-02 00:00:00+00:00	10 days 06:00:00
2	item3	2021-01-03 00:00:00+00:00	11 days 06:00:00
3	item4	2021-01-04 00:00:00+00:00	12 days 06:00:00
4	item5	2021-01-05 00:00:00+00:00	13 days 06:00:00

Figure 6.9 – A DataFrame with a Timedelta column

See also

- To learn more about the `pandas.timedelta_range()` function, please refer to the official documentation here: `https://pandas.pydata.org/docs/reference/api/pandas.timedelta_range.html`.

- To learn more about the `pandas.Timedelta` class, please visit the official documentation here: `https://pandas.pydata.org/docs/reference/api/pandas.Timedelta.html`.

Converting DateTime with time zone information

When working with time-series data that requires attention to different time zones, things can get out of hand and become more complicated. For example, when developing data pipelines, building a data warehouse, or integrating data between systems, dealing with time zones requires attention and consensus amongst the different stakeholders in the project. For example, in Python, there are several libraries and modules dedicated to working with time zone conversion; these include `pytz`, `dateutil`, and `zoneinfo`, to name a few.

Let's discuss an inspiring example regarding time zones within time-series data. It is common for large companies that span their products and services across continents to include data from different places around the globe. For example, it would be hard to make data-driven business decisions if we neglect time zones. Let's say you want to determine whether most customers come to your e-commerce site in the morning or evening, and whether shoppers browse during the day and then make a purchase in the evening after work. For this analysis, you need to be aware of time zone differences and their interpretation on an international scale.

How to do it...

In this recipe, you will work with a hypothetical scenario – a small dataset that you will generate to represent website visits at different time intervals from various locations worldwide. The data will be standardized to UTC, and you will work with time-zone conversions.

1. You will start by importing the pandas library and creating the time-series DataFrame:

```
df = pd.DataFrame(
        {
        'Location': ['Los Angeles',
                      'New York',
                      'Berlin',
                      'New Delhi',
                      'Moscow',
                      'Tokyo',
                      'Dubai'],
        'tz': ['US/Pacific',
                'US/Eastern',
                'Europe/Berlin',
                'Asia/Kolkata',
                'Europe/Moscow',
                'Asia/Tokyo',
                'Asia/Dubai'],
        'visit_dt': pd.date_range(start='22:00',periods=7,
freq='45min'),
        }).set_index('visit_dt')
df
```

This will produce a DataFrame where visit_dt is the index of the DatetimeIndex type and two columns, Location and tz, indicate the time zone:

visit_dt	Location	tz
2021-10-28 22:00:00	Los Angeles	US/Pacific
2021-10-28 22:45:00	New York	US/Eastern
2021-10-28 23:30:00	Berlin	Europe/Berlin
2021-10-29 00:15:00	New Delhi	Asia/Kolkata
2021-10-29 01:00:00	Moscow	Europe/Moscow
2021-10-29 01:45:00	Tokyo	Asia/Tokyo
2021-10-29 02:30:00	Dubai	Asia/Dubai

Figure 6.10 – The DataFrame with visit_dt in UTC as an index

2. Assume that you need to convert this DataFrame to be in the same time zone as the company's headquarters in Tokyo. You can do this easily using `DataFrame.tz_convert()` against the DataFrame, but you will get a `TypeError` exception if you do this. That is because your time-series DataFrame is not time zone-aware. So, you need to localize it first using `tz_localize()` to make it time-zone aware. In this case, you will localize it to UTC:

```
df = df.tz_localize('UTC')
```

3. You will now convert the DataFrame to the headquarters' time zone (Tokyo):

```
df_hq = df.tz_convert('Asia/Tokyo')
df_hq
```

The DataFrame index, `visit_dt`, will be converted to the new time zone:

visit_dt	Location	tz
2021-10-29 07:00:00+09:00	Los Angeles	US/Pacific
2021-10-29 07:45:00+09:00	New York	US/Eastern
2021-10-29 08:30:00+09:00	Berlin	Europe/Berlin
2021-10-29 09:15:00+09:00	New Delhi	Asia/Kolkata
2021-10-29 10:00:00+09:00	Moscow	Europe/Moscow
2021-10-29 10:45:00+09:00	Tokyo	Asia/Tokyo
2021-10-29 11:30:00+09:00	Dubai	Asia/Dubai

Figure 6.11 – The DataFrame index converted to the headquarters' time zone (Tokyo)

Note that you were able to access the `tz_localize()` and `tz_convert()` methods because the DataFrame had an index of type `DatetimeIndex`. If that was not the case, you would get a `TypeError` exception with the following message:

```
TypeError: index is not a valid DatetimeIndex or
PeriodIndex
```

4. Now, you will localize each row to the appropriate time zone. You will add a new column reflecting the time zone, based on the location of the user that accessed the website. You will leverage the `tz` column to accomplish this:

```
df['local_dt'] = df.index
df['local_dt'] = df.apply(lambda x: pd.Timestamp.tz_
convert(x['local_dt'], x['tz']), axis=1)
df
```

This should produce a new column, `local_dt`, which is based on the UTC datetime from `visit_dt` and converted based on the time zone provided in the `tz` column:

visit_dt	Location	tz	local_dt
2021-10-28 22:00:00+00:00	Los Angeles	US/Pacific	2021-10-28 15:00:00-07:00
2021-10-28 22:45:00+00:00	New York	US/Eastern	2021-10-28 18:45:00-04:00
2021-10-28 23:30:00+00:00	Berlin	Europe/Berlin	2021-10-29 01:30:00+02:00
2021-10-29 00:15:00+00:00	New Delhi	Asia/Kolkata	2021-10-29 05:45:00+05:30
2021-10-29 01:00:00+00:00	Moscow	Europe/Moscow	2021-10-29 04:00:00+03:00
2021-10-29 01:45:00+00:00	Tokyo	Asia/Tokyo	2021-10-29 10:45:00+09:00
2021-10-29 02:30:00+00:00	Dubai	Asia/Dubai	2021-10-29 06:30:00+04:00

Figure 6.12 – The updated DataFrame with local_dt based on a localized time zone for each visit

You may wonder, what if you did not have a `tz` column? Where would you find the right `tz` string? Well, these are called **Time Zone (TZ)** database names. These are standard names, and you can find a subset of these in the Python documentation, or for a more comprehensive list, you can visit this link: `https://en.wikipedia.org/wiki/List_of_tz_database_time_zones`.

How it works...

Converting a time-series DataFrame from one time zone to another was achieved using `DataFrame.tz_convert()`, providing it with a time-zone string argument such as `US/Pacific`. There are a few assumptions when using `DataFrame.tz_convert()` that you need to keep in mind:

- The DataFrame should have an index of the `DatetimeIndex` type.

- `DatetimeIndex` needs to be time zone-aware.

You used the `DataFrame.tz_localize()` function to make the index time zone aware. It is a good practice to standardize on *UTC* if you are dealing with different time zones and daylight saving, since UTC is always consistent and never changes (regardless of where you are or if daylight saving time is applied or not). Once in UTC, converting to other time zones is very straightforward.

We first localized the data in the previous steps and then converted it to a different time zone in two steps. You can also do this in one step by chaining the two methods, as shown in the following code:

```
df.tz_localize('UTC').tz_convert('Asia/Tokyo')
```

If your index is already time zone-aware, then using `tz_localize()` will produce a `TypeError` exception with the following message:

```
TypeError: Already tz-aware, use tz_convert to convert
```

This indicates that you do not need to localize it again. Instead, just convert it to another time zone.

There's more...

Looking at the DataFrame in *Figure 6.11*, it is hard to tell immediately whether the time was in the morning (AM) or evening (PM). You can format `datetime` using `strftime` (which we discussed in the *Providing a format argument to DateTime* recipe).

You will construct the same DataFrame, localize it to UTC, then convert it to the headquarters' time zone, and apply the new format:

```
df = pd.DataFrame(
        {
        'Location': ['Los Angeles',
                    'New York',
```

```
                          'Berlin',
                          'New Delhi',
                          'Moscow',
                          'Tokyo',
                          'Dubai'],
            'tz': ['US/Pacific',
                   'US/Eastern',
                   'Europe/Berlin',
                   'Asia/Kolkata',
                   'Europe/Moscow',
                   'Asia/Tokyo',
                   'Asia/Dubai'],
            'visit_dt': pd.date_range(start='22:00',periods=7,
freq='45min'),
            }).set_index('visit_dt').tz_localize('UTC').tz_
convert('Asia/Tokyo')
```

We have combined the steps, and this should produce a DataFrame similar to the one in *Figure 6.11*.

Now, you can update the formatting to use the pattern – YYYY-MM-DD HH:MM AM/PM:

```
df.index = df.index.strftime('%Y-%m-%d %H:%M %p')
df
```

The index will be updated from a format/layout perspective. However, it is still time zone-aware, based on Tokyo's time zone, and the index is still DatetimeIndex. The only change is to the datetime layout:

visit_dt	Location	tz
2021-10-29 07:00 AM	Los Angeles	US/Pacific
2021-10-29 07:45 AM	New York	US/Eastern
2021-10-29 08:30 AM	Berlin	Europe/Berlin
2021-10-29 09:15 AM	New Delhi	Asia/Kolkata
2021-10-29 10:00 AM	Moscow	Europe/Moscow
2021-10-29 10:45 AM	Tokyo	Asia/Tokyo
2021-10-29 11:30 AM	Dubai	Asia/Dubai

Figure 6.13 – The updated DataFrame index, formatted based on the date format string provided

I am sure you will agree that this is easier to present to users to determine whether the visit was AM or PM quickly.

See also

To learn more about `tz_convert` you can read the official documentation at `https://pandas.pydata.org/docs/reference/api/pandas.Series.dt.tz_convert.html` and `https://pandas.pydata.org/docs/reference/api/pandas.Timestamp.tz_convert.html`.

Working with date offsets

When working with time series, it is critical that you learn more about the data you are working with and how it relates to the problem you are attempting to solve. For example, when working with manufacturing or sales data, you cannot assume that an organization's working day is Monday to Friday or whether it uses the standard calendar year or fiscal year. You should also consider understanding any holiday schedule, annual shutdowns, and other matters related to the business operation.

This is where offsets can be handy. They can help transform your dates into something more meaningful and relatable to a business. They can also help correct data entries that may not be logical.

We will work through a hypothetical example in this recipe and see how to leverage pandas offsets.

How to do it...

In this recipe, you will generate a time-series DataFrame to represent some daily logs of production quantity. The company, a US-based firm, would like to analyze data to better understand production capacity for future forecasting:

1. Start by importing the `pandas` library and then generate our DataFrame:

```
np.random.seed(10)
df = pd.DataFrame(
        {
        'purchase_dt': pd.date_range('2021-01-01',
periods=6, freq='D'),
        'production' : np.random.randint(4, 20, 6)
        }).set_index('purchase_dt')
```

```
df
>>
            production
purchase_dt
2021-01-01         13
2021-01-02         17
2021-01-03          8
2021-01-04         19
2021-01-05          4
2021-01-06          5
```

2. Let's add the name of the days:

```
df['day'] = df.index.day_name()
df
>>
            production         day
purchase_dt
2021-01-01         13      Friday
2021-01-02         17    Saturday
2021-01-03          8      Sunday
2021-01-04         19      Monday
2021-01-05          4     Tuesday
2021-01-06          5   Wednesday
```

When working with any data, always understand the business context behind it. Without domain knowledge or business context, it would be difficult to determine whether a data point is acceptable or not. In this scenario, the company was described as a US-based firm, and thus, working days are Monday to Friday. If there is data on a Saturday or Sunday (the weekend), you should not make assumptions without validating with the business. You should confirm whether there was any exception made for production on those specific weekend dates. Also, realize that January 1 was a holiday. After investigation, it was confirmed that production did occur due to an emergency exception. The business executives do not want to account for weekend or holiday work in the forecast. In other words, it was a one-time non-occurring event that they do not want to model or build a hypothesis on.

3. The firm asks you to push the weekend/holiday production numbers to the next business day instead. Here, you will use `pandas.offsets.BDay()`, which represents business days:

```
df['BusinessDay'] = df.index + pd.offsets.BDay(0)
df['BDay Name'] = df['BusinessDay'].dt.day_name()
df
>>
                production       day  BusinessDay   BDay Name
purchase_dt
2021-01-01              13    Friday   2021-01-01      Friday
2021-01-02              17  Saturday   2021-01-04      Monday
2021-01-03               8    Sunday   2021-01-04      Monday
2021-01-04              19    Monday   2021-01-04      Monday
2021-01-05               4   Tuesday   2021-01-05     Tuesday
2021-01-06               5 Wednesday   2021-01-06   Wednesday
```

Because Saturday and Sunday were weekends, their production numbers were pushed to the next business day, Monday, January 4.

4. Let's perform a summary aggregation that adds production numbers by business days to understand the impact of this change better:

```
df.groupby(['BusinessDay', 'BDay Name']).sum()
>>
                               production
BusinessDay BDay Name
2021-01-01  Friday                     13
2021-01-04  Monday                     44
2021-01-05  Tuesday                     4
2021-01-06  Wednesday                  5
```

Now, Monday shows to be the most productive day for that week, given it was the first business day after the holiday and a long weekend.

5. Finally, the business has made another request – they would like to track production monthly (MonthEnd) and quarterly (QuarterEnd). You can use `pandas.offsets` again to add two new columns:

```
df['QuarterEnd'] = df.index + pd.offsets.QuarterEnd(0)
df['MonthEnd'] = df.index + pd.offsets.MonthEnd(0)
df['BusinessDay'] = df.index + pd.offsets.BDay(0)


>>
            production QuarterEnd    MonthEnd BusinessDay
purchase_dt
2021-01-01          13 2021-03-31 2021-01-31  2021-01-01
2021-01-02          17 2021-03-31 2021-01-31  2021-01-04
2021-01-03           8 2021-03-31 2021-01-31  2021-01-04
2021-01-04          19 2021-03-31 2021-01-31  2021-01-04
2021-01-05           4 2021-03-31 2021-01-31  2021-01-05
2021-01-06           5 2021-03-31 2021-01-31  2021-01-06
```

Now, you have a DataFrame that should satisfy most of the reporting requirements of the business.

How it works...

Using date offsets made it possible to increment, decrement, and transform your dates to a new date range following specific rules. There are several offsets provided by pandas, each with its own rules, which can be applied to your dataset. Here is a list of the common offsets available in pandas:

- BusinessDay or Bday
- MonthEnd
- BusinessMonthEnd or BmonthEnd
- CustomBusinessDay or Cday
- QuarterEnd
- FY253Quarter

For a more comprehensive list and their descriptions, you can visit the documentation here: `https://pandas.pydata.org/pandas-docs/stable/user_guide/timeseries.html#dateoffset-objects`.

Applying an offset in pandas is as simple as doing an addition or subtraction, as shown in the following example:

```
df.index + pd.offsets.BDay()
df.index - pd.offsets.BDay()
```

There's more...

Following our example, you may have noticed when using the `BusinessDay` (`BDay`) offset that it did not account for the New Year's Day holiday (January 1). So, what can be done to account for both the New Year's Day holiday and weekends?

To accomplish this, pandas provides two approaches to handle standard holidays. The first method is by defining a custom holiday. The second approach (when suitable) uses an existing holiday offset.

Let's start with an existing offset. For this example, dealing with New Year, you can use the `USFederalHolidayCalendar` class, which has standard holidays such as New Year, Christmas, and other holidays specific to the United States. So, let's see how this works.

First, generate a new DataFrame and import the needed library and classes:

```
import pandas as pd
from pandas.tseries.holiday import (
    USFederalHolidayCalendar
)


df = pd.DataFrame(
        {
        'purchase_dt': pd.date_range('2021-01-01', periods=6,
freq='D'),
            'production' : np.random.randint(4, 20, 6)
        }).set_index('purchase_dt')
```

USFederalHolidayCalendar has some holiday rules that you can check using the following code:

```
USFederalHolidayCalendar.rules
>>
[Holiday: New Years Day (month=1, day=1, observance=<function
nearest_workday at 0x7fedf3ec1a60>),
 Holiday: Martin Luther King Jr. Day (month=1, day=1,
offset=<DateOffset: weekday=MO(+3)>),
 Holiday: Presidents Day (month=2, day=1, offset=<DateOffset:
weekday=MO(+3)>),
 Holiday: Memorial Day (month=5, day=31, offset=<DateOffset:
weekday=MO(-1)>),
 Holiday: July 4th (month=7, day=4, observance=<function
nearest_workday at 0x7fedf3ec1a60>),
 Holiday: Labor Day (month=9, day=1, offset=<DateOffset:
weekday=MO(+1)>),
 Holiday: Columbus Day (month=10, day=1, offset=<DateOffset:
weekday=MO(+2)>),
 Holiday: Veterans Day (month=11, day=11, observance=<function
nearest_workday at 0x7fedf3ec1a60>),
 Holiday: Thanksgiving (month=11, day=1, offset=<DateOffset:
weekday=TH(+4)>),
 Holiday: Christmas (month=12, day=25, observance=<function
nearest_workday at 0x7fedf3ec1a60>)]
```

To apply these rules, you will use the CustomerBusinessDay or CDay offset:

```
df['USFederalHolidays'] = df.index + pd.offsets.
CDay(calendar=USFederalHolidayCalendar())
df
```

The output is as follows:

purchase_dt	production	USFederalHolidays
2021-01-01	5	2021-01-04
2021-01-02	14	2021-01-04
2021-01-03	12	2021-01-04
2021-01-04	13	2021-01-05
2021-01-05	4	2021-01-06
2021-01-06	14	2021-01-07

Figure 6.14 – The USFederalHolidays column added to the DataFrame,
which recognizes New Year's Day

The custom holiday option will behave in the same way. You will need to import the
Holiday class and the nearest_workday function. You will use the Holiday class to
define your specific holidays. In this case, you will determine the New Year's rule:

```
from pandas.tseries.holiday import (
    Holiday,
    nearest_workday,
    USFederalHolidayCalendar
)
newyears = Holiday("New Years",
                    month=1,
                    day=1,
                    observance=nearest_workday)
newyears
>>
Holiday: New Years (month=1, day=1, observance=<function
nearest_workday at 0x7fedf3ec1a60>)
```

Similar to how you applied the USFederalHolidayCalendar class to the CDay offset,
you will apply your new newyears object to Cday:

```
df['NewYearsHoliday'] = df.index + pd.offsets.
CDay(calendar=newyears)
df
```

You will get the following output:

purchase_dt	production	USFederalHolidays	NewYearsHoliday
2021-01-01	5	2021-01-04	2021-01-04
2021-01-02	14	2021-01-04	2021-01-04
2021-01-03	12	2021-01-04	2021-01-04
2021-01-04	13	2021-01-05	2021-01-05
2021-01-05	4	2021-01-06	2021-01-06
2021-01-06	14	2021-01-07	2021-01-07

Figure 6.15 – The NewYearsHoliday column, added using a custom holiday offset

If you are curious about the `nearest_workday` function and how it was used in both the `USFederalHolidayCalendar` rules and your custom holiday, then the following code illustrates how it works:

```
nearest_workday(pd.to_datetime('2021-1-3'))
>>
Timestamp('2021-01-04 00:00:00')


nearest_workday(pd.to_datetime('2021-1-2'))
>>
Timestamp('2021-01-01 00:00:00')
```

As illustrated, the function mainly determines whether the day is a weekday or not, and based on that, it will either use the day before (if it falls on a Saturday) or the day after (if it falls on a Sunday). There are other rules available as well as `nearest_workday`, including the following:

- `Sunday_to_Monday`
- `Next_Monday_or_Tuesday`
- `Previous_Friday`
- `Next_monday`

See also

For more insight regarding `pandas.tseries.holiday`, you can view the actual code, which highlights all the classes and functions and can serve as an excellent reference, at `https://github.com/pandas-dev/pandas/blob/master/pandas/tseries/holiday.py`.

Working with custom business days

Companies have different working days worldwide, influenced by the region or territory they belong to. For example, when working with time-series data and depending on the analysis you need to make, knowing whether certain transactions fall on a workday or weekend can make a difference. For example, suppose you are doing anomaly detection, and you know that certain types of activities can only be done during working hours. In that case, any activities beyond these boundaries may trigger some further analysis.

In this recipe, you will see how you can customize an offset to fit your requirements when doing an analysis that depends on defined business days and non-business days.

How to do it...

In this recipe, you will create custom business days and holidays for a company headquartered in Dubai, UAE. In the UAE, the working week is from Sunday to Thursday, whereas Friday to Saturday is a 2-day weekend. Additionally, their National Day (a holiday) is on December 2 each year:

1. You will start by importing pandas and defining the workdays and holidays for the UAE:

    ```
    dubai_uae_workdays = "Sun Mon Tue Wed Thu"


    # UAE national day
    nationalDay = [pd.to_datetime('2021-12-2')]
    ```

Note that `nationalDay` is a Python list. This allows you to register multiple dates as holidays. When defining workdays, it will be a string of abbreviated weekday names. This is called `weekmask`, and it's used in both pandas and NumPy when customizing weekdays.

2. You will apply both variables to the `CustomBusinessDay` or `CDay` offset:

```
dubai_uae_bday = pd.offsets.CDay(
    holidays=nationalDay,
    weekmask=dubai_uae_workdays,
)
```

3. You can validate that the rules were registered properly:

```
dubai_uae_bday.holidays
>>
(numpy.datetime64('2021-12-02'),)
dubai_uae_bday.weekmask
>>
'Sun Mon Tue Wed Thu'
```

4. Now, you can use the new offset to generate custom dates using `pandas.date_range()`:

```
df = pd.DataFrame({'Date': pd.date_range('12-1-2021',
periods=10, freq=dubai_uae_bday )})
```

5. To make it easier to determine whether things are working as expected, add a new column that represents the day name:

```
df['Day_name'] = df.Date.dt.day_name()
df
```

The generated time series has a new custom rule for UAE in terms of workdays and holidays. For example, if you list the workdays in UAE, the custom rule will skip December 2 (a national holiday) and December 3 and 4, since they are weekends. The week will resume on December 5 (Sunday). This is demonstrated in the following output:

	Date	Day_name
0	2021-12-01	Wednesday
1	2021-12-05	Sunday
2	2021-12-06	Monday
3	2021-12-07	Tuesday
4	2021-12-08	Wednesday
5	2021-12-09	Thursday
6	2021-12-12	Sunday
7	2021-12-13	Monday
8	2021-12-14	Tuesday
9	2021-12-15	Wednesday

Figure 6.16 – The time series generated based on the UAE custom working days and holidays

This can be extended to include different countries and holidays to fit the type of analysis you are working with.

How it works...

This recipe builds on the *Working with date offsets* recipe but focuses on customizing offsets. pandas provides several offsets that can take a custom calendar, holiday, and weekmask. These include the following:

- CustomBusinessDay or Cday
- CustomBusinessMonthEnd or CBMonthEnd
- CustomBusinessMonthBegin or CBMonthBegin
- CustomBusinessHour

They behave like any other offset; the only difference is that they allow you to create your own rules.

There's more...

Let's extend the previous example and add custom business hours to the DataFrame. This will be another custom offset that you can use in a similar way to `Cday`:

```
cust_hours = pd.offsets.CustomBusinessHour(
    start="8:30",
    end="15:30",
    holidays=nationalDay,
    weekmask=dubai_uae_workdays)
```

Here, you are applying the same rules, the custom `holidays`, `weekmask` to indicate custom workdays, and now the custom hours by providing the `start` and `end` times (in 24-hour format):

```
df['Bhours'] = df['Date'] + cust_hours
df
```

You will get output as follows:

	Date	Day_name	Bhours
0	2021-12-01	Wednesday	2021-12-01 09:30:00
1	2021-12-05	Sunday	2021-12-05 09:30:00
2	2021-12-06	Monday	2021-12-06 09:30:00
3	2021-12-07	Tuesday	2021-12-07 09:30:00
4	2021-12-08	Wednesday	2021-12-08 09:30:00
5	2021-12-09	Thursday	2021-12-09 09:30:00
6	2021-12-12	Sunday	2021-12-12 09:30:00
7	2021-12-13	Monday	2021-12-13 09:30:00
8	2021-12-14	Tuesday	2021-12-14 09:30:00
9	2021-12-15	Wednesday	2021-12-15 09:30:00

Figure 6.17 – Custom business hours added to the DataFrame

Note that even though the DataFrame is not time zone-aware, we did not use `tz.localize()` or `tz.convert()`, which allowed the application of the custom offset. Ideally, you should make your DataFrame time zone-aware (localize it and then convert it to your time zone) before applying the custom offset to get better results.

See also

To learn more about pandas' `CustomBusinessDay`, you can read the official documentation here:

`https://pandas.pydata.org/docs/reference/api/pandas.tseries.offsets.CustomBusinessDay.html`

7
Handling Missing Data

As a data scientist, data analyst, or business analyst, you have probably discovered that obtaining a *perfect* clean dataset is too optimistic. What is more common, though, is that the data you are working with suffers from flaws such as missing values, erroneous data, duplicate records, insufficient data, or the presence of outliers in the data.

Time series data is no different, and before plugging the data into any analysis or modeling workflow, you must investigate the data first. It is vital to understand the *business context around the time series data* to detect and identify these problems successfully. For example, if you work with stock data, the context is very different from COVID data or sensor data.

Having that intuition or domain knowledge will allow you to anticipate what to expect and what is considered acceptable when analyzing the data. Always try to understand the business context around the data. For example, why is the data collected in the first place? How was the data collected? What business rules, logic, or transformations have been applied to the data? Were these modifications applied during the data acquisition process or built into the systems that generate the data?

During the discovery phase, such prior knowledge will help you determine the best approach to clean and prepare your dataset for analysis or modeling. Missing data and outliers are two common problems that need to be dealt with during data cleaning and preparation. You will dive into outlier detection in *Chapter 8, Outlier Detection Using Statistical Methods*, and *Chapter 14, Outlier Detection Using Unsupervised Machine Learning*. In this chapter, you will explore techniques to handle missing data through **imputation** and **interpolation**.

Here is the list of recipes that we will cover in this chapter:

- Performing data quality checks

- Handling missing data with univariate imputation using pandas

- Handling missing data with univariate imputation using scikit-learn

- Handling missing data with multivariate imputation

- Handling missing data with interpolation

Technical requirements

You can download the Jupyter notebooks and the requisite datasets from the GitHub repository to follow along:

- Jupyter notebooks: `https://github.com/PacktPublishing/Time-Series-Analysis-with-Python-Cookbook./blob/main/code/Ch7/Chapter%207.ipynb`

- Datasets: `https://github.com/PacktPublishing/Time-Series-Analysis-with-Python-Cookbook./tree/main/datasets/Ch7`

In this chapter and beyond, you will extensively use pandas 1.4.2 (released April 2, 2022). There will be four additional libraries that you will be using:

- NumPy (≥ 1.20.3)

- Matplotlib (≥ 3.5.0)

- statsmodels (≥ 0.11.0)

- scikit-learn (≥ 1.0.1)

- SciPy (≥ 1.7.1)

If you are using `pip`, then you can install these packages from your terminal with the following command:

```
pip install matplotlib numpy statsmodels scikit-learn scipy
```

If you are using `conda`, then you can install these packages with the following command:

```
conda install matplotlib numpy statsmodels scikit-learn scipy
```

In this chapter, two datasets will be used extensively for the imputation and interpolation recipes: the *CO2 Emissions* dataset, and the *e-Shop Clickstream* dataset. The source for the Clickstream dataset comes from *clickstream data for online shopping* from the *UCI machine learning repository*, which you can find here:

https://archive.ics.uci.edu/ml/datasets/clickstream+data+for
+online+shopping

The source for the CO2 emissions dataset comes from the Annual *CO2 emissions* report from *Our World in Data*, which you can find here: https://ourworldindata.org/
co2-emissions.

For demonstration purposes, the two datasets have been modified by removing observations (missing data). The original versions are provided, in addition to the modified versions, to be used for evaluating the different techniques discussed in this chapter.

Throughout this chapter, you will follow similar steps for handling missing data: ingest the data into a DataFrame, identify missing data, impute missing data, evaluate it against the original data, and finally, visualize and compare the different imputation techniques.

These steps can be translated into functions for reusability. You can create functions for these steps in the process: a function to read the data into a DataFrame, a function to evaluate using the RMSE score, and a function to plot the results.

Start by loading the standard libraries that you will be using throughout this chapter:

```
import pandas as pd
from pathlib import Path
import matplotlib.pyplot as plt
import numpy as np
```

Function 1 – read_datasets

The `read_datasets` function takes a path to the folder, CSV filename, and the column name that contains the date variable.

The `read_datasets` function is defined as follows:

```
def read_dataset(folder, file, date_col=None):
    '''
    folder: is a Path object
    file: the CSV filename
    date_col: specify a date_col to use for index_col

    returns: a pandas DataFrame with a DatetimeIndex
    '''
    df = pd.read_csv(folder / file,
                     index_col=date_col,
                     parse_dates=[date_col])
    return df
```

Function 2 – plot_dfs

The `plot_dfs()` function takes two DataFrames: the original DataFrame (`df1`) with no missing data (as the baseline), and the imputed DataFrame (`df2`) to compare against. The function creates multiple time series subplots using the specified response column (`col`). Note that the imputed DataFrame will contain additional columns (a column for the output of each imputation technique), and the plotting function accommodates this fact. This is done by looping through the columns. The function will plot each imputation technique for visual comparison and will be utilized throughout this chapter.

This `plot_dfs` function is defined as follows:

```
def plot_dfs(df1, df2, col, title=None, xlabel=None,
ylabel=None):
    '''
    df1: original dataframe without missing data
    df2: dataframe with missing data
    col: column name that contains missing data
    '''
```

```
    df_missing = df2.rename(columns={col: 'missing'})


    columns = df_missing.loc[:, 'missing':].columns.tolist()
    subplots_size = len(columns)
    fig, ax = plt.subplots(subplots_size+1, 1, sharex=True)
    plt.subplots_adjust(hspace=0.25)
    fig.suptitle = title

    df1[col].plot(ax=ax[0], figsize=(10, 12))
    ax[0].set_title('Original Dataset')
    ax[0].set_xlabel(xlabel)
    ax[0].set_ylabel(ylabel)

    for i, colname in enumerate(columns):
        df_missing[colname].plot(ax=ax[i+1])
        ax[i+1].set_title(colname.upper())
    plt.show()
```

Function 3 – rmse_score

In addition to a visual comparison between imputation techniques using the `plot_dfs` function, you will need a method to compare the different imputation techniques numerically (using a statistical measure).

This is where the `rmse_score` function will come in handy. It takes two DataFrames: the original DataFrame (`df1`) as the baseline and the imputed DataFrame (`df2`) to compare against. The function allows you to specify which column contains the response column (`col`) used as the basis for the calculation.

The `rmse_score` function is defined as follows:

```
def rmse_score(df1, df2, col=None):
    '''
    df1: original dataframe without missing data
    df2: dataframe with missing data
    col: column name that contains missing data
    returns: a list of scores
    '''
    df_missing = df2.rename(columns={col: 'missing'})
```

```
    columns = df_missing.loc[:, 'missing':].columns.tolist()
    scores = []
    for comp_col in columns[1:]:
        rmse = np.sqrt(np.mean((df1[col] - df_missing[comp_
col])**2))
        scores.append(rmse)
        print(f'RMSE for {comp_col}: {rmse}')
    return scores
```

Understanding missing data

Data can be missing for a variety of reasons, such as unexpected power outages, a device that got accidentally unplugged, a sensor that just became defective, a survey respondent declined to answer a question, or the data was intentionally removed for privacy and compliance reasons. In other words, missing data is inevitable.

Generally, missing data is very common, yet sometimes it is not given the proper level of attention in terms of formulating a strategy on how to handle the situation. One approach for handling rows with missing data is to drop those observations (delete the rows). However, this may not be a good strategy if you have limited data in the first place, for example, if collecting the data is a complex and expensive process. Additionally, the drawback of deleting records, if done prematurely, is that you will not know if the missing data was due to censoring (an observation is only partially collected) or due to bias (for example, high-income participants declining to share their total household income in a survey).

A second approach may involve tagging the rows with missing data by adding a column describing or labeling the missing data. For example, suppose you know that there was a power outage on a particular day. In that case, you can add Power Outage to label the missing data and differentiate it from other missing data labeled with Missing Data if the cause is unknown.

A third approach, which this chapter is about, is estimating the missing data values. The methods can range from simple and naive to more complex techniques leveraging machine learning and complex statistical models. But how can you measure the accuracy of the estimated values for data missing in the first place?

There are different options and measures to consider, and the answer is not as simple. Therefore, you should explore different approaches, emphasizing a thorough evaluation and validation process to ensure the selected method is ideal for your situation. In this chapter, you will use **Root Mean Squared Error (RMSE)** to evaluate the different imputation techniques.

The process to calculate the RMSE can be broken down into a few simple steps: first, computing the error, which is the difference between the actual values and the predicted or estimated values. This is done for each observation. Since the errors may be either negative or positive, and to avoid having a zero summation, the errors (differences) are squared. Finally, all the errors are summed and divided by the total number of observations to compute the mean. This gives you the **Mean Squared Error (MSE)**. RMSE is just the square root of the MSE.

The RMSE equation can be written as:

$$\text{RMSE} = \sqrt{\frac{\sum_{i=1}^{N}(x_i - \hat{x}_i)^2}{N}}$$

In our estimate of the missing observations, $\hat{x}_i$ is the imputed value, x_i is the actual (original) value, and N is the number of observations.

RMSE for Evaluating Multiple Imputation Methods

I want to point out that RMSE is commonly used to measure the performance of *predictive* models (for example, comparing regression models). Generally, a *lower* RMSE is desirable; it tells us that the model can fit the dataset. Simply stated, it tells us the average distance (error) between the predicted value and the actual value. You want this distance minimized.

When comparing different imputation methods, we want our imputed values to resemble (as close as possible) the actual data, which contains random effects (uncertainty). This means we are not seeking a perfect prediction, and thus a lower RMSE score does not necessarily indicate a better imputation method. Ideally, you would want to find a balance, hence, in this chapter, the use of RMSE is combined with visualization to help illustrate how the different techniques compare and work.

As a reminder, we have intentionally removed some values (synthetically causing missing data) but retained the original data to compare against for when using RMSE.

Performing data quality checks

Missing data are values not captured or observed in the dataset. Values can be missing for a *particular feature* (column), or an *entire observation* (row). When ingesting the data using pandas, missing values will show up as either NaN, NaT, or NA.

Sometimes, missing observations are replaced with other values in the source system; for example, this can be a numeric filler such as 99999 or 0, or a string such as missing or N/A. When missing values are represented by 0, you need to be cautious and investigate further to determine whether those zero values are legitimate or they are indicative of missing data.

In this recipe, you will explore how to identify the presence of missing data.

Getting ready

You can download the Jupyter notebooks and requisite datasets from the GitHub repository. Please refer to the *Technical requirements* section of this chapter.

You will be using two datasets from the Ch7 folder: clicks_missing_multiple.csv and co2_missing.csv.

How to do it...

The **pandas** library provides convenient methods for discovering missing data and for summarizing data in a DataFrame:

1. Start by reading the two CSV files, co2_missing.csv and clicks_missing.csv:

```
co2 = Path('../../datasets/Ch7/co2_missing.csv')
ecom = Path('../../datasets/Ch7/clicks_missing.csv')
co2_df = pd.read_csv(co2,
                        index_col='year',
                        parse_dates=True)
ecom_df = pd.read_csv(ecom,
                        index_col='date',
                        parse_dates=True)
ecom_df.head()
```

This should display the first five rows from the `ecom_df` DataFrame:

	date	price	location	clicks
0	2008-04-01	43.155647	2.0	18784.0
1	2008-04-02	43.079056	1.0	24738.0
2	NaT	43.842609	NaN	15209.0
3	NaT	NaN	1.0	14018.0
4	NaT	43.941176	1.0	11974.0

Figure 7.1 – First five rows from the ecom_df DataFrame showing NaN and NaT

The output from the preceding code shows that there are five missing values from the source dataset. NaN is how pandas represents empty *numeric* values (**NaN** is short for **Not a Number**). NaT is how pandas represents missing `Datetime` values (**NaT** is short for **Not a Time**).

2. To count the number of missing values in both DataFrames, you can use the `DataFrame.isnull()` method. This will return `True` (if missing) or `False` (if not missing) for each value. For example, to get the total count of missing values for each column, you can use `DataFrame.isnull().sum()`.

In Python, Booleans (`True` or `False`) are a subtype of integers. `True` is equivalent to `1`, and `False` is equivalent to `0`. To validate this concept, try the following:

```
isinstance(True, int)
>> True
int(True)
>> 1
```

Now, let's get the total number of missing values for each DataFrame:

```
co2_df.isna().sum()
>>
year       0
co2       25
dtype: int64

ecom_df.isnull().sum()
>>
date        3
```

```
price          1
location       1
clicks        14
dtype: int64
```

Notice in the preceding code that both .isnull() and .isna() were used. They both can be used interchangeably since .isnull() is an alias of .isna().

From the results, co2_df has 25 missing values from the co2 column, while ecom_df has 19 missing values in total (3 from the date column, 1 from the price column, 1 from the location column, and 14 from the clicks column).

3. To get the grand total for the entire ecom_df DataFrame, just chain another .sum() function to the end of the statement:

```
ecom_df.isnull().sum().sum()
>> 19
```

4. If you inspect the co2_missing.csv file using a text/code editor, Excel, or Jupyter (Notebook or Lab) and scroll down to *rows 192-194*, you will notice that there are string placeholder values in there: NA, N/A, and null:

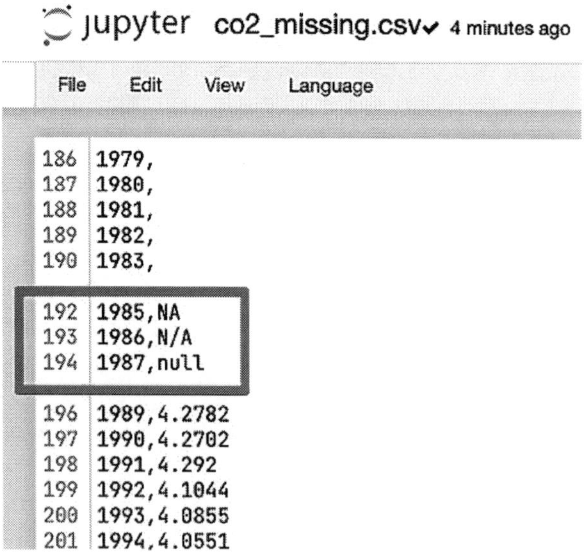

Figure 7.2 – co2_missing.csv shows string values that were converted to NaN (missing) by pandas

Figure 7.2 shows the three string values. Interestingly, `pandas.read_csv()` interpreted the three string values as NaN. This is the default behavior in `read_csv()`, which can be modified through the `na_values` parameter. To see how pandas represents these values, you can run the following command:

```
co2_df[190:195]
```

This should produce the following output:

```
co2_df[190:195]
```

	year	missing
190	1985	NaN
191	1986	NaN
192	1987	NaN
193	1988	4.2953
194	1989	4.2782

Figure 7.3 – pandas.read_csv() interpreted the NA, N/A, and null strings as a NaN type

5. If all you need is to check whether the DataFrame contains any missing values, use `isnull().values.any()`. This will output `True` if there are any missing values in the DataFrame:

```
ecom_df.isnull().values.any()
>> True
co2_df.isnull().values.any()
>> True
```

6. So far, `.isnull()` helped identify all the missing values in the DataFrames. But what if the missing values were masked or replaced by other placeholder values such as ? or 99999. The presence of these values will be skipped and considered missing (NaN) in pandas. Technically, they are not empty cells (missing) and hold values. On the other hand, domain or prior knowledge will tell us that the CO2 emission dataset is measured annually and should have values greater than 0.

Similarly, we expect the number of clicks to be numeric for the Clickstream data. If the column is not numeric, it should trigger an investigation as to why pandas could not parse the column as numeric. For example, this could be due to the presence of string values.

To gain a better insight into the DataFrame schema and data types, you can use `DataFrame.info()` to display the schema, total records, column names, column dtypes, count of non-missing values per column, index dtype, and the DataFrame's total memory usage:

```
ecom_df.info()
>>
<class 'pandas.core.frame.DataFrame'>
RangeIndex: 135 entries, 0 to 134
Data columns (total 4 columns):
 #    Column     Non-Null Count   Dtype
---   ------     --------------   -----
 0    date       132 non-null     datetime64[ns]
 1    price      134 non-null     float64
 2    location   134 non-null     float64
 3    clicks     121 non-null     object
dtypes: datetime64[ns](1), float64(2), object(1)
memory usage: 4.3+ KB


co2_df.info()
>>
<class 'pandas.core.frame.DataFrame'>
RangeIndex: 226 entries, 0 to 225
Data columns (total 2 columns):
 #    Column     Non-Null Count   Dtype
---   ------     --------------   -----
 0    year       226 non-null     int64
 1    co2        201 non-null     float64
dtypes: float64(1), int64(1)
memory usage: 3.7 KB
```

The `co2_df` summary output looks reasonable, confirming that we have 25 (226-221=25) missing values in the co2 column.

On the other hand, the summary for `ecom_df` indicates that the `clicks` column is of the `object` dtype, and not the expected `float64`. Let's investigate further using basic summary statistics.

7. To get the summary statistics for a DataFrame, use the `DataFrame.describe()` method:

```
co2_df.describe(include='all',
                datetime_is_numeric=True)
```

The output is as follows:

	year	missing
count	226.000000	201.000000
mean	1906.902655	1.590015
std	66.543281	1.644182
min	1750.000000	0.000000
25%	1851.250000	0.076400
50%	1907.500000	0.935100
75%	1963.750000	2.807600
max	2020.000000	4.907900

Figure 7.4 – co2_df summary statistics indicating zero values present in the data

Note the use of `include='all'` to replace the default value None. The default behavior is to show summary statistics for only numeric columns. By changing the value to `'all'`, the results will include all column types.

The summary statistics for the co2_df DataFrame confirms that we have zero values under the missing column (min = 0.00). As pointed out earlier, prior knowledge tells us that 0 represents a null (or missing) value. Therefore, the zeros will need to be replaced with NaN to include such values in the imputation process. Now, review the summary statistics for ecom_df:

```
ecom_df.describe(include='all',
                 datetime_is_numeric=True)
```

The output is as follows:

	date	price	location	clicks
count	132	134.000000	134.000000	121
unique	NaN	NaN	NaN	119
top	NaN	NaN	NaN	?
freq	NaN	NaN	NaN	2
mean	2008-06-08 10:54:32.727272704	43.480221	1.694030	NaN
min	2008-04-01 00:00:00	42.207018	1.000000	NaN
25%	2008-05-06 18:00:00	43.038050	1.000000	NaN
50%	2008-06-08 12:00:00	43.498842	1.000000	NaN
75%	2008-07-11 06:00:00	43.889935	2.000000	NaN
max	2008-08-13 00:00:00	45.801613	5.000000	NaN
std	NaN	0.610578	1.118724	NaN

Figure 7.5 – ecom_df summary statistics indicating the ? value in the clicks column

As you can see, the summary statistics for the ecom_df DataFrame indicate that we have a ? value under the clicks column. This explains why pandas did not parse the column as numeric (due to mixed types). Similarly, the ? values will need to be replaced with NaN to be treated as missing values for imputation.

8. Convert the 0 and ? values to NaN types. This can be accomplished using the DataFrame.replace() method:

```
co2_df.replace(0, np.NaN, inplace=True)
ecom_df.replace('?', np.NaN, inplace=True)
ecom_df['clicks'] = ecom_df['clicks'].astype('float')
```

To validate, run .isnull().sum() and you should notice that the missing value counts have increased:

```
co2_df.isnull().sum()
>>
year          0
missing      35
dtype: int64
ecom_df.isnull().sum()
>>
```

```
date          3
price         1
location      1
clicks       16
dtype: int64
```

The new numbers do a better job of reflecting the number of actual missing values in both DataFrames.

How it works...

When reading the CSV files using `pandas.read_csv()`, the default behavior is to recognize and parse certain string values, such as NA, N/A, and `null`, to the NaN type (missing). Thus, once these values became NaN, the CSV reader could parse the CO_2 column as `float64` (numeric) based on the remaining non-null values.

This is possible due to two parameters: `na_values` and `keep_default_na`. The `na_values` parameter, by default, contains a list of strings that are interpreted as NaN. The list includes #N/A, #N/A N/A, #NA, -1.#IND, -1.#QNAN, -NaN, -nan, 1.#IND, 1.#QNAN, <NA>, N/A, NA, NULL, NaN, n/a, nan, and `null`.

You can append to this list by providing additional values to the `na_values` parameter. Additionally, `keep_default_na` is set to `True` by default, thus using `na_values` with the default list for parsing.

If you change `keep_default_na` to `False` without providing new values to na_ values, then none of the strings (NA, N/A, and `null`) would be parsed to NaN unless you provide a custom list. For example, if `keep_default_na` was set to `False` and no values provided to `na_values`, then the entire CO_2 column would be parsed as a `string` (object), and any missing values will show up as strings; in other words, they will be coming in as ' ', which is an empty string.

Here is an example:

```
co2_df = pd.read_csv(co2, keep_default_na=False)
co2_df.isna().sum()
>>
year     0
co2      0
dtype: int64
```

```
co2_df.shape
>> (226, 2)
```

Notice that we did not lose any data (226 records) but showed no NaN (or missing) values. Let's inspect the DataFrame structure:

```
co2_df.info()
>>
<class 'pandas.core.frame.DataFrame'>
RangeIndex: 226 entries, 0 to 225
Data columns (total 2 columns):
 #   Column  Non-Null Count  Dtype
---  ------  --------------  -----
 0   year    226 non-null    int64
 1   co2     226 non-null    object
dtypes: int64(1), object(1)
memory usage: 3.7+ KB
```

Notice the change in *dtype* for the co2 columns. Let's check the data from index 190 to 195 again:

```
co2_df[190:195]
```

The output is as follows:

	year	co2
190	1985	NA
191	1986	N/A
192	1987	null
193	1988	4.2953
194	1989	4.2782

Figure 7.6 – Output from the co2_df DataFrame without NaN parsing

Finally, you can check how the missing values were handled:

```
co2_df.iloc[132:139]  (style as SC-source)
```

You will notice all seven rows have blank values (empty string).

In this recipe you explored the `.isna()` method. Once the data is read into a DataFrame or series, you get access to the `.isna()` and `.isnull()` methods, which return `True` if data is missing and `False` otherwise. To get the counts for each column, we just chain a `.sum()` function, and to get the grand total, we chain another `.sum()` function following that:

```
co2_df.isnull().sum()
co2_df.isnull().sum().sum()
```

There's more...

If you know that the data will always contain ?, which should be converted to NaN (or any other value), then you can utilize the `pd.read_csv()` function and update the `na_values` parameter. This will reduce the number of steps needed to clean the data after creating the DataFrame:

```
pd.read_csv(ecom, parse_dates=['date'], na_values={'?'})
```

This will replace all instances of ? with NaN.

See also

- To learn more about the `na_values` and `keep_default_na` parameters from `pandas.read_csv()`, please visit the official documentation here:

  https://pandas.pydata.org/docs/reference/api/pandas.read_csv.html

- To learn more about the `DataFrame.isna()` function, please visit the official documentation here:

  https://pandas.pydata.org/docs/reference/api/pandas.DataFrame.isna.html

Handling missing data with univariate imputation using pandas

Generally, there are two approaches to imputing missing data: **univariate imputation** and **multivariate imputation**. This recipe will explore univariate imputation techniques available in pandas.

In univariate imputation, you use non-missing values in a single variable (think a column or feature) to impute the missing values for that variable. For example, if you have a sales column in the dataset with some missing values, you can use a univariate imputation method to impute missing sales observations using average sales. Here, a single column (`sales`) was used to calculate the mean (from non-missing values) for imputation.

Some basic univariate imputation techniques include the following:

- Imputing using the **mean**.
- Imputing using the last observation forward (**forward fill**). This can be referred to as **Last Observation Carried Forward** (**LOCF**).
- Imputing using the next observation backward (**backward fill**). This can be referred to as **Next Observation Carried Backward** (**NOCB**).

You will use two datasets to impute missing data using different techniques and then compare the results.

Getting ready

You can download the Jupyter notebooks and requisite datasets from the GitHub repository. Please refer to the *Technical requirements* section of this chapter.

You will be using four datasets from the Ch7 folder: `clicks_original.csv`, `clicks_missing.csv`, `clicks_original.csv`, and `co2_missing_only.csv`. The datasets are available from the GitHub repository.

How to do it...

You will start by importing the libraries and then read all four CSV files. You will use the original versions of datasets to compare the results of the imputations to gain a better intuition of how they perform. For the comparison measure, you will use *RMSE* to evaluate each technique and then visualize the outputs to compare the imputation results visually:

1. Use the `read_dataset()` function to read the four datasets:

    ```
    folder = Path('../../datasets/Ch7/')
    co2_original = pd.read_csv(folder / 'co2_original.csv')
    co2_missing = pd.read_csv(folder / 'co2_missing_only.
    csv')
    clicks_original = pd.read_csv(folder / 'clicks_original.
    csv')
    clicks_missing = pd.read_csv(folder / 'clicks_missing.
    csv')
    ```

2. Visualize the CO2 DataFrames (original and missing) and specify the column with missing values (co2):

    ```
    plot_dfs(co2_original,
             co2_missing,
             'co2',
             title="Annual CO2 Emission per Capita",
             xlabel="Years",
             ylabel="x100 million tons")
    ```

The `plot_dfs` function will produce two plots: the original CO2 dataset without missing values, and the altered dataset with missing values.

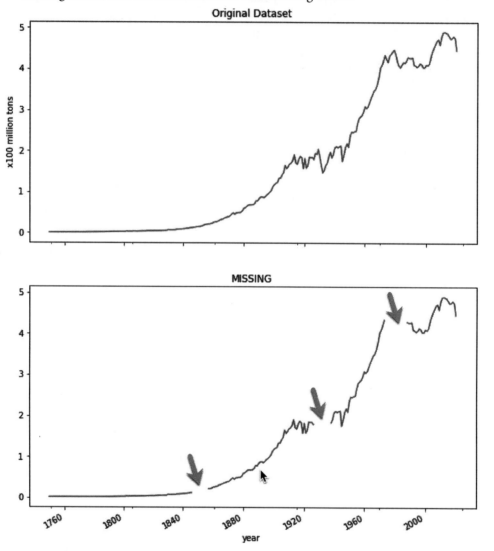

Figure 7.7 – CO2 dataset showing a comparison between the missing values and the original

From *Figure 7.7*, you can see a noticeable upward trend in CO2 levels over time. There is missing data in three different spots. Now, visualize the Clickstream DataFrames:

```
plot_dfs(clicks_original,
         clicks_missing,
```

```
        'clicks',
        title="Page Clicks per Day",
        xlabel="date",
        ylabel="# of clicks")
```

The `plot_dfs` function will produce two plots: the original Clickstream dataset without missing values, and the altered dataset with missing values.

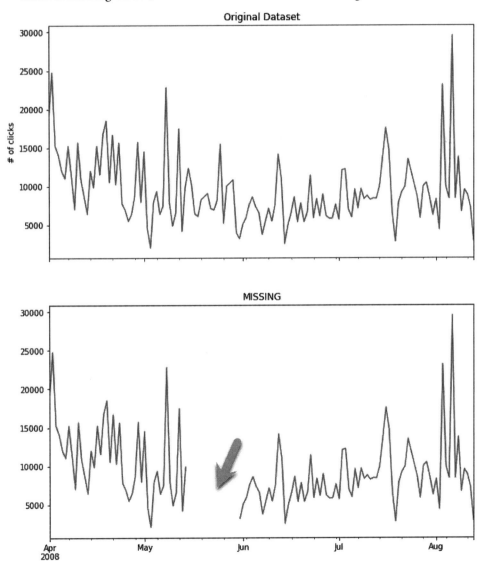

Figure 7.8 – Clickstream dataset showing a comparison between the missing values and the original

Notice, the output shows missing data from May 15 to May 31. You can confirm this by running the following code:

```
clicks_missing[clicks_missing['clicks'].isna()]
```

3. Now you are ready to perform your first imputation. You will use the `fillna()` method which has a `value` parameter that takes either a numeric or a string value to substitute for all the NaN instances. Alternatively, instead of using the `value` parameter, `.fillna()` has a `method` parameter that can take specific string values such as `ffill` for forward fill, or `bfill` for backward fill.

Let's impute the missing values utilizing the `method` parameter and append the results as new columns in the DataFrame. Start with the CO2 DataFrame:

```
co2_missing['ffil'] = co2_missing['co2'].
fillna(method='ffill')
co2_missing['bfill'] = co2_missing['co2'].
fillna(method='bfill')
co2_missing['mean'] = co2_missing['co2'].fillna(co2_
missing['co2'].mean())
```

Use the `rmse_score` function to get the scores:

```
_ = rmse_score(co2_original,
                co2_missing,
                'co2')
>>
RMSE for ffil: 0.05873012599267133
RMSE for bfill: 0.05550012995280968
RMSE for mean: 0.7156383637041684
```

Now, visualize the results using the `plot_dfs` function:

```
plot_dfs(co2_original, co2_missing, 'co2')
```

The preceding code produces the results as follows:

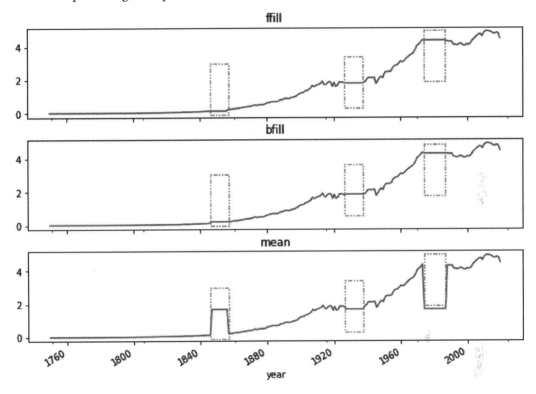

Figure 7.9 – Comparison between the three imputation methods for the CO2 DataFrame

Compare the results in *Figure 7.9* with the original data in *Figure 7.7*. Notice that both `ffill` and `bfill` produce better results than when using the mean. Both techniques have favorable RMSE scores and visual representation.

4. Now, perform the same imputation methods on the Clickstream DataFrame:

```
clicks_missing['ffil'] = clicks_missing['clicks'].
fillna(method='ffill')
clicks_missing['bfill'] = clicks_missing['clicks'].
fillna(method='bfill')
clicks_missing['mean'] = clicks_missing['clicks'].
fillna(clicks_missing['clicks'].mean())
```

Now, calculate the RMSE scores:

```
_ = rmse_score(clicks_original,
                     clicks_missing,
                     'clicks')
>>
RMSE for ffil: 1034.1210689204554
RMSE for bfill: 2116.6840489225033
RMSE for mean: 997.7600138929953
```

Interestingly, for the Clickstream dataset, the mean imputation had the lowest RMSE score, in contrast to the results from the CO2 dataset. Let's visualize the results to get another perspective on performance:

```
plot_dfs(clicks_original, clicks_missing, 'clicks')
```

You get the plots as follows:

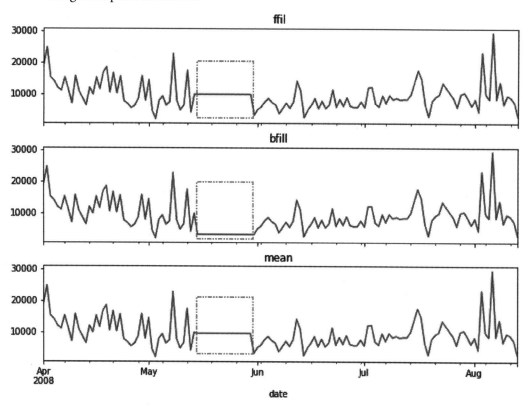

Figure 7.10 – Comparison between the three imputation methods for the Clickstream DataFrame

Compare the results in *Figure 7.10* with the original data in *Figure 7.8*. Notice that from imputing two different datasets (CO2 and Clickstream), there is no *one-size-fits-all strategy* when it comes to handling missing data. Instead, each dataset requires a different strategy. Therefore, you should always inspect your results and align the outputs with the expectations based on the nature of your data.

How it works...

Using `DataFrame.fillna()` is the simplest imputation method. The function can be used in two ways depending on which parameter you are using:

- The `value` parameter, where you can pass a scalar value (numeric or string) to use to fill for all missing values
- The `method` parameter, which takes specific string values:
  - Backward filling: `backfill` or `bfill`, uses the next observation, after the missing spot(s) and fills the gaps backward
  - Forward filling: `ffill` or `pad`, uses the last value before the missing spot(s) and fills the gaps forward

There's more...

There is a convenient shortcut for forward filling and backward filling in pandas. For example, instead of using `DataFrame.fillna(method="ffill")`, you can use `DataFrame.ffill()`. The same applies to `bfill` as well. The following shows how this can be implemented:

```
co2_missing['co2'].ffill()
co2_missing['co2'].bfill()
```

These shortcuts can be convenient when testing different imputation strategies.

See also

To learn more about `DataFrame.fillna()`, please visit the official documentation page here: `https://pandas.pydata.org/docs/reference/api/pandas.DataFrame.fillna.html`.

In the following recipe, you will perform similar univariate imputation, but this time using the scikit-learn library.

Handling missing data with univariate imputation using scikit-learn

scikit-learn is a very popular machine learning library in Python. The scikit-learn library offers a plethora of options for everyday machine learning tasks and algorithms such as classification, regression, clustering, dimensionality reduction, model selection, and preprocessing.

Additionally, the library offers multiple options for univariate and multivariate data imputation.

Getting ready

You can download the Jupyter notebooks and requisite datasets from the GitHub repository. Please refer to the *Technical requirements* section of this chapter.

This recipe will utilize the three functions prepared earlier (`read_dataset`, `rmse_score`, and `plot_dfs`). You will be using four datasets from the `Ch7` folder: `clicks_original.csv`, `clicks_missing.csv`, `clicks_original.csv`, and `co2_missing_only.csv`. The datasets are available from the GitHub repository.

How to do it...

You will start by importing the libraries and then read all four CSV files:

1. You will be using the `SimpleImputer` class from the scikit-learn library to perform univariate imputation:

```
from sklearn.impute import SimpleImputer


folder = Path('../../datasets/Ch7/')
co2_original = read_dataset(folder,
                            'co2_original.csv', 'year')
co2_missing = read_dataset(folder,
                            'co2_missing_only.csv',
'year')
clicks_original = read_dataset(folder,
                            'clicks_original.csv',
'date')
clicks_missing = read_dataset(folder,
```

```
                                    'clicks_missing.csv',
    'date')
```

2. `SimpleImputer` accepts different values for the `strategy` parameter, including mean, median, and `most_frequent`. Let's explore all three strategies and see how they compare. Create a list of tuples for each method:

    ```
    strategy = [
        ('Mean Strategy', 'mean'),
        ('Median Strategy', 'median'),
        ('Most Frequent Strategy', 'most_frequent')]
    ```

    You can loop through the `Strategy` list to apply the different imputation strategies. `SimpleImptuer` has a `fit_transform` method. It combines two steps into one: fitting to the data (`.fit`), and then transforming the data (`.transform`).

    Keep in mind that `SimpleImputer` accepts a NumPy array, so you will need to use the `Series.values` property followed by the `.reshape(-1, 1)` method to create a 2D NumPy array. Simply, what this is doing is transforming the 1D array from `.values` of shape `(226, )` to a 2D array of shape `(226, 1)`, which is a column vector:

    ```
    co2_vals = co2_missing['co2'].values.reshape(-1,1)
    clicks_vals = clicks_missing['clicks'].values.reshape(-
    1,1)
    for s_name, s in strategy:
        co2_missing[s_name] = (
            SimpleImputer(strategy=s).fit_transform(co2_
    vals))
        clicks_missing[s_name] = (
            SimpleImputer(strategy=s).fit_transform(clicks_
    vals))
    ```

    Now, both the `clicks_missing` and `co2_missing` DataFrames have three additional columns, one for each of the imputation strategies implemented.

3. Using the `rmse_score` function, you can now evaluate each strategy. Start with the CO2 data. You should get an output like the following:

    ```
    _ = rmse_score(co2_original, co2_missing, 'co2')
    >>
    RMSE for Mean Strategy: 0.7156383637041684
    ```

```
RMSE for Median Strategy: 0.8029421606859859
RMSE for Most Frequent Strategy: 1.1245663822743381
```

For the Clickstream data, you should get an output like the following:

```
_ = rmse_score(clicks_original, clicks_missing, 'clicks')
>>
RMSE for Mean Strategy: 997.7600138929953
RMSE for Median Strategy: 959.3580492530756
RMSE for Most Frequent Strategy: 1097.6425985146868
```

Notice how the RMSE strategy rankings vary between the two datasets. For example, the Mean strategy performed best on the CO2 data, while the Median strategy did best on the Clickstream data.

4. Finally, use the plot_dfs function to plot the results. Start with the CO2 dataset:

```
plot_dfs(co2_original, co2_missing, 'co2')
```

It produces the following plots:

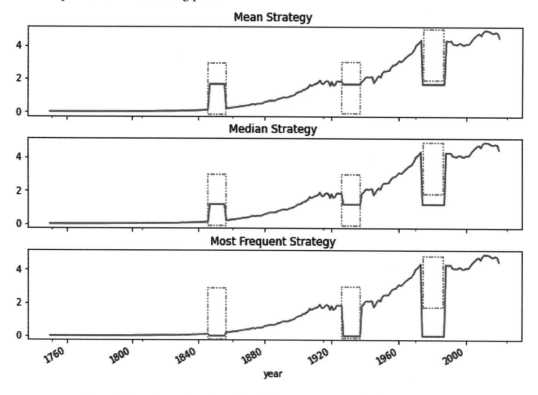

Figure 7.11 – Comparing three SimpleImputer strategies for the CO2 dataset

Compare the results in *Figure 7.11* with the original data in *Figure 7.7*. For the Clickstream dataset, you should use the following:

```
plot_dfs(clicks_original, clicks_missing, 'clicks')
```

This should plot all three strategies:

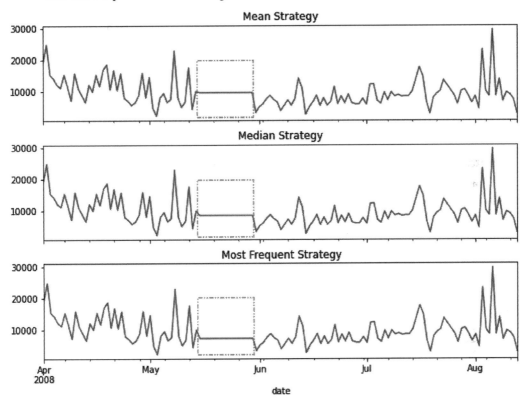

Figure 7.12 – Comparing three SimpleImputer strategies for the Clickstream dataset

Compare the results in *Figure 7.12* with the original data in *Figure 7.8*.

SimpleImputer provides basic strategies that may be suitable with some data but not others. The advantage of these simple imputation strategies (including the ones from the previous *Handling missing data with univariate imputation using pandas*) recipe is that they are fast and straightforward to implement.

How it works...

You used the `SimpleImputer` class to implement three simple strategies to impute missing values: mean, median, and most frequent (mode).

This is a univariate imputation technique, meaning only one feature or column was used to compute the mean, median, and most frequent value.

The `SimpleImptuer` class has three parameters that you need to know:

- `missing_values`, which, by default, is set to nan, and, more specifically, `np.nan`. NumPy nan and pandas NaN are similar, as you can see from the following example:

```
test = pd.Series([np.nan, np.nan, np.nan])
test

>>
0    NaN
1    NaN
2    NaN
dtype: float64
```

SimpleImputer will impute all occurrences of the `missing_values`, which you can update with `pandas.NA`, an integer, float, or a string value.

- `strategy`, which defaults to mean, and takes string values.
- `fill_value` can be used to replace all instances from `missing_values` with a specific value. This can either be a string or a numeric value. If the `Strategy` was set to `constant`, then you will need to provide your custom `fill_value`.

There's more...

The pandas DataFrame, `.fillna()`, can provide the same functionality as `SimpleImputer`. For example, the mean strategy can be accomplished by using the pandas `DataFrame.mean()` method and passing to `.fillna()`.

The following example illustrates this:

```
avg = co2_missing['co2'].mean()
co2_missing['pands_fillna'] = co2_missing['co2'].fillna(avg)

cols = ['co2', 'Mean Strategy', 'pands_fillna']
_ = rmse_score(co2_original, co2_missing[cols], 'co2')
```

```
>>
RMSE for Mean Strategy: 0.7156383637041684
RMSE for pands_fillna: 0.7156383637041684
```

Notice how you were able to accomplish the same results as the `SimpleImputer` class from scikit-learn. The `.fillna()` method makes it easier to scale the imputation across the entire DataFrame (column by column). For example, if you have a `sales_report_data` DataFrame with multiple columns containing missing data, you can perform a mean imputation with a single line, `sales_report_data.fillna(sales_report_data.mean())`.

See also

To learn more about scikit-learn's `SimpleImputer` class, please visit the official documentation page here: `https://scikit-learn.org/stable/modules/generated/sklearn.impute.SimpleImputer.html#sklearn.impute.SimpleImputer`.

So far, you have been dealing with univariate imputation. A more powerful approach is multivariate imputation, which you will learn in the following recipe.

Handling missing data with multivariate imputation

Earlier, we discussed the fact that there are two approaches to imputing missing data: univariate imputation and multivariate imputation.

As you have seen in the previous recipes, univariate imputation involves using one variable (column) to substitute for the missing data, disregarding other variables in the dataset. Univariate imputation techniques are usually faster and simpler to implement, but a multivariate approach may produce better results in most situations.

Instead of using a single variable (column), in a multivariate imputation, the method uses multiple variables within the dataset to impute missing values. The idea is simple: Have more variables within the dataset chime in to improve the predictability of missing values.

In other words, univariate imputation methods handle missing values for a particular variable in isolation of the entire dataset and just focus on that variable to derive the estimates. In multivariate imputation, the assumption is that there is some synergy within the variables in the dataset, and collectively, they can provide better estimates to fill in for the missing values.

In this recipe, you will be working with the Clickstream dataset since it has additional variables (*clicks*, *price*, and *location* columns) to perform multivariate imputation for *clicks*.

Getting ready

You can download the Jupyter notebooks and requisite datasets from the GitHub repository. Please refer to the *Technical requirements* section of this chapter.

In addition, you will leverage the three functions defined earlier in the chapter (`read_dataset`, `rmse_score`, and `plot_dfs`).

How to do it...

In this recipe, you will use scikit-learn for the multivariate imputation. The library provides the `IterativeImputer` class, which allows you to pass a regressor to predict the missing values from other variables (columns) within the dataset:

1. Start by importing the necessary libraries, methods, and classes:

    ```
    from sklearn.experimental import enable_iterative_imputer
    from sklearn.impute import IterativeImputer
    from sklearn.ensemble import ExtraTreesRegressor,
    BaggingRegressor
    from sklearn.linear_model import ElasticNet,
    LinearRegression
    from sklearn.neighbors import KneighborsRegressor
    ```

    Load the two Clickstream datasets into DataFrames:

    ```
    folder = Path('../../datasets/Ch7/')


    clicks_original = read_dataset(folder,
                                   'clicks_original.csv',
    'date')
    clicks_missing = read_dataset(folder,
                                  'clicks_missing.csv', 'date')
    ```

2. With `IterativeImputer`, you can test different estimators. So, let's try different regressors and compare the results. Create a list of the regressors (estimators) to be used in `IterativeImputer`:

    ```
    estimators = [
        ('extra_trees', ExtraTreesRegressor(n_
    ```

```
estimators=10)),
    ('bagging', BaggingRegressor(n_estimators=10)),
    ('elastic_net', ElasticNet()),
    ('linear_regression', LinearRegression()),
    ('knn', KNeighborsRegressor(n_neighbors=3))
]
```

3. Loop through the estimators and train on the dataset using `.fit()`, thereby building different models, and finally apply the imputation using `.transform()` on the variable with missing data. The results of each estimator will be appended as a new column to the `clicks_missing` DataFrame so that it can be used for scoring and compare the results visually:

```
clicks_vals = clicks_missing.iloc[:,0:3].values
for e_name, e in estimators:
    est = IterativeImputer(
                random_state=15,
                estimator=e).fit(clicks_vals)
    clicks_missing[e_name] = est.transform(clicks_vals)[:
, 2]
```

4. Using the `rmse_score` function, evaluate each estimator:

```
_ = rmse_score(clicks_original, clicks_missing, 'clicks')
```

This should print the following scores:

```
RMSE for bayesianRidge: 949.439397345585
RMSE for extra_trees: 1491.4107552296964
RMSE for bagging: 1315.5222743444128
RMSE for elastic_net: 945.4075209343101
RMSE for linear_regression: 938.9419831427186
RMSE for knn: 1336.8798392251822
```

Observe that Bayesian Ridge, ElasticNet, and Linear Regression produce similar results.

5. Finally, plot the results for a visual comparison between the best three:

```
plot_dfs(clicks_original, clicks_missing, 'clicks')
```

The output is as follows:

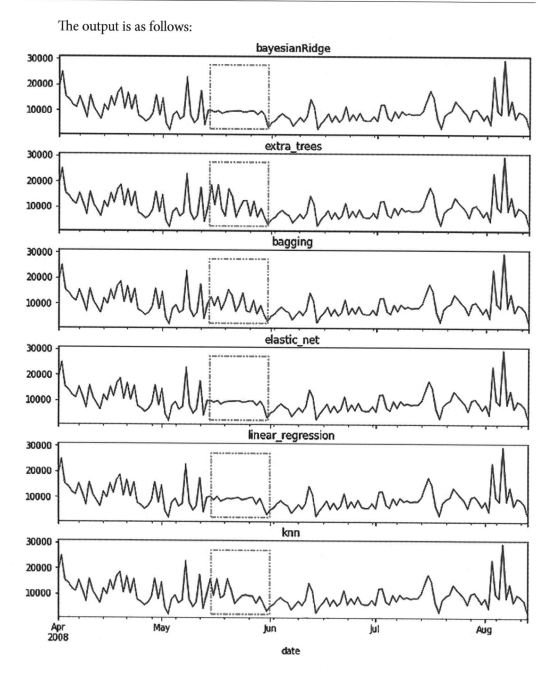

Figure 7.13 – Comparing different estimators using IterativeImputation

Compare the results in *Figure 7.13* with the original data in *Figure 7.8*.

Early in the chapter, we noted that the RMSE could be misleading because we did not seek the best score (smallest value) since we are not scoring a prediction model but rather an imputation model to fill for missing data. Later, you may use the data (with imputed values) to build another model for making predictions (forecasting). Thus, we do not mind some imperfections to better resemble real data. Additionally, since we may not know the true nature of the missing data, the goal is to get a decent estimate. For example, the three with the lowest RMSE scores (BayesianRidge, ElasticNet, and Linear Regression) did not capture some of the randomness in the data.

How it works...

The R MICE package inspired the `IterativeImputer` class from the scikit-learn library to implement **Multivariate Imputation by Chained Equation** (`https://www.jstatsoft.org/article/view/v045i03`). `IterativeImputer` does differ from the original implementation, which you can read more about here: `https://scikit-learn.org/stable/modules/impute.html#id2`.

Keep in mind that `IterativeImputer` is still in experimental mode. In the next section, you will use another implementation of MICE from the `statsmodels` library.

There's more...

The `statsmodels` library has an implementation of MICE that you can test and compare with `IterariveImputer`. This implementation is closer to the MICE implementation in R.

You will use the same DataFrames (`clicks_original` and `clicks_missing`) and append the `statsmodels` MICE imputation output to the `clicks_missing` DataFrame as an additional column.

Start by loading the required libraries:

```
from statsmodels.imputation.mice import MICE, MICEData,
MICEResults
import statsmodels.api as sm
```

Since your goal is to impute missing data, you can use the `MICEData` class to wrap the `clicks_missing` DataFrame. Start by creating an instance of `MICEData` and store it in a `mice_data` variable:

```
# create a MICEData object
fltr = ['price', 'location','clicks']
mice_data = MICEData(clicks_missing[fltr],
                     perturbation_method='gaussian')
# 20 iterations
mice_data.update_all(n_iter=20)
mice_data.set_imputer('clicks', formula='~ price + location',
model_class=sm.OLS)
```

Store the results in a new column and call it *MICE*. This way, you can compare the scores with results from `IterativeImputer`:

```
clicks_missing['MICE']   = mice_data.data['clicks'].values.
tolist()
_ = rmse_score(clicks_original, clicks_missing, 'clicks')
>>
RMSE for bayesianRidge: 949.439397345585
RMSE for extra_trees: 1756.0413495722155
RMSE for bagging: 1311.7040013605147
RMSE for elastic_net: 945.4075209343101
RMSE for linear_regression: 938.9419831427186
RMSE for knn: 1336.8798392251822
RMSE for MICE: 1204.8443667744593
```

Finally, visualize the results for a final comparison. This will include some of the imputations from `IterativeImputer`:

```
cols = ['clicks','bayesianRidge', 'bagging', 'knn', 'MICE']
plot_dfs(clicks_original, clicks_missing[cols], 'clicks')
```

The output is as follows:

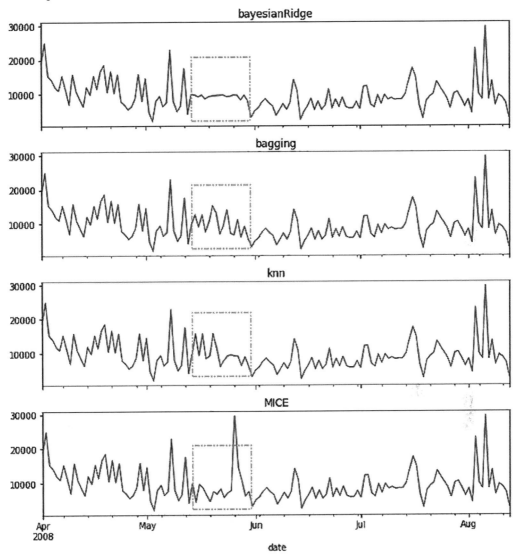

Figure 7.14 – Comparing the statsmodels MICE implementation with the scikit-learn IterativeImputer

Compare the results in *Figure 7.14* with the original data in *Figure 7.8*.

Overall, multivariate imputation techniques generally produce better results than univariate methods. This is true when working with more complex time-series datasets in terms of the number of features (columns) and records. Though univariate imputers are more efficient in terms of speed and simplicity to interpret, there is a need to balance complexity, quality, and analytical requirements.

See also

- To learn more about `IterativeImputer`, please visit the official documentation page here: `https://scikit-learn.org/stable/modules/generated/sklearn.impute.IterativeImputer.html#sklearn.impute.IterativeImputer`.

- To learn more about `statsmodels` MICE implementation, please visit the official documentation page here: `https://www.statsmodels.org/dev/imputation.html`.

- An interesting library, `FancyImpute`, that originally inspired scikit-learn's `IterativeImputer` offers a variety of imputation algorithms that you can check out here: `https://github.com/iskandr/fancyimpute`.

Handling missing data with interpolation

Another commonly used technique for imputing missing values is *interpolation*. The pandas library provides the `DataFrame.interpolate()` method for more complex univariate imputation strategies.

For example, one of the interpolation methods available is linear interpolation. **Linear interpolation** can be used to impute missing data by drawing a straight line between the two points surrounding the missing value (in time series, this means for a missing data point, it looks at a prior past value and the next future value to draw a line between them). A polynomial interpolation, on the other hand, will attempt to draw a curved line between the two points. Hence, each method will have a different mathematical operation to determine how to fill in for the missing data.

The interpolation capabilities in pandas can be extended further through the **SciPy** library, which offers additional univariate and multivariate interpolations.

In this recipe, you will use the pandas `DataFrame.interpolate()` function to examine different interpolation methods, including linear, polynomial, quadratic, nearest, and spline.

Getting ready

You can download the Jupyter notebooks and requisite datasets from the GitHub repository. Please refer to the *Technical requirements* section of this chapter.

You will utilize the three functions prepared earlier (`read_dataset`, `rmse_score`, and `plot_dfs`).

You will be using four datasets from the Ch7 folder: `clicks_original.csv`, `clicks_missing.csv`, `clicks_origina.csv`, and `co2_missing_only.csv`. The datasets are available from the GitHub repository.

How to do it...

You will perform multiple interpolations on two different datasets and then compare the results using RMSE and visualization:

1. Start by importing the libraries and reading the data into DataFrames:

```
folder = Path('../../datasets/Ch7/')
co2_original = read_dataset(folder,
                            'co2_original.csv', 'year')
co2_missing = read_dataset(folder,
                           'co2_missing_only.csv',
'year')
clicks_original = read_dataset(folder,
                               'clicks_original.csv',
'date')
clicks_missing = read_dataset(folder,
                              'clicks_missing.csv',
'date')
```

2. Create a list of the interpolation methods to be tested: `linear`, `quadratic`, `nearest`, and `cubic`:

```
interpolations = [
    'linear',
    'quadratic',
    'nearest',
    'cubic'
]
```

3. You will loop through the list to run different interpolations using `.interpolate()`. Append a new column for each interpolation output to be used for comparison:

```
for intp in interpolations:
    co2_missing[intp] = co2_missing['co2'].
interpolate(method=intp)
```

```
    clicks_missing[intp] = clicks_missing['clicks'].
interpolate(method=intp)
```

4. There are two additional methods that it would be interesting to test: *spline* and *polynomial*. To use these methods, you will need to provide an integer value for the order parameter. You can try `order = 2` for the spline method, and `order = 5` for the polynomial method. For the spline method, for example, it would look like this: `.interpolate(method="spline", order = 2)`:

```
co2_missing['spline'] = \
        co2_missing['co2'].interpolate(method='spline',
order=2)
clicks_missing['spline'] = \
        clicks_missing['clicks'].
interpolate(method='spline',order=2)

co2_missing['polynomial'] = \
        co2_missing['co2'].
interpolate(method='polynomial',order=5)
clicks_missing['polynomial'] = \
        clicks_missing['clicks'].
interpolate(method='polynomial',order=5)
```

5. Use the `rmse_score` function to compare the results from the different interpolation strategies. Start with CO2 data:

```
_ = rmse_score(co2_original, co2_missing, 'co2')
>>
RMSE for linear: 0.05507291327761665
RMSE for quadratic: 0.08367561505614347
RMSE for nearest: 0.05385422309469095
RMSE for cubic: 0.08373627305833133
RMSE for spline: 0.187602347541416
RMSE for polynomial: 0.06728323553134927
```

Now, let's check the Clickstream data:

```
_ = rmse_score(clicks_original, clicks_missing, 'clicks')
>>
RMSE for linear: 1329.1448378562811
RMSE for quadratic: 5224.641260626975
```

```
RMSE for nearest: 1706.1853705030173
RMSE for cubic: 6199.304875782831
RMSE for spline: 5222.922993448641
RMSE for polynomial: 56757.29323647127
```

6. Lastly, visualize the results to gain a better idea of how each interpolation worked. Start with the CO2 dataset:

```
cols = ['co2', 'linear', 'nearest', 'polynomial']
plot_dfs(co2_original, co2_missing[cols], 'co2')
```

This should plot the selected columns:

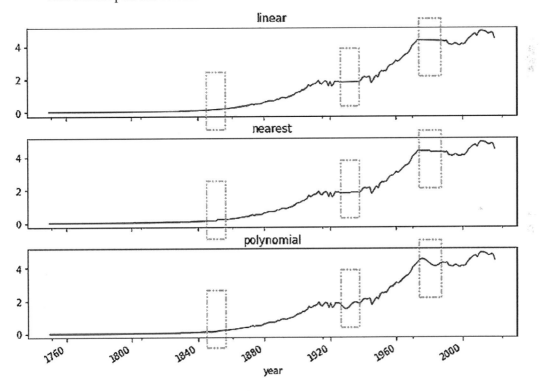

Figure 7.15 – Comparing the different interpolation strategies on the CO2 dataset

Compare the results in *Figure 7.15* with the original data in *Figure 7.7*.

Both the `linear` and `nearest` methods seem to have a similar effect regarding how the missing values were imputed. This can be seen from the RMSE scores and plot.

Now, create the plots for the Clickstream dataset:

```
cols = ['clicks', 'linear', 'nearest', 'polynomial',
'spline']
plot_dfs(clicks_original, clicks_missing[cols], 'clicks')
```

This should plot the selected columns:

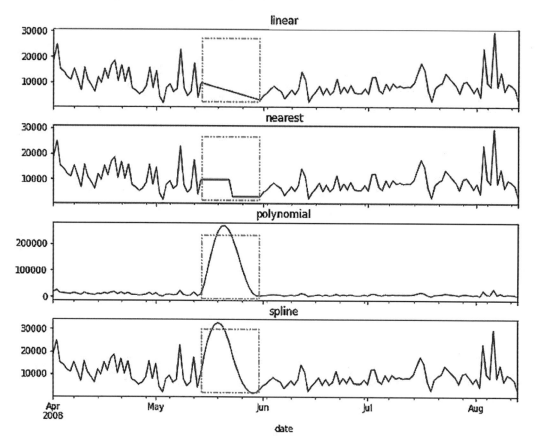

Figure 7.16 – Comparing the different interpolation strategies on the Clickstream dataset

Compare the results in *Figure 7.16* with the original data in *Figure 7.8*.

From the output, you can see how the `polynomial` method exaggerated the curve when using 5 as the polynomial order. On the other hand, the `Linear` method attempts to draw a straight line.

One thing to note is that between the strategies implemented, only linear interpolation ignores the index, while the rest use numerical values for the index.

How it works...

Overall, the interpolation technique detects patterns in neighboring data points (to the missing points) to predict what the missing values should be. The simplest form is linear interpolation, which assumes a straight line between two neighboring data points. On the other hand, a polynomial defines a curve between the two adjacent data points. Each interpolation method uses a different function and mechanism to predict the missing data.

In pandas, you will use the DataFrame.interpolate function. The default interpolation method is the linear interpolation (method = "linear"). There are additional parameters to provide more control over how the imputation with interpolation is done.

The limit parameter allows you to set the maximum number of consecutive NaN to fill. Recall in the previous recipe, *Handling missing data with univariate imputation using pandas*, that the Clickstream dataset had 16 consecutive missing points. You can limit the number of consecutive NaN, for example, to 5:

```
clicks_missing['clicks'].isna().sum()
>> 16
example = clicks_missing['clicks'].interpolate(limit = 5)
example.isna().sum()
>> 11
```

Only 5 data points were imputed; the remaining 11 were not.

There's more...

Other libraries also offer interpolation, including the following:

- SciPy provides a more extensive selection covering univariate and multivariate techniques: https://docs.scipy.org/doc/scipy/reference/interpolate.html.

- NumPy offers a couple of interpolation options; the most widely used is the numpy.interp() function: https://numpy.org/doc/stable/reference/generated/numpy.interp.html?highlight=interp#numpy.interp.

See also

To learn more about DataFrame.interpolate, please visit the official documentation page here: https://pandas.pydata.org/docs/reference/api/pandas.DataFrame.interpolate.html.

8

Outlier Detection Using Statistical Methods

In addition to missing data, as discussed in *Chapter 7, Handling Missing Data,* a common data issue you may face is the presence of **outliers**. Outliers can be point outliers, collective outliers, or contextual outliers. For example, a **point outlier** occurs when a data point deviates from the rest of the population—sometimes referred to as a **global outlier**. **Collective outliers**, which are groups of observations, differ from the population and don't follow the expected pattern. Lastly, **contextual outliers** occur when an observation is considered an outlier based on a particular condition or context, such as deviation from neighboring data points. Note that with contextual outliers, the same observation may not be considered an outlier if the context changes.

In this chapter, you will be introduced to a handful of practical statistical techniques that cover parametric and non-parametric methods. In *Chapter 14, Outlier Detection Using Unsupervised Machine Learning,* you will dive into more advanced machine learning and deep learning-based techniques.

In the literature, you will find another popular term, **anomaly detection**, which can be synonymous with **outlier detection**. The methods and techniques to identify outlier or anomaly observations are similar; the difference lies in the context and the actions that follow once these points have been identified. For example, an outlier transaction in financial transactions may be referred to as an anomaly and trigger a fraud investigation to stop them from re-occurring. Under a different context, survey data with outlier data points may simply be removed by the researchers once they examine the overall impact of keeping versus removing such points. Sometimes you may decide to keep these outlier points if they are part of the natural process. In other words, they are legitimate and opt to use robust statistical methods that are not influenced by outliers.

Another concept, known as **change point detection (CPD)**, relates to outlier detection. In CPD, the goal is to anticipate abrupt and impactful fluctuations (increasing or decreasing) in the time series data. CPD covers specific techniques, for example, **cumulative sum (CUSUM)** and **Bayesian online change point detection (BOCPD)**. Detecting change is vital in many situations. For example, a machine may break if the internal temperature reaches a certain point or if you are trying to understand whether the discounted price did increase sales or not. This distinction between outlier detection and CPD is vital since you sometimes want the latter. Where the two disciplines converge, depending on the context, sudden changes may indicate the potential presence of outliers (anomalies).

The recipes that you will encounter in this chapter are as follows:

- Resampling time series data
- Detecting outliers using visualizations
- Detecting outliers using the Tukey method
- Detecting outliers using a z-score
- Detecting outliers using a modified z-score

Technical requirements

You can download the Jupyter Notebooks and needed datasets from the GitHub repository:

- Jupyter Notebook: `https://github.com/PacktPublishing/Time-Series-Analysis-with-Python-Cookbook./blob/main/code/Ch8/Chapter%208.ipynb`

- Datasets: `https://github.com/PacktPublishing/Time-Series-Analysis-with-Python-Cookbook./tree/main/datasets/Ch8`

Throughout the chapter, you will be using a dataset from the **Numenta Anomaly Benchmark (NAB)**, which provides outlier detection benchmark datasets. For more information about NAB, please visit their GitHub repository here: `https://github.com/numenta/NAB`.

The *New York Taxi dataset* captures the number of NYC taxi passengers at a specific timestamp. The data contains known anomalies that are provided to evaluate the performance of our outlier detectors. The dataset contains 10,320 records between July 1, 2014, to May 31, 2015. The observations are captured in a 30-minute interval, which translates to `freq = '30T'`.

To prepare for the outlier detection recipes, start by loading the libraries that you will be using throughout the chapter:

```
import pandas as pd
import numpy as np
import matplotlib.pyplot as plt
from pathlib import Path

import warnings
warnings.filterwarnings('ignore')
plt.rcParams["figure.figsize"] = [16, 3]
```

Load the `nyc_taxi.csv` data into a pandas DataFrame as it will be used throughout the chapter:

```
file = Path("../../datasets/Ch8/nyc_taxi.csv")
nyc_taxi = pd.read_csv(folder / file,
                        index_col='timestamp',
                        parse_dates=True)
nyc_taxi.index.freq = '30T'
```

You can store the known dates containing outliers, also known as **ground truth labels**:

```
nyc_dates =   [
        "2014-11-01",
        "2014-11-27",
        "2014-12-25",
        "2015-01-01",
        "2015-01-27"
]
```

If you investigate these dates to gain more insight into their significance, you will find similar information to the following summary:

- Saturday, November 1, 2014, was before the New York Marathon, and the official marathon event was on Sunday, November 2, 2014.

- Thursday, November 27, 2014, was Thanksgiving Day.

- Thursday, December 25, 2014, was Christmas Day.

- Thursday, January 1, 2015, was New Year's Day.

- Tuesday, January 27, 2015, was the North American Blizzard where all vehicles were ordered off the street from January 26 to January 27, 2015.

You can plot the time series data to gain an intuition on the data you will be working with for outlier detection:

```
nyc_taxi.plot(title="NYC Taxi", alpha=0.6)
```

This should produce a time series with a 30-minute frequency:

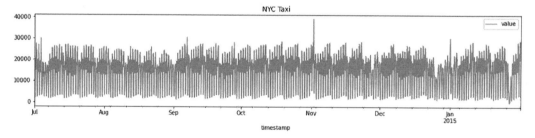

Figure 8.1 – Plot of the New York City taxi time series data

Finally, create the `plot_outliers` function that you will use throughout the recipes:

```
def plot_outliers(outliers, data, method='KNN',
                  halignment = 'right',
                  valignment = 'bottom',
                  labels=False):

    ax = data.plot(alpha=0.6)

    if labels:
        for i in outliers['value'].items():
            plt.plot(i[0], i[1], 'rx')
```

```
                plt.text(i[0], i[1], f'{i[0].date()}',
                            horizontalalignment=halignment,
                            verticalalignment=valignment)
    else:
        data.loc[outliers.index].plot(ax=ax, style='rx')

    plt.title(f'NYC Taxi - {method}')
    plt.xlabel('date'); plt.ylabel('# of passengers')
    plt.legend(['nyc taxi','outliers'])
    plt.show()
```

As we proceed with the outlier detection recipes, the goal is to see how the different techniques capture outliers and compare them to the ground truth labels.

Understanding outliers

The presence of outliers requires special handling and further investigation before hastily jumping to decisions on how to handle them. First, you will need to detect and spot their existence, which this chapter is all about. Domain knowledge can be instrumental in determining whether these identified points are outliers, their impact on your analysis, and how you should deal with them.

Outliers can indicate bad data due to a random variation in the process, known as noise, or due to data entry error, faulty sensors, bad experiment, or natural variation. Outliers are usually undesirable if they seem synthetic, for example, bad data. On the other hand, if outliers are a natural part of the process, you may need to rethink removing them and opt to keep these data points. In such circumstances, you can rely on non-parametric statistical methods that do not make assumptions on the underlying distribution.

Generally, outliers can cause side effects when building a model based on strong assumptions on the data distribution; for example, the data is from a Gaussian (normal) distribution. Statistical methods and tests based on assumptions of the underlying distribution are referred to as **parametric methods**.

There is no fixed protocol for dealing with outliers, and the magnitude of their impact will vary. For example, sometimes you may need to test your model with outliers and again without outliers to understand the overall impact on your analysis. In other words, not all outliers are created, nor should they be treated equally. However, as stated earlier, having domain knowledge is essential when dealing with these outliers.

Now, before using a dataset to build a model, you will need to test for the presence of such outliers so you can further investigate their significance. Spotting outliers is usually part of the data cleansing and preparation process before going deep into your analysis.

A common approach to handling outliers is to delete these data points and not have them be part of the analysis or model development. Alternatively, you may wish to replace the outliers using similar techniques highlighted in *Chapter 7, Handling Missing Data*, such as imputation and interpolation. Other methods, such as smoothing the data, could minimize the impact of outliers. Smoothing, such as exponential smoothing, is discussed in *Chapter 10, Building Univariate Time Series Models Using Statistical*. You may also opt to keep the outliers and use more resilient algorithms to their effect.

There are many well-known methods for outlier detection. The area of research is evolving, ranging from basic statistical techniques to more advanced approaches leveraging neural networks and deep learning. In statistical methods, you have different tools that you can leverage, such as the use of visualizations (boxplots, QQ-plots, histograms, and scatter plots), z-score, **interquartile range** (**IQR**) and Tukey fences, and statistical tests such as Grubb's test, the Tietjen-Moore test, or the generalized **Extreme Studentized Deviate** (**ESD**) test. These are basic, easy to interpret, and effective methods.

In your first recipe, you will be introduced to a crucial time series transformation technique known as resampling before diving into outlier detection.

Resampling time series data

A typical transformation that is done on time series data is **resampling**. The process implies changing the frequency or level of granularity of the data.

Usually, you will have limited control over how the time series is generated in terms of frequency. For example, the data can be generated and stored in small intervals, such as milliseconds, minutes, or hours. In some cases, the data can be in larger intervals, such as daily, weekly, or monthly.

The need for resampling time series can be driven by the nature of your analysis and at what granular level you need your data to be. For instance, you can have daily data, but your analysis requires the data to be weekly, and thus you will need to resample. This process is known as **downsampling**. When you are downsampling, you will need to provide some level of aggregation, such as mean, sum, min, or max, to name a few. On the other hand, some situations require you to resample your data from daily to hourly. This process is known as **upsampling**. When upsampling, you will have null rows, which you must fill either using imputation or interpolation techniques. See *Chapter 7, Handling Missing Data*, where both imputation and interpolation methods were discussed in more detail.

In this recipe, you will explore how resampling is done using the pandas library.

How to do it...

In this recipe, you will work with the nyc_taxis DataFrame created earlier in the *Technical requirements* section. The data captures the number of passengers in 30-minute intervals.

1. Downsample the data to a daily frequency. Currently, you have 10,320 records, and when you resample the data to daily, you will need to aggregate the data. In this example, you will use the .mean() function. This will reduce the number of samples to 215 records, hence the name *downsampling* (the number of samples went down).

    Inspect the first five rows of the original DataFrame:

    ```
    nyc_taxi.head()
    >>
                    value
    timestamp
    2014-07-01 00:00:00      10844
    2014-07-01 00:30:00      8127
    2014-07-01 01:00:00      6210
    2014-07-01 01:30:00      4656
    2014-07-01 02:00:00      3820
    ```

    Resampling is done using the DataFrame.resample() function. For daily, you will use 'D' as the date offset rule, followed by .mean():

    ```
    df_downsampled = nyc_taxi.resample('D').mean()
    df_downsampled.head()
    >>
                    value
    timestamp
    2014-07-01      15540.979167
    2014-07-02      15284.166667
    2014-07-03      14794.625000
    2014-07-04      11511.770833
    2014-07-05      11572.291667
    ```

Notice how `DatetimeIndex` is now at a daily frequency, and the number of passengers now reflects the daily average. Inspect the first `DatetimeIndex` to check its frequency:

```
df_downsampled.index[0]
>>
Timestamp('2014-07-01 00:00:00', freq='D')
```

You can also check frequency directly using the `.freq` property:

```
df_downsampled.index.freq
>>
<Day>
```

Check the number of records now after downsampling:

```
df_downsampled.shape
>>
(215, 1)
```

Indeed, now you have `215` records.

2. Resample the data one more time, but this time as a 3-day frequency. You can do this by using `'3D'`. This time, use the `.sum()` method instead:

```
df_downsampled = machine_temp.resample('3D').sum()
df_downsampled.head()
>>
                value
timestamp
2013-12-02    50382.133560
2013-12-05    70382.125169
2013-12-08    59704.334577
2013-12-11    81755.895600
2013-12-14    73672.877837
```

Check the frequency of `DatetimeIndex`:

```
df_downsampled.index.freq
>>
<3 * Days>
```

If you use `df_downsampled.shape`, then you will notice the number of records got reduced to 27 records.

3. Now, change the frequency to 3 business days instead. The default in pandas is Monday to Friday. In the *Working with custom business days* recipe in *Chapter 6, Working with Date and Time in Python,* You learned how to create custom business days. For now, you will use the default definition of business days. If you observe the output from the previous step, 2013-12-08 falls on a Sunday. Using '3B' will push it to the following Tuesday, 2013-12-10:

```
df_downsampled = machine_temp.resample('3B').sum()
df_downsampled.head()
>>
              value
timestamp
2013-12-02    50382.133560
2013-12-05    113685.006053
2013-12-10    70050.163937
2013-12-13    127476.152590
2013-12-18    137601.305150
```

Interesting output in how it skips 5 days from 12-05 to 12-10, and then again from 12-13 to 12-18. The reason is the *Business Day rule* which specifies we have 2 days of the week as weekends. Since the function is calendar-aware, it knows a weekend is coming after the first 3-day increment, so it adds a 2-day weekend to skip them, and thus, it makes a 6-day jump. Starting from 12-5, thus moving to 12-10, and from 12-13 moving to 12-18. And similarly, from 12-18 to 12-23, and so on.

4. Lastly, let's upsample the data from a 30-minute interval (frequency) to a 15-minutes frequency. This will create an empty entry (NaN) between every other entry. You will use 'T' for minutes, since 'M' is used for monthly aggregation:

```
nyc_taxi.resample('15T').mean().head()
>>
                        value
timestamp
2014-07-01 00:00:00     10844.0
2014-07-01 00:15:00     NaN
2014-07-01 00:30:00     8127.0
2014-07-01 00:45:00     NaN
2014-07-01 01:00:00     6210.0
```

Notice that upsampling creates NaN rows. Unlike downsampling, when upsampling, you need to give instructions on how to fill the NaN rows. You might be wondering why we used .mean() here? The simple answer is because it would not matter whether you used .sum(), .max(), or .min(), for example. You will need to augment the missing rows using imputation or interpolation techniques when you upsample. For example, you can specify an imputation method in .fillna() or by using the shortcut methods such as .ffill() or .bfill().

Notice the two statements are equivalent:

```
nyc_taxi.resample('15T').fillna('ffill')
## OR
nyc_taxi.resample('15T').ffill()
>>
                value
timestamp
2014-07-01 00:00:00     10844
2014-07-01 00:15:00     10844
2014-07-01 00:30:00     8127
2014-07-01 00:45:00     8127
2014-07-01 01:00:00     621
```

The first five records show the use of forward filling. For more information on using .fillna() or imputation in general, refer to *Chapter 7, Handling Missing Data*.

Overall, resampling in pandas is very convenient and straightforward. This can be a handy tool when you want to change the frequency of your time series.

How it works...

The DataFrame.resample() method allows you to group rows in a specified time frame, for example, by day, week, month, year, or any DateTime attribute. The way .resample() works is by grouping the data using the DatetimeIndex and the frequency provided, hence, this method is specific to time series DataFrames.

The .resample() function works in a very similar manner to the .groupby() function; the difference is that .resample() is specific to time series data and groups at the DatetimeIndex.

There's more...

You can supply more than one aggregation at once when downsampling using the
.agg() function.

For example, using 'M' for monthly, you can supply the .agg() function with a list of
aggregations you want to perform:

```
nyc_taxi.resample('M').agg(['mean', 'min',
                            'max', 'median', 'sum'])
```

This should produce a DataFrame with five columns, one for each aggregation method
specified. The index column, a timestamp column, will be grouped at monthly intervals:

					value
timestamp	mean	min	max	median	sum
2014-07-31	14994.084677	1769	29985	16625.5	22311198
2014-08-31	14580.438844	1841	26062	16184.0	21695693
2014-09-30	15623.374306	1431	30373	17244.5	22497659
2014-10-31	16086.851478	1691	28626	17767.5	23937235
2014-11-30	15492.125000	1683	39197	17287.0	22308660
2014-12-31	14813.428763	1459	27804	16587.0	22042382
2015-01-31	14399.790995	8	30236	16061.0	21426889

Figure 8.2 – Multiple aggregations using the .agg() method

Notice that the default behavior for 'M' or monthly frequency is at the month's end
(example 2014-07-31). You can change to month's start instead by using 'MS'. For
example, this will produce 2014-07-01 instead (the beginning of each month).

See also

To learn more about pandas DataFrame.resample(), please visit the official
documentation here: https://pandas.pydata.org/docs/reference/api/
pandas.DataFrame.resample.html.

Detecting outliers using visualizations

There are two general approaches for using statistical techniques to detect outliers: **parametric** and **non-parametric** methods. Parametric methods assume you know the underlying distribution of the data. For example, if your data follows a normal distribution. On the other hand, in non-parametric methods, you make no such assumptions.

Using histograms and box plots are basic non-parametric techniques that can provide insight into the distribution of the data and the presence of outliers. More specifically, box plots, also known as **box and whisker** plots, provide a five-number summary: the minimum, first quartile (25th percentile), median (50th percentile), third quartile (75th percentile), and the maximum. There are different implementations for how far the whiskers extend, for example, the whiskers can extend to the *minimum* and *maximum* values. In most statistical software, including Python's `matplotlib` and `seaborn` libraries, the whiskers extend to what is called **Tukey's lower and upper fences**. Any data point outside these boundaries is considered an outlier. You will dive into the actual calculation and implementation in the *Detecting outliers using the Tukey method* recipe. For now, let's focus on the visualization aspect of the analysis.

In this recipe, you will use `seaborn` as another Python visualization library that is based on `matplotlib`.

Getting ready

You can download the Jupyter Notebooks and required datasets from the GitHub repository. Please refer to the *Technical requirements* section of this chapter.

You will be using the `nyc_taxi` DataFrame that you loaded earlier in the *Technical requirements* section.

You will be using `seaborn` version *0.11.2*, which is the latest version as of this writing.

To install `seaborn` using `pip`, use the following:

```
pip install seaborn
```

To install `seaborn` using `conda`, use the following:

```
conda install seaborn
```

How to do it...

In this recipe, you will explore different plots available from `seaborn` including `histplot()`, `displot()`, `boxplot()`, `boxenplot()`, and `violinplot()`. You will notice that these plots tell a similar story but visually, each plot represents the information differently. Eventually, you will develop a preference toward some of these plots for your own use when investigating your data;

1. Start by importing the `seaborn` library to begin exploring how these plots work to help you detect outliers:

   ```
   Import seaborn as sns
   sns.__version__
   >> '0.11.2'
   ```

2. Recall from *Figure 8.1*, the `nyc_taxi` DataFrame contains passenger counts recorded every 30 minutes. Keep in mind that every analysis or investigation is unique and so should be your approach to align with the problem you are solving for. This also means that you will need to consider your data preparation approach, for example, determine what transformations you need to apply to your data.

   For this recipe, your goal is to find which days have outlier observations, not at which interval within the day, so you will resample the data to a daily frequency. You will start by downsampling the data using the `mean` aggregation. Even though such a transformation will smooth out the data, you will not lose too much of the detail as it pertains to finding outliers since the `mean` is very sensitive to outliers. In other words, if there was an extreme outlier on a specific interval (there are 48 intervals in a day), the mean will still carry that information.

   Downsample the data to a daily frequency. This will reduce the number of observations from 10,320 to 215, or (`10320/48 = 215`):

   ```
   tx = nyc_taxi.resample('D').mean()
   ```

3. Plot the new `tx` DataFrame with the ground truth labels to use as a reference. You will call the `plot_outliers` function that you created from the *Technical requirements* section:

   ```
   known_outliers= tx.loc[nyc_dates]
   plot_outliers(known_outliers, tx, 'Known Outliers')
   ```

This should produce a time series plot with X markers for known outliers.

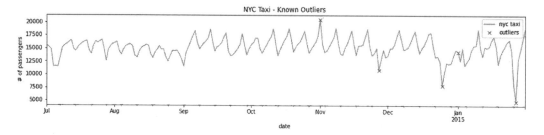

Figure 8.3 – Plotting the NYC Taxi data after downsampling with ground truth labels (outliers)

4. Now, let's start with your first plot for inspecting your time series data using the histplot() function:

```
sns.histplot(tx)
```

This should produce the following:

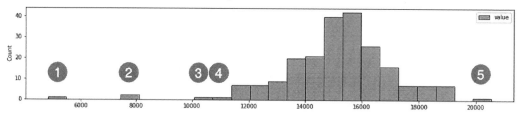

Figure 8.4 – Histogram showing extreme daily mean passenger rides

In *Figure 8.4*, the observations labeled as *1, 2, 3, 4,* and *5* seem to represent extreme passenger values. Recall, these numbers represent the average daily passengers after resampling. The question you should ask is whether these observations are outliers. The center of the histogram is close to 15,000 daily average passengers. This should make you question whether the extreme value close to 20,000 (*label 5*) is that extreme. Similarly, the observations labeled *3* and *4* (since they are close to the tail of the distribution), are they actually extreme values? How about labels *1* and *2* with average passenger rides at 3,000 and 8,000 daily average passengers respectively? These do seem more extreme compared to the rest and may potentially be actual outliers. Again, determining what is an outlier and what is not requires domain knowledge and further analysis. There is no specific rule, and you will see throughout this chapter that some of the generally accepted rules are arbitrary and subjective. You should not jump to conclusions immediately.

5. You can achieve a similar plot using `displot()`, which has a `kind` parameter. The `kind` parameter can take one of three values: `hist` for the histogram plot, `kde` for the kernel density estimate plot, and `ecdf` for the empirical cumulative distribution function plot.

    You will use `displot(kind='hist')` to plot a similar histogram as the one in *Figure 8.4*:

    ```
    sns.displot(tx, kind='hist', height=3, aspect=4)
    ```

6. A box plot provides more information than a histogram and can be a better choice for spotting outliers. In a box plot, observations that are outside the whiskers or boundaries are considered outliers. The whiskers represent the visual boundary for the upper and lower fences as proposed by mathematician John Tukey in 1977.

    The following code shows how to create a box plot using `seaborn`:

    ```
    sns.boxplot(tx['value'])
    ```

    The following figure shows the potential outliers:

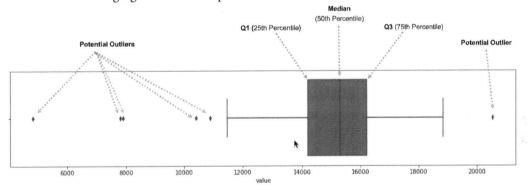

Figure 8.5 – A box plot showing potential outliers that are outside the boundaries (whiskers)

The width of the box (**Q1** to **Q3**) is called **interquartile range** (**IQR**) calculated as the difference between the 75th and 25th percentiles (**Q3 – Q1**). The lower fence is calculated as *Q1 - (1.5 x IQR)*, and the upper fence as *Q3 + (1.5 x IQR)*. Any observation less than the lower boundary or greater than the upper boundary is considered a potential outlier. More on that in the *Detecting outliers using the Tukey method* recipe. The `whis` parameter in the `boxplot` function is set to `1.5` by default (1.5 times IQR), which controls the width or distance between the upper and lower fences. Larger values mean fewer observations will be deemed as outliers, and smaller values will make non-outlier points seem outside of boundaries (more outliers).

```
sns.boxplot(tx['value'], whis=1.5)
```

7. There are two more variations for box plots in `seaborn` (`boxenplot` and `violinplot`). They provide similar insight as to the boxplot but are presented differently. The *boxen plot*, which in literature is referred to as a *letter-value* plot, can be considered as an enhancement to regular box plots to address some of their shortcomings, as described in the paper *Heike Hofmann, Hadley Wickham & Karen Kafadar (2017) Letter-Value Plots: Boxplots for Large Data, Journal of Computational and Graphical Statistics, 26:3, 469-477.* More specifically, boxen (letter-value) plots are better suited when working with larger datasets (higher number of observations for displaying data distribution and more suitable for differentiating outlier points for larger datasets). The `seaborn` implementation in `boxenplot` is based on that paper.

The following code shows how to create a boxen (letter-value) plot using `seaborn`:

```
sns.boxenplot(tx['value'])
```

This should produce a plot that looks like the box plot in *Figure 8.5*, but with boxes extending beyond the quartiles (**Q1, Q2,** and **Q3**). The 25th percentile is at the 14,205 daily average passengers mark, and the 75th percentile is at the 16,209 daily average passengers mark.

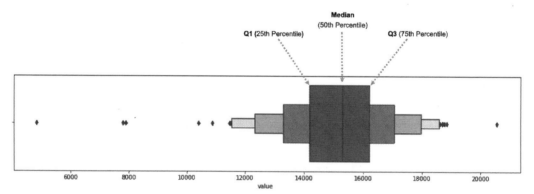

Figure 8.6 – A boxen (letter-value) plot for the average daily taxi passengers in NYC

> **Percentile Values**
>
> Are you wondering how I was able to determine the exact value for the 25th, 50th, and 75th percentiles?
>
> You can obtain these values for a DataFrame or series with the `describe` method. For example, if you run `tx.describe()`, you should see a table of descriptive statistics that includes count, mean, standard deviation, minimum, maximum, 25th, 50th, and 75th percentile values for the dataset.

In *Figure 8.6*, you are getting additional insight into the distribution of passengers beyond the quantiles. In other words, it extends the box plot to show additional distributions to give more insight into the tail of the data. The boxes in theory could keep going to accommodate all the data points, but in order to show outliers, there needs to be a stopping point, referred to as depth. In `seaborn`, this parameter is called `k_depth`, which can take a numeric value, or you can specify different methods such as `tukey`, `proportion`, `trustworthy`, or `full`. For example, a `k_depth=1` numeric value will show a similar box to the boxplot in *Figure 8.5* (one box). As a reference, *Figure 8.6* shows four boxes determined using the Tukey method, which is the default value (`k_depth="tukey"`). Using `k_depth=4` would produce the same plot.

These methods are explained in the referenced paper by *Heike Hofmann, Hadley Wickham & Karen Kafadar (2017)*. To explore the different methods, you can try the following code:

```
for k in ["tukey", "proportion", "trustworthy", "full"]:
    sns.boxenplot(tx['value'], k_depth=k)
    plt.title(k)
    plt.show()
```

This should produce four plots; notice the different numbers of boxes that were determined by each method. Recall, you can also specify `k_depth` numerically as well.

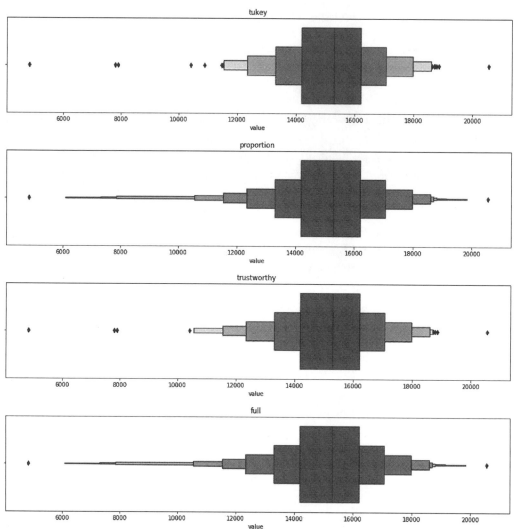

Figure 8.7 – The different k_depth methods available in seaborn for the boxenplot function

8. Now, the final variation is the violin plot, which you can display using the
    `violinplot` function:

```
sns.violinplot(tx['value'])
```

This should produce a plot that is a hybrid between a box plot and a **kernel density
estimation (KDE)**. A kernel is a function that estimates the probability density
function, the larger peaks (wider area), for example, show where the majority of
the points are concentrated. This means that there is a higher probability that a data
point will be in that region as opposed to the much thinner regions showing much
lower probability.

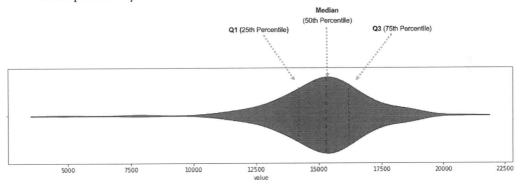

Figure 8.8 – A violin plot for the average daily taxi passengers in NYC

Notice that *Figure 8.8* shows the distribution for the entire dataset. Another observation
is the number of peaks; in this case, we have one peak, which makes it a unimodal
distribution. If there is more than one peak, we call it a multimodal distribution, which
should trigger a further investigation into the data. A KDE plot will provide similar
insight as a histogram but with a more smoothed curve.

How it works...

In the recipe, we were introduced to several plots that help visualize the distribution of the
data and show outliers. Generally, histograms are great for showing distribution, but a box
plot (and its variants) are much better for outlier detection. We also explored the boxen
(letter-value) plot, which is more suited for larger datasets and is more appropriate than
regular box plots.

There's more...

The lag plot is another useful visualization for spotting outliers. A lag plot is essentially a scatter plot, but instead of plotting two variables to observe correlation, as an example, we plot the same variable against its lagged version. This means, it is a scatter plot using the same variable, but the *y* axis represents passenger count at the current time (*t*) and the *x* axis will show passenger count at a prior period (*t-1*), which we call lag. The lag parameter determines how many periods to go back; for example, a lag of 1 means one period back, while a lag of 2 means two periods back. In our resampled data (downsampled to daily), a lag of 1 represents the prior day.

The pandas library provides the `lag_plot` function, which you can use as shown in the following example:

```
from pandas.plotting import lag_plot
lag_plot(tx)
```

This should produce the following scatter plot:

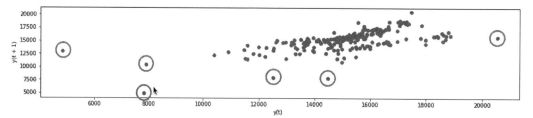

Figure 8.9 – A lag plot of average daily taxi passengers in NYC

The circled data points highlight interesting points that can be potential outliers. Some seem more extreme than others. Further, you can see some linear relationship between the passenger counts and its lagged version (prior day) indicating the existence of an autocorrelation. Recall from basic statistics that correlation shows the relationship between two independent variables, so you can think of autocorrelation as a correlation of a variable at a time (*t*) and its prior version at a time (*t-1*). More on this in *Chapter 9, Exploratory Data Analysis and Diagnosis*, and *Chapter 10, Building Univariate Time Series Models Using Statistical Methods*.

The labels for the *x* axis and the *y* axis in *Figure 8.9* can be a bit confusing, with the *y* axis being labeled as *y(t+1)*. Essentially it is saying the same thing we described earlier: the *x* axis represents prior values (the predictor) to its future self at *t+1*, which is what the *y* axis represents. To make it clearer, you can recreate the exact visualization produced by `lag_plot` using `seaborn` manually, as shown in the following code:

```
y = tx[1:].values.reshape(-1)
x = tx[:-1].values.reshape(-1)
sns.scatterplot(x=x, y=y)
```

This should produce a similar plot to that in *Figure 8.9*.

Notice in the code that the `y` values start from *t+1* (we skipped the value at index 0) up to the last observation, and the `x` values start from index 0 up to index -1 (we skip the last observation). This makes the values in the *y* axis ahead by one period.

In the next recipe, we will dive further into IQR and Tukey fences that we briefly discussed when talking about box plots.

See also

You can learn more about the plots we used and the different options available from the `seaborn` documentation. To learn more about the following, visit the associated URLs:

- For box plots (`boxplot`), you can visit https://seaborn.pydata.org/generated/seaborn.boxplot.html.

- For boxen plots (`boxenplot`), you can visit https://seaborn.pydata.org/generated/seaborn.boxenplot.html.

- For violin plots (`violinplot`), you can visit https://seaborn.pydata.org/generated/seaborn.violinplot.html#seaborn.violinplot.

- For histograms (`histpolot`), you can visit https://seaborn.pydata.org/generated/seaborn.histplot.html.

- For distribution plots (`distplot`), you can visit https://seaborn.pydata.org/generated/seaborn.displot.html#seaborn.displot.

Detecting outliers using the Tukey method

This recipe will extend on the previous recipe, *Detecting outliers using visualizations*. In *Figure 8.5*, the box plot showed the quartiles with whiskers extending to the upper and lower fences. These boundaries or fences were calculated using the Tukey method.

Let's expand on *Figure 8.5* with additional information on the other components:

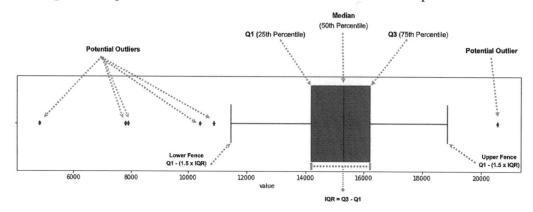

Figure 8.10 – Box plot for the daily average taxi passengers data

Visualizations are great to give you a high-level perspective on the data you are working with, such as the overall distribution and potential outliers. Ultimately you want to identify these outliers programmatically so you can isolate these data points for further investigation and analysis. This recipe will teach how to calculate IQR and define points that fall outside the lower and upper Tukey fences.

How to do it...

Most statistical methods allow you to spot extreme values beyond a certain threshold. For example, this could be the mean, standard deviation, the 10th or 90th percentile, or some other value that you want to compare against. You will start the recipe by learning how to obtain basic descriptive statistics and more specifically, the quantiles.

1. Both DataFrame and Series have the `describe` method that outputs summary descriptive statistics. By default, it shows the quartiles: the first quartile, which is the 25th percentile, the second quartile (median), which is the 50th percentile, and the third quartile, which is the 75th percentile. You can customize the percentiles by providing a list of values to the `percentiles` parameter. The following code shows how you can get values for additional percentiles:

```
percentiles = [0, 0.05, .10, .25, .5, .75, .90, .95, 1]
tx.describe(percentiles= percentiles)
```

This should produce the following DataFrame:

	value
count	215.000000
mean	15137.569380
std	1937.391020
min	4834.541667
Minimum ➔ 0%	4834.541667
5%	11998.181250
10%	13043.854167
1st Quartile or Lower Quartile ➔ 25%	14205.197917
2nd Quartile or Median ➔ 50%	15299.937500
3rd Quartile or Upper Quartile ➔ 75%	16209.427083
90%	17279.300000
95%	18321.616667
Maximum ➔ 100%	20553.500000
max	20553.500000

Figure 8.11 – Descriptive statistics with custom percentiles for the daily tax passenger data

> **Quantiles versus Quartiles versus Percentiles**
>
> The terms can be confusing, but essentially both percentiles and quartiles are quantiles. Sometimes you will see people use percentiles more loosely and interchangeably with quantiles.
>
> Quartiles divide your distribution into four segments (hence the name) marked as *Q1* (25th percentile), *Q2* (50th percentile or Median), and *Q3* (75th percentile). Percentiles, on the other hand, can take any range from 0 to 100 (in pandas from 0 to 1, while in NumPy from 0 to 100), but most commonly refer to when the distribution is partitioned into 100 segments. These segments are called quantiles.
>
> The names pretty much indicate the type of partitioning (number of quantiles) applied on the distribution; for example, with four quantiles we call it quartiles, with two quantiles we call it median, with 10 quantiles we call it deciles, and with 100 quantiles we call it percentiles.

2. The NumPy library also offers the `percentile` function, which would return the value(s) for the specified percentiles. The following code explains how this can be used:

```
percentiles = [0, 5, 10, 25, 50, 75, 90, 95, 100]
np.percentile(tx, percentiles)
>>
array([ 4834.54166667, 11998.18125    , 13043.85416667,
14205.19791667,
       15299.9375    , 16209.42708333, 17279.3        ,
18321.61666667,
       20553.5        ])
```

3. In *Figure 8.10*, notice that most extreme values, potential outliers, fall below the lower fence calculated as *Q1 – (1.5 x IQR)* or above the upper fence calculated as *Q3 + (1.5 x IQR)*. IQR is calculated as the difference between *Q3* and *Q1* (*IQR = Q3 – Q1*), which determines the width of the box in the box plot. These upper and lower fences are known as **Tukey's fences**, and more specifically, they are referred to as **inner boundaries**. The **outer boundaries** also have lower *Q1 - (3.0 x IQR)* and upper *Q3 + (3.0 x IQR)* fences. We will focus on the inner boundaries and describe anything outside of those as potential outliers.

You will create a function, `iqr_outliers`, which calculates the IQR, upper (inner) fence, lower (inner) fence, and then filters the data to return the outliers. These outliers are any data points that are below the lower fence or above the upper fence:

```
def iqr_outliers(data):
    q1, q3 = np.percentile(data, [25, 75])
    IQR = q3 - q1
    lower_fence = q1 - (1.5 * IQR)
    upper_fence = q3 + (1.5 * IQR)
    return data[(data.value > upper_fence) | (data.value
< lower_fence)]
```

4. Test the function by passing the `tx` DataFrame:

```
outliers = iqr_outliers(tx)
outliers
>>
                    value
timestamp
2014-11-01   20553.500000
2014-11-27   10899.666667
2014-12-25    7902.125000
2014-12-26   10397.958333
2015-01-26    7818.979167
2015-01-27    4834.541667
```

These dates (points) are the same ones identified in *Figure 8.5* and *Figure 8.10* as outliers based on Tukey's fences.

5. Use the `plot_outliers` function defined earlier in the *Technical requirements* section:

```
plot_outliers(outliers, tx, "Outliers using IQR with
Tukey's Fences")
```

This should produce a plot similar to that in *Figure 8.3*, except the x markers are based on the outliers identified using the Tukey method:

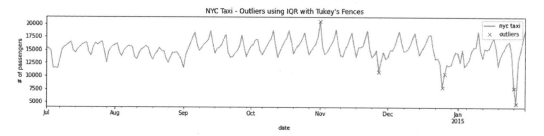

Figure 8.12 – Daily average taxi passengers and outliers identified using the Tukey method

Compare *Figures 8.12* and *8.3* and you will see that this simple method did a great job at identifying four of the five known outliers. In addition, Tukey's method identified two additional outliers on *2014-12-26* and *2015-01-26*.

How it works...

Using IQR and Tukey's fences is a simple non-parametric statistical method. Most box plot implementations use *1.5x(IQR)* to define the upper and lower fences.

There's more...

The use of *1.5x(IQR)* is common when it comes to defining outliers; the choice is still arbitrary, even though there is a lot of discussion about its reasoning. You can change the value for more experimentation. For example, in seaborn, you can change the default 1.5 value by updating the whis parameter in the boxplot function. The choice of 1.5 makes the most sense when the data follows a Gaussian distribution (normal), but this is not always the case. Generally, the larger the value, the fewer outliers you will capture as you expand your boundaries (fences). Similarly, the smaller the value, the more non-outliers will be defined as outliers, as you are shrinking the boundaries (fences).

Let's update the iqr_outliers function to accept a p parameter so you can experiment with different values:

```
def iqr_outliers(data, p):
    q1, q3 = np.percentile(data, [25, 75])
    IQR = q3 - q1
    lower_fence = q1 - (p * IQR)
    upper_fence = q3 + (p * IQR)
```

```
    return data[(data.value > upper_fence) | (data.value <
lower_fence)]
```

Run the function on different values:

```
for p in [1.3, 1.5, 2.0, 2.5,  3.0]:
    print(f'with p={p}')
    print(iqr_outliers(tx, p))
    print('-'*15)
>>
with p=1.3
                      value
timestamp
2014-07-04   11511.770833
2014-07-05   11572.291667
2014-07-06   11464.270833
2014-09-01   11589.875000
2014-11-01   20553.500000
2014-11-08   18857.333333
2014-11-27   10899.666667
2014-12-25    7902.125000
2014-12-26   10397.958333
2015-01-26    7818.979167
2015-01-27    4834.541667

---------------
with p=1.5
                      value
timestamp
2014-11-01   20553.500000
2014-11-27   10899.666667
2014-12-25    7902.125000
2014-12-26   10397.958333
2015-01-26    7818.979167
2015-01-27    4834.541667

---------------
with p=2.0
                      value
```

```
timestamp
2014-11-01   20553.500000
2014-12-25    7902.125000
2015-01-26    7818.979167
2015-01-27    4834.541667
--------------
with p=2.5
                value
timestamp
2014-12-25   7902.125000
2015-01-26   7818.979167
2015-01-27   4834.541667
--------------
with p=3.0
                value
timestamp
2014-12-25   7902.125000
2015-01-26   7818.979167
2015-01-27   4834.541667
--------------
```

The best value will depend on your data and how sensitive you need the outlier detection to be.

See also

To learn more about Tukey's fences for outlier detection, you can refer to this Wikipedia page: https://en.wikipedia.org/wiki/Outlier#Tukey's_fences.

We will explore another statistical method based on a z-score in the following recipe.

Detecting outliers using a z-score

The **z-score** is a common transformation for standardizing the data. This is common when you want to compare different datasets. For example, it is easier to compare two data points from two different datasets relative to their distributions. This can be done because the z-score standardizes the data to be centered around a zero mean and the units represent standard deviations away from the mean. For example, in our dataset, the unit is measured in daily taxi passengers (in thousands). Once you apply the z-score transformation, you are no longer dealing with the number of passengers, but rather, the units represent standard deviation, which tells us how far an observation is from the mean. Here is the formula for the z-score:

$$z = \frac{x - \mu}{\sigma}$$

Where x is a data point (an observation), mu (μ) is the mean of the dataset, and sigma (σ) is the standard deviation for the dataset.

Keep in mind that the z-score is a lossless transformation, which means you will not lose information such as its distribution (shape of the data) or the relationship between the observations. All that is changing is the units of measurement as they are being scaled (standardized).

Once the data is transformed using the z-score, you can pick a threshold. So, any data point above or below that threshold (in standard deviation) is considered an outlier. For example, your threshold can be +3 and -3 standard deviations away from the mean. Any point lower than -3 or higher than +3 standard deviation can be considered an outlier. In other words, the further a point is from the mean, the higher the probability of it being an outlier.

The z-score has one major shortcoming due to it being a parametric statistical method based on assumptions. It assumes a Gaussian (normal) distribution. So, suppose the data is not normal. In that case, you will need to use a modified version of the z-score, which is discussed in the following recipe, Detecting outliers using a modified z-score.

How to do it...

You will start by creating the `zscore` function that takes in a dataset and a threshold value that we will call `degree`. The function will return the standardized data and the identified outliers. These outliers are any points above the positive threshold or below the negative threshold.

1. Create the `zscore()` function to standardize the data and filter out the extreme values based on a threshold. Recall, the threshold is based on the standard deviation:

```
def zscore(df, degree=3):
    data = df.copy()
    data['zscore'] = (data - data.mean())/data.std()
    outliers = data[(data['zscore'] <= -degree) |
(data['zscore'] >= degree)]


    return outliers['value'], data
```

2. Now, use the `zscore` function and store the returned objects:

```
threshold = 2.5
outliers, transformed = zscore(tx, threshold)
```

3. To see the effect of the z-score transformation, you can plot a histogram. The transformed DataFrame contains two columns, the original data labeled `value` and the standardized data labeled `zscore`:

```
transformed.hist()
```

This should produce two histograms for the two columns:

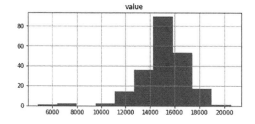 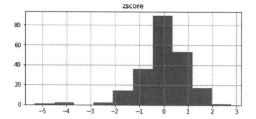

Figure 8.13 – Histogram to compare the distribution of the original and standardized data

Notice how the shape of the data did not change, hence why the z-score is called a *lossless transformation*. The only difference between the two is the scale (units).

4. You ran the `zscore` function using a threshold of `2.5`, meaning any data point that is 2.5 standard deviations away from the mean in either direction. For example, any data point that is above the `+2.5` standard deviations or below the `-2.5` standard deviations will be considered an outlier. Print out the results captured in the `outliers` object:

```
print(outliers)
>>
timestamp
2014-11-01    20553.500000
2014-12-25     7902.125000
2015-01-26     7818.979167
2015-01-27     4834.541667
Name: value, dtype: float64
```

This simple method managed to capture three out of the five known outliers.

5. Use the `plot_outliers` function defined earlier in the *Technical requirements* section:

```
plot_outliers(outliers, tx, "Outliers using Z-score")
```

This should produce a plot similar to that in *Figure 8.3*, except the x markers are based on the outliers identified using the z-score method:

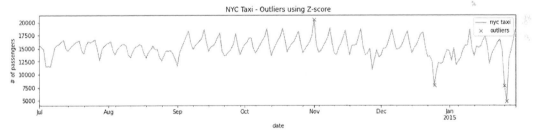

Figure 8.14 – Daily average taxi passengers and outliers identified using the z-score method

You will need to play around to determine the best threshold value. The larger the threshold, the fewer outliers you will capture, and the smaller the threshold, the more non-outliers will be labeled as outliers.

6. Finally, let's create a `plot_zscore` function that takes the standardized data to plot the data with the threshold lines. This way you can visually see how the threshold is isolating extreme values:

```
def plot_zscore(data, d=3):
```

```
n = len(data)
plt.figure(figsize=(8,8))
plt.plot(data,'k^')
plt.plot([0,n],[d,d],'r--')
plt.plot([0,n],[-d,-d],'r--')
```

Run the function using a threshold of 2.5:

```
data = transformed['zscore'].values
plot_zscore(data, d=2.5)
```

This should produce a scatter plot with two horizontal lines:

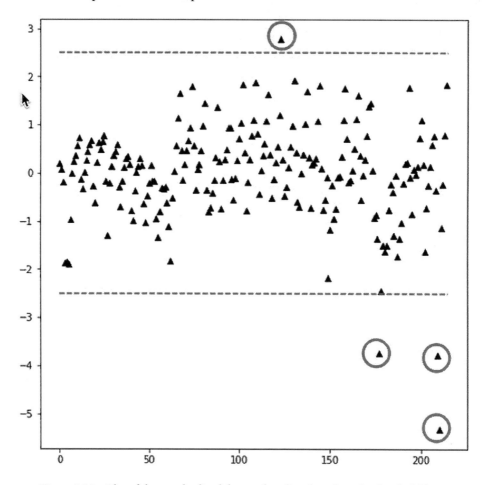

Figure 8.15 – Plot of the standardized data and outliers based on the threshold lines

The four circled data points represent the outliers that were returned by the `zscore` function. Run the function using different threshold values to gain a deeper understanding of this simple technique.

How it works...

The z-score method is a very simple and interpretable method. The z-scores are interpreted as standard deviation units away from the mean, which is the center of the distribution. Since we are subtracting the mean from all observations, we are essentially mean-centering the data. We also divide by the standard deviation to standardize the data.

Figure 8.15 pretty much explains the understanding of this method. Once the data is standardized, it became easy to just use the standard deviation threshold. If the data was not standardized, it may have been challenging to determine the threshold based on daily passengers.

There's more...

The z-score is a parametric method and assumes the data comes from a Gaussian (normal) distribution. There are several tests available in the `statsmodels` library to test if the data is normally distributed. One of these tests is the *Kolmogorov-Smirnov* test. The null hypothesis is that the data comes from a normal distribution. The test returns the test statistics and a p-value; if the p-value is less than 0.05, you can reject the null hypothesis (data is not normally distributed). Otherwise, you would fail to reject the null hypothesis (data is normally distributed).

You will use the `kstest_normal` function from the `statsmodels` library. To make the results easier to interpret, create the `test_normal` function as follows:

```
from statsmodels.stats.diagnostic import kstest_normal
def test_normal(df):
    t_test, p_value = kstest_normal(df)
    if p_value < 0.05:
        print("Reject null hypothesis. Data is not normal")
    else:
"       print("Fail to reject null hypothesis. Data is normal")
```

Run the test using the `test_normal` function:

```
test_normal(tx)
>>
Reject null hypothesis. Data is not normal
```

As expected, the dataset is not normally distributed. In *Chapter 9*, *Exploratory Data Analysis and Diagnosis*, you will learn about additional normality tests under the *Applying power transformations* recipe. But do be cautious; these tests will usually fail in the presence of outliers. If your data fails a normality test, then use some of the plotting methods discussed in the *Detecting outliers using visualizations* recipe to examine any outliers that may be causing the test to fail.

See also

To read more about z-scores and standardization, you can refer to this Wikipedia page: `https://en.wikipedia.org/wiki/Standard_score`.

In the following recipe, you will explore a very similar method to the z-score that is more robust to outliers and is more suitable with non-normal data.

Detecting outliers using a modified z-score

In the *Detecting outliers using a z-score* recipe, you experienced how simple and intuitive the method is. But it has one major drawback: it assumes your data is normally distributed.

But, what if your data is not normally distributed? Luckily, there is a modified version of the z-score to work with non-normal data. The main difference between the regular z-score and the modified z-score is that we replace the mean with the median:

$$Modified\ Z = \frac{0.6745(x_i - \tilde{x})}{\text{MAD}}$$

Where $\tilde{x}$ (*tilde x*) is the median of the dataset, and MAD is the median absolute deviation of the dataset:

$$MAD = median\big(abs(x_i - \tilde{x})\big)$$

The `0.6745` value is the standard deviation unit that corresponds to the 75th percentile (*Q3*) in a Gaussian distribution and is used as a normalization factor. In other words, it is used to approximate the standard deviation. This way, the units you obtain from this method are measured in standard deviation, similar to how you would interpret the regular z-score.

You can obtain this value using SciPy's **percent point function** (**PPF**), also known as the inverse of the **cumulative distribution function** (**CDF**). Simply give the PPF function a percentile, for example, 75%, and it will return the quantile corresponding to the lower tail probability.

```
import scipy.stats as stats
stats.norm.ppf(0.75)
>>
0.6744897501960817
```

This is the normalization factor used in the formula.

Lastly, the modified z-score is sometimes referred to as the **robust z-score**.

How to do it...

Overall, the approach will work exactly as the steps used when using the standard z-score method. You will start by creating the modified_zscore function that takes in a dataset, and a threshold value we will call degree, and the function will return the standardized data as well as the identified outliers. These outliers are any points above the positive threshold or below the negative threshold.

1. Create the modified_zscore () function to standardize the data and filter out the extreme values based on a threshold. Recall, the threshold is based on the standard deviation:

```
def modified_zscore(df, degree=3):
    data = df.copy()
    s = stats.norm.ppf(0.75)
    numerator = s*(data - data.median())
    MAD = np.abs(data - data.median()).median()
    data['m_zscore'] = numerator/MAD
    outliers = data[(data['m_zscore'] > degree) |
(data['m_zscore'] < -degree)]

    return outliers['value'], data
```

2. Now, use the modified_zscore function and store the returned objects:

```
threshold = 3
outliers, transformed = modified_zscore (tx, threshold)
```

3. To see the effect of the modified z-score transformation, let's plot a histogram. The transformed DataFrame contains two columns, the original data labeled `value` and the standardized data labeled `zscore`.

```
transformed.hist()
```

This should produce two histograms for the two columns:

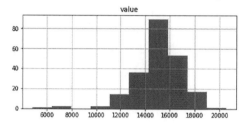 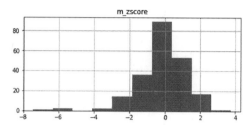

Figure 8.16 – Histogram to compare the distribution of the original and modified z-score standardized data

Compare the results from *Figure 8.16* with *Figure 8.13*. Both approaches, the z-score and modified z-score approaches, do not change the shape of the data. The difference is in the scaling factor.

4. Run the `modified_zscore` function using a threshold of 3, meaning any data point three standard deviations away from the mean in either direction. For example, any data point above +3 standard deviations or below –3 standard deviations will be considered an outlier. Print out the results captured in the `outliers` object:

```
print(outliers)
>>
timestamp
2014-11-01    20553.500000
2014-11-27    10899.666667
2014-12-25     7902.125000
2014-12-26    10397.958333
2015-01-26     7818.979167
2015-01-27     4834.541667
Name: value, dtype: float64
```

Interestingly, the modified z-score did a much better job capturing four out of the five known outliers.

5. Use the `plot_outliers` function defined earlier in the *Technical requirements* section:

```
plot_outliers(outliers, tx, "Outliers using Modified
Z-score")
```

This should produce a plot similar to that in *Figure 8.3*, except the **x** markers are based on the outliers identified using the modified z-score method:

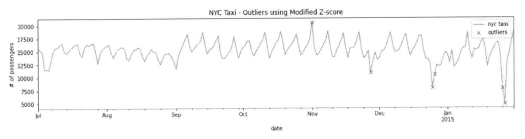

Figure 8.17 – Daily average taxi passengers and outliers identified using the z-score method

You will need to play around to determine the best threshold value. The larger the threshold, the fewer outliers you will capture, and the smaller the threshold, the more non-outliers will be labeled as outliers.

6. Finally, let's create a `plot_zscore` function that takes the standardized data to plot the data with the threshold lines. This way you can visually see how the threshold is isolating extreme values:

```
def plot_m_zscore(data, d=3):
    n = len(data)
    plt.figure(figsize=(8,8))
    plt.plot(data,'k^')
    plt.plot([0,n],[d,d],'r--')
    plt.plot([0,n],[-d,-d],'r--')
```

Run the function using a threshold of 3:

```
data = transformed['m_zscore'].values
plot_m_zscore(data, d=2.5)
```

This should produce a scatter plot with two horizontal lines:

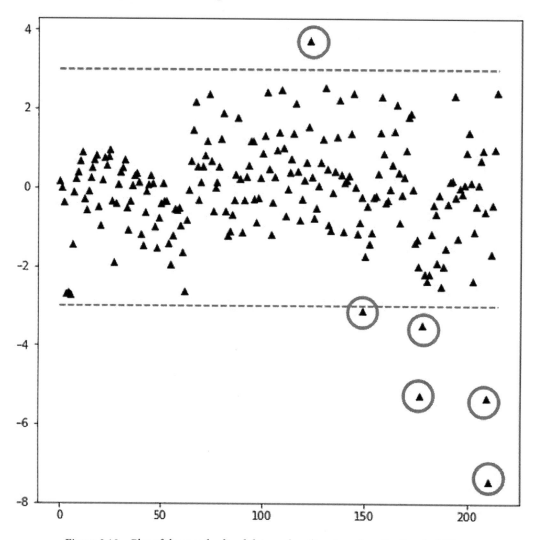

Figure 8.18 – Plot of the standardized data and outliers based on the threshold lines

The six circled data points represent the outliers that were returned by the `modified_score` function. Run the function using different threshold values to gain more profound intuition into this simple technique.

Notice in *Figure 8.18* how we have a data point that is right at the threshold line. Would you consider this an outlier? Generally, when it comes to outlier detection you will still need to apply due diligence to inspect the results.

How it works...

The modified z-score (robust z-score) method is very similar to the z-score approach, as it depends on defining a standard deviation threshold. What makes this method more robust to outliers is the use of the median instead of the mean. We also use the **median absolute deviation** (**MAD**) instead of the standard deviation.

There's more...

In the previous recipe, *Detecting outliers using a z-score*, we used `kstest_normal` from `statsmodels` to test normality.

Another helpful plot that is specifically designed to test for normality and sometimes can help detect outliers is the **Quantile-Quantile plot** (**QQ-plot**).

You can plot a QQ-plot using SciPy or `statsmodels`. Both will produce the same plot. The following code will show you can plot using either.

This shows how you can plot using SciPy:

```
import scipy
import matplotlib.pyplot as plt
res = scipy.stats.probplot(tx.values.reshape(-1), plot=plt)
```

This shows how you can plot using `statsmodels`:

```
from statsmodels.graphics.gofplots import qqplot
qqplot(tx.values.reshape(-1), line='s')
plt.show()
```

Both SciPy and `statsmodels` will produce the following plot:

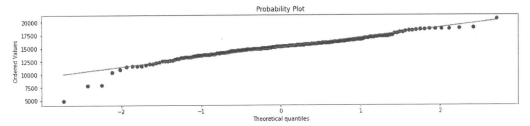

Figure 8.19 – QQ-plot comparing the taxi passenger data against a hypothetical normal distribution

The solid line represents a reference line for what normally distributed data would look like. If the data you are comparing is normally distributed, all the points will lie on that straight line. In *Figure 8.19*, we can see that the distribution is almost normal (not perfect), and we see issues toward the distribution's tails. This also aligns with what we have seen in *Figure 8.16* and *Figure 8.13*, showing the majority of the outliers are at the bottom tail end (less than -2 standard deviation).

See also

To learn more about MAD, you can refer to the Wikipedia page here: `https://en.wikipedia.org/wiki/Median_absolute_deviation`.

9
Exploratory Data Analysis and Diagnosis

So far, we have covered techniques to extract data from various sources. This was covered in *Chapter 2, Reading Time Series Data from Files*, and *Chapter 3, Reading Time Series Data from Databases*. *Chapter 6, Working with Date and Time in Python*, and *Chapter 7, Handling Missing Data*, covered several techniques to help prepare, clean, and adjust data.

You will continue to explore additional techniques to better understand the time series process behind the data. Before modeling the data or doing any further analysis, an important step is to inspect the data at hand. More specifically, there are specific time series characteristics that you need to check for, such as stationarity, effects of trend and seasonality, and autocorrelation, to name a few. These characteristics that describe the time series process you are working with need to be combined with domain knowledge behind the process itself.

This chapter will build on what you have learned from previous chapters to prepare you for creating and evaluating forecasting models starting from *Chapter 10, Building Univariate Time Series Models Using Statistical Methods*.

In this chapter, you will learn how to visualize time series data, decompose a time series into its components (trend, seasonality, and residuals), test for different assumptions that your models may rely on (such as stationarity, normality, and homoskedasticity), and explore techniques to transform the data to satisfy some of these assumptions.

The recipes that you will encounter in this chapter are as follows:

- Plotting time series data using pandas

- Plotting time series data with interactive visualizations using hvPlot

- Decomposing time series data

- Detecting time series stationarity

- Applying power transformations

- Testing for autocorrelation in time series data

Technical requirements

You can download the Jupyter notebooks and datasets needed from the GitHub repository to follow along:

- Jupyter notebooks: `https://github.com/PacktPublishing/Time-Series-Analysis-with-Python-Cookbook./blob/main/code/Ch9/Chapter%209.ipynb`

- Datasets: `https://github.com/PacktPublishing/Time-Series-Analysis-with-Python-Cookbook./tree/main/datasets/Ch9`

In this chapter and onward, we will extensively use pandas 1.4.2 (released April 2, 2022). This applies to all the recipes in the chapter.

There are four additional libraries that we will be using:

- `hvplot` and `PyViz`

- `seaborn`

- `matplotlib`

If you are using `pip`, then you can install these packages from your terminal with the following:

```
pip install hvplot seaborn matplotlib jupyter plotly==5.5.0
```

If you are using `conda`, then you can install these packages with the following:

```
conda install -c conda-forge seaborn
conda install -c plotly plotly=5.5.0
conda install -c pyviz hvplot
```

The visualizations should work in Jupyter notebooks, but if you plan to use JupyterLab, then you will need to install an additional extension, `jupyterlab_pyviz`:

```
conda install jupyterlab
jupyter labextension install @pyviz/jupyterlab_pyviz
```

Throughout this chapter, you will be using three datasets (*Closing Price Stock Data*, *CO2*, and *Air Passengers*). The CO2 and Air Passengers datasets are provided with the `statsmodels` library. The Air Passengers dataset contains monthly airline passenger numbers from 1949 to 1960. The CO2 dataset contains weekly atmospheric carbon dioxide levels on Mauna Loa. The Closing Price Stock Data dataset includes Microsoft, Apple, and IBM stock prices from November 2019 to November 2021.

To get started, you will need to load the datasets and store them as pandas DataFrames and load any libraries or methods that are needed throughout:

```
import pandas as pd
from pathlib import Path
import matplotlib.pyplot as plt
from statsmodels.datasets import co2, get_rdataset

file = Path('../../datasets/Ch9/closing_price.csv')
closing_price = pd.read_csv(file,
                            index_col='Date',
                            parse_dates=True)

co2_df = co2.load_pandas().data
co2_df = co2_df.ffill()
```

```
air_passengers = get_rdataset("AirPassengers")
airp_df = air_passengers.data
airp_df.index = pd.date_range('1949', '1961', freq='M')
airp_df.drop(columns=['time'], inplace=True)
```

Now, you should have three DataFrames: `airp_df`, `closing_price`, and `co2_df`.

Plotting time series data using pandas

The pandas library offers built-in plotting capabilities for visualizing data stored in a DataFrame or Series data structure. In the backend, these visualizations are powered by the **Matplotlib** library, which is also the default option.

The pandas library offers many convenient methods to plot data. Simply calling `DataFrame.plot()` or `Series.plot()` will generate a line plot by default. You can change the type of the plot in two ways:

- Using the `.plot(kind="<sometype>")` parameter to specify the type of plot by replacing `<sometype>` with a chart type. For example, `.plot(kind="hist")` will plot a histogram while `.plot(kind="bar")` will produce a bar plot.

- Alternatively, you can extend `.plot()`. This can be achieved by chaining a specific plot function, such as `.hist()` or `.scatter()`, for example, using `.plot.hist()` or `.plot.line()`.

This recipe will use the standard pandas `.plot()` method with Matplotlib backend support.

Getting ready

You can download the Jupyter notebooks and datasets needed from the GitHub repository. Please refer to the *Technical requirements* section of this chapter.

You will be using the stock data for Microsoft, Apple, and IBM, which you can find in the `closing_price.csv` file.

How to do it...

In this recipe, you will explore how to plot time series data, change themes, produce subplots, and customize the output visualization:

1. Plotting in pandas can be done by simply adding `.plot()` to the end of the DataFrame or Series name:

    ```
    closing_price.plot()
    ```

    This will produce a line plot, which is the default option for the `kind` parameter, which looks like `.plot(kind="line")`:

Figure 9.1 – Multiline time series plot using pandas

2. If you want to see how the prices fluctuate (up or down) in comparison to each other, one easy approach is to **normalize** the data. To accomplish this, just divide the stock prices by the first-day price (first row) for each stock. This will make all the stocks have the same starting point:

    ```
    closing_price_n = closing_price.div(closing_price.
    iloc[0])
    closing_price_n.plot(figsize=fig_dims)
    ```

This would produce the following plot:

Figure 9.2 – Simple normalizing technique to make it visually easier to compare price fluctuation

From the output, you can observe that the lines now have the same starting point (origin), set to 1. The plot shows how the prices in the time series plot deviate from each other:

```
closing_price_n.head()
```

Notice that the first row from the output table is set to 1.0:

	AAPL	MSFT	IBM
Date			
2019-11-01	1.000000	1.000000	1.000000
2019-11-04	1.006567	1.005775	1.015790
2019-11-05	1.005121	1.005149	1.017413
2019-11-06	1.005551	1.002366	1.023980
2019-11-07	1.017156	1.003757	1.027937

Figure 9.3 – Output of normalized time series with a common starting point at 1

3. Additionally, Matplotlib allows you to change the style of the plots. To do that, you can use the `style.use` function. You can specify a style name from an existing template or use a custom style. For example, the following code shows how you can change from the `default` style to the `ggplot` style:

```
plt.style.use('ggplot')
closing_price_n.plot()
```

The preceding code should produce the same plot in terms of data content but a different style.

Figure 9.4 – Using the ggplot style from Matplotlib

The ggplot style was inspired by the ggplot2 package from **R**.

You can explore other attractive styles: fivethirtyeight, which is inspired by **fivethirtyeight.com**, dark_background, seaborn-dark, and tableau-colorblind10. For a comprehensive list of available style sheets, you can reference the Matplotlib documentation here: https://matplotlib.org/stable/gallery/style_sheets/style_sheets_reference.html.

If you want to revert to the original theme, you specify plt.style.use("default").

4. You can customize the plot further by adding a title, updating the axes labels, and customizing the *x* ticks and *y* ticks, to name a few.

    Add a title and a label to the *y* axis, then save it as a .jpg file:

```
plot = closing_price_n.plot(figsize=fig_dims,
            title=f'Stock Prices from {start_date} -
{end_date}',
            ylabel= 'Norm. Price')
plot.get_figure().savefig('plot_1.jpg')
```

The plot should be saved as a plot_1.jpg image file on your local directory.

How it works...

There is good collaboration between pandas and Matplotlib, with an ambition to integrate and add more plotting capabilities within pandas.

There are many plotting styles that you can use within pandas simply by providing a value to the `kind` argument. For example, you can specify the following:

- `line` for line charts commonly used to display time series
- `bar` or `barh` (horizontal) for bar plots
- `hist` for histogram plots
- `box` for boxplots
- `kde` or `density` for kernel density estimation plots
- `area` for area plots
- `pie` for pie plots
- `scatter` for scatter plots
- `hexbin` for hexagonal bin plots

There's more...

As observed in the previous section, we plotted all three columns in the time series in one plot (three line charts in the same plot). What if you want each symbol (column) plotted separately?

This can be done by simply changing the `subplots` parameter to `True`:

```
closing_price.plot(figsize=fig_dims, subplots=True)
```

The preceding code will generate a subplot for each column in the DataFrame. For the `closing_price` DataFrame, this will generate three subplots.

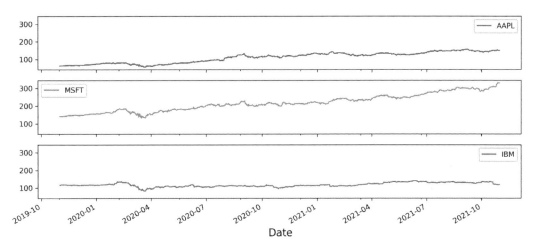

Figure 9.5 – Using the pandas subplot feature

See also

To learn more about pandas charting and plotting capabilities, please visit the official documentation here: `https://pandas.pydata.org/pandas-docs/stable/user_guide/visualization.html`.

Plotting time series data with interactive visualizations using hvPlot

In this recipe, you will explore the hvPlot library to create interactive visualizations. hvPlot works well with pandas DataFrames to render interactive visualizations with minimal effort. You will be using the same `closing_price.csv` dataset to explore the library.

Getting ready

You can download the Jupyter notebooks and datasets needed from the GitHub repository. Please refer to the *Technical requirements* section of this chapter.

How to do it...

1. Start by importing the libraries needed. Notice that hvPlot has a pandas extension, which makes it more convenient. This will allow you to use the same syntax as in the previous recipe:

```
import pandas as pd
import hvplot.pandas
import hvplot as hv


closing_price_n = closing_price.div(closing_price.
iloc[0])
```

When plotting using pandas, you use the `.plot()` method, for example, `closing_price_n.plot()`. Similarly, hvPlot allows you to render an interactive plot simply by substituting `.plot()` with `.hvplot()`. This can be useful if you have a dense chart in terms of content. You can zoom in to a specific portion of the chart and then, with the panning feature, move to different portions of the chart:

```
closing_price_n.hvplot(
    title='Time Series plot using hvplot'
)
```

By substituting `.plot` with `.hvplot`, you get an interactive visualization with a hover effect:

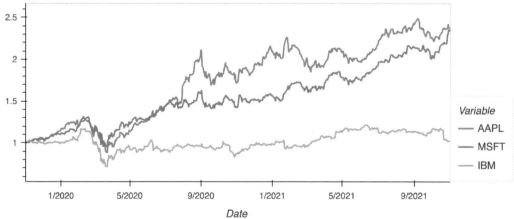

Figure 9.6 – hvPlot interactive visualization

The same result could be accomplished simply by switching the pandas plotting backend. The default backend is `matplotlib`. To switch it to hvPlot, you can just update `backend='hvplot'`:

```
closing_price_n.plot(backend='hvplot',
                     title='Time Series plot using
hvplot')
```

This should produce the same plot as in *Figure 9.6*.

Notice the widget bar to the right, which has a set of modes for interaction, including pan, box zoom, wheel zoom, save, reset, and hover.

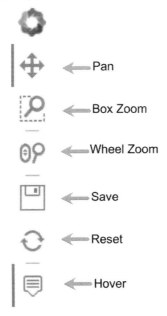

Figure 9.7 – Widget bar with six modes of interaction

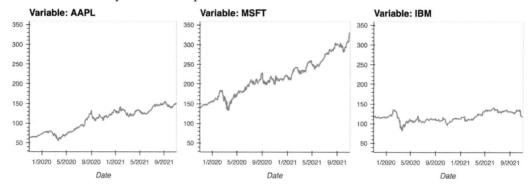

2. You can split each time series into separate plots per symbol (column). For example, to split into three columns one for each symbol (or ticker): MSFT, AAPL, and IBM. Subplotting can be done by specifying `subplots=True`:

```
closing_price.hvplot(width=300, subplots=True)
```

This should produce a subplot for each column:

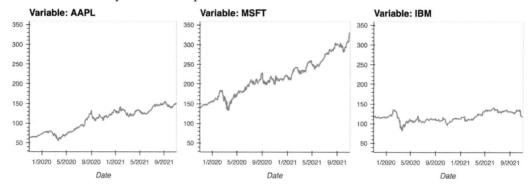

Figure 9.8 – hvPlot subplot example

You can use the `.cols()` method for more control over the layout. The method allows you to control the number of plots per row. For example, `.cols(1)` means one plot per row, whereas `.cols(2)` indicates two plots per line:

```
closing_price.hvplot(width=300, subplots=True).cols(2)
```

This should produce a figure with two subplots in the first row and the third subplot on the second row, as follows:

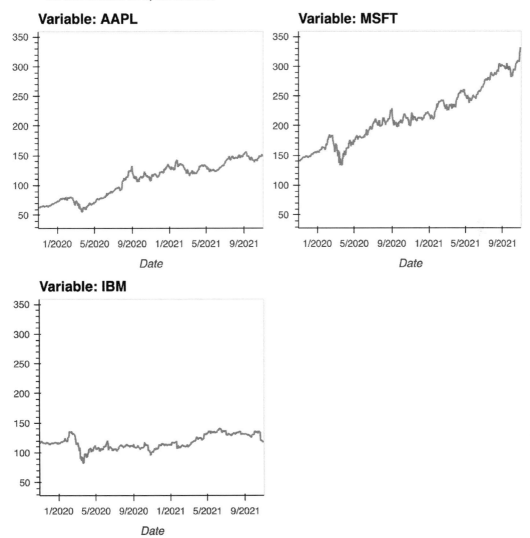

Figure 9.9 – Example hvPlot with two columns per row using .col(2)

Keep in mind that the .cols() method only works if the subplots parameter is set to True. Otherwise, you will get an error.

How it works...

Due to pandas' popularity, you will notice that many libraries now support pandas DataFrames and Series as inputs. Furthermore, the integration between Matplotlib and hvPlot makes switching the plotting engine for pandas easy.

hvPlot offers convenient options for plotting your DataFrame: switching the backend, extending pandas with `DataFrame.hvplot()`, or using hvPlot's native API.

There's more...

hvPlot allows you to use two arithmetic operators, + and *, to configure the layout of the plots.

The plus sign (+) allows you to add two charts side by side, while multiply (*) will enable you to combine charts (merge one graph with another). In the following example, we will add two plots, so they are aligned side by side on the same row:

```
(closing_price_n['AAPL'].hvplot(width=400) +
  closing_price_n['MSFT'].hvplot(width=400))
```

This should produce what is shown in the following figure:

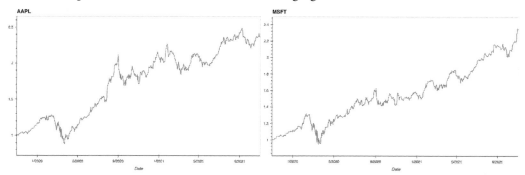

Figure 9.10 – Two plots side by side using the addition operator

Notice that the two plots will share the same widget bar. If you filter or zoom into one of the charts, the other chart will have the same action applied.

Now, let's see how multiplication will combine the two plots into one:

```
(closing_price_n['AAPL'].hvplot(width=400) *
 closing_price_n['MSFT'].hvplot(width=400))
```

The preceding code should produce one plot that combines both AAPL and MSFT:

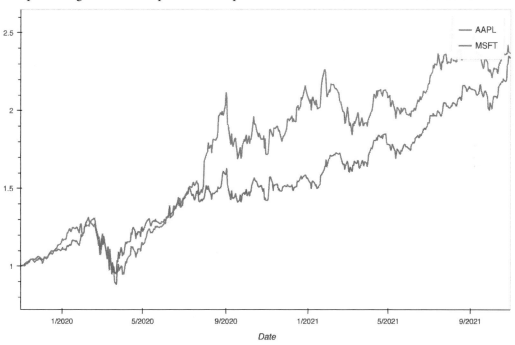

Figure 9.11 – Two plots combined into one using the multiplication operator

See also

For more information on hvPlot, please visit their official page here: `https://hvplot.holoviz.org/`.

Decomposing time series data

When performing time series analysis, one of your objectives may be forecasting, where you build a model to make a future prediction. Before starting the modeling process, you will need to extract the components of the time series process for analysis. This will help you make informed decisions during the modeling process. In addition, there are three major components for any time series process: trend, seasonality, and residual.

Trend gives a sense of the long-term direction of the time series and can be either upward, downward, or horizontal. For example, a time series of sales data can show an upward (increasing) trend. **Seasonality** is repeated patterns over time. For example, a time series of sales data might show an increase in sales around Christmas time. This phenomenon can be observed every year (annually) as we approach Christmas. The **residual** is simply the remaining or unexplained portion once we extract trend and seasonality.

The **decomposition** of a time series is the process of extracting the three components and representing them as their models. The modeling of the decomposed components can be either additive or multiplicative.

You have an *additive* model when the original time series can be reconstructed by adding all three components:

$$y_t = T_t + S_t + R_t$$

An additive decomposition model is reasonable when the seasonal variations do not change over time. On the other hand, if the time series can be reconstructed by multiplying all three components, you have a *multiplicative* model:

$$y_t = T_t \times S_t \times R_t$$

A *multiplicative* model is suitable when the seasonal variation fluctuates over time.

Furthermore, you can group these into predictable versus non-predictable components. Predictable components are consistent, repeating patterns that can be captured and modeled. Seasonality and trend are examples. On the other hand, every time series has an unpredictable component that shows irregularity, often called **noise**, though it is referred to as **residual** in the context of decomposition.

In this recipe, you will explore different techniques for **decomposing** your time series using the `seasonal_decompose`, **Seasonal-Trend decomposition with LOESS (STL)**, and `hp_filter` methods available in the `statsmodels` library.

Getting ready

You can download the Jupyter notebooks and datasets needed from the GitHub repository. Please refer to the *Technical requirements* section of this chapter.

How to do it...

You will start with statsmodels' `seasonal_decompose` approach:

1. Import the libraries needed and set `.rcParams` for the visuals to make them large enough. Generally, plots produced by statsmodels are small. You can fix this by adjusting `.rcParams` for `figure.figsize` to apply for all the plots in this recipe:

```
from statsmodels.tsa.seasonal import seasonal_decompose,
STL
plt.rcParams["figure.figsize"] = (10,3)
```

This will make all the charts in the notebook the same size: width at 10 inches and height at 3 inches (*W x H*).

2. You can decompose both datasets using the `seasonal_decompose()` function. But before doing so, you should plot your time series first to understand whether the seasonality shows *multiplicative* or *additive* behavior:

```
co2_df.plot()
```

This should display a line chart showing weekly carbon dioxide levels measured in **parts per million (ppm)** from 1960 to 2000. When using the `.plot()` method, the default chart type is a line chart with the `kind="line"` parameter. For more information about pandas' plotting capabilities, refer to the *Plotting time series data using pandas* recipe.

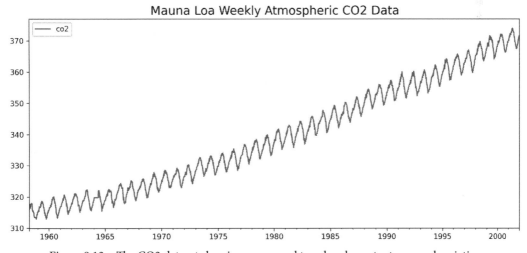

Figure 9.12 – The CO2 dataset showing an upward trend and constant seasonal variation

The `co2_df` data shows a long-term linear (upward) trend, with a repeated seasonal pattern at a constant rate (seasonal variation). This indicates that the CO2 dataset is an additive model.

Similarly, you can explore the `airp_df` DataFrame for the Air Passengers dataset to observe whether the seasonality shows *multiplicative* or *additive* behavior:

```
airp_df['value'].plot()
```

This should produce a line chart showing the number of passengers per month from 1949 to 1960:

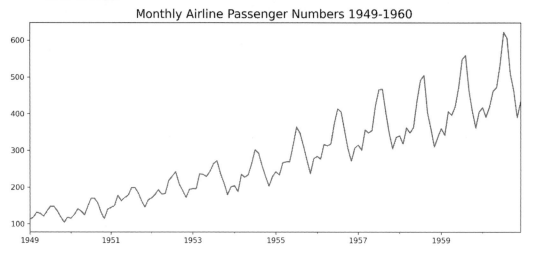

Figure 9.13 – The Air Passengers dataset showing trend and increasing seasonal variation

The `airp_df` data shows a long-term linear (upward) trend and seasonality. However, the seasonality fluctuations seem to be increasing as well, indicating a multiplicative model.

3. Use `seasonal_decompose` on the two datasets. For the CO2 data, use an additive model and a multiplicative model for the air passenger data:

```
co2_decomposed = seasonal_decompose(co2_
df,model='additive')
air_decomposed = seasonal_decompose(airp_
df,model='multiplicative')
```

Both `co2_decomposed` and `air_decomposed` have access to several methods, including `.trend`, `.seasonal`, and `.resid`. You can plot all three components by using the `.plot()` method:

```
air_decomposed.plot(); plt.show()
```

The following plot is the result:

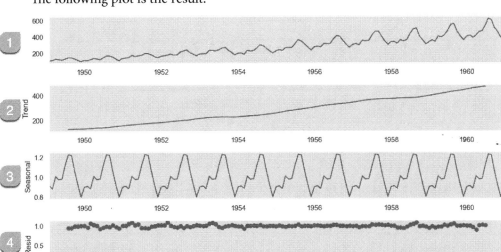

Figure 9.14 – Air Passengers multiplicative decomposed into trend, seasonality, and residual

Let's break down the resulting plot into four parts:

1. This is the original observed data that we are decomposing.

2. The *trend* component shows an upward direction. The trend indicates whether there is positive (increasing or upward), negative (decreasing or downward), or constant (no trend or horizontal) long-term movement.

3. The *seasonal* component shows the seasonality effect and the repeating pattern of highs and lows.

4. Finally, the *residual* (*noise*) component shows the random variation in the data after applying the model. In this case, a multiplicative model was used.

Similarly, you can plot the decomposition of the CO2 dataset:

```
co2_decomposed.plot(); plt.show()
```

This should produce the following plots:

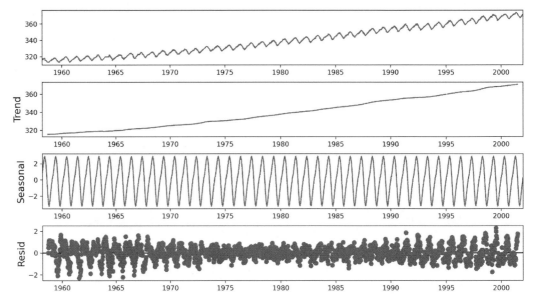

Figure 9.15 – CO2 additive decomposed into trend, seasonality, and residual

5. When reconstructing the time series, for example, in a multiplicative model, you will be multiplying the three components. To demonstrate this concept, use `air_decomposed`, an instance of the `DecomposeResult` class. The class provides the `seasonal`, `trend`, and `resid` attributes as well as the `.plot()` method.

In the following code, you can multiply the components to reconstruct the time series:

```
(air_decomposed.trend *
 air_decomposed.seasonal *
 air_decomposed.resid).plot()
```

It gives the following plot as output:

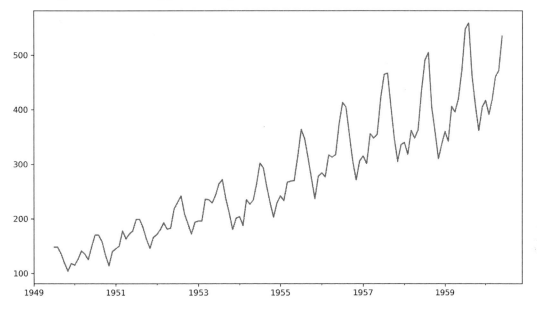

Figure 9.16 – Reconstructing the Air Passengers time series dataset

6. Another decomposition option within statsmodels is STL, which is a more advanced decomposition technique. In statsmodels, the STL class requires additional parameters than the seasonal_decompose function. The two other parameters you will use are seasonal and robust. The seasonal parameter is for the seasonal smoother and can *only take odd integer values greater than or equal to 7*. Similarly, the STL function has a trend smoother (the trend parameter).

The second parameter is robust, which takes a Boolean value (True or False). Setting robust=True helps remove the impact of outliers on seasonal and trend components when calculated. You will use STL to decompose the co2_df DataFrame:

```
co2_stl = STL(
    co2_df,
    seasonal=13,
    robust=True).fit()
co2_stl.plot(); plt.show()
```

This should produce similar subplots to the `seasonal_decompose` function, showing the trend, seasonality, and residuals:

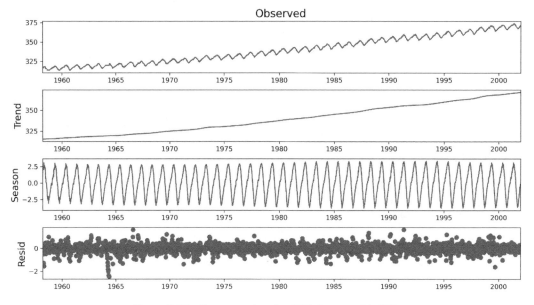

Figure 9.17 – Decomposing the CO2 dataset with STL

Compare the output in *Figure 9.16* to that in *Figure 9.15*. You will notice that the residual plots look different, indicating that both methods capture similar information using distinct mechanisms. When you used STL, you provided `seasonal=13` because the data has an annual seasonal effect.

How it works...

You used two different approaches for time series decomposition. Both methods decompose a time series into trend, seasonal, and residual components.

The STL class uses the **LOESS** seasonal smoother, which stands for **Locally Estimated Scatterplot Smoothing**. STL is more robust than `seasonal_decompose` for measuring non-linear relationships. On the other hand, STL assumes additive composition, so you do not need to indicate a model, unlike with `seasonal_decompose`.

Both approaches can extract seasonality from time series to better observe the overall trend in the data.

There's more...

The Hodrick-Prescott filter is a smoothing filter that can be used to separate short-term fluctuations (cyclic variations) from long-term trends. This is implemented as hp_filter in the statsmodels library.

Recall that STL and seasonal_decompose returned three components (trend, seasonal, and residual). On the other hand, hp_filter returns two components: a *cyclical* component and a *trend* component.

Start by importing the hpfilter function from the statsmodels library:

```
from statsmodels.tsa.filters.hp_filter import hpfilter
plt.rcParams["figure.figsize"] = (20,3)
co2_cyclic, co2_trend = hpfilter(co2_df)
```

The hpfilter function returns two pandas Series: the first Series is for the cycle and the second Series is for the trend. Plot co2_cyclic and co2_trend side by side to gain a better idea of what information the Hodrick-Prescott filter was able to extract from the data:

```
fig, ax = plt.subplots(1,2)
co2_cyclic.plot(ax=ax[0], title='CO2 Cyclic Component')
co2_trend.plot(ax=ax[1], title='CO2 Trend Component')
ax[0].title.set_size(20); ax[1].title.set_size(20)
```

This should produce two subplots on the same row (side by side), as shown:

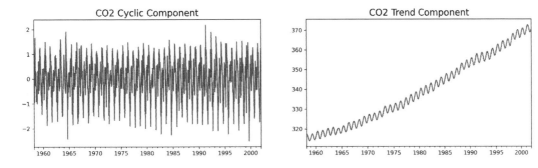

Figure 9.18 – Cyclical and trend components using the Hedrick-Prescott filter

Note that the two components from hp_filter are additive. In other words, to reconstruct the original time series, you would add co2_cyclic and co2_trend.

See also

- To learn more about `hpfilter()`, please visit the official documentation page here: `https://www.statsmodels.org/dev/generated/statsmodels.tsa.filters.hp_filter.hpfilter.html#statsmodels.tsa.filters.hp_filter.hpfilter`.

- To learn more about `seasonal_decompose()`, please visit the official documentation page here: `https://www.statsmodels.org/dev/generated/statsmodels.tsa.seasonal.seasonal_decompose.html`.

- To learn more about `STL()`, please visit the official documentation page here: `https://www.statsmodels.org/dev/generated/statsmodels.tsa.seasonal.STL.html#statsmodels.tsa.seasonal.STL`.

Detecting time series stationarity

Several time series forecasting techniques assume **stationarity**. This makes it essential to understand whether the time series you are working with is **stationary** or **non-stationary**.

A stationary time series implies that specific statistical properties do not vary over time and remain steady, making the processes easier to model and predict. On the other hand, a non-stationary process is more complex to model due to the dynamic nature and variations over time (for example, in the presence of trend or seasonality).

There are different approaches for defining stationarity; some are strict and may not be possible to observe in real-world data, referred to as *strong stationarity*. In contrast, other definitions are more modest in their criteria and can be observed in (or transformed into) real-world data, known as *weak stationarity*.

In this recipe, and for practical reasons, a stationary time series is defined as a time series with a constant mean (μ), a constant variance (σ^2), and a consistent covariance (or autocorrelation) between identical distanced periods (*lags*). Having the mean and variance as constants simplifies modeling since you are not solving for them as functions of time.

Generally, a time series with trend or seasonality can be considered non-stationary. Usually, spotting trends or seasonality visually in a plot can help you determine whether the time series is stationary or not. In such cases, a simple line plot would suffice. But in this recipe, you will explore statistical tests to help you identify a stationary or non-stationary time series numerically. You will explore testing for stationarity and techniques for making a time series stationary.

You will explore two statistical tests, the **Augmented Dickey-Fuller (ADF)** test and the **Kwiatkowski-Phillips-Schmidt-Shin (KPSS)** test, using the `statsmodels` library. Both ADF and KPSS test for unit roots in a univariate time series process. Note that unit roots are just one cause for a time series to be non-stationary, but generally, the presence of unit roots indicates non-stationarity.

Both ADF and KPSS are based on linear regression and are a type of statistical hypothesis test. For example, the **null hypothesis** for ADF states that there is a unit root in the time series, and thus, it is non-stationary. On the other hand, KPSS has the opposite null hypothesis, which assumes the time series is stationary. Therefore, you will need to interpret the test results to determine whether you can reject or fail to reject the null hypothesis. Generally, you can rely on the p-values returned to decide whether you reject or fail to reject the null hypothesis. Remember, the interpretation for ADF and KPSS results is different given their opposite null hypotheses.

Getting ready

You can download the Jupyter notebooks and datasets needed from the GitHub repository. Please refer to the *Technical requirements* section of this chapter.

In this recipe, you will be using the CO2 dataset, which was previously loaded as a pandas DataFrame under the *Technical requirements* section of this chapter.

How to do it...

In addition to the visual interpretation of a time series plot to determine stationarity, a more concrete method would be to use one of the *unit root tests*, such as the ADF KPSS test.

In *Figure 9.13*, you can spot an upward trend and a reoccurring seasonal pattern (annual). However, when trend or seasonality exists (in this case, both), it makes the time series non-stationary. It's not always this easy to identify stationarity or lack of it visually, and therefore, you will rely on statistical tests.

You will use both the `adfuller` and `kpss` tests from the statsmodels library and interpret their results knowing they have opposite null hypotheses:

1. Start by importing both the `adfuller` and `kpss` functions from statsmodels:

    ```
    from statsmodels.tsa.stattools import adfuller, kpss
    ```

To simplify the interpretation of the test results, create a function that outputs the results in a user-friendly way. Let's call the function `print_results`:

```python
def print_results(output, test='adf'):
    pval = output[1]
    test_score = output[0]
    lags = output[2]
    decision = 'Non-Stationary'
    if test == 'adf':
        critical = output[4]
        if pval < 0.05:
            decision = 'Stationary'
    elif test=='kpss':
        critical = output[3]
        if pval >= 0.05:
            decision = 'Stationary'
    output_dict = {
    'Test Statistic': test_score,
    'p-value': pval,
    'Numbers of lags': lags,
    'decision': decision
    }
    for key, value in critical.items():
        output_dict["Critical Value (%s)" % key] = value

    return pd.Series(output_dict, name=test)
```

The function takes the output from the `adfuller` and `kpss` functions and returns a dictionary that adds labels to the output.

2. Run both the `kpss` and `adfuller` tests. Use the default parameter values for both functions:

```python
adf_output = adfuller(co2_df)
kpss_output = kpss(co2_df)
```

3. Pass both outputs to the `print_results` function and concatenate them into a pandas DataFrame for easier comparison:

```python
pd.concat([
print_results(adf_output, 'adf'),
```

```
print_results(kpss_output, 'kpss')
], axis=1)
```

This should produce the following DataFrame:

	adf	kpss
Test Statistic	0.046051	8.183188
p-value	0.962179	0.01
Numbers of lags	27	27
decision	Non-Stationary	Non-Stationary
Critical Value (1%)	-3.433252	0.739
Critical Value (5%)	-2.862822	0.463
Critical Value (10%)	-2.567452	0.347
Critical Value (2.5%)	NaN	0.574

Figure 9.19 – Result output from the ADF and KPSS unit root tests

For ADF, the p-value is at 0.96, which is greater than 0.05, so you *cannot reject* the null hypothesis, and therefore, the time series is non-stationary. For KPSS, the p-value is at 0.01, which is less than 0.05, so you *reject* the null hypothesis, and therefore, the time series is non-stationary.

You will explore six techniques for making the time series stationary, such as transformations and differencing. The techniques covered are first-order differencing, second-order differencing, subtracting moving average, log transformation, decomposition, and Hodrick-Prescott filter.

Essentially, stationarity can be achieved by removing trend (detrending) and seasonality effects. For each transformation, you will run the stationarity tests and compare the results between the different techniques. To simplify the interpretation and comparison, you will create two functions:

- `check_stationarity` takes a DataFrame, performs both KPSS and ADF tests, and returns the outcome.

- `plot_comparison` takes a list of methods and compares their plots. The function takes `plot_type`, so you can explore a line chart and a histogram. The function calls the `check_stationarity` function to capture the results for the subplot titles.

Create the `check_stationarity` function, which is a simplified rewrite of the
`print_results` function used earlier:

```python
def check_stationarity(df):
    kps = kpss(df)
    adf = adfuller(df)

    kpss_pv, adf_pv = kps[1], adf[1]
    kpssh, adfh = 'Stationary', 'Non-stationary'

    if adf_pv < 0.05:
        # Reject ADF Null Hypothesis
        adfh = 'Stationary'
    if kpss_pv < 0.05:
        # Reject KPSS Null Hypothesis
        kpssh = 'Non-stationary'
    return (kpssh, adfh)
```

Create the `plot_comparison` function:

```python
def plot_comparison(methods, plot_type='line'):
    n = len(methods) // 2
    fig, ax = plt.subplots(n,2, sharex=True, figsize=(20,10))
    for i, method in enumerate(methods):
        method.dropna(inplace=True)
        name = [n for n in globals() if globals()[n] is method]
        v, r = i // 2, i % 2

        kpss_s, adf_s = check_stationarity(method)

        method.plot(kind=plot_type,
                    ax=ax[v,r],
                    legend=False,
                    title=f'{name[0]} --> KPSS: {kpss_s}, ADF
{adf_s}')
        ax[v,r].title.set_size(20)
        method.rolling(52).mean().plot(ax=ax[v,r],
legend=False)
```

Let's implement some of the methods for making the time series stationary or extracting a stationary component. Then, combine the methods into a Python list:

1. **First-order differencing**: Also known as detrending, which is calculated by subtracting an observation at time t from the previous observation at time t-1 ($y_t - y_{t-1}$). In pandas this can be done using the .diff() function, which defaults to period=1. Note that the differenced data will contain one less data point (row) than the original data, hence the use of the .dropna() method:

```
first_order_diff = co2_df.diff().dropna()
```

2. **Second-order differencing**: This is useful if seasonality exists or if the first-order differencing was insufficient. This is essentially differencing twice – differencing to remove seasonality followed by differencing to remove trend:

```
differencing_twice = co2_df.diff(52).diff().dropna()
```

3. **Subtracting moving average** (rolling window) from the time series using DataFrame.rolling(window=52).mean() since it is weekly data:

```
rolling = co2_df.rolling(window=52).mean()
subtract_rolling_mean = co2_df - rolling
```

4. **Log transformation** using np.log() is a common technique to stabilize the variance in a time series and sometimes enough to make the time series stationary. Simply, all it does is replace each observation with its log value:

```
log_transform = np.log(co2_df)
```

5. Using time series **decomposition** to remove the trend component, such as seasonal_decompose. From *Figure 9.12,* it seems the process is additive. This is the default parameter in seasonal_decompose, so you do not need to make any changes here:

```
decomp = seasonal_decompose(co2_df)
sd_detrend = decomp.observed - decomp.trend
```

6. Using the **Hodrick-Prescott filter** to remove the trend component, for example, using hp_filter:

```
cyclic, trend = hpfilter(co2_df)
```

Now, let's combine the methods into a Python list, then pass the list to the `plot_comparison` function:

```
methods = [first_order_diff, differencing_twice,
           subtract_rolling_mean, log_transform,
           sd_detrend, cyclic]
plot_comparison(methods)
```

This should display 3 x 2 subplots, which defaults to line charts:

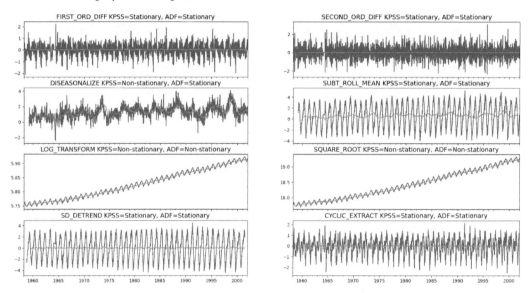

Figure 9.20 – Plotting the different methods to make the CO2 time series stationary

Generally, you do not want to over-difference your time series as some studies have shown that models based on over-differenced data are less accurate. For example, `first_order_diff` already made the time series stationary, and thus there was no need to *difference* it any further. In other words, `differencing_twice` was not needed. Additionally, notice how `log_transform` is still non-stationary.

Notice the center line representing the time series average (moving average). The mean should be constant for a stationary time series and look more like a straight line.

How it works...

Stationarity is an essential concept in time series forecasting, and more relevant when working with financial or economic data. The mean is considered stable and constant if the time series is stationary. In other words, there is an equilibrium as values may deviate from the mean (above or below), but eventually, it always returns to the mean. Some trading strategies rely on this core assumption, formally called a *mean reversion* strategy.

The statsmodels library offers stationarity tests, such as the `adfuller` and `kpss` functions. Both are considered unit root tests and are used to determine whether differencing or other transformations are needed to make the time series stationary.

Remember, ADF and KPSS tests are based on different null hypotheses. For example, `adfuller` and `kpss` have an opposite null hypothesis. So, the p-value that you use to reject (or fail to reject) the null hypothesis will be interpreted differently between the two.

In *Figure 9.19*, there is additional information returned by the tests. This includes the following:

- The `Test Statistic` value is 0.046 for ADF and 8.18 for KPSS, which are above the 1% critical value threshold. This indicates that the time series is non-stationary. It confirms that you cannot reject the null hypothesis. The critical values for ADF come from a Dickey-Fuller table. Luckily, you do not have to reference the Dickey-Fuller table since all statistical software/libraries that offer the ADF test use the table internally. The same applies to KPSS.

- The `p-value` result is associated with the test statistic. Generally, you can reject the null hypothesis if the p-value is less than 0.05 (5%). Again, when using ADF, KPSS, or other stationarity tests, make sure to understand the null hypothesis to accurately interpret the results.

- `Number of lags` represents the number of lags used in the autoregressive process in the test (ADF and KPSS). In both tests, 27 lags were used. Since our CO2 data is weekly, a lag represents 1 week back. So, 27 lags represent 27 weeks in our data.

- The number of observations used is the number of data points, excluding the number of lags.

- The maximized info criteria are based on the `autolag` parameter. The default is `autolag="aic"` for the **Akaike information criterion**. Other acceptable `autolag` parameter values are `bic` for the **Bayesian information criterion** and `t-stat`.

You also explored some techniques for detrending (removing trend) in a time series to make it stationary. For example, you used first-order differencing, decomposition, and log transform to remove the effect of the trend. Detrending stabilizes the mean of the time series and sometimes can be all that is needed to make it stationary. When you decide to detrend your data, you are essentially removing an element of distraction so you can focus on hidden patterns that are not as obvious. Hence, you can build a model to capture these patterns and not be overshadowed by the long-term trend (upward or downward movement).

An example was the first differencing approach. However, in the presence of seasonal patterns you will need to remove the seasonal effect as well, which can be done through seasonal differencing. This is done in addition to the first-order differencing for detrending; hence it can be called second-order differencing, twice-differencing, or differencing twice as you use differencing to remove seasonality effect first and again to remove the trend. This assumes the seasonal differencing was insufficient to make the time series stationary. Your goal is to use the minimal amount of differencing needed and avoid over-differencing. You will rarely need to go beyond differencing twice.

There's more...

In the introduction section of this recipe, we mentioned that both ADF and KPSS use **Ordinary Least Squares** (OLS) regression. More specifically, OLS regression is used to compute the model's coefficients. To view the OLS results for ADF, you use the store parameter and set it to True:

```
adf_result = adfuller(first_order_diff, store=True)
```

The preceding code will return a tuple that contains the test results. The regression summary will be appended as the last item. There should be four items in the tuple: the first item, adf_result[0], contains the t-statistic, the second item, adf_result[1], includes the p-value, and the third item, adf_result[2], contains the critical values for 1%, 5%, and 10% intervals. The last item, adf_result[3], includes a ResultStore object. You can access the last item by using adf_result[-1], as shown in the following code:

```
adf_result[-1].resols.summary()
```

The `ResultStore` object gives you access to `.resols`, which contains the `.summary()` method. This should produce the following output:

OLS Regression Results

Dep. Variable:	y	R-squared:	0.586
Model:	OLS	Adj. R-squared:	0.580
Method:	Least Squares	F-statistic:	112.4
Date:	Mon, 03 Jan 2022	Prob (F-statistic):	0.00
Time:	09:19:41	Log-Likelihood:	-1300.1
No. Observations:	2255	AIC:	2658.
Df Residuals:	2226	BIC:	2824.
Df Model:	28		
Covariance Type:	nonrobust		

	coef	std err	t	P>|t|	[0.025	0.975]
x1	-1.2089	0.078	-15.517	0.000	-1.362	-1.056
x2	0.0694	0.074	0.934	0.351	-0.076	0.215
x3	0.0549	0.071	0.771	0.441	-0.085	0.194
x4	0.2661	0.068	3.894	0.000	0.132	0.400
x5	0.4363	0.066	6.603	0.000	0.307	0.566

Figure 9.21 – ADF OLS regression summary and the first five lags and their coefficients

The ADF test uses OLS.

See also

To learn more about stationarity and detrending, visit the official statsmodels page here: `https://www.statsmodels.org/dev/examples/notebooks/generated/stationarity_detrending_adf_kpss.html`.

Applying power transformations

Time series data can be complex, and embedded within the data is critical information that you will need to understand and peek into to determine the best approach for building a model. For example, you have explored time series decomposition, understood the impact of trend and seasonality, and tested for stationarity. In the previous recipe, *Detecting time series stationarity*, you examined the technique to transform data from non-stationary to stationary. This includes the idea of detrending, which attempts to stabilize the mean over time.

Depending on the model and analysis you are pursuing, you may need to test for additional assumptions against the observed dataset or the model's residuals. For example, testing for **homoskedasticity** (also spelled homoscedasticity) and **normality**. Homoskedasticity means that the variance is stable over time. More specifically, it is the variance of the residuals. When the variance is not constant, changing over time, we call it **heteroskedasticity** (also spelled heteroscedasticity). Another assumption you will need to test for is normality; does the specific observation come from a normal (Gaussian) distribution? Sometimes, you may want to check the normality of the residuals as well, which can be part of the model diagnostics stage. Therefore, it is important to be aware of the assumptions made by specific models or techniques so you can determine which test to use and against which dataset. If you do not do this, you may end up with a flawed model or an outcome that may be overly optimistic or overly pessimistic.

Additionally, in this recipe, you will learn about **Box-Cox transformation**, which you can use to transform the data to satisfy normality and homoskedasticity. Box-Cox transformation takes the following form:

$$T(x) = \begin{cases} \frac{(x^\lambda - 1)}{\lambda} & \text{if} \quad \lambda \neq 0 \\ \ln(x) & \text{if} \quad \lambda = 0 \end{cases}$$

Figure 9.22 – Box-Cox transformation

The Box-Cox transformation relies on just one parameter, lambda (λ), and covers both logarithm and power transformations. If λ is 0, then you get a **natural log transformation**; otherwise, it's a power transformation. The approach is to try different values of λ and then test for normality and homoskedasticity. For example, the **SciPy** library has the boxcox function, and you can specify different λ values using the lmbda parameter (interestingly, this is how it is spelled in the implementation since lambda is a reserved Python keyword). If the lmbda parameter is set to None, the function will find the optimal lambda (λ) value for you.

Getting ready

You can download the Jupyter notebooks and datasets needed from the GitHub repository. Please refer to the *Technical requirements* section of this chapter.

In this recipe, you will be using the Air Passengers dataset, which was previously loaded as a pandas DataFrame under the *Technical requirements* section of this chapter.

You will be using the SciPy and `statsmodels`.

For `pip` installation, use the following command:

```
> pip install scipy
```

For `conda` installation, use the following command:

```
> conda install -c anaconda scipy
```

In addition to the preparation highlighted in the *Technical requirements* section, you will need to import these common libraries that you will use throughout this recipe:

```
import numpy as np
from statsmodels.graphics.tsaplots import plot_acf, plot_pacf
import statsmodels.api as sm
```

To make the plots a lot bigger and easier to read, use the following command to establish a fixed size (20, 8) – a width of 20 inches and a height of 8 inches:

```
plt.rcParams["figure.figsize"] = (20,8)
```

How to do it...

In this recipe, you will extend what you learned from the previous recipe, *Detecting time series stationarity*, and test for two additional assumptions: normality and homoskedasticity.

> **Note**
>
> Usually, stationarity is the most crucial assumption you will need to worry about but being familiar with additional diagnostic techniques will serve you well.

Sometimes, you can determine normality and homoskedasticity from plots, for example, a histogram or a **Q-Q plot**. This recipe aims to teach you how to perform these diagnostic tests programmatically in Python. In addition, you will be introduced to the **White test** and the **Breusch-Pagan Lagrange** statistical test for *homoskedactisity*.

For normality diagnostics, you will explore the **Shapiro-Wilk**, **D'Agostino-Pearson**, and **Kolmogorov-Smirnov** statistical tests. Overall, Shapiro-Wilk tends to perform best and handles a broader set of cases.

Testing normality

The statsmodels library and the SciPy library have overlapping implementations. For example, the Kolmogorov-Smirnov test is implemented as `ktest` in SciPy and `ktest_normal` in statsmodels. In SciPy, the D'Agostino-Pearson test is implemented as `normaltest` and the Shapiro-Wilk test as `shapiro`:

1. Start by importing the normality tests provided by the SciPy and statsmodels libraries:

```
from scipy.stats import shapiro, kstest, normaltest
from statsmodels.stats.diagnostic import kstest_normal
```

2. The normality diagnostic is a statistical test based on a null hypothesis that you need to determine whether you can accept or reject. Conveniently, the following tests that you will implement have the same null hypothesis. *The null hypothesis states that the data is normally distributed*; for example, you would reject the null hypothesis if the p-value is less than 0.05, making the time series not normally distributed. Let's create a simple function, `is_normal()`, that will return either `Normal` or `Not Normal` based on the p-value:

```
def is_normal(test, p_level=0.05):
    stat, pval = test

    return 'Normal' if pval > 0.05 else 'Not Normal'
```

Run each test to check the results:

```
normal_args = (np.mean(co2_df),np.std(co2_df))
print(is_normal(shapiro(co2_df)))
print(is_normal(normaltest(co2_df)))
print(is_normal(normal_ad(co2_df)))
print(is_normal(kstest_normal(co2_df)))
print(is_normal(kstest(co2_df,
```

```
                              cdf='norm',
                              args=(np.mean(co2_df), np.std(co2_
df)))))
    >>
    Not Normal
    Not Normal
    Not Normal
    Not Normal
    Not Normal
```

The output from the tests confirms the data does not come from a normal distribution. You do not need to run that many tests. The `shapiro` test, for example, is a very common and popular test that you can rely on. Generally, as with any statistical test, you need to read the documentation regarding the implementation to gain an understanding of the test. More specifically, you will need to understand the null hypothesis behind the test to determine whether you can reject or fail to reject the null hypothesis.

3. Sometimes, you may need to test normality as part of model evaluation and diagnostics. For example, you would evaluate the residuals (defined as the difference between actual and predicted values) if they follow a normal distribution. In *Chapter 10, Building Univariate Time Series Models Using Statistical Methods*, you will explore building forecasting models using autoregressive and moving average models. For now, you will run a simple autoregressive (AR(1)) model to demonstrate how you can use a normality test against the residuals of a model:

```
from statsmodels.tsa.api import AutoReg
model = AutoReg(co2_df.dropna(), lags=1).fit()
```

You can run the `shapiro` test against the residuals. To access the residuals, you would use the `.resid` property as in `model.resid`. This is common in many models you will build in *Chapter 10, Building Univariate Time Series Models Using Statistical Methods*:

```
print(is_normal(shapiro(model.resid)))
>>
'Not Normal'
```

The output indicates the residuals are not normally distributed. This fact, residuals not being normally distributed, is not enough to determine the model's validity or potential improvements. But taken into context with the other tests, it should help you determine how good your model is. This is a topic you will explore further in the next chapter.

Testing homoskedactisity

You will be testing for the stability of the variance against the model's residuals. This will be the same AR(1) model used in the previous normality test:

1. Let's start by importing the method needed for this recipe:

    ```
    from statsmodels.stats.api import (het_breuschpagan,
                                       het_goldfeldquandt)
    ```

2. You will perform a homoskedasticity test on the model's residuals. As stated earlier regarding statistical tests, it is vital to understand the hypothesis behind these tests. The null hypothesis states that *the data is homoskedastic* for the two tests. For example, you would reject the null hypothesis if the p-value is less than 0.05, making the time series heteroskedastic.

    Let's create a small function, calling it `het_test(model, test)`, that takes in a model and the test function and returns either `Heteroskedastic` or `Homoskedastic` based on the p-value to determine whether the null hypothesis is accepted or rejected:

    ```
    def het_test(model, test=het_breuschpagan):
        lm, lm_pvalue, fvalue, f_pvalue = (
            het_breuschpagan(model.resid,
                             sm.add_constant(
                                 model.fittedvalues)
            ))

        return "Heteroskedastic" if f_pvalue < 0.05 else
    "Homoskedastic"
    ```

3. Start with the Breusch-Pagan Lagrange multiplier test to diagnose the residuals. In statsmodels, you will use the `het_breuschpagan` function, which takes `resid`, the model's residual, and `exog_het`, where you provide the original data (explanatory variables) related to the heteroskedasticity in the residual:

    ```
    het_test(model, test=het_breuschpagan)
    >> 'Homoskedastic'
    ```

    This result indicates that the residual is homoskedastic, with a constant variance (stable).

4. A very similar test is White's Lagrange multiplier test. In statsmodels, you will use the het_white function, which has the same two parameters that you used with het_breuschpagan:

```
het_test(model, test=het_white)
>> 'Homoskedastic'
```

Both tests indicate that the residuals of the autoregressive model have constant variance (homoskedastic). Both tests estimate the auxiliary regression against the squared residuals and all the explanatory variables.

Keep in mind that both normality and homoskedasticity are some of the tests you may need to conduct on the residuals as you diagnose your model. Another essential test is testing for autocorrelation, which is discussed in the following recipe, *Testing for autocorrelation in time series data.*

Applying Box-Cox transform

Box-Cox transformation can be a useful tool, and it's good to be familiar with. Box-Cox transforms a non-normally distributed dataset into a normally distributed one. At the same time, it stabilizes the variance, making the data homoskedastic. To gain a better understanding of the effect of Box-Cox transformation, you will use the Air Passengers dataset, which contains both trend and seasonality:

1. Start by importing the boxcox function from the SciPy library:

```
from scipy.stats import boxcox
```

2. Recall, from the introduction section of this recipe and *Figure 9.22*, there is a lambda parameter used to determine which transformation to apply (logarithm or power transform). Use the boxcox function with the default parameter value for lmbda, which is None. Just provide the dataset to satisfy the required x parameter:

```
xt, lmbda = boxcox(airp['passengers'])
xts = pd.Series(xt, index=airp.index)
```

By not providing a value to lmbda and keeping it at None, the function will find the optimal lambda (λ) value. From the introduction of this recipe, you'll remember lambda is spelled lmbda in the boxcox implementation. The function returns two values captured by xt for the transformed data and lmda for the optimal lambda value found.

A histogram can visually show the impact of the transformation:

```
fig, ax = plt.subplots(1, 2)
airp.hist(ax=ax[0])
xts.hist(ax=ax[1])
plt.show()
```

This should produce the following two plots:

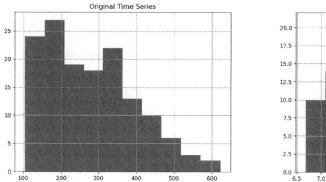
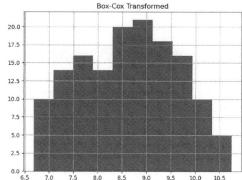

Figure 9.23 – Box-Cox transformation and effect on the distribution

The second histogram shows that the data was transformed, and the overall distribution changed. It would be interesting to examine the dataset as a time series plot.

Plot both datasets to compare before and after the transformation:

```
fig, ax = plt.subplots(1, 2)
airp.plot(ax=ax[0])
xts.plot(ax=ax[1])
plt.show()
```

This should produce the following two plots:

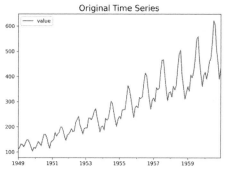
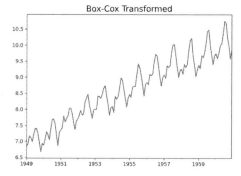

Figure 9.24 – Box-Cox transformation and overall effect on time series data

Notice how the seasonal effect on the transformed dataset looks more stable than before.

3. Finally, build two simple autoregressive models to compare the effect on the residuals before and after the transformation:

```
model_airp = AutoReg(airp, lags=1, trend='n').fit()
model_bx = AutoReg(xts, lags=1, trend='n').fit()
fig, ax = plt.subplots(1, 2)
model_airp.resid.plot(ax=ax[0])
model_bx.resid.plot(ax=ax[1])
```

This should produce the following two plots:

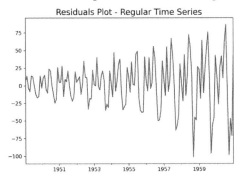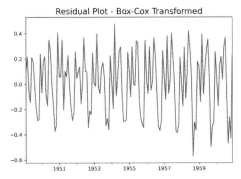

Figure 9.25 – Box-Cox transformation and effect on residuals

How it works...

Box-Cox allows us to make the data both normal and homoskedastic and is part of a family of power transforms that includes log transform and square root transform. Box-Cox is a powerful transform because it supports both root and log transforms, and others are made possible by changing the lambda values.

> **Note**
>
> One thing to point out is that the boxcox function requires the data to be positive.

There's more...

The AutoReg model comes with two useful methods: diagnostic_summary() and plot_diagnostics(). They will save you time from having to write additional code to test the model's residuals for normality, homoskedasticity, and autocorrelation.

The following code shows how you can get the diagnostic summary for `model_bx`:

```
print(model_bx.diagnostic_summary())
```

This should display the results from the Ljung-Box test for autocorrelation and the homoskedasticity test against the model's residuals.

```
              Test of No Serial Correlation
==================================================
     Lag  Ljung-Box LB P-value           DF
--------------------------------------------------
       1      8.800          0.003         1
       2     12.729          0.002         2
       3     28.040          0.000         3
       4     29.202          0.000         4
       5     29.205          0.000         5
       6     31.021          0.000         6
       7     47.992          0.000         7
       8     50.468          0.000         8
       9     52.247          0.000         9
      10     59.828          0.000        10
      11    172.816          0.000        11
      12    181.177          0.000        12


                 Test of Normality
==================================================
Jarque-Bera     P-value    Skewness    Kurtosis
--------------------------------------------------
     5.987        0.050      -0.128       2.031


         Test of Conditional Homoskedasticity
==================================================
     Lag     ARCH-LM     P-value           DF
--------------------------------------------------
       1       0.116       0.733            1
       2       1.243       0.537            2
       3       4.112       0.250            3
       4       4.058       0.398            4
       5       6.836       0.233            5
       6       7.203       0.302            6
       7      14.755       0.039            7
       8      15.157       0.056            8
       9      15.993       0.067            9
      10      17.963       0.056           10
      11      19.322       0.056           11
      12      64.563       0.000           12
      13      63.975       0.000           13
--------------------------------------------------
```

Figure 9.26 – diagnostic_summary for autocorrelation

To get the visual summary, you can use the following code:

```
model_bx.plot_diagnostics(); plt.show()
```

The `.plot_diagnostics()` function will show four plots so you can examine the model's residuals. Mainly, the plots will show whether the residuals are normally distributed from the Q-Q plot and histogram. Additionally, the **autocorrelation function plot (ACF)** will allow you to examine for autocorrelation. You will examine ACF plots in more detail in the *Plotting ACF and PACF* recipe in *Chapter 10, Building Univariate Time Series Models Using Statistical Methods*.

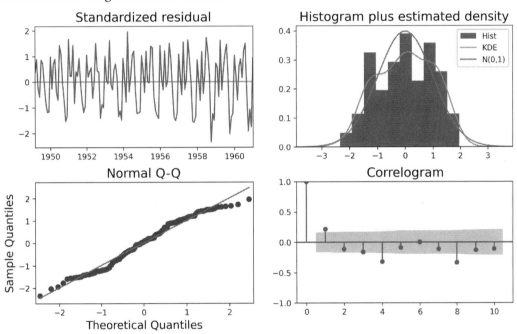

Figure 9.27 – Output from the plot_diagnostics() method

See also

To learn more about the `boxcox` function, visit the official SciPy documentation here: `https://docs.scipy.org/doc/scipy/reference/generated/scipy.stats.boxcox.html`.

Testing for autocorrelation in time series data

Autocorrelation is like statistical correlation (think **Pearson correlation** from high school), which measures the strength of a linear relationship between two variables, except that we measure the linear relationship between *time series values separated by a lag*. In other words, we are comparing a variable with its lagged version of itself.

In this recipe, you will perform a **Ljung-Box test** to check for autocorrelations up to a specified lag and whether they are significantly far off from 0. *The null hypothesis for the Ljung-Box test states that the previous lags are not correlated with the current period*. In other words, you are testing for the absence of autocorrelation.

When running the test using `acorr_ljungbox` from statsmodels, you need to provide a lag value. The test will run for all lags up to the specified lag (maximum lag).

The autocorrelation test is another helpful test for model diagnostics. As discussed in the previous recipe, *Applying power transformations*, there are assumptions that you need to test against the model's residuals. For example, when testing for autocorrelation on the residuals, the expectation is that there should be no autocorrelation between the residuals. This ensures that the model has captured all the necessary information. The presence of autocorrelation in the residuals can indicate that the model missed an opportunity to capture critical information and will need to be evaluated.

Getting ready

You can download the Jupyter notebooks and datasets needed from the GitHub repository. Please refer to the *Technical requirements* section of this chapter.

You will be using `acorr_ljungbox` from the statsmodels library.

How to do it...

You will use the CO2 dataset stored in the `co2_df` DataFrame:

1. Load `acorr_ljungbox` from the `statsmodels` library:

    ```
    from statsmodels.stats.diagnostic import acorr_ljungbox
    ```

2. Since the data is not stationary (review the *Detecting time series stationarity* recipe), you will perform a log transform this time (log differencing):

    ```
    co2_diff= np.log(co2_df).diff().dropna()
    ```

3.   Run the Ljung-Box test. Start with `lags=10`:

```
acorr_ljungbox(co2_diff, lags=10, return_df=True)
```

This should print the results for the first 10 lags.

	lb_stat	lb_pvalue
1	16.193898	5.717801e-05
2	78.485798	9.057856e-18
3	287.050787	6.311581e-62
4	383.291716	1.132455e-81
5	493.588582	1.932434e-104
6	536.683057	1.047943e-112
7	598.257880	5.776363e-125
8	620.615981	8.637442e-129
9	626.775866	3.739862e-129
10	631.630413	2.925751e-129

Figure 9.28 – The first 10 lags for the autocorrelation test

This shows that the test statistic for all lags up to lag 10 are significant (p-value < 0.05), so you can reject the null hypothesis. Rejecting the null hypothesis means you reject the claim that there is no autocorrelation.

How it works...

`acorr_ljungbox` is a function that accumulates autocorrelation up until the lag specified. Therefore, it is helpful to determine whether the structure is worth modeling in the first place.

There's more...

Let's use the Ljung-Box test against the residual from `model_bx` that was created in the *Applying power transformations* recipe:

```
acorr_ljungbox(model_bx.resid, return_df=True, lags=10)
```

This should print the results for the first 10 lags:

	lb_stat	lb_pvalue
1	6.891379	8.661245e-03
2	8.799865	1.227817e-02
3	12.728606	5.261829e-03
4	28.039695	1.224399e-05
5	29.201881	2.116595e-05
6	29.204901	5.563811e-05
7	31.021143	6.161812e-05
8	47.991784	9.915323e-08
9	50.468158	8.794752e-08
10	52.247452	1.026842e-07

Figure 9.29 – The first 10 lags for the autocorrelation test against residuals

From the preceding example, the p-values are less than 0.05, so you reject the null hypothesis, and there is autocorrelation.

See also

To learn more about the `acorr_ljungbox` function, visit the official documentation here: `https://www.statsmodels.org/dev/generated/statsmodels.stats.diagnostic.acorr_ljungbox.html`.

10

Building Univariate Time Series Models Using Statistical Methods

In *Chapter 9*, *Exploratory Data Analysis and Diagnosis*, you were introduced to several concepts to help you understand the time series process. Such recipes included *Decomposing time series data*, *Detecting time series stationarity*, *Applying power transformations*, and *Testing for autocorrelation in time series data*. These techniques will come in handy in the statistical modeling approach that will be discussed in this chapter.

When working with time series data, different methods and models can be used, depending on whether the time series is univariate or multivariate, seasonal or non-seasonal, stationary or non-stationary, and linear or nonlinear. If you list the assumptions you need to consider and examine – for example, stationarity and autocorrelation – it will become apparent why time series data is deemed to be complex and challenging. Thus, to model such a complex system, your goal is to get a good enough approximation that captures the critical factors of interest. These factors will vary by industry domain and the study's objective, such as forecasting, analyzing a process, or detecting abnormalities.

Some popular statistical modeling methods include **exponential smoothing**, non-seasonal **autoregressive integrated moving average (ARIMA)**, **Seasonal ARIMA (SARIMA)**, **Vector Autoregressive (VAR)**, and other variants of these models. Many practitioners, such as economists and data scientists, have used these models. Additionally, these models can be found in popular software packages such as EViews, MATLAB, Orange, and Alteryx, as well as libraries in Python and R.

In this chapter, you will learn how to build these statistical models in Python. In other words, I will provide a brief introduction to the theory and math since the focus is on the implementation. I will provide references where it makes sense if you are interested in diving deeper into the math and theory of such models.

In this chapter, we will cover the following recipes:

- Plotting ACF and PACF

- Forecasting univariate time series data with exponential smoothing

- Forecasting univariate time series data with non-seasonal ARIMA

- Forecasting univariate time series data with seasonal ARIMA

Before diving into these recipes, pay special attention to the upcoming *Technical requirements* section, in which you will perform upfront preparation. This will remove any distractions and repetitive coding so that you can focus on the recipe's core goals and the concepts behind each implementation.

Technical requirements

You can download the Jupyter Notebooks and necessary datasets from this book's GitHub repository:

- Jupyter Notebook: `https://github.com/PacktPublishing/Time-Series-Analysis-with-Python-Cookbook./blob/main/code/Ch10/Chapter%2010.ipynb`

- Datasets: `https://github.com/PacktPublishing/Time-Series-Analysis-with-Python-Cookbook./tree/main/datasets/Ch10`

Before you start working through the recipes in this chapter, please run the following code to load the datasets and functions that will be referenced throughout:

1. Start by importing the basic libraries that will be shared across all the recipes in this chapter:

```
import pandas as pd
import numpy as np
import matplotlib.pyplot as plt
import warnings
from statsmodels.tsa.api import (kpss, adfuller,
                                 seasonal_decompose, STL)
from statsmodels.tools.eval_measures import rmspe, rmse
from sklearn.metrics import mean_absolute_percentage_
error as mape
from statsmodels.graphics.tsaplots import plot_acf, plot_
pacf
from itertools import product
from pathlib import Path


warnings.filterwarnings('ignore')
plt.rcParams["figure.figsize"] = [12, 5]
```

2. You will be working with two datasets throughout this chapter: *Life Expectancy from Birth* and *Monthly Milk Production*. Import these datasets, which are stored in CSV format (life_expectancy_birth.csv, and milk_production.csv), into pandas DataFrames. Each dataset comes from a different time series process, so they will contain a different trend or seasonality. Once you've imported the datasets, you will have two DataFrames called life and milk:

```
life_file = Path('../../datasets/Ch10/life_expectancy_
birth.csv')
milk_file = Path('../../datasets/Ch10/milk_production.
csv')


life = pd.read_csv(life_file,
                   index_col='year',
                   parse_dates=True,
                   skipfooter=1)
```

```
milk = pd.read_csv(milk_file,
                   index_col='month',
                   parse_dates=True)
```

Inspect the data visually and observe if the time series contains any trend or seasonality. You can always come back to the plots shown in this section for reference:

```
fig, ax = plt.subplots(2, 1, figsize=(16, 12))
life.plot(title='Annual Life Expectancy',
                   legend=False, ax=ax[0])
milk.plot(title='Monthly Milk Production',
                   legend=False, ax=ax[1])
```

This should display two time series plots:

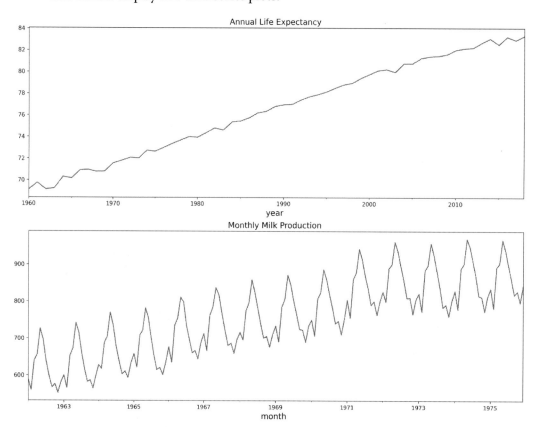

Figure 10.1 – Time series plots for Annual Life Expectancy and Monthly Milk Production

The preceding figure shows a time series plot for the `life` DataFrame showing a positive (upward) trend and no seasonality. The life expectancy data contains *annual* life expectancy records at birth from 1960 to 2018 (59 years). The original dataset contained records for each country, but you will be working with `world` records in this chapter. The time series plot for the `milk` DataFrame shows a positive (upward) trend and a repeating seasonality (every summer). The milk production data is recorded monthly from January 1962 to December 1975 (168 months). The seasonal magnitudes and variations over time seem to be steady, indicating an additive nature. Having a seasonal decomposition that specifies the level, trend, and season of an additive model will reflect this as well. For more insight on seasonal decomposition, please review the *Decomposing time series data* recipe in *Chapter 9, Exploratory Data Analysis and Diagnosis.*

3. You will need to split the data into *test* and *train* datasets. Then, you must train the models (fitting) on the training dataset and use the test dataset to evaluate the model and compare your predictions. A forecast that's created for the data that will be used in training is called an *in-sample* forecast, while forecasting for unseen data such as a test set is called an *out-of-sample* forecast. When you're evaluating the different models, you will be using the out-of-sample or test sets.

   Create a generalized function, `split_data`, which splits the data based on a test split factor. This way, you can experiment on different splits as well. We will be referencing this function throughout this chapter:

   ```
   def split_data(data, test_split):
       l = len(data)
       t_idx = round(l*(1-test_split))
       train, test = data[ : t_idx], data[t_idx : ]
       print(f'train: {len(train)} , test: {len(test)}')
       return train, test
   ```

4. Call the `split_data` function to split the two DataFrames into `test` and `train` datasets (start with 15% test and 85% train). You can always experiment with different split factors:

   ```
   test_split = 0.15
   milk_train, milk_test = split_data(milk, test_split)
   life_train, life_test = split_data(life, test_split)
   >>
   train: 143 , test: 25
   train: 50 , test: 9
   ```

5. You will be checking for stationarity often since it is an essential assumption for many of the models you will build. For example, in *Chapter 9, Exploratory Data Analysis and Diagnosis*, in the *Detecting time series stationarity* recipe, we discussed the importance of testing for stationarity and using the *Augmented Dickey-Fuller* test. Create a function that you can refer to throughout this chapter to perform the test and interpret the results:

```
def check_stationarity(df):
    results = adfuller(df)[1:3]
    s = 'Non-Stationary'
    if results[0] < 0.05:
        s = 'Stationary'
    print(f"'{s}\t p-value:{results[0]} \t
lags:{results[1]}")
    return (s, results[0])
```

6. There will be recipes in which you will run multiple variations of a model as you search for the optimal configuration, a practice commonly called *hyperparameter tuning*. For example, you may train an ARIMA model with different parameter values and thus produce multiple variations of the ARIMA model (multiple models). The get_best_model function will compare the different models – for example, ARIMA models – to select the best model and the set of parameters associated with that model. The get_best_model function will take a dictionary that contains the produced model, parameters used, and the scores for each model. The function will return the winning model based on a scoring (metric) criterion of your choice. This is the c parameter of the function, which defaults to AIC. For instance, you may choose the evaluation (the c parameter) to be based on the **Root Mean Squared Percentage Error (RMSPE)**, **Root Mean Square Error (RMSE)**, **Mean Square Error (MSE)**, **Akaike's Information Criteria (AIC)**, **Corrected Akaike's Information Criteria (AICc)**, and **Bayesian Information Criteria (BIC)**, which will be used as evaluation metrics for each model:

```
def get_best_model(score, c='AIC'):
    initial_score = score[0][c]
    best_model = 0
    for k,v in score.items():
        if v[c] < initial_score:
            initial_score = v[c]
```

```
                best_model = k
        print(f'Best model: {best_model} with lowest {c}
score: {initial_score}')
        return score[best_model]['model']
```

7. Create the `plot_forecast` function, which takes a model object that you have trained, a starting position, and both the train and test datasets to create a plot that compares the forecast (predicted values) against actuals. This will become clearer as you dive into this chapter's recipes:

```
def plot_forecast(model, start, train, test):
    forecast = pd.DataFrame(model.forecast(test.
shape[0]),
                            index=test.index)
    ax = train.loc[start:].plot(style='--')
    test.plot(ax=ax)
    forecast.plot(ax=ax, style = '-.')
    ax.legend(['orig_train', 'orig_test', 'forecast'])
    plt.show()
```

8. Lastly, create a `combinator` utility function that takes a list of parameter values and returns a Cartesian product of these choices. You will use this when performing a grid search for hyperparameter tuning. In grid search, you specify a combination of parameter values to train multiple models on each set and then evaluate the winning model using the `get_best_model` function. For example, suppose your list contains three possible values for three different parameters. In such a case, the `combinator` function will return a list containing 3x3 or nine possible combinations. This will become clearer as you dive into this chapter's recipes:

```
def combinator(items):
    combo = [i for i in product(*items)]
    return combo
```

Now, let's dive into the recipes.

In the first recipe, you will be introduced to the ACF and PACF plots, which are used to determine the **orders (parameters)** for some of the models that will be used in this chapter, such as the ARIMA model.

Plotting ACF and PACF

When building statistical forecasting models such as AR, MA, ARMA, ARIMA, or SARIMA, you will need to determine the type of time series model that is most suitable for your data and the values for some of the required parameters, called orders. More specifically, these are called the *lag orders* for the **autoregressive (AR)** or **moving average (MA)** components. This will be explored further in the *Forecasting univariate time series data with non-seasonal ARIMA* recipe of this chapter.

To demonstrate this, for example, an **Autoregressive Moving Average (ARMA)** model can be written as ARMA(p, q), where p is the autoregressive order or AR(p) component, and q is the moving average order or MA(q) component. Hence, an ARMA model combines an AR(p) and an MA(q) model.

The core idea behind these models is built on the assumption that the current value of a particular variable, x, can be estimated from past values of itself. For example, in an autoregressive model of order p or AR(p), we assume that the current value, x_t, at time t can be estimated from its past values $(x_{t-1}, x_{t-2}, ..., x_{t-p})$ up to p, where p determines how many lags (steps back) we need to go. If $p = 2$, this means we must use two previous periods (x_{t-1}, x_{t-2}) to predict x_t. Depending on the granularity of your time series data, p=2 can be 2 hours, 2 days, 2 months, or 2 quarters.

To build an ARMA model, you will need to provide values for the p and q orders (known as lags). These are considered hyperparameters since they are supplied by you to influence the model.

The terms parameters and hyperparameters are sometimes used interchangeably. However, they have different interpretations and you need to understand the distinction.

Parameters versus Hyperparameters

When training an ARIMA model, the outcome will produce a set of parameters called coefficients – for example, a coefficient value for AR Lag 1 or sigma – that are estimated by the algorithm during the model training process and are used for making predictions. They are referred to as the model's parameters.

On the other hand, the (p, d, q) parameters are the ARIMA(p, q, d) orders for AR, differencing, and MA, respectively. These are called hyperparameters. They are set manually and influence the model parameters that are produced (for example, the coefficients). These hyperparameters, as we have seen previously can be tuned using grid search, for example, to find the best set of values that produce the best model.

Now, you might be asking yourself, how do I find the significant lag values for AR and MA models?

This is where the **Autocorrelation Function (ACF)** and the **Partial Autocorrelation Function (PACF)** and their plots come into play. The ACF and PACF can be plotted to help you identify if the time series process is an AR, MA, or an ARMA process (if both are present) and the *significant* lag values (for p and q). Both PACF and ACF plots are referred to as **correlograms** since the plots represent the correlation statistics.

The difference between an ARMA and ARIMA, written as ARIMA(p, d, q), is in the stationarity assumption. The d parameter in ARIMA is for the differencing order. An ARMA model assumes a stationary process, while an ARIMA model does not since it handles differencing. An ARIMA model is a more generalized model since it can satisfy an ARMA model by making the differencing factor d=0. Hence, ARIMA(1,0,1) is ARMA(1,1).

> **AR Order versus MA Order**
>
> You will use the PACF plot to estimate the AR order and the ACF plot to estimate the MA order. Both the ACF and PACF plots show values that range from -1 to 1 on the vertical axis (y-axis), while the horizontal axis (x-axis) indicates the size of the lag. A *significant* lag is any lag that goes outside the shaded confidence interval, as you shall see from the plots.

The statsmodels library provides two functions: acf_plot and pacf_plot. The correlation (for both ACF and PACF) at lag zero is always *one* (since it represents autocorrelation of the first observation on itself). Hence, both functions provide the zero parameter, which takes a Boolean. Therefore, to exclude the zero lag in the visualization, you can pass zero=False instead.

In *Chapter 9, Exploratory Data Analysis and Diagnosis*, in the *Testing autocorrelation in time series data* recipe, you used the Ljung-Box test to evaluate autocorrelation on the residuals. In this recipe, you will learn how to use the ACF plot to examine residual autocorrelation visually as well.

How to do it...

In this recipe, you will explore acf_plot and pacf_plot from the statsmodels library. Let's get started:

1. You will use the life expectancy data in this recipe. As shown in *Figure 10.1*, the data is not stationary due to the presence of a long-term trend. In such a case, you will need to difference (detrend) the time series to make it stationary before applying the ACF and PACF plots.

Start by differencing and then create the plots without the zero lag:

```
life_diff = life.diff().dropna()
fig, ax = plt.subplots(2,1, figsize=(12,8))
plot_acf(life_diff, zero=False, ax=ax[0])
plot_pacf(life_diff, zero=False, ax=ax[1])
plt.show()
```

This should produce the following two plots:

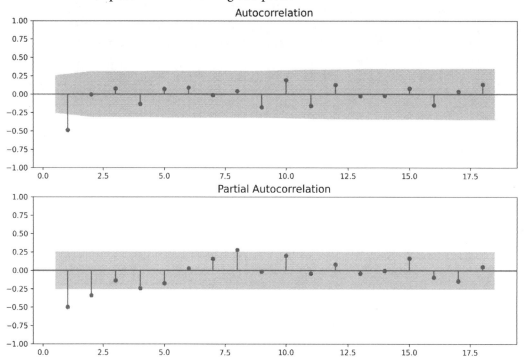

Figure 10.2 – The ACF and PACF plots for the life expectancy data after differencing

The ACF plot shows a significant spike at lag (order) 1. Significance is represented when a lag (vertical line) goes above or below the shaded area. The shaded area represents the confidence interval, which is set to 95% by default. In the ACF plot, only the first lag is significant, which is below the lower confidence interval, and then *cuts off* right after. All the remaining lags are not significant. This indicates a moving average of order one or MA(1).

The PACF plot shows a *gradual* decay with oscillation. Generally, if PACF shows a gradual decay, it indicates a moving average model. For example, if you are using an ARMA or ARIMA model, it would be represented as ARMA(0, 1) once the data has been differenced to make it stationary, or ARIMA(0, 1, 1), indicating a first-order differencing with d=1. In both ARMA and ARIMA, the AR order is p=0, and the MA order is q=1.

2. Now, let's see how PACF and ACF can be used with a more complex dataset containing strong trends and seasonality. In *Figure 10.1*, the Monthly Milk Production plot shows an annual seasonal effect and a positive upward trend indicating a non-stationary time series. It is more suitable with a SARIMA model. In a SARIMA model, you have two components: a non-seasonal and a seasonal component. For example, in addition to the AR and MA processes for the non-seasonal components represented by lower case p and q, which you saw earlier, you will have AR and MA orders for the seasonal component, which are represented by upper case P and Q, respectively. This can be written as SARIMA(p,d,q) (P,D,Q,S). You will learn more about the SARIMA model in the *Forecasting univariate time series data with seasonal ARIMA* recipe.

To make such time series stationary, you must start with seasonal differencing to remove the seasonal effect. Since the observations are taken monthly, the seasonal effects are observed annually (every 12 months or period):

```
milk_diff_12 = milk.diff(12).dropna()
```

3. Use the check_stationarity function that you created earlier in this chapter to perform an Augmented Dickey-Fuller test to check for stationarity:

```
check_stationarity(milk_diff_12)
>> 'Non-Stationary      p-value:0.1607988052771138
2          lags:12
```

4. The differenced time series is still not stationary, so you still need to perform a second differencing. This time, you must perform first-order differencing (detrend). When the time series data contains seasonality and trend, you may need to difference it twice to make it stationary. Store the resulting DataFrame in the milk_diff_12_1 variable and run check_stationarity again:

```
milk_diff_12_1 = milk.diff(12).diff(1).dropna()
check_stationarity(milk_diff_12_1)
```

```
>> 'Stationary      p-value:1.865423431878876e-05
lags:11
```

Great – now, you have a stationary process.

5. Plot ADF and PACF for the stationary time series in `milk_diff_12_1`:

```
fig, ax = plt.subplots(1,2)
plot_acf(milk_diff_12_1, zero=False, ax=ax[0], lags=36)
plot_pacf(milk_diff_12_1, zero=False, ax=ax[1], lags=36)
;plt.show()
```

This should produce the following ACF and PACF plots:

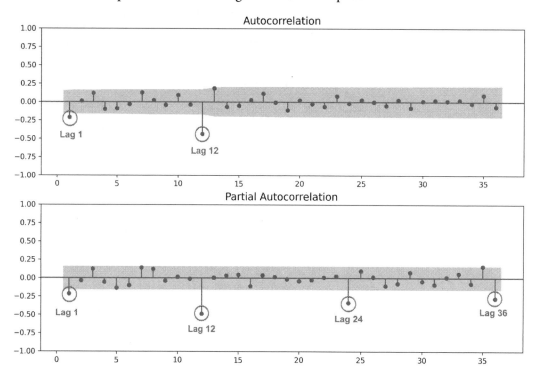

Figure 10.3 – PACF and ACF for Monthly Milk Production after differencing twice

For the seasonal orders, P and Q, you should diagnose spikes or behaviors at lags s, 2s, 3s, and so on, where s is the number of periods in a season. For example, in the milk production data, s=12 (since there are 12 monthly periods in a season). Then, we observe for significance at 12 (s), 24 (2s), 36 (3s), and so on.

Starting with the ACF plot, there is a significant spike at lag 1, which represents the *non-seasonal* order for the MA process as q=1. The spike at lag 12 represents the *seasonal* order for the MA process as Q=1. Notice that there is a cut-off right after lag 1, then a spike at lag 12, followed by a cut-off (no other significant lags afterward). These indicate a moving average model: an MA(1) for the non-seasonal component and an MA(1) for the seasonal component. The PACF plot confirms this as well; an exponential decay at lags 12, 24, and 36 indicates an MA model. So, the SARIMA model would be ARIMA (0, 1,1)(0, 1, 1, 12).

How it works...

The ACF and PACF plots can help you understand the strength of the linear relationship between past observations and their significance at different lags.

The ACF and PACF plots show significant autocorrelation or partial autocorrelation above the **confidence interval**. The shaded portion represents the confidence interval, which is controlled by the alpha parameter in both pacf_plot and acf_plot functions. The default value for alpha in statsmodels is 0.05 (or a 95% confidence interval). Being significant could be in either direction; strongly positive the closer to 1 (above) or strongly negative the closer to -1 (below).

The following table shows an example guide for identifying the stationary AR and MA orders from PACF and ACF plots:

Process	ACF	PACF
AR(p)	Gradual decay after lag p, which can be oscillating	Cut-off after lag p
MA(q)	Cut-off at lag q	Gradual decay after lag q, which can be oscillating
ARMA(p,q)	Gradual decay after lag p, which can be oscillating	Gradual decay after lag q, which can be oscillating

Table 10.1 – Identifying the AR, MA, and ARMA models using ACF and PACF plots

There's more...

In this recipe, you used ACF and PACF plots to understand what order values (lags) to use for the seasonal and non-seasonal ARIMA models. Let's see how ACF plots can be used to diagnose the model's residuals. Let's build the seasonal ARIMA model we identified earlier in this recipe as SARIMA(0,1,1)(0,1,1,12), then use the ACF to diagnose the residuals. If the model captured all the information that's been embedded within the time series, you would expect the residuals to have *no autocorrelation*:

```
from statsmodels.tsa.statespace.sarimax import SARIMAX
model = SARIMAX(milk, order=(0,1,1),
                seasonal_order=(0,1,1, 12)).fit(disp=False)
plot_acf(model.resid[1:], zero=False)
plt.show()
```

This should produce the following autocorrelation plot:

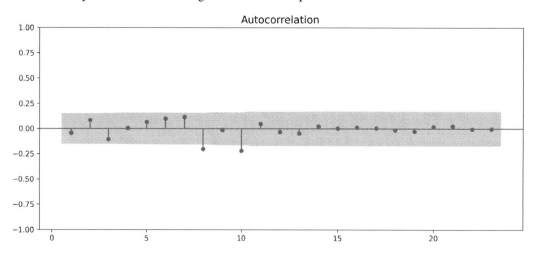

Figure 10.4 – Autocorrelation plot for seasonal ARIMA residuals

Overall, there are a couple of slightly significant lags, indicating the existence of some autocorrelation in the residuals. When the residuals show autocorrelation, this can mean that the model did not capture all the information, and there is potential for further improvement.

You can further tune the model and experiment with other values for the seasonal and non-seasonal orders. In this chapter and later recipes, you will explore a grid search method for selecting the best hyperparameters to find the best model.

See also

To learn more about ACF plots, visit the official documentation at `https://www.statsmodels.org/dev/generated/statsmodels.graphics.tsaplots.plot_acf.html`.

To learn more about PACF plots, visit the official documentation at `https://www.statsmodels.org/dev/generated/statsmodels.graphics.tsaplots.plot_pacf.html`.

With that, you know how to use ACF and PACF plots when building an ARIMA model and its variants – for example, an ARMA or SARIMA model. In the next recipe, you will be introduced to this chapter's first time series forecasting technique.

Forecasting univariate time series data with exponential smoothing

In this recipe, you will explore the exponential smoothing technique using the statsmodels library. The `ExponentialSmoothing` classes in statsmodels resemble popular implementations from the R *forecast* package, such as `ets()` and `HoltWinters()`. In statsmodels, there are three different implementations (*classes*) of exponential smoothing, depending on the nature of the data you are working with:

- `SimpleExpSmoothing`: Simple exponential smoothing is used when the time series process lacks seasonality and trend. This is also referred to as single exponential smoothing.

- `Holt`: Holt's exponential smoothing is an enhancement of the simple exponential smoothing and is used when the time series process contains only trend (but no seasonality). It is referred to as double exponential smoothing.

- `ExponentialSmoothing`: Holt-Winters' exponential smoothing is an enhancement of Holt's exponential smoothing and is used when the time series process has both seasonality and trend. It is referred to as triple exponential smoothing.

The statsmodels implementation follows the definitions from *Forecasting: principles and practice*, by *Hyndman, Rob J., and George Athanasopoulos*, which you can reference here: `https://otexts.com/fpp3/expsmooth.html`.

How to do it...

In this recipe, you will perform exponential smoothing on both datasets. Since both the `Holt` class and the `SimpleExpSmoothing` class are restricted versions of the `ExponentialSmoothing` class, you will be using the latter. Instead of using all three, you can use the `ExponentialSmoothing` class to run the three different types since `ExponentialSmoothing` is a more generic implementation. You still need to determine whether your time series has trend, seasonality, or both. Let's get started:

1. Import the `ExponentialSmoothing` class:

    ```
    from statsmodels.tsa.api import ExponentialSmoothing
    ```

2. Start with the life expectancy dataset and use the `ExponentialSmoothing` class. `ExponentialSmoothing` takes several parameters (referred to as hyperparameters):

    - `smoothing_level`: A float value for the smoothing factor for the level known as *alpha* (α), where $0 \le \alpha \le 1$.

    - `smoothing_trend`: A float value for the smoothing factor for the trend known as *beta* (β), where $0 \le \beta \le 1$.

    - `smoothing_seasonal`: A float value for the smoothing factor for the seasonal trend known as *gamma* (γ), where $0 \le \gamma \le 1$.

    - `trend`: A single choice from (`multiplicative` or `mul`), (`additive` or `add`), or None.

    - `seasonal`: A single choice from (`multiplicative` or `mul`), (`additive` or `add`), or None.

    - `seasonal_periods`: Takes an integer value representing the seasonality period, for example, 12 if the data is monthly or 4 if the information is quarterly.

    - `damped_trend`: A Boolean value that is either `True` or `False`.

    - `use_boxcox`: A Boolean value that is either `True` or `False` to determine if a Box-Cox transform should be applied.

    Later, in the *How it works...* section, you will explore the Holt-Winters' formulas for level, trend, and seasonality and how these parameters are used.

Start by creating a list that contains different combinations of values for these hyperparameters. This way, you get to evaluate a different combination at each run. In other words, at each iteration, you will be training a different model and capturing its scores. Once every combination has been evaluated, you will use the `get_best_model` function (from the *Technical requirements* section) to determine the best performing model and its associated hyperparameters values (optimal values through this exhaustive grid search). This can be a time-consuming process, but luckily, there is an alternative hybrid technique to shorten the search.

You can use the `ExponentialSmoothing` class to find the optimal values for *alpha*, *beta*, and *gamma* (α, β, γ). This eliminates the need to provide their values in the grid (you still can if you want to own the process). This will simplify the search process and you will only provide values for the remaining hyperparameters for the grid search. For example, the trend and seasonal types supply *multiplicative* and *additive*. You can visually determine if the components are multiplicative or additive by plotting their decomposition using the `seasonal_decompose()` function. But if you are still unsure, this exhaustive grid search method would be an alternate approach.

For the `life` DataFrame, you only have *trend*, so you only need to explore different values for the *two* parameters; that is, `trend` and `damped`:

```
trend = ['add', 'mul']
damped = [True, False]
life_ex_comb = combinator([trend, damped])
life_ex_comb
[('add', True), ('add', False), ('mul', True), ('mul',
False)]
```

Here, we have two parameters that take two different values, each providing us with a 2x2 or four total combinations to evaluate for.

3. Loop through the combination list and train (fit) a different model at each iteration. Capture the evaluation metrics in a dictionary to compare the results later. Example scores you will capture include RMSE, RMSPE, MAPE, AIC, and BIC, to name a few. Keep in mind that most automated tools and software will use the AIC and BIC scores behind the scenes to determine the best model:

```
train = life_train.values.ravel()
y = life_test.values.ravel()
score = {}
for i, (t, dp) in enumerate(life_ex_comb):
```

```
exp = ExponentialSmoothing(train,
                trend=t,
                damped_trend=dp,
                seasonal=None)
model = exp.fit(use_brute=True, optimized=True)
y_hat = model.forecast(len(y))
score[i] = {'trend':t,
                'damped':dp,
                'AIC':model.aic,
                'BIC':model.bic,
                'AICc':model.aicc,
                'RMSPE': rmspe(y, y_hat),
                'RMSE' : rmse(y, y_hat),
                'MAPE' : mape(y, y_hat),
                'model': model}
```

To retrieve the best model using the `get_best_model` function, just pass the scores dictionary. For now, keep the default criteria set to `c=AIC` to be consistent:

```
life_best_model = get_best_model(score, 'AIC')
Best model: 1 with lowest AIC score: -137.03060179180176
```

4. The `get_best_model` function returns the winning model object, a `HoltWintersResultsWrapper` class that you stored in the `life_best_model` variable. You have access to additional methods and attributes such as summary, predict, and forecast, to name a few. To access the model's summary, you can use the following code. To print the summary, you can use the `summary` method:

```
life_best_model.summary()
```

This should produce a tabular layout summarizing the model – for example, the parameter values that were used and the calculated coefficients:

ExponentialSmoothing Model Results

Dep. Variable:	endog	**No. Observations:**	50
Model:	ExponentialSmoothing	**SSE**	2.749
Optimized:	True	**AIC**	-137.031
Trend:	Additive	**BIC**	-129.383
Seasonal:	None	**AICC**	-135.077
Seasonal Periods:	None	**Date:**	Thu, 23 Dec 2021
Box-Cox:	False	**Time:**	17:04:55
Box-Cox Coeff.:	None		

	coeff	code	optimized
smoothing_level	0.1621954	alpha	True
smoothing_trend	0.1621954	beta	True
initial_level	68.748480	l.0	True
initial_trend	0.2422271	b.0	True

Figure 10.5 – Exponential Smoothing summary for the life expectancy data

Notice that the optimal α and β values have been deduced.

5. You can forecast future values using the `forecast` method and then evaluate the results against the test set (unseen data by the model). The `plot_forecast()` function that we created earlier in this chapter in the *Technical requirements* section will produce the forecast and plot the results against the test data. Pass the model object stored in `life_best_model` and both the train and test sets for plotting:

```
plot_forecast(life_best_model, '2000', life_train, life_
test)
```

The `start` argument in the `plot_forecast` function slices the data from that point forward to make it easier to compare the results. Think of it as zooming in. For example, instead of showing data from 1960 to 2018 (59 months), you are just requesting the slice starting from `2000` and later.

This should produce a plot with the x-axis starting from the year 2000. There should be three lines: the actual data is split into two lines, one for the training data and another for test data, and a third for the forecast (predicted values):

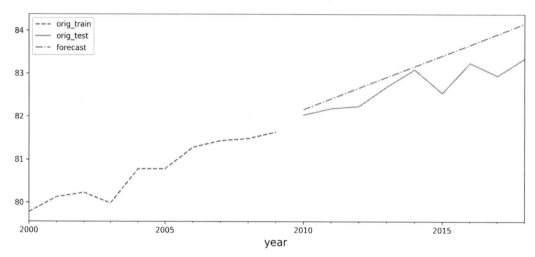

Figure 10.6 – Plotting the exponential smoothing forecast versus
the actual data for the life expectancy dataset

The forecast from the simple exponential smoothing produced a straight line extending the upward trend from the trained data.

6. Replicate the same process but using the `milk` DataFrame. Keep in mind that the most significant difference here is the addition of the seasonal parameters. This means you will be adding two additional hyperparameters to evaluate for – that is, `seasonal` and `seasonal_periods`.

Build a Cartesian product for the different options. For `seasonal_periods`, you can explore three periods – 4, 6, and 12 months. This should give you a total of 24 models (2 x 2 x 2 x 3 = 24) that you will need to evaluate:

```
trend , damped= ['add', 'mul'], [True, False]
seasonal, periods = ['add' , 'mul'], [4, 6, 12]
milk_exp_comb = combinator([trend, damped, seasonal,
periods])
```

Loop through the list of combinations to train multiple models and capture their scores:

```
train = milk_train.values.ravel()
y = milk_test.values.ravel()
milk_model_scores = {}
for i, (t, dp, s, sp) in enumerate(milk_exp_comb):
    exp = ExponentialSmoothing(train,
                        trend=t,
                        damped_trend=dp,
                        seasonal=s,
                        seasonal_periods=sp)
    model = exp.fit(use_brute=True, optimized=True)
    y_hat = model.forecast(len(y))
    milk_model_scores[i] = {'trend':t,
                'damped':dp,
                'AIC':model.aic,
                'BIC':model.bic,
                'AICc': model.aicc,
                'RMSPE': rmspe(y, y_hat),
                'RMSE' : rmse(y, y_hat),
                'MAPE' : mape(y, y_hat),
                'model': model}
```

7. Upon completion, run the `get_best_model` function to obtain the winning model:

```
milk_model = get_best_model(milk_model_scores)
>>
Best model: 8 with lowest AIC score: 593.7138896839506
```

8. Let's print the model's summary:

```
milk_model.summary()
```

This should produce a tabular layout summarizing the model – for example, the parameter values that were used to build the model and the calculated coefficients:

ExponentialSmoothing Model Results

Dep. Variable:	endog	No. Observations:	143
Model:	ExponentialSmoothing	SSE	7265.655
Optimized:	True	AIC	593.714
Trend:	Additive	BIC	641.119
Seasonal:	Additive	AICC	599.230
Seasonal Periods:	12	Date:	Thu, 23 Dec 2021
Box-Cox:	False	Time:	01:50:56
Box-Cox Coeff.:	None		

	coeff	code	optimized
smoothing_level	0.6859127	alpha	True
smoothing_trend	8.7159e-10	beta	True
smoothing_seasonal	0.1477057	gamma	True

Figure 10.7 – Exponential Smoothing summary for the Monthly Milk Production data

Notice the optimal combination of values for **Trend**, **Seasonal**, and **Seasonal Periods**. The optimal **Seasonal Periods** was at 12 months or lags. The summary results table will show the coefficients for all those lags, and it will be a long list. The preceding screenshot only shows the top section. Notice how the ExponentialSmoothing class was able to determine the optimal coefficients for alpha (α), beta (β), and gamma (γ).

Recall that the model is selected based on the AIC score. Therefore, you should explore the different metrics that have been captured, for example, using get_best_model(milk_scores, c='BIC').

9. Compare your forecast using the best model against the test data:

```
plot_forecast(milk_model, '1969', milk_train, milk_test)
```

This should produce a plot with the x-axis starting from the year 1969. There should be three lines: the actual data is split into two lines, one for the training data and another for test data, and a third line for the forecast (predicted values):

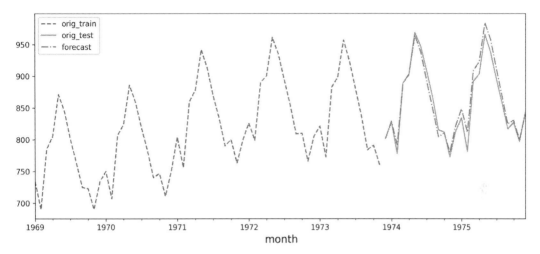

Figure 10.8 – Plotting the exponential smoothing forecast versus actual
the Monthly Milk Production data

Overall, the model did a decent job of capturing the effect of trend and seasonality and they looked close to the actual values from the test set.

How it works...

There are different techniques for smoothing time series data, such as simple moving average, simple exponential smoothing, Holt's exponential smoothing, and Holt-Winter's exponential smoothing, to name a few.

The moving average model treats past values equally, while exponential smoothing type models put more emphasis (weight) on more recent observations. In other words, older observations decay in weight exponentially, hence the "exponential" term. This is based on the logical assumption that more recent events are likely to be more important than much older events; for example, what happened yesterday or the day before is more relevant than what happened 2 months ago for a daily time series.

The formula for simple exponential smoothing (single) for time series processes without trend or seasonality is as follows:

$$S_t = \alpha x_t + (1 - \alpha)S_{t-1}$$
$$F_{t+1} = S_t$$

The `ExponentialSmoothing` class is finding the optimal value for alpha (α), S_t is the expected (smoothed) level at the current time, t, S_{t-1} is the previous smoothed level value at time $t - 1$, and x_t is the observed value at the current time, t.

The alpha (α) parameter is the level smoothing parameter and plays a vital role in determining whether the model should trust the past or S_{t-1} versus the present or x_t. Hence, as α gets closer to zero, the first term, αx_t, gets closer to zero, and more weight is put on the past. And as α gets closer to one, then the $(1 - \alpha)S_{t-1}$ term gets closer to zero and more emphasis or weight is put on the present. Some of the influencing factors depend on how much randomness is in the system. The output value for the coefficient, α, is the weight to determine how the model uses current and past observations to forecast future events or F_{t+1}.

The explanation theme is similar to the rest of the formulas, so we will not dive into every detail, but the general idea holds.

The formula for Holt's exponential smoothing (double) incorporates the addition of the trend (T) and its smoothing parameter, beta (β). Hence, once a trend is included, the model will output the values for both coefficients – that is, alpha and beta (α, β):

$$S_t = \alpha x_t + (1 - \alpha)(S_{t-1} + T_{t-1})$$
$$T_t = \beta(S_t - S_{t-1}) + (1 - \beta)T_{t-1}$$
$$F_{t+1} = S_t + T_t$$

The Holt-Winters exponential smoothing (triple) formula incorporates both trend (T) and seasonality (C). The following equation shows multiplicative seasonality as an example:

$$S_t = \frac{\alpha x_t}{C_{t-L}} + (1 - \alpha)(S_{t-1} + T_{t-1})$$
$$T_t = \beta(S_t - S_{t-1}) + (1 - \beta)T_{t-1}$$
$$C_t = \gamma\left(\frac{x_t}{S_t}\right) + (1 - \gamma)C_{t-L}$$
$$F_{t+1} = (S_t + T_t)C_{(t+1)-L}$$

When using `ExponentialSmoothing` to find the best α, β, γ parameter values, it does so by minimizing the error rate (the **sum of squared error** or **SSE**). So, every time in the loop you were passing new parameters values (for example, damped as either `True` or `False`), the model was solving for the optimal set of values for the α, β, γ coefficients by minimizing for SSE. This can be written as follows:

$$\min(F_t - x_t)^2$$

In some textbooks, you will see different letters used for level, trend, and seasonality, but the overall structure of the formulas holds.

Generally, exponential smoothing is a fast and effective technique for smoothing a time series for improved analysis, dealing with outliers, data imputation, and forecasting (prediction).

There's more...

An exciting library known as `darts` has a wrapper on top of statsmodels's `ExponentialSmoothing`.

It is always advisable to create a separate virtual Python environment for `darts`, whether you are using `conda` or `venv` (please refer to *Chapter 1, Getting Started with Time Series Analysis*).

To install using `pip`, run the following command:

```
pip install darts
```

To install using `conda`, run the following command:

```
conda install -c conda-forge -c pytorch u8darts-all
```

Load the `ExponentialSmoothing` and `TimeSeries` classes:

```
from darts.models import ExponentialSmoothing
from darts import TimeSeries
```

`darts` expects the data to be an instance of the `TimeSeries` class, so you need to convert your pandas DataFrame before using it to train the model. The `TimeSeries` class provides the `from_dataframe` method, which you will be using:

```
model = ExponentialSmoothing(seasonal_periods=12)
ts = TimeSeries.from_dataframe(milk.reset_index(),
                               time_col='month', value_
cols='production', freq='MS')
```

When creating the `TimeSeries` object, you must specify which column name is the date and which column contains the observations (values). You can train the model using the `.fit()` method. Once trained, you can forecast using the `.predict()` method. To plot the results, you can use the `.plot()` method:

```
train, test = split_data(ts, 0.15)
model.fit(train)
forecast = model.predict(len(test), num_samples=100)
train.plot()
forecast.plot(label='forecast', low_quantile=0.05, high_
quantile=0.95)
```

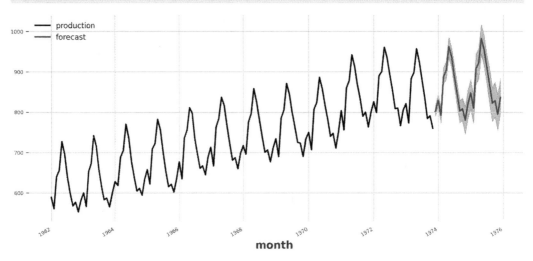

Figure 10.9 – Forecasting plot generated from Darts for the Monthly Milk Production data

The `darts` library automated the evaluation process to find the optimal configuration (hyperparameters). Darts' `ExponentialSmoothing` class is a wrapper to statsmodels's `ExponentialSmoothing` class, which means you have access to familiar methods and attributes, such as the `.summary()` method:

```
model.model.summary()
```

This should produce the familiar statsmodels tabular summary of the model and the optimized parameter values. As a challenge, compare the summary using Dart with the results shown in *Figure 10.7*. Though you will notice you achieved similar results, it was with less effort using Darts.

See also

To learn more about the `ExponentialSmoothing` class, you can visit statsmodels's official documentation at `https://www.statsmodels.org/dev/generated/statsmodels.tsa.holtwinters.ExponentialSmoothing.html`.

> **Note**
>
> Did you notice that you did not have to test for stationarity with exponential smoothing? Exponential smoothing is appropriate for non-stationary time series (for example, a time series with trend or seasonality).

In the next section, while building an ARIMA model, you will be testing for stationarity to determine the differencing factor and leverage the ACF and PACF plots that were discussed earlier in this chapter.

Forecasting univariate time series data with non-seasonal ARIMA

In this recipe, you will explore non-seasonal ARIMA and use the implementation in the statsmodels package. ARIMA stands for Autoregressive Integrated Moving Average, which combines three main components: the autoregressive or AR(p) model, the moving average or MA(q) model, and an integrated (differencing) factor or I(d).

An ARIMA model can be defined by the p, d, and q parameters, so for a non-seasonal time series, it is described as ARIMA(p, d, q). The p and q parameters are called *orders*; for example, in AR of order p and MA of order q. They can also be called lags since they represent the number of periods we need to lag for. You may also come across another reference for p and q, namely *polynomial degree*.

ARIMA models can handle non-stationary time series data through differencing, a time series transformation technique, to make a non-stationary time series stationary. The integration or order of differencing, d, is one of the parameters that you will need to pick a value for when building the model. For a refresher on stationarity, please refer to the *Detecting time series stationarity* recipe in *Chapter 9, Exploratory Data Analysis and Diagnosis*.

Even though ARIMA models do not assume stationarity, they do assume no seasonality in the data. On the other hand, an ARIMA model can handle trends in the data through the integrated factor, d. For example, first-order differencing can make a time series stationary by removing the trend effect (detrending) but not the seasonality effect. When seasonality is present, you can use the **Seasonal ARIMA (SARIMA)** model.

Getting ready

Start by loading this recipe's necessary classes and functions from the `statsmodels` library:

```
from statsmodels.tsa.arima.model import ARIMA
from statsmodels.stats.diagnostic import acorr_ljungbox
```

How to do it...

There are different models for handling different types of time series data. Therefore, it is essential to ensure the model you've selected is ideal for the kind of data and problem you are trying to solve. In this recipe, you will use the `life` DataFrame since it has trend and no seasonality.

You will combine visual inspection (using the ACF and PACF plots) and statistical tests to make an informed decision for the AR and MA orders. These topics were covered in *Chapter 9, Exploratory Data Analysis and Diagnosis*, in the *Testing data for autocorrelation, Decomposing time series data*, and *Detecting time series stationarity* recipes. Let's get started:

1. Start by performing decomposition to break the data into the three main components – trend, seasonality, and the residual (noise):

```
decomposed = seasonal_decompose(life)
decomposed.plot(); plt.show()
```

You can see the plot as follows:

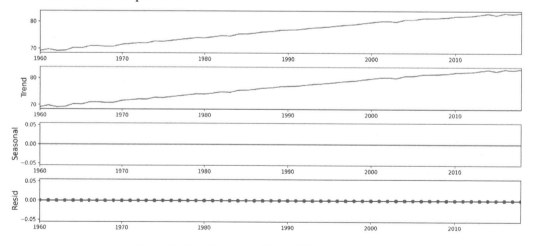

Figure 10.10 – Decomposition of life expectancy data

Notice that the dataset shows a positive trend but no seasonality effect, as expected.

2. You will need to detrend the data first. Perform a first-order differencing and then test for stationarity by using the `check_stationarity` function you created earlier in this chapter:

```
life_df1 = life.diff().dropna()
check_stationarity(life_df1)
>>
Stationary     p-value:1.5562189676003248e-14     lags:1
```

Now, the data is *stationary*. The p-value is significant, and you can reject the null hypothesis. Note that the default `periods` value for `diff` is `1`. Generally, `diff(periods=n)` is the difference between the current observation at period t and its lagged version at period t-n. In the case of `diff(1)` or `diff()`, the lagged version is t-1 (for example, the prior month's observation).

You can plot the differenced time series data using the `plot` method:

```
life_df1.plot()
```

This produces the following plot:

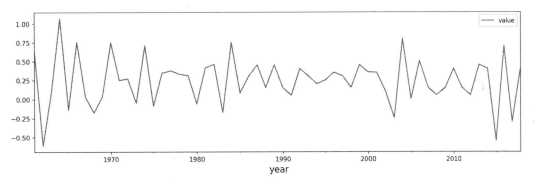

Figure 10.11 – First-order differencing for life expectancy data (detrending)

Next, you will need to determine the p and q parameters for the ARIMA (p, d, q) model.

3. The ACF and PACF plots will help you estimate the appropriate p and q values for the AR and MA models, respectively. Use `plot_acf` and `plot_pacf` on the stationary `life_df1` data:

```
fig, ax = plt.subplots(1,2)
plot_acf(life_df1, ax=ax[0])
plot_pacf(life_df1, ax=ax[1]); plt.show()
```

It produces the following plots:

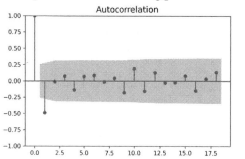
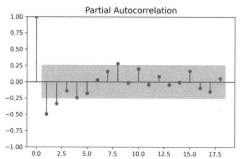

Figure 10.12 – First-order differencing for life expectancy data (detrending)

In the preceding example, the zero lag was kept in the plot to help you visually compare past lags. The ACF and PACF at lag(0) are always one, so sometimes, it is removed from the plot since it does not provide any significance. Therefore, you must focus on lag(1) to determine its significance, as well as other prior lags that are of significance.

The ACF plot provides the significant lags for the MA(q) model. The ACF plot shows a cut-off after lag 1, indicating an MA(1) model. The PACF plot provides the significant lags for the AR(p) model. There is a gradual decay with oscillation after lag 1, indicating a MA model at lag 1 or MA(1). This indicates a lack of an AR model, so the p order is zero or AR(0). Please refer to *Table 10.1* for more details.

An MA(1) process is also called a first-order process, indicating that the current value (at time `t`) is based on the value immediately preceding it (at time `t-1`).

Now, you can build the ARIMA(p, d, q) model using these values to get an `ARIMA(0,1,1)`. Sometimes, it is not clear what the optimal lag values are (the order values for p and q), so you may need to run different ARIMA models with different values for the p, d, and q parameters, similar to what you did for the grid search method in the *Forecasting univariate time series data with Exponential Smoothing* recipe.

4.   Train the ARIMA model on the training set, `life_train`, and inspect the model's summary. Don't use the differenced `life_df1` version here since ARIMA will apply differencing based on the value of the d parameter. In this example, first-order differencing was satisfactory to detrend and make the data stationary, and you set `d=1`:

```
model = ARIMA(life_train, order=(0,1,1))
results = model.fit()
results.summary()
```

You will see the summary as follows:

SARIMAX Results

Dep. Variable:	value	No. Observations:	50
Model:	ARIMA(0, 1, 1)	Log Likelihood	-24.161
Date:	Wed, 12 Jan 2022	AIC	52.321
Time:	23:13:50	BIC	56.105
Sample:	01-01-1960	HQIC	53.757
	- 01-01-2009		
Covariance Type:	opg		

	coef	std err	z	P>|z|	[0.025	0.975]
ma.L1	0.0827	0.200	0.413	0.680	-0.310	0.475
sigma2	0.1569	0.032	4.918	0.000	0.094	0.219

Ljung-Box (L1) (Q):	12.54	Jarque-Bera (JB):	0.56
Prob(Q):	0.00	Prob(JB):	0.76
Heteroskedasticity (H):	0.43	Skew:	0.07
Prob(H) (two-sided):	0.10	Kurtosis:	3.51

Figure 10.13 – Summary of ARIMA(0,1,1) for the life expectancy data

Notice that the AIC and BIC scores are provided, but they do not mean much in isolation; they are more meaningful when you're comparing multiple models.

Since the ARIMA model is mainly an MA process with an integration (differencing) factor, d, the summary results only provide the coefficient values for the MA(1) model. More on that in the *How it works...* section.

5. You will need to validate the model's residuals to determine if the ARIMA model you built captured the signals in the time series. The assumption is that if the model captured all the information, the residuals from the model's prediction are random (noise) and do not follow a pattern. For example, you expect no autocorrelation in the residuals. Start by using the `acorr_ljungbox` test on the residuals. You should expect no autocorrelation:

```
(acorr_ljungbox(results.resid,
                lags=25,
                return_df=True) < 0.05)['lb_pvalue'].
```

```
sum()
>> 0
```

The result shows 0, which is an aggregate of the results for the first 25 lags, indicating no autocorrelation.

Try the ACF plot as well:

```
plot_acf(results.resid, zero=False);plt.show()
```

This should produce an ACF plot. Here you would expect the plot to show no significant lags. In other words, all the vertical lines should be closer to zero or at zero for all lags:

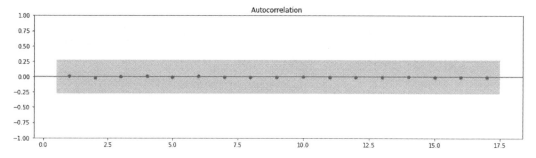

Figure 10.14 – ACF plot showing no autocorrelation for the residuals

This plot confirms no signs of autocorrelation (visually).

6. You can also inspect the distribution of the residuals. For example, you would expect normally distributed residuals with a mean of zero. You can use the QQPlot and **Kernel Density Estimation** (**KDE**) plot to observe the distribution and assess normality. You can accomplish this with the `plot_diagnostics` method:

```
results.plot_diagnostics();plt.show()
```

The preceding code will produce following plots:

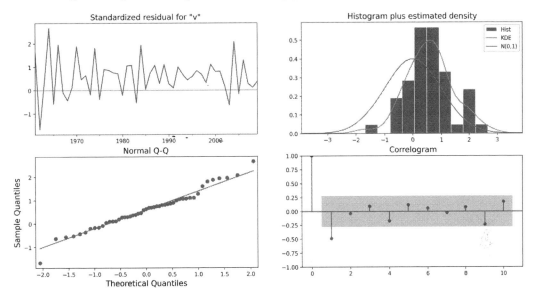

Figure 10.15 – Visual diagnostics for the ARIMA(0,1,1) model

The plots show a slight deviation from a normal distribution. For example, a perfect normally distributed dataset will have a perfect bell-curved KDE plot and all the points will be perfectly aligned on the line in the QQPlot.

So far, the results and diagnostics indicate a decent model, though there might be room for improvements. Building an ARIMA model can be an iterative process that involves creating and testing different models.

7. The final step is to create a forecast (prediction) and compare it with your test dataset (unseen or out of sample data). Use the `plot_forecast()` function you created earlier in this chapter in the *Technical requirements* section:

```
plot_forecast(results, '1998', life_train, life_test)
```

This should produce a plot with the x-axis starting from the year 1998. There should be three lines: the actual data is split into two lines, one for the training data and another for the test data, and a third line for the forecast (predicted values):

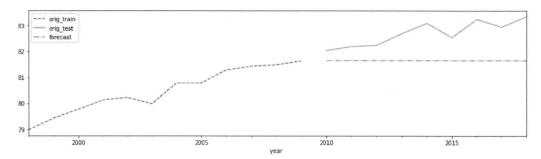

Figure 10.16 – ARIMA(0,1,1) forecast versus the actual Monthly Milk Production data

The dashed line (forecast) doesn't seem to follow the expected trend. Compare this with the results from the exponential smoothing model in *Figure 10.6*, which did a much better job. To resolve this, you can run multiple ARIMA models with different (p, d, q) values and compare the RMSE, MAPE, AIC, or BIC scores to pick the best-fitted model. You will explore this option in the *There's more...* section.

How it works...

An autoregressive model or AR(p) is a linear model that uses observations from previous time steps as inputs into a regression equation to determine the predicted value of the next step. Hence, the *auto* part in autoregression indicates *self* and can be described as the regression of a variable on a past version of itself. A typical linear regression model will have this equation:

$$y = m + \theta_1 x_1 + \theta_2 x_2 + \cdots + \theta_n x_n +$$

Here, y is the predicted variable, m is the intercept, $(x_1, x_2, \ldots, x_n)$ are the features or independent variables, and $(\theta_1, \theta_2, \ldots, \theta_n)$ are the coefficients for each of the independent variables. In regression, your goal is to solve these coefficients, including the intercept (think of them as weights), since they are later used to make predictions. The error term, ϵ, denotes the residual or noise (the unexplained portion of the model).

Compare that with the autoregressive equation and you will see the similarities:

$$AR(p) = y_t = \alpha + \theta_1 y_{t-1} + \theta_2 y_{t-2} + \cdots + \theta_p y_{t-p} + \epsilon_t$$

This is an AR model of order p written as AR (p). The main difference between an autoregressive and regression model is that the predicted variable is y_t, which is y at the current time, t, and that the $y_{t-1}, y_{t-2}, \dots, y_{t-p}$ variables are lagged (previous) versions of y. In this recipe, you used an ARIMA(0,1,1), which translates into an AR(0), indicating no autoregressive model being used.

Unlike an autoregressive model that uses past values, the moving average or MA(q) uses past errors (from past estimates) to make a prediction:

$$MA(q) = y_t = \beta + \theta_1 \epsilon_{t-1} + \theta_2 \epsilon_{t-2} + \dots + \theta_p \epsilon_{t-q} + \epsilon_t$$

Combining the AR(p) and MA(q) models would produce an ARMA(p,q) model (autoregressive moving average). Both the AR and ARMA processes assume a stationary time series. However, suppose the time series is not stationary due to the presence of a trend. In that case, you cannot use the AR or ARMA models on non-stationary data, unless you perform some transformations, such as differencing. This was the case with the life data.

Differencing is just subtracting a current value from its previous (lagged) version. For example, a differencing order of one (lag=1) can be written as $y_t - y_{t-1}$. In pandas, you used the diff method, which is set to periods=1 by default.

The ARIMA model improves on the ARMA model by adding an integrated (differencing) factor to make the time series stationary.

You leveraged both ACF plots and PACF plots to estimate the order values for the AR and MA models. The autocorrelation function measures the correlation between a current observation and its lagged version. The purpose of the ACF plot is to determine how reliable past observations are in making predictions.

On the other hand, a **partial autocorrelation function (PACF)** is like autocorrelation but with the relationships of intervening observations removed.

ACF versus PACF Through an Example

If there is a strong correlation between past observations at lags 1, 2, 3, and 4, this means that the correlation measure at lag 1 is influenced by the correlation with lag 2, lag 2 is influenced by the correlation with lag 3, and so on.

The ACF measure at lag 1 will include these influences of prior lags if they are correlated. In contrast, a PACF at lag 1 will remove these influences to measure the pure relationship at lag 1 with the current observation.

One of the reasons ARIMA is popular is because it generalizes to other simpler models, as follows:

- ARIMA(1, 0, 0) is a first-order autoregressive or AR(1) model
- ARIMA(1, 1, 0) is a *differenced* first-order autoregressive model
- ARIMA(0, 0, 1) is a first-order moving average or MA(1) model
- ARIMA(1, 0, 1) is an ARMA (1,1) model
- ARIMA(0, 1, 1) is a simple exponential smoothing model

There's more...

Sometimes, it isn't easy to identify if the time series is an MA or AR process or determine the optimal order (lag) values for p or q. You can look at the following example of a naive grid search approach by trying different combinations for p, d, and q to train other ARIMA models before picking a winning model.

Here, you will leverage the combinator() function that you created in the *Technical requirements* section. You will train multiple ARIMA models and then use get_best_model() to find the best model. As a starter, try a combination of (0,1,2) for each of the three hyperparameters (p, d, and q). You will be testing 3x3x3 or 27 ARIMA models:

```
pv, dv, qv = [list(range(3))]*3
vals = combinator([pv, dv, qv ])
score = {}
for i, (p, d, q) in enumerate(vals):
    m = ARIMA(life_train, order=(p,d,q))
    res = m.fit()
    y = life_train.values.ravel()
    y_hat = res.forecast(steps=len(y))
    score[i] = {'order': (p,d,q),
                'AIC':res.aic,
                'RMSPE': rmspe(y, y_hat),
                'BIC': res.bic,
                'AICc':res.aicc,
                'RMSE' : rmse(y, y_hat),
```

```
                    'MAPE' : mape(y, y_hat),
                    'model': res}
best_m = get_best_model(score, 'AIC')
>>
Best model: 8 with lowest AIC score: 7.698477131195528
```

If you run `best_m.summary()` to view the model's summary, you will notice that it is an ARIMA(0,2, 2). This confirms our earlier assumption that this is a moving average process, but we missed the orders.

To view the results of all 27 models in a DataFrame (tabular format), you can use the following command:

```
pd.DataFrame(score).T.sort_values(by='AIC').reset_index()
```

This should produce a DataFrame sorted by AIC. The following table shows the first five models:

index	order	AIC	BIC	AICc	RMSPE	RMSE	MAPE
0	8 (0, 2, 2)	7.697471	13.311074	8.242925	0.055956	0.463577	0.004494
1	14 (1, 1, 2)	9.533201	17.100482	10.442292	0.054758	0.453636	0.004395
2	17 (1, 2, 2)	9.675276	17.16008	10.605508	0.055728	0.461687	0.004469
3	23 (2, 1, 2)	11.510423	20.969525	12.905772	0.054477	0.451309	0.004365
4	26 (2, 2, 2)	13.832574	23.188579	15.261146	0.074281	0.615756	0.006201
5	25 (2, 2, 1)	19.672789	27.157593	20.603021	0.054426	0.451322	0.003985

Figure 10.17 – Results from the 27 ARIMA models sorted by AIC score

The **Akaike Information Criterion (AIC)** is a metric that aims to find a balance between a model's maximum likelihood and a model's simplicity. Overly complex models can sometimes overfit, meaning they can look like they learned but once they are presented with unseen data, they perform poorly. The AIC score penalizes as the number of parameters increases since they increase complexity:

$$\text{AIC} = 2k - 2\ln(L^*)$$

Here, $2k$ is considered the penalty term.

The **Bayesian Information Criteria** (**BIC**) is very similar to AIC but has a higher penalty term on the model's complexity. In general, the BIC penalty term is more significant, so it can encourage models with fewer parameters than AIC does. Therefore, if you change the sorting or evaluation criteria from AIC to BIC, you may see different results. Simpler models are preferred more with BIC:

$$\text{BIC} = k \ln(n) - 2 \ln(L^*)$$

Here, L^* is the maximum likelihood, k is the number of estimated parameters, and n is the number of data points.

To plot a forecast using the best model, you can run the following command:

```
plot_forecast(best_m, '1998', life_train, life_test)
```

As a challenge, compare the output from the preceding code with *Figure 10.16* from the ARIMA(0, 1, 1) model and *Figure 10.6* from the Exponential Smoothing model.

See also

To learn more about the ARIMA class, you can visit statsmodels's official documentation at https://www.statsmodels.org/dev/generated/statsmodels.tsa.arima.model.ARIMA.html.

How about the `milk` data, which has trend and seasonality? The next recipe will explore working with a SARIMA model to handle such data.

Forecast versus Predict Methods

In the `plot_forecast` function, we used the forecast method. In statsmodels, the SARIMA family of models, such as ARMA and ARIMA, have two methods for making predictions: `predict` and `forecast`.

The `predict` method allows you to include both *in-sample* and *out-of-sample* predictions, hence why the method takes the `start` and `end` parameters. On the other hand, the `forecast` method only takes `steps`, which is the number of *out-of-sample* forecasts, starting from the end of the sample or the training set.

Forecasting univariate time series data with seasonal ARIMA

In this recipe, you will be introduced to an enhancement to the ARIMA model for handling seasonality, known as the **Seasonal Autoregressive Integrated Moving Average** or **SARIMA**. Like an ARIMA(p, d, q), a SARIMA model also requires (p, d, q) to represent non-seasonal orders. Additionally, a SARIMA model requires the orders for the seasonal component, which is denoted as (P, D, Q, s). Combining both components, the model can be written as a SARIMA(p, d, q)(P, D, Q, s). The letters still mean the same, and the letter case indicates which component. For example, the lowercase letters represent the non-seasonal orders, while the uppercase letters represent the seasonal orders. The new parameter, s, is the number of steps per cycle – for example, s=12 for monthly data or s=4 for quarterly data.

In statsmodels, you will use the SARIMAX class to build a SARIMA model.

In this recipe, you will be working with the milk data, which contains both trend and seasonality. This was prepared in the *Technical requirements* section.

How to do it...

Follow these steps:

1. Start by importing the necessary libraries:

    ```
    from statsmodels.tsa.statespace.sarimax import SARIMAX
    ```

2. From *Figure 10.1*, we determined that both seasonality and trend exist. We could also see that the seasonal effect is additive. The periodicity or number of periods in a season is 12 since the data is monthly. This can be confirmed with an ACF plot:

    ```
    plot_acf(milk, lags=40, zero=False);plt.show()
    ```

This should produce an ACF plot for the `milk` data with a noticeable cyclical pattern of spikes at specific lags:

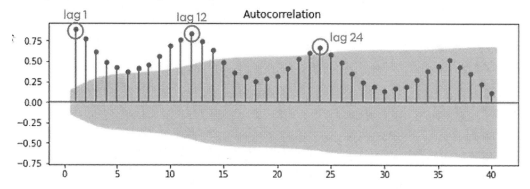

Figure 10.18 – ACF plot showing significant spikes at lags 1, 12, and 24

Notice that there is a repeating pattern every 12 months (lags). If the pattern is not easy to spot, you can try the ACF plot after you difference the data – for example, detrend (first-order differencing) the data first, then plot the ACF plot:

```
plot_acf(milk.diff(1).dropna(), lags=40, zero=False);
plt.show()
```

This should produce an ACF plot on the differenced data that makes the seasonal spikes more apparent:

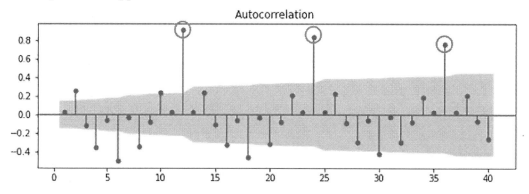

Figure 10.19 – ACF plot after differencing shows significant spikes at lags 1, 12, 24, and 36

You can also extract the seasonal component and use that for the ACF plot, as shown in the following code:

```
decomposed = seasonal_decompose(milk, period=12,
model='multiplicative')

milk_s = decomposed.seasonal

plot_acf(milk_s, zero=False, lags=40);plt.show()
```

The ACF plot will show the autocorrelation using the seasonal component after decomposition and will tell a similar story to what's shown in *Figure 10.18* and *Figure 10.19*.

Generally, you can assume a 12-month cycle when working with monthly data. For example, for the non-seasonal ARIMA portion, start with d=1 for detrending, and for the seasonal ARIMA portion, start with D=1 as well, given s=12.

3. Suppose you are not sure about the values for d (non-seasonal differencing) and D (seasonal differencing). In that case, you can use the check_stationarity function after differencing to determine if seasonal differencing was enough or not. In most cases, if the time series has both trend and seasonality, you may need to difference twice. First, you perform seasonal differencing, followed by a first-order differencing for detrending.

Start with seasonal differencing by using diff(12) (*deseasonalize*) and test if that is enough to make the time series stationarity. If not, then you will need to follow it with a first-order differencing, diff():

```
milk_dif_12 = milk.diff(12).dropna()
milk_dif_12_1 = milk.diff(12).diff(1).dropna()
sets = [milk, milk_dif_12, milk_dif_12_1]
desc = ['Original', 'Deseasonalize (Difference Once)',
'Differencing Twice']

fig, ax = plt.subplots(2,2, figsize=(20,10))
index, l = milk.index, milk.shape[0]
for i, (d_set, d_desc) in enumerate(zip(sets, desc)):
    v, r = i // 2, i % 2
    outcome, pval = check_stationarity(d_set)
    d_set.plot(ax= ax[v,r], title=f'{d_desc}: {outcome}',
legend=False)
    pd.Series(d_set.mean().values.tolist()*l,
index=index).plot(ax=ax[v,r])
    ax[v,r].title.set_size(20)
ax[1,1].set_visible(False)
plt.show()
```

This should produce 2x2 subplots (two plots per row), where the extra subplot is hidden:

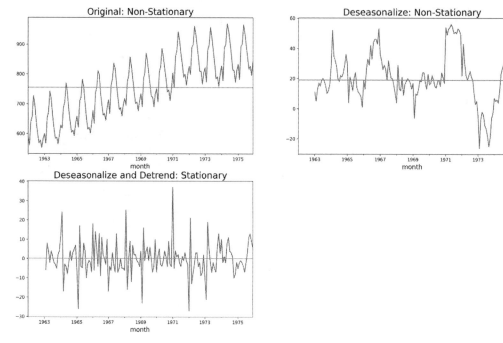

Figure 10.20 – Stationarity comparison for original, seasonally differenced, and differenced twice time series

4. Now, you will need to estimate the AR and MA orders for the non-seasonal (p, q) and seasonal components (P, Q). To do this, you must use the ACF and PACF plots on the stationary data, which can be found in the `milk_dif_12_1` DataFrame:

```
fig, ax = plt.subplots(1,2)
plot_acf(milk_dif_12_1, zero=False, lags=36, ax=ax[0],
title=f'ACF - {d_desc}')
plot_pacf(milk_dif_12_1, zero=False, lags=36, ax=ax[1],
title=f'PACF - {d_desc}')
plt.show()
```

This should produce ACF and PACF plots on the same row:

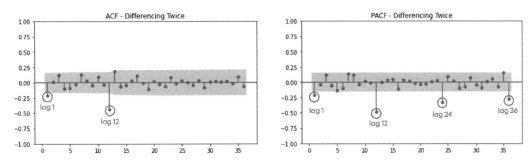

Figure 10.21 – ACF and PACF plots for the milk data after becoming stationary

Starting with the ACF plot, there is a significant spike at lag 1, which represents the non-seasonal order for the MA process. The spike at lag 12 represents the seasonal order for the MA process. Notice that there is a cut-off right after lag 1, then a spike at lag 12, followed by another cut-off (no other significant lags afterward). These are indications of a moving average model – more specifically, an order of $q=1$ and $Q=1$.

The PACF plot confirms this as well; an exponential decay at lags 12, 24, and 36 indicates an MA model. Here, the seasonal ARIMA would be ARIMA(0, 1,1) (0, 1, 1, 12).

Build the SARIMA model based on the initial information that was extracted for the AR and MA orders. The following code will fit a SARIMA(0, 1, 1)(0, 1, 1, 12) model on the training dataset. Note that the results may differ from those shown in the *Plotting ACF and PACF* recipe since the data was not split in that recipe, but it has been split here:

```
sarima_model = SARIMAX(milk_train,
                       order=(0,1,1),
                       seasonal_order=(0,1,1,12))
model = sarima_model.fit(disp=0)
```

Now, use the `plot_diagnostics` method, which becomes available after fitting the model:

```
model.plot_diagnostics(figsize=(15,7)); plt.show()
```

This will provide four plots – a standardized residual plot, a QQPlot, an ACF residual plot, and a histogram with kernel density plot:

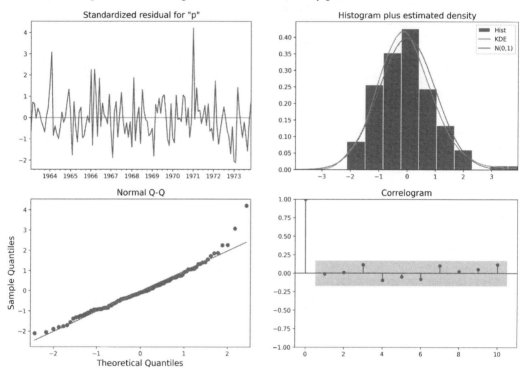

Figure 10.22 – SARIMA(0,1,1)(0,1,1,12) diagnostic plots

The residual's ACF plot (correlogram) does not show autocorrelation (ignoring the spike at lag 0 since it is always 1). However, the histogram and QQPlot show that the residuals do not fit a perfectly normal distribution. These are not critical assumptions compared to random residuals (no autocorrelation). Overall, the results look very promising.

You can obtain the summary using the `summary` method:

```
model.summary()
```

This should print out additional information regarding the model in a tabular format.

5. Use the `plot_forecast` function to plot the forecast from the SARIMA model and compare it with the test set:

```
plot_forecast(model, '1971', milk_train, milk_test)
```

This should produce a plot with the x-axis starting from the year 1971:

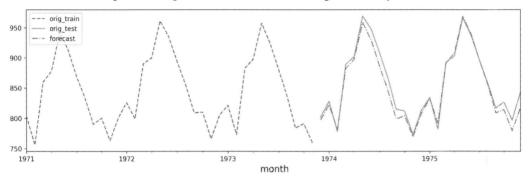

Figure 10.23 – Milk production forecast versus actual production using SARIMA(0,1,1)(0,1,1,12)

Overall, the SARIMA model did a great job of capturing the seasonal and trend effects. You can always iterate and test different values for (p, q) and (P, Q) by evaluating the results using other metrics such as RMSE, MAPE, or AIC, to name a few.

How it works...

The SARIMA model is very similar to the ARIMA model, except that it can handle seasonality and requires a seasonal order. For example, SARIMA(1,1,1)(0,0,0,0) is an ARIMA model of order (1, 1, 1).

You can think of the SARIMAX implementation as a generalized implementation for running AR, MA, ARMA, ARIMA, and SARIMA models. As shown in the *Forecasting univariate time series data with Exponential Smoothing* recipe, the `ExponentialSmoothing` class is a generalized implementation for running `SimpleExpSmoothing` and `Holt`.

There's more...

Similar to what you did in the *Forecasting univariate time series data with non-seasonal ARIMA* recipe, you can perform a naive grid search by evaluating different combinations of the (p, d, q) and (P, D, Q, s) parameters to pick the best model.

Leverage the `combinator()` function, loop through the list, and fit a different SARIMA model at every iteration. Finally, use the `get_best_model()` function to get the best model.

Let's try the combination of (0,1,2) for each of the non-seasonal order parameters, (p, d, q) and (0,1), for the seasonal order parameters, (P, D, Q). For s, you can keep it at 12 for now. This means you will be testing (3x3x3x2x2x2) or 216 models. Again, this is a naive approach and not resource-efficient, but it's still a valid option. Automated time series libraries such as `Auto_ARIMA` support this naive *brute* force grid search over combinations:

```
P_ns, D_ns, Q_ns = [list(range(3))]*3
P_s, D_s, Q_s = [list(range(2))]*3
vals = combinator([P_ns, D_ns, Q_ns, P_s, D_s, Q_s])
score = {}
for i, (p, d, q, P, D, Q) in enumerate(vals):
    if i%15 == 0:
        print(f'Running model #{i} using SARIMA({p},{d},{q})
({P},{D},{Q},12)')
    m = SARIMAX(milk_train,
                order=(p,d,q),
                seasonal_order=(P, D, Q, 12),
                enforce_stationarity=False)
    res = m.fit(disp=0)
    y = milk_test.values.ravel()
    y_hat = res.forecast(steps=len(y))
    score[i] = {'non-seasonal order': (p,d,q),
                'seasonal order': (P, D, Q),
                'AIC':res.aic,
                'AICc': res.aicc,
                'BIC': res.bic,
                'RMSPE': rmspe(y, y_hat),
                'RMSE' : rmse(y, y_hat),
                'MAPE' : mape(y, y_hat),
                'model': res}
```

Notice the `enforce_stationarity=False` parameter to avoid a `LinAlgError` that may occur when running a naive grid search.

It will take a little more time (compared to running one SARIMA model) to run all 216 models. This took approximately 55 seconds (about 1 minute) on my machine. Once completed, you can evaluate the winning model using `get_best_model`:

```
best_model = get_best_model(score, 'AIC')
>>
Best model: 211 with lowest AIC score: 795.4217652895388
```

Let's inspect model number `211`:

```
score[211]
{'non-seasonal order': (2, 2, 2),
 'seasonal order': (0, 1, 1),
 'AIC': 795.4217652895388,
 'RMSPE': 0.17818982960206564,
 'RMSE': 15.135855599359052,
 'MAPE': 0.014454255464947679,
 'model': <statsmodels.tsa.statespace.sarimax.
SARIMAXResultsWrapper at 0x7fd090ba9880>}
```

The best model was a SARIMA(2, 2, 2)(0, 1, 1, 12). This is different from the earlier model we estimated as SARIMA(0, 1, 1)(0, 1, 1, 12). Finally, you can forecast and plot the model using the `plot_forecast` function:

```
plot_forecast(best_model, '1962', milk_train, milk_test)
```

This should produce a plot with the x-axis starting from the year 1962:

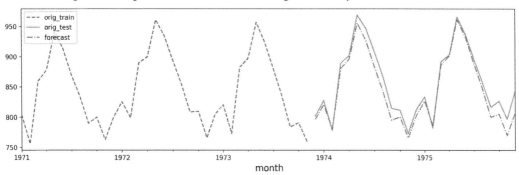

Figure 10.24 – Milk production forecast versus actual production using SARIMA(2,2,2)(0,1,1,12)

Here's an exercise for you: compare the plots from *Figure 10.23* and *Figure 10.24*. What do you notice?

You can also store the results from training the models in a tabular format using the following command:

```
pd.DataFrame(score).T.sort_values(by='AIC').reset_index()
```

This should produce an output similar to what's shown in *Figure 10.17*. You can change the sort_values criteria and use any other columns, such as BIC or AIC.

See also

To learn more about the SARIMAX class, you can visit statsmodels's official documentation at https://www.statsmodels.org/dev/generated/statsmodels.tsa.statespace.sarimax.SARIMAX.html.

11

Additional Statistical Modeling Techniques for Time Series

In *Chapter 10, Building Univariate Time Series Models Using Statistical Methods*, you were introduced to exponential smoothing, non-seasonal ARIMA, and seasonal ARIMA for building forecasting models. These are popular techniques and are referred to as classical or statistical forecasting methods. They are fast, simple to implement, and easy to interpret.

In this chapter, you will dive head-first and learn about additional statistical methods that build on the foundation you gained from the previous chapter. This chapter will introduce a few libraries that can automate time series forecasting and model optimization—for example, **auto_arima** and Facebook's **Prophet** library. Additionally, you will explore statsmodels' **vector autoregressive (VAR)** class for working with multivariate time series and the arch library, which supports **GARCH** for modeling volatility in financial data.

The main goal of this chapter is to introduce you to the Prophet library (which is also an algorithm) and the concept of multivariate time series modeling with VAR models.

In this chapter, we will cover the following recipes:

- Forecasting time series data using auto_arima

- Forecasting time series data using Facebook Prophet

- Forecasting multivariate time series data using VAR

- Evaluating vector autoregressive (VAR) models

- Forecasting volatility in financial time series data with GARCH

Technical requirements

You can download the Jupyter Notebooks to follow along and the necessary datasets for this chapter from this book's GitHub repository:

- Jupyter Notebooks: `https://github.com/PacktPublishing/Time-Series-Analysis-with-Python-Cookbook./blob/main/code/Ch11/Chapter%2011.ipynb`

- Datasets: `https://github.com/PacktPublishing/Time-Series-Analysis-with-Python-Cookbook./tree/main/datasets/Ch11`

There are common libraries that you will be using throughout the recipes in this chapter. You can import them in advance by using the following code:

```
import pandas as pd
import numpy as np
import matplotlib.pyplot as plt
from statsmodels.graphics.tsaplots import plot_acf, plot_pacf
from statsmodels.tsa.statespace.tools import diff
from pathlib import Path
import warnings
warnings.filterwarnings('ignore')
plt.rc("figure", figsize=(16, 5))
```

Forecasting time series data using auto_arima

For this recipe, you must install `pmdarima`, a Python library that includes `auto_arima` for automating ARIMA hyperparameter optimization and model fitting. The `auto_arima` implementation in Python is inspired by the popular `auto.arima` from the `forecast` package in R.

In *Chapter 10, Building Univariate Time Series Models Using Statistical Methods*, you learned that finding the proper orders for the AR and MA components is not simple. Although you explored useful techniques for estimating the orders, such as interpreting the **partial autocorrelation function** (**PACF**) and **autocorrelation function** (**ACF**) plots, you may still need to train different models to find the optimal configurations (referred to as *hyperparameter tuning*). This can be a time-consuming process and is where `auto_arima` shines.

Instead of the naive approach of training multiple models through grid search to cover every possible combination of parameter values, `auto_arima` automates the process for finding the optimal parameters. The `auto_arima` function uses a `stepwise` algorithm that is faster and more efficient than a full grid search or random search:

- When `stepwise=True`, `auto_arima` performs a stepwise search (which is the default).

- With `stepwise=False`, it performs a brute-force grid search (full search).

- With `random=True`, it performs a random search.

The stepwise algorithm was proposed in 2008 by Rob Hyndman and Yeasmin Khandakar in the paper *Automatic Time Series Forecasting: The forecast Package for R*, which was published in the Journal of Statistical Software 27, no. 3 (2008) (`https://doi.org/10.18637/jss.v027.i03`). In a nutshell, stepwise is an optimization technique that utilizes grid search more efficiently. This is accomplished using unit root tests and minimizing information criteria (for example, **Akaike Information Criterion** (**AIC**) and **Maximum Likelihood Estimation** (**MLE**).

Additionally, `auto_arima` can handle seasonal and non-seasonal ARIMA models. If seasonal ARIMA is desired, then you will need to set `seasonal=True` for `auto_arima` to optimize over the (P, D, Q) values.

Getting ready

You can download the Jupyter Notebooks and necessary datasets from this book's GitHub repository. Please refer to the *Technical requirements* section of this chapter for more information.

You will need to install pmdarima before you can proceed with this recipe.

To install it using pip, use the following command:

```
pip install pmdarima
```

To install it using conda, use the following command:

```
conda install -c conda-forge pmdarima
```

You will use the milk_production.csv data used in *Chapter 10, Building Univariate Time Series Models Using Statistical Methods*. Recall that the data contains both trend and seasonality, so you will be training a SARIMA model.

How to do it...

The pmdarima library wraps over the statsmodels library, so you will see familiar methods and attributes as you proceed. You will follow a similar process by loading the data, splitting the data into train and test sets, train the model, and evaluate the results.

1. Start by importing the necessary libraries and load the Monthly Milk Production dataset from the milk_production.csv file:

    ```
    import pmdarima as pm
    ```

    Ingest the milk_prodiction.csv into a pandas DataFrame:

    ```
    milk_file = Path('../../datasets/Ch11/milk_production.
    csv')
    milk = pd.read_csv(milk_file,
                       index_col='month',
                       parse_dates=True)
    ```

2. Split the data into train and test sets using the train_test_split function from pmdarima. This is a wrapper to scikit-learn's train_test_split function but without shuffling. The following code shows how to use both; they will produce the same results:

    ```
    from sklearn.model_selection import train_test_split
    train, test = train_test_split(milk, test_size=0.10,
    ```

```
shuffle=False)
# same results using pmdarima
train, test = pm.model_selection.train_test_split(milk,
test_size=0.10)
print(f'Train: {train.shape}')
print(f'Test: {test.shape}')
>>
Train: (151, 1)
Test: (17, 1)
```

There are 151 months in the training set and 17 months in the test set. You will use the test set to evaluate the model using out-of-sample data.

3. You will use the auto_arima function from pmdarima to optimize and find the best configuration for your SARIMA model. Prior knowledge about the milk data is key to obtaining the best results from auto_arima. You know the data has a seasonal pattern, so you will need to provide values for the two parameters: seasonal=True and m=12 (the number of periods in a season). If these values are not set, the model will only search for the non-seasonal orders (p, d, q).

    The test parameter specifies the type of unit root test to use to detect stationarity to determine the differencing order (d). The default test is kpss. You will change the parameter to use adf instead (to be consistent with what you did in *Chapter 10, Building Univariate Time Series Models Using Statistical Methods.*) Similarly, seasonal_test is used to determine the order (D) for seasonal differencing. The default seasonal_test is OCSB, which you will keep as-is:

```
auto_model = pm.auto_arima(train,
                           seasonal=True,
                           m=12,
                           test='adf',
                           stepwise=True)
auto_model.summary()
```

The summary will show the configuration of the selected SARIMA model and the information criteria scores (for example, AIC and BIC):

SARIMAX Results

Dep. Variable:		y	No. Observations:	151
Model:	SARIMAX(0, 1, 1)x(0, 1, 1, 12)		Log Likelihood	-475.008
Date:	Thu, 24 Mar 2022		AIC	956.016
Time:	00:33:43		BIC	964.798
Sample:	0		HQIC	959.585
	- 151			
Covariance Type:	opg			

	coef	std err	z	P>|z|	[0.025	0.975]
ma.L1	-0.2714	0.082	-3.326	0.001	-0.431	-0.111
ma.S.L12	-0.6233	0.079	-7.908	0.000	-0.778	-0.469
sigma2	54.7638	5.498	9.960	0.000	43.987	65.540

Ljung-Box (Q):	24.04	Jarque-Bera (JB):	31.78
Prob(Q):	0.98	Prob(JB):	0.00
Heteroskedasticity (H):	1.22	Skew:	0.74
Prob(H) (two-sided):	0.50	Kurtosis:	4.83

Figure 11.1 – Summary of the best SARIMA model selected using auto_arima

Interestingly, the best model is a SARIMA(0,1,1)(0,1,1,12), which is the same model you obtained in the *Forecasting univariate time series data with non-seasonal ARIMA* recipe in the previous chapter. You estimated the non-seasonal order (p, q) and seasonal orders (P, Q) using the ACF and PACF plots.

4. If you want to observe the score of the trained model at each iteration, you can use `trace=True`:

```
auto_model = pm.auto_arima(train,
                           seasonal=True,
                           m=12,
                           test='adf',
                           stepwise=True,
                           trace=True)
```

This should print the AIC results for each model from the step-wise algorithm:

```
Performing stepwise search to minimize aic
 ARIMA(2,1,2)(1,1,1)[12]             : AIC=961.878, Time=0.68 sec
 ARIMA(0,1,0)(0,1,0)[12]             : AIC=1005.341, Time=0.01 sec
 ARIMA(1,1,0)(1,1,0)[12]             : AIC=971.814, Time=0.09 sec
 ARIMA(0,1,1)(0,1,1)[12]             : AIC=956.016, Time=0.13 sec
 ARIMA(0,1,1)(0,1,0)[12]             : AIC=996.508, Time=0.04 sec
 ARIMA(0,1,1)(1,1,1)[12]             : AIC=957.982, Time=0.21 sec
 ARIMA(0,1,1)(0,1,2)[12]             : AIC=957.967, Time=0.43 sec
 ARIMA(0,1,1)(1,1,0)[12]             : AIC=971.938, Time=0.07 sec
 ARIMA(0,1,1)(1,1,2)[12]             : AIC=960.016, Time=0.54 sec
 ARIMA(0,1,0)(0,1,1)[12]             : AIC=964.474, Time=0.10 sec
 ARIMA(1,1,1)(0,1,1)[12]             : AIC=957.884, Time=0.20 sec
 ARIMA(0,1,2)(0,1,1)[12]             : AIC=957.783, Time=0.19 sec
 ARIMA(1,1,0)(0,1,1)[12]             : AIC=956.436, Time=0.18 sec
 ARIMA(1,1,2)(0,1,1)[12]             : AIC=959.701, Time=0.40 sec
 ARIMA(0,1,1)(0,1,1)[12] intercept   : AIC=958.000, Time=0.16 sec

Best model:  ARIMA(0,1,1)(0,1,1)[12]
Total fit time: 3.462 seconds
```

Figure 11.2 – auto_arima evaluating different SARIMA models

The best model was selected based on AIC, which is controlled by the information_criterion parameter. This can be changed to any of the four supported information criterias aic (*default*), bic, hqic, and oob.

In *Figure 11.2* two models are highlighted with similar (close enough) AIC scores but with drastically different non-seasonal (p, q) orders. The winning model (marked with a star) does not have a non-seasonal autoregressive AR(p) component; instead, it assumes a moving average MA(q) process. On the other hand, the second highlighted model shows only an AR(p) process, for the non-seasonal component. This demonstrates that even the best auto ARIMA still require your best judgment and analysis to evaluate the results.

Choose bic as the information criteria, as shown in the following code:

```
auto_model = pm.auto_arima(train,
                           seasonal=True,
                           m=12,
                           test='adf',
                           information_criterion='bic',
                           stepwise=True,
                           trace=True)
```

The output will display the BIC for each iteration. Interestingly, the winning model will be the same as the one shown in *Figure 11.2*.

5. Inspect the residuals to gauge the overall performance of the model by using the `plot_diagnostics` method. This should produce the same results that were shown in *Figure 10.24* from *Chapter 10, Building Univariate Time Series Models Using Statistical Methods*.

6. `auto_model` stored the winning SARIMA model. To make a prediction, you can use the `predict` method. You need to provide the number of periods to forecast forward into the future. You can obtain the confidence intervals with the prediction by updating the `return_conf_int` parameter from `False` to `True`. This allows you to plot the lower and upper confidence intervals using matplotlib's `fill_between` function. The following code uses the `predict` method, returns the confidence intervals, and plots the predicted values against the test set:

```
n = test.shape[0]
forecast, conf_interval = auto_model.predict(n_periods=n,
return_conf_int=True)
lower_ci, upper_ci = zip(*conf_interval)

index = test.index
ax = test.plot(style='--', alpha=0.6, figsize=(12,4))
pd.Series(forecast, index=index).plot(style='-', ax=ax)
plt.fill_between(index, lower_ci, upper_ci, alpha=0.2)
plt.legend(['test', 'forecast']); plt.show()
```

The shaded area is based on the lower and upper bounds of the confidence intervals:

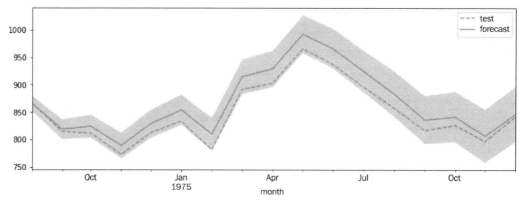

Figure 11.3 – Plotting the forecast from auto_arima against actual test data with the confidence intervals

The default confidence interval is set to 95% and can be controlled using the alpha parameter (alpha=0.05, which is 95% confidence interval) from the predict() method. The shaded area represents the likelihood that the real values would lie between this range. Ideally, you would prefer a narrower confidence interval range.

Notice that the forecast line lies in the middle of the shaded area. This represents the mean of the upper and lower bounds. The following code demonstrates this:

```
sum(forecast) == sum(conf_interval.mean(axis=1))
>> True
```

How it works...

The auto_arima function from the pmdarima library is a wrapper for the statsmodels SARIMAX class. auto_arima intelligently attempts to automate the process of optimizing the training process to find the best model and parameters. There are three ways to do so:

- The naive brute-force grid search method (full search)
- Random grid search
- The stepwise search algorithm

This is controlled by the stepwise parameter, which defaults to True.

There's more...

The pmdarima library offers a plethora of useful functions to help you make informed decisions so that you can understand the data you are working with.

For example, the ndiff function performs stationarity tests to determine the differencing order, d, to make the time series stationary. The tests include the Augmented Dickey-Fuller (adf) test, the Kwiatkowski–Phillips–Schmidt–Shin (kpss) test, and the Phillips-Perron (pp) test.

Similarly, the nsdiff function helps estimate the number of seasonal differencing orders (D) that are needed. The implementation covers two tests – the Osborn-Chui-Smith-Birchenhall (ocsb) and Canova-Hansen (ch) tests:

```
from pmdarima.arima.utils import ndiffs, nsdiffs
n_adf = ndiffs(milk, test='adf')
# KPSS test (the default in auto_arima):
n_kpss = ndiffs(milk, test='kpss')
```

```
n_pp = ndiffs(milk, test='pp')
n_ch = nsdiffs(milk, test='ocsb', m=10, max_D=12,)
n_ocsb = nsdiffs(milk, test='ch' , m=10, max_D=12,)
```

auto_arima() gives you more control over the evaluation process by providing a min and max constraints. For example, you can provide min and max constraints for the non-seasonal autoregressive order, p, or the seasonal moving average, Q. The following code shows how some of these parameters and constraints can be used:

```
model = pm.auto_arima(train,
                      seasonal=True,
                      with_intercept=True,
                      d=1,
                      max_d=2,
                      start_p=0, max_p=2,
                      start_q=0, max_q=2,
                      m=12,
                      D=1,
                      max_D=2,
                      start_P=0, max_P=2,
                      start_Q=0, max_Q=2,
                      information_criterion='aic',
                      stepwise=False,
                      out_of_sample_siz=25,
                      test = 'kpss',
                      score='mape',
                      trace=True)
```

If you run the preceding code, auto_arima will create different models for every combination of the parameter values based on the constraints you provided. Because stepwise is set to False, it becomes a brute-force grid search in which every permutation for the different variable combinations is tested one by one. Hence, this is generally a much slower process, but by providing these constraints, you can improve the search performance.

With `trace=True`, executing the preceding code will show the AIC score for each fitted model. The following code shows the seasonal ARIMA model and the AIC scores for the last three models:

```
. . .
ARIMA(2,1,2)(0,1,0)[12] intercept    : AIC=993.327, Time=0.31
sec
  ARIMA(2,1,2)(0,1,1)[12] intercept   : AIC=961.890, Time=0.56
sec
  ARIMA(2,1,2)(1,1,0)[12] intercept   : AIC=976.662, Time=0.72
sec
```

Once completed, it should print out the best model.

The approach that was taken here, with `stepwise=False`, should resemble the approach you took in *Chapter 10, Building Univariate Time Series Models Using Statistical Methods,* in the *Forecasting univariate time series data with seasonal ARIMA* recipe, in the *There's more...* section.

See also

To learn more about the `auto_arima` implementation, please visit the official documentation at `https://alkaline-ml.com/pmdarima/modules/generated/pmdarima.arima.auto_arima.html`.

In the next recipe, you will learn about a new algorithm that provides a simpler API for model tuning and optimization. In other words, there are far fewer parameters that you need to worry about.

Forecasting time series data using Facebook Prophet

The **Prophet** library is a popular open source project that was originally developed at Facebook (Meta) based on a 2017 paper that proposed an algorithm for time series forecasting titled *Forecasting at Scale*. The project soon gained popularity due to its simplicity, its ability to create compelling and performant forecasting models, and its ability to handle complex seasonality, holiday effects, missing data, and outliers. The Prophet library automates many aspects of designing a forecasting model while providing additional out-of-the-box visualizations. The library offers additional capabilities, such as building growth models (saturated forecasts), working with uncertainty in trend and seasonality, and changepoint detection.

In this recipe, you will use the Milk Production dataset used in the previous recipe. This will help you understand the different forecasting approaches while using the same dataset for benchmarking.

The Prophet algorithm is an additive regression model that can handle non-linear trends and works well with strong seasonal effects. The algorithm decomposes a time series into three main components: *trend*, *seasonality*, and *holidays*. The model can be written as follows:

$$y(t) = g(t) + s(t) + h(t) + \epsilon_t$$

Here, $g(t)$ is the trend function, $s(t)$ represents the periodic seasonality function, $h(t)$ covers effects of holidays, and ϵ_t is the error term (residual).

The algorithm uses Bayesian inferencing to automate many aspects of tuning the model and finding the optimized values for each component. Behind the scenes, Prophet uses **Stan**, a library for Bayesian inferencing, through the **PyStan** library as the Python interface to Stan.

Getting ready

You can the Jupyter Notebooks and necessary datasets from this book's GitHub repository. Please refer to the *Technical requirements* section of this chapter for more information.

It is recommended that you create a new virtual Python environment for Prophet to avoid issues with your current environment. If you need a quick refresher on how to create a virtual Python environment, check out the *Development environment setup* recipe from *Chapter 1, Getting Started with Time Series Analysis*. That chapter covers two methods: using conda and venv.

Let's learn how to use conda. You can give the environment any name you like. For the following example, we will name our environment prophet:

```
>> conda create -n prophet python=3.8 -y
>> conda activate prophet
```

To make the new prophet environment visible within Jupyter, run the following code:

```
python -m ipykernel install --user --name prophet --display-
name "fbProphet"
```

To install Prophet using `pip`, you will need to install `pystan` first. Make sure you install the supported PyStan version. You can check the documentation at `https://facebook.github.io/prophet/docs/installation.html#python` for the latest instructions:

```
pip install pystan==2.19.1.1
```

Once installed, run the following command:

```
pip install prophet
```

For additional information or troubleshooting when installing with `pip`, please refer to their official documentation.

To install Prophet use Conda, which takes care of all the necessary dependencies, use the following command:

```
conda install -c conda-forge prophet
```

How to do it...

The Prophet library is very opinionated when it comes to column names. The Prophet class does not expect a `DatetimeIndex` but rather a datetime column called `ds` and a variable column (that you want to forecast) called `y`. Note that if you have more than two columns, Prophet will only pick the `ds` and `y` columns and ignore the rest. If these two columns do not exist, it will throw an error. Follow these steps:

1. Start by reading the `milk_productions.csv` file and rename the columns `ds` and `y`:

    ```
    from prophet import Prophet
    milk_file = Path('../../datasets/Ch11/milk_production.
    csv')


    milk = pd.read_csv(milk_file, parse_dates=['month'])
    milk.columns = ['ds', 'y']
    ```

    Split the data into test and train sets. Let's go with a 90/10 split by using the following code:

    ```
    idx = round(len(milk) * 0.90)
    train = milk[:idx]
    test = milk[idx:]
    ```

```
print(f'Train: {train.shape}')
print(f'Test: {test.shape}')
>>
Train: (151, 2)
Test: (17, 2)
```

2. You can create an instance of the Prophet class and fit it on the train set in one line using the `fit` method. The milk production time series is monthly, with both trend and a steady seasonal fluctuation (additive). The default `seasonality_mode` in Prophet is `additive`, so leave it as-is:

```
From prophet import Prophet
model = Prophet().fit(train)
```

3. Some setup needs to be done before you can use the model to make predictions. Use the `make_future_dataframe` method to extend the `train` DataFrame forward for a specific number of periods and at a specified frequency:

```
Future = m_milk.make_future_dataframe(len(test_milk),
freq='MS')
```

This extends the training data by 17 months (the number of periods in the test set). In total, you should have the exact number of periods that are in the milk DataFrame (train and test). The frequency is set to month start with `freq='MS'`. The `future` object only contains one column, `ds`, of the `datetime64 [ns]` type, which is used to populate the predicted values:

```
len(milk) == len(future)
>> True
```

4. Now, use the `predict` method to take the future DataFrame and make predictions. The result will be a DataFrame that's the same length as `forecast` but now with additional columns:

```
forecast = model.predict(future)
forecast.columns
>>
Index(['ds', 'trend', 'yhat_lower', 'yhat_upper', 'trend_
lower', 'trend_upper',
        'multiplicative_terms',
        'multiplicative_terms_lower',
        'multiplicative_terms_upper', 'yearly',
```

```
        'yearly_lower', 'yearly_upper',
        'additive_terms', 'additive_terms_lower',
        'additive_terms_upper',
        'yhat'],
      dtype='object')
```

Notice that Prophet returned a lot of details to help you understand how the model performs. Of interest are ds and the predicted value, yhat. Both yhat_lower and yhat_upper represent the uncertainty intervals for the prediction (yhat).

Create a cols object to store the columns of interest so that you can use them later:

```
cols = ['ds', 'yhat', 'yhat_lower', 'yhat_upper']
```

5. The model object provides two plotting methods: plot and plot_components. Start by using plot to visualize the forecast from Prophet:

```
model.plot(forecast, ylabel='Milk Production in Pounds')
plt.show()
```

This should produce a time series plot with two forecasts (predictions): the first segment can be distinguished by the dots (one for each training data point), while the line represents the estimated forecast for the historical data. This is followed by another segment that shows future predictions beyond the training data (no dots present):

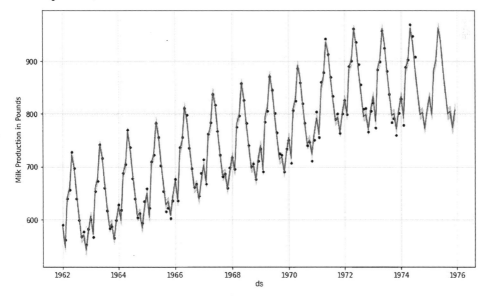

Figure 11.4 – Plotting the forecast (historical and future) using Prophet

Here, you can see the distinction between past and future estimates (forecast) more concretely by only plotting the future periods beyond the training set. You can accomplish this with the following code:

```
predicted = model.predict(test)
model.plot(predicted, ylabel='Milk Production in
      Pounds')
plt.show()
```

This should produce a plot that's similar to the one shown in *Figure 11.4*, but it will only show the forecast line for the second segment – that is, the future forecast.

The shaded area in *Figure 11.4* represents the uncertainty intervals. This is represented by the yhat_lower and yhat_upper columns in the forecast DataFrame.

6. The next important plot deals with the forecast components. Use the plot_components method to plot the components:

```
Model.plot_components(forecast); plt.show()
```

The number of subplots will depend on the number of components that have been identified in the forecast. For example, if holiday was included, then it will show the holiday component. In our example, there will be two subplots: trend and yearly:

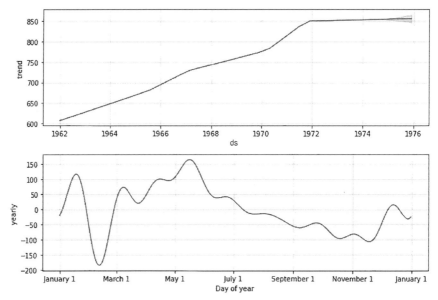

Figure 11.5 – Plotting the components showing trend and seasonality (annual)

Figure 11.5 breaks down the trend and seasonality of the training data. If you look at *Figure 11.4*, you will see a positive upward trend that becomes steady (slows down) starting from 1972. The seasonal pattern shows an increase in production around summertime (this peaks in *Figure 11.4*).

The shaded area in the trend plot represents the uncertainty interval for estimating the trend. The data is stored in the `trend_lower` and `trend_upper` columns of the `forecast` DataFrame.

7. Finally, compare with out-of-sample data (the test data) to see how well the model performs:

```
ax = test.plot(x='ds', y='y',
                label='Actual',
                style='-.',
                figsize=(12,4))
predicted.plot(x='ds', y='yhat',
                label='Predicted',
                ax=ax)
plt.title('Milk Production Actual vs Forecast')
plt.show()
```

Compare the following plot with *Figure 11.3* to see how Prophet compares to the SARIMA model that you obtained using `auto_arima`:

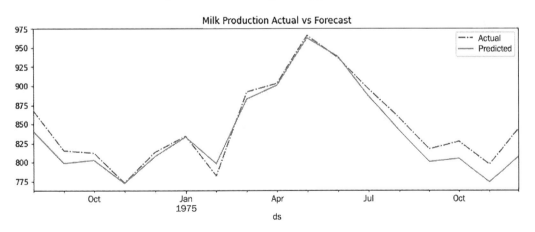

Figure 11.6 – Comparing Prophet's forecast against test data

Notice that for the highly seasonal milk production data, the model did a great job. Generally, Prophet shines when it's working with strong seasonal time series data.

How it works...

Overall, Prophet automated many aspects of building and optimizing the model. Building a complex model was straightforward with Prophet. However, you still had to provide some instructions initially to ensure the model was tuned properly. For example, you had to determine if the seasonal effect was additive or multiplicative when initializing the model. You also had to specify a monthly frequency when extending the periods into the future with `freq='MS'` in the `make_future_dataframe` method.

When you used `.fit` to build the model, you probably noticed two messages, as follows:

```
INFO:prophet:Disabling weekly seasonality. Run prophet with
weekly_seasonality=True to override this.
INFO:prophet:Disabling daily seasonality. Run prophet with
daily_seasonality=True to override this.
```

Because `yearly_seasonality`, `weekly_seasonality`, and `daily_seasonality` are set to `auto` by default, this allows Prophet to determine which ones to turn on or off based on the data.

As per Prophet's documentation, there are three components for the uncertainty intervals (for example, `yhat_lower` and `yhat_upper`):

- Observation noise
- Parameter uncertainty
- Future trend uncertainty

By default, the `uncertainty_samples` parameter is set to `1000`, which is the number of simulations to estimate the uncertainty using the **Hamiltonian Monte Carlo (HMC)** algorithm. You can always reduce the number of samples that are simulated or set it to `0` or `False` to speed up the performance. If you set `uncertainty_samples=0` or `uncertainty_samples=False`, the forecast's output will not contain any uncertainty interval calculations. For example, you will not have `yhat_lower` or `yhat_upper`.

Prophet automatically detects changes or sudden fluctuations in the trend. Initially, it will place 25 points using the first 80% of the training data. You can change the number of changepoints with the `n_changepoints` parameter. Similarly, the proportion of past data to use to estimate the changepoints can be updated using `changepoint_range`, which defaults to 0.8 (or 80%). You can observe the 25 changepoints using the `changepoints` attribute from the `model` object. The following code shows the first five:

```
model.changepoints.head()
>>
```

5	1962-06-01
10	1962-11-01
14	1963-03-01
19	1963-08-01
24	1964-01-01

You can plot these points as well, as shown in the following code:

```
ax = milk.set_index('ds').plot(figsize=(12,5))
milk.set_index('ds').loc[model.changepoints].plot(style='o',
ax=ax)
plt.legend(['original data', 'changepoints'])
plt.show()
```

This should produce a plot that contains the original time series data and the 25 potential changepoints that indicate changes in trend:

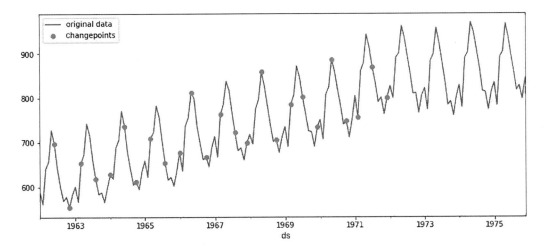

Figure 11.7 – The 25 potential changepoints, as identified by Prophet

These potential changepoints were estimated from the first 80% of the training data.

In the next section, you will explore changepoint detection in more detail.

There's more...

To plot the *significant* changepoints that capture the impactful changes in trend, you can use the `add_changepoints_to_plot` function, as shown in the following code:

```
from prophet.plot import add_changepoints_to_plot

fig = model.plot(forecast, ylabel='Milk Production in Pounds')
add_changepoints_to_plot(fig.gca(), model, forecast)
plt.show()
```

This should produce a plot similar to *Figure 11.7*, but with the additional changepoint lines and the trend line. 8 significant changepoints are shown out of the 25. The linear trend line should be the same as the trend component shown in *Figure 11.5*:

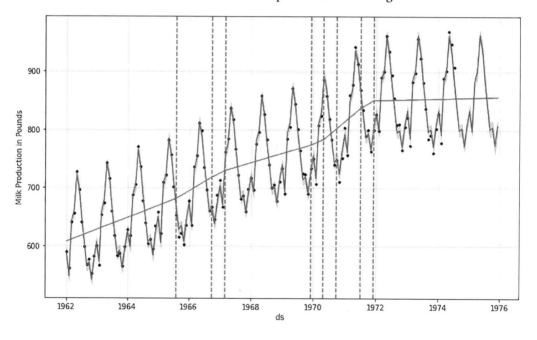

Figure 11.8 – Showing the eight significant change points and the trend line

Notice how the trend line changes at the identified changepoints. This is how Prophet can detect changes in trends. Notice that the line is not an exact straight line since *piecewise regression* was used to build the trend model. When thinking about piecewise linear models, you can think of multiple linear regression lines between the significant changepoints (segments) that are then connected. This gives the model the flexibility to capture non-linear changes in trends and make future predictions.

See also

Prophet supports both Python and R. For more information on the Python API, please visit the following documentation: `https://facebook.github.io/prophet/docs/quick_start.html#python-api`.

If you are interested in reading the original paper behind the Prophet algorithm, which is publicly available, go to `https://peerj.com/preprints/3190/`.

So far, you have been working with univariate time series. In the next recipe, you will learn how to work with multivariate time series.

Forecasting multivariate time series data using VAR

In this recipe, you will explore the **Vector Autoregressive (VAR)** model for working with multivariate time series. In *Chapter 10, Building Univariate Time Series Models Using Statistical Methods,* we discussed AR, MA, ARIMA, and SARIMA as examples of univariate one-directional models. VAR, on the other hand, is bi-directional and multivariate.

> **VAR versus AR Models**
>
> You can think of a VAR of order p, or VAR(P), as a generalization of the univariate AR(p) mode for working with multiple time series. Multiple time series are represented as a vector, hence the name vector autoregression. A VAR of lag one can be written as VAR(1) across two or more variables.

There are other forms of multivariate time series models, including **Vector Moving Average (VMA)**, **Vector Autoregressive Moving Average (VARMA)**, and **Vector Autoregressive Integrated Moving Average (VARIMA)**, that generalize other univariate models. In practice, you will find that VAR is used the most due to its simplicity. VAR models are very popular in economics, but you will find them being used in other areas, such as social sciences, natural sciences, and engineering.

The premise behind multivariate time series is that you can add more power to your forecast when leveraging multiple time series (or inputs variables) as opposed to a single time series (single variable). Simply put, VAR is used when you have two or more time series that have (or are assumed to have) an influence on each other's behavior. These are normally referred to as **endogenous** variables and the relationship is bi-directional. If the variables or time series are not directly related, or we do not know if there is a direct influence within the same system, we refer to them as **exogenous** variables.

Exogenous versus Endogenous Variables

When you start researching more about VAR models, you will come across references to endogenous and exogenous variables. At a high level, the two are the opposite of each other and in *statsmodels*, you will see them referenced as endog and exog, respectively.

Endogenous variables are influenced by other variables within the system. In other words, we expect that a change in one's state affects the other. Sometimes, these can be referred to as dependent variables in machine learning literature. You can use the Granger causality tests to determine if there is such a relationship between multiple endogenous variables. For example, in statsmodels, you can use grangercausalitytests.

On the other hand, exogenous variables are outside the system and do not have a direct influence on the variables. They are external influencers. Sometimes, these can be referred to as independent variables in machine learning literature.

A VAR model, like an AR model, assumes the stationarity of the time series variables. This means that each endogenous variable (time series) needs to be stationary.

To illustrate how VAR works and the mathematical equation behind it, let's start with a simple VAR(1) with *two* endogenous variables, referred to as $(y_{1,t}, y_{2,t})$. Recall from *Chapter 10, Building Univariate Time Series Models Using Statistical Methods*, that an AR(1) model would take the following form:

$$AR(1) = y_t = \alpha + \theta_1 y_{t-1} + \epsilon_t$$

Generally, an AR(p) model is a linear model of past values of itself and the (p) parameter tells us how far back we should go. Now, assume you have two AR(1) models for two different time series data. This will look as follows:

$$y_{(1),t} = \alpha_1 + \theta_{11} y_{(1),t-1} + \epsilon_{(1),t}$$
$$y_{(2),t} = \alpha_2 + \theta_{21} y_{(2),t-1} + \epsilon_{(2),t}$$

However, these are two separate models that do not show any relationship or that influence each other. If we create a linear combination of the two models (the past values of itself and the past values of the other time series), we would get the following formula:

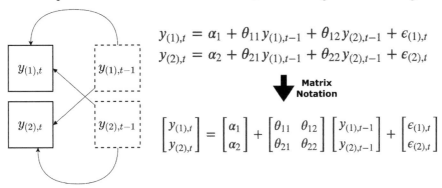

$$y_{(1),t} = \alpha_1 + \theta_{11} y_{(1),t-1} + \theta_{12} y_{(2),t-1} + \epsilon_{(1),t}$$
$$y_{(2),t} = \alpha_2 + \theta_{21} y_{(1),t-1} + \theta_{22} y_{(2),t-1} + \epsilon_{(2),t}$$

Matrix Notation

$$\begin{bmatrix} y_{(1),t} \\ y_{(2),t} \end{bmatrix} = \begin{bmatrix} \alpha_1 \\ \alpha_2 \end{bmatrix} + \begin{bmatrix} \theta_{11} & \theta_{12} \\ \theta_{21} & \theta_{22} \end{bmatrix} \begin{bmatrix} y_{(1),t-1} \\ y_{(2),t-1} \end{bmatrix} + \begin{bmatrix} \epsilon_{(1),t} \\ \epsilon_{(2),t} \end{bmatrix}$$

Figure 11.9 – Formula for a VAR model with lag one or VAR(1)

The preceding equation may seem complex, but in the end, like an AR model, it is still simply a linear function of past lags. In other words, in a VAR(1) model, you will have a linear function of lag 1 for each variable. When fitting a VAR model, as you shall see in this recipe, the **Ordinary Least Squares (OLS)** method is used for each equation to estimate the VAR model.

How to do it...

In this recipe, you will use the `.FredReader()` class from the `pandas_datareader` library. You will request three different datasets by passing three symbols. As mentioned on FRED's website, the first symbol, FEDFUNDS, for the federal funds rate *"is the interest rate at which depository institutions trade federal funds (balances held at Federal Reserve Banks) with each other overnight."* Simply put, the federal funds rate influences the cost of borrowing. It is *the target interest rate set by the Federal Open Market Committee (FOMC) for what banks can charge other institutions for lending excess cash from their reserve balances.* The second symbol is `unrate` for the *Unemployment Rate.*

Citations

Board of Governors of the Federal Reserve System (US), Federal Funds Effective Rate [FEDFUNDS], retrieved from FRED, Federal Reserve Bank of St. Louis; `https://fred.stlouisfed.org/series/FEDFUNDS`, April 6, 2022.

U.S. Bureau of Labor Statistics, Unemployment Rate [UNRATE], retrieved from FRED, Federal Reserve Bank of St. Louis; `https://fred.stlouisfed.org/series/UNRATE`, April 6, 2022.

Follow these steps:

1. Start by loading the necessary libraries and pulling the data. Note that both FEDFUNDS and unrate are reported monthly:

```
import pandas_datareader.data as web
from statsmodels.tsa.api import VAR,adfuller, kpss
from statsmodels.tsa.stattools import
grangercausalitytests
```

2. Pull the data using panda_datareader, which wraps over the FRED API and returns a pandas DataFrame. For the FEDFUNDS and unrate symbols, you will pull close to 32 years' worth of data:

```
start = "01-01-1990"
end = "04-01-2022"
economic_df = web.FredReader(symbols=["FEDFUNDS",
                                      "unrate"],
                             start=start,
                             end=end).read()
file = '../../datasets/Ch11/economic_df.pickle'
economic_df.to_pickle(file)
```

Store the DataFrame as a pickle object, as shown in the last line of the preceding code. This way, you do not have make an API call to rerun the example. You can read the pickle file using economic_df = pd.read_pickle(file).

3. Inspect the data and make sure there are no null values:

```
economic_df.isna().sum()
>>
FEDFUNDS    0
unrate      0
dtype: int64
```

4. Change the DataFrame's frequency to month start (MS) to reflect how the data is being stored:

```
economic_df.index.freq = 'MS'
```

5. Plot the datasets for visual inspection and understanding:

```
economic_df.plot(subplots=True); plt.show()
```

Since `subplots` is set to `True`, this will produce two subplots for each column:

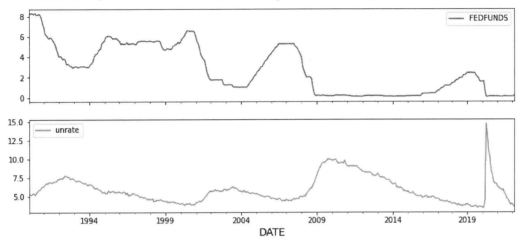

Figure 11.10 – Plotting both Federal Funds Effective Rate and Unemployment Rate

There is some sort of inverse relationship between `FEDFUND` and `unrate` – as `FEDFUNDS` increases, `unrate` decreases. There is interesting anomalous behavior starting in 2020 due to the COVID-19 pandemic.

6. An important assumption in VAR is stationarity. Both variables (the two endogenous time series) need to be stationary. Create the `check_stationarity()` function, which returns the stationarity results from the Augmented Dickey-Fuller (`adfuller`) and Kwiatkowski-Phillips-Schmidt-Shin (`kpss`) tests. Start by creating the `check_stationarity` function:

```
def check_stationarity(df):
    kps = kpss(df)
    adf = adfuller(df)
    kpss_pv, adf_pv = kps[1], adf[1]
    kpssh, adfh = 'Stationary', 'Non-stationary'
    if adf_pv < 0.05:
        # Reject ADF Null Hypothesis
        adfh = 'Stationary'
    if kpss_pv < 0.05:
        # Reject KPSS Null Hypothesis
        kpssh = 'Non-stationary'
    return (kpssh, adfh)
```

Use the `check_stationarity` function to evaluate each endogenous variable (column):

```
for i in economic_df:
    kps, adf = check_stationarity(economic_df[i])
    print(f'{i} adf: {adf}, kpss: {kps}')
>>
FEDFUNDS adf: Stationary, kpss: Non-stationary
unrate adf: Stationary, kpss: Stationary
```

Overall, both seem to be stationary. We will stick with the ADF results here; there is no need to do any stationary-type transformation.

Next, examine the causality to determine if one time series influences the other (can FEDFUNDS be used to forecast our time series of interest, which is unemp?).

7. Granger causality tests are implemented in statsmodels with the `grangercausalitytests` function, which performs *four* tests across each past lag. You can control this using the `maxlag` parameter. Granger causality tests are used to determine if past values from one variable influence the other variable. In statsmodels, at each lag, it will show the tests that have been performed and their results: the test statistics score, the *p-value*, and the degrees of freedom. Let's focus on the *p-value* to decide if you should reject or accept the null hypothesis.

The *null hypothesis* in the Granger causality tests is that the *second* variable or column (that is, FEDFUNDS) does not Granger cause the first variable or column (that is, unrate). In other words, it assumes there is no *statistical significance in terms of influence or effect*. If you are trying to predict unrate and determine if FEDFUNDS influences unrate, you will need to switch the order of the columns before applying the test. This is because `grangercausalitytests` examines the second column against the first column:

```
granger = grangercausalitytests(economic_df[['unrate',
'FEDFUNDS']], maxlag=12)
```

The test is set for a maximum of 12 lags (12 months). The following code shows the output for the last lag:

```
Granger Causality
number of lags (no zero) 12
ssr based F test:          F=7.1137  , p=0.0000  , df_
denom=350, df_num=12
ssr based chi2 test:    chi2=91.4612 , p=0.0000  , df=12
likelihood ratio test: chi2=81.8433 , p=0.0000  , df=12
```

```
parameter F test:          F=7.1137  , p=0.0000  , df_
denom=350, df_num=12
```

Here, all the lags (except for lag 1) have a p-value less than 0.05, which indicates that we can *reject* the null hypothesis. This means that the effect of FEDFUNDS is statistically significant. We can say that FEDFUNDS does Granger cause unrate.

8. Plot both ACF and PACF to gain an intuition over each variable and which process they belong to – for example, an AR or MA process:

```
for col in econ_scaled.columns:
    fig, ax = plt.subplots(1,2, figsize=(15,2))
    plot_acf(economic_df[col], zero=False,
             lags=30, ax=ax[0], title=f'ACF - {col}')
    plot_pacf(economic_df[col], zero=False,
             lags=30, ax=ax[1], title=f'PACF -
{col}');plt.show()
```

This should produce two ACF plots and two PACF plots:

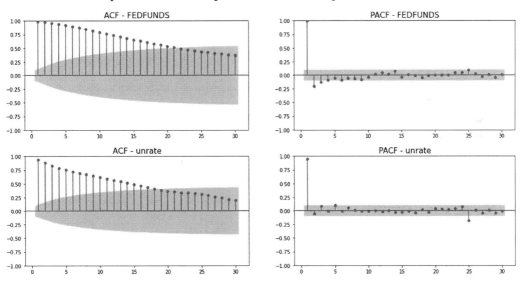

Figure 11.11 – ACF and PACF plots for FEDFUNDS and unrate

Notice that for FEDFUNDS and unrate, the plots indicate we are dealing with an **autoregressive (AR)** process. The ACF is gradually decaying, while both PACF plots show a sharp cutoff after lag 1. The PACF for FEDFUNDS shows slightly significant (above or below the shaded area) lags at 2 and 3, while the PACF for unrate shows some significance at lag 24. We can ignore those for now.

9. There is often a debate if the variables need to be scaled (standardized) or not when implementing VAR. Generally, when it comes to VAR, the algorithm does not require the variables to be scaled (some algorithms, on the other hand, will require the data to be scaled). Since you will be working with multivariate time series (multiple variables) that may have different scales, it would be easier to interpret the residuals from each if the data is scaled. Similarly, the coefficients will become easier to compare since the units will be in standard deviation (for more insight, please refer to the *Detecting outliers using Z-score* recipe in *Chapter 8, Outlier Detection Using Statistical Methods*). In this step, you will perform scaling as a best practice. You will use the `StandardScalar` class from Scikit-Learn since it will provide you with the `inverse_transform` method so that you can return to the original scale. In *Chapter 13, Deep Learning for Time Series Forecasting*, in the *Preparing time series data for deep learning* recipe, you will implement a class to scale and inverse transform.

    Before you use `StandardScalar`, split the data into train and test sets:

    ```
    train = economic_df.loc[:'2019']
    test = economic_df.loc['2020':]
    print(f'Train: {len(train)}, Test: {len(test)}')
    >>
    Train: 360, Test: 27
    ```

10. Scale the data using `StandardScalar` by fitting the train set using the `fit` method. Then, apply the scaling transformation to both the train and test sets using the `transform` method. The transformation will return a NumPy `ndarray`, which you will then return as pandas DataFrames. This will make it easier for you to plot and examine the DataFrames further:

    ```
    from sklearn.preprocessing import StandardScaler
    scale = StandardScaler()
    scale.fit(train)
    train_sc = pd.DataFrame(scale.transform(train),
                            index=train.index,
                            columns=train.columns)
    test_sc = pd.DataFrame(scale.transform(test),
                           index=test.index,
                           columns=test.columns)
    ```

11. But how can you pick the VAR order P? Luckily, the VAR implementation in statsmodels will pick the best VAR order. You only need to define the maximum number of lags (threshold); the model will determine the best p values that minimize each of the four information criteria scores: AIC, BIC, FPE, and HQIC. The `select_order` method will compute the scores at each lag order, while the `summary` method will display the scores for each lag. The results will help when you train (fit) the model to specify which information criteria the algorithm should use:

```
model = VAR(endog=train_stage1_sc, freq='MS')
res = model.select_order(maxlags=10)
res.summary()
```

This should show the results for all `10` lags. The lowest scores are marked with an `*`:

VAR Order Selection (* highlights the minimums)

	AIC	BIC	FPE	HQIC
0	-0.3448	-0.3227	0.7084	-0.3360
1	-9.987	-9.921	4.598e-05	-9.961
2	-10.51	-10.40	2.735e-05	-10.46
3	-10.55	-10.40	2.607e-05	-10.49
4	-10.60	-10.40*	2.486e-05	-10.52*
5	-10.60	-10.36	2.496e-05	-10.50
6	-10.62	-10.33	2.446e-05	-10.50
7	-10.65*	-10.32	2.375e-05*	-10.52
8	-10.63	-10.26	2.417e-05	-10.48
9	-10.62	-10.20	2.444e-05	-10.45
10	-10.60	-10.14	2.491e-05	-10.42

Figure 11.12 – The Var Order Selection summary

The `res` object is a `LagOrderResults` class. You can print the selected lag number for each score using the `selected_orders` attribute:

```
res.selected_orders
>>
{'aic': 7, 'bic': 4, 'hqic': 4, 'fpe': 7}
```

At lag 7, both *AIC* and *FPE* were the lowest. On the other hand, both *BIC* and *HQ* were the lowest at lag 4.

12. To train the model, you must use the *AIC* score. You can always experiment with a different information criterion. Accomplish this by updating the `ic` parameter. The `maxlags` parameter is optional – for example, if you leave it blank, it will still pick the lag order at 7 because it is based on minimizing the `ic` parameter, which in this case is `aic`:

```
results = model.fit(maxlags=7, ic='aic')
```

Running `results.summary()` will print a long summary – one for each autoregressive process. *Figure 11.9* showed a VAR(1) for *two* variables; in a VAR(7), this will equate to two functions (for each variable), each having 14 coefficients. *Figure 11.13* and *Figure 11.14* show the first portion of the summary:

```
Summary of Regression Results
==================================================
Model:                          VAR
Method:                         OLS
Date:            Tue, 26, Apr, 2022
Time:                      21:49:02
--------------------------------------------------
No. of Equations:      2.00000    BIC:                 -10.3164
Nobs:                   353.000    HQIC:                -10.5142
Log likelihood:         907.070    FPE:             2.38224e-05
AIC:                   -10.6450    Det(Omega_mle):  2.19199e-05
--------------------------------------------------
```

Figure 11.13 – VAR model summary of the regression (OLS) results showing the AIC score

Toward the end of the summary, the correlation matrix for the residuals is displayed. It provides insight into whether all the information was captured by the model or not. The following output does not show a correlation. Ideally, we want it to be as close to zero as possible:

```
Correlation matrix of residuals
              FEDFUNDS      unrate
FEDFUNDS      1.000000    0.007212
unrate        0.007212    1.000000
```

13. Store the VAR lag order using the k_ar attribute so that we can use it later when we use the forecast method:

```
lag_order = results.k_ar
lag_order
>> 7
```

Finally, you can forecast using either the forecast or forecast_interval method. The latter will return the forecast, as well as the upper and lower confidence intervals. Both methods will require past values and the number of steps ahead. The prior values will be used as the initial values for the forecast:

```
past_y = train_sc[-lag_order:].values
n = test_sc.shape[0]
forecast, lower, upper = results.forecast_
interval(past_y, steps=n)
```

14. Plot the forecast with the confidence intervals:

```
forecast, lower, upper = results.forecast_
interval(past_y, steps=n)
idx = test.index; style = 'k--'
ax = train_sc.iloc[:-lag_order, 1].plot(style='k')
pred_forecast  = pd.Series(forecast[:, 1], index=idx).
plot(ax=ax, style=style)
pred_lower = pd.Series(lower[:, 1], index=idx).
plot(ax=ax, style=style)
pred_upper  = pd.Series(upper[:, 1], index=idx).
plot(ax=ax, style=style)
plt.fill_between(idx, lower[:,1], upper[:,1], alpha=0.12)
plt.title('Forecasting Unemployment Rate (unrate)')
plt.legend(['Train','Forecast']);plt.show()
```

This should plot the training data and the forecast (middle dashed line) for unrate, along with the upper and lower confidence intervals:

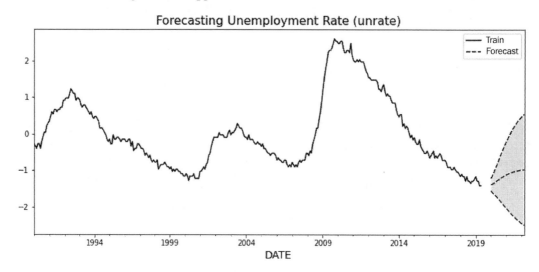

Figure 11.14 – Plotting the forecast with confidence intervals

Compare the results with *Figure 11.10* for unrate.

Recall that the training data was set up until the end of 2019 without any insight into the impact COVID-19 had in 2020. Thus, the results may not be as good as you would expect. You may need to adjust the train and test split to accommodate this fact and perform different experiments with the model. This is something you will be dealing with when a major event, maybe an anomaly, has a big economic impact and you need to determine if such an impact is truly an anomaly (a one-time unique event and its effects fade or if it's not) and whether you need to model for it. This is where domain knowledge is key when making such decisions.

How it works...

Vector autoregressive models are very useful, especially in econometrics. When evaluating the performance of a VAR model, it is common to report the results from Granger causality tests, residual or error analysis, and the analysis of the impulse response. As shown in *Figure 11.9*, a VAR(1) for two variables results in two equations with four coefficients that we are solving for. Each equation is estimated using OLS, as shown in the results from *Figure 11.13*.

The two functions in *Figure 11.9* show contributions from the variable's past values and the second (endogenous) variable. In a VAR model, unlike an AR model, there is a different dynamic between the multiple variables. Hence, in this recipe, once the model was built, a significant portion was spent plotting VAR-specific plots – for example, the **impulse responses (IRs)** and the **forecast error variance decomposition (FEVD)** – to help us understand these contributions and the overall interaction between the variables.

There's more...

Since we are focusing on comparing the forecasting results, it would be interesting to see if our VAR(7) model, with two endogenous variables, is better than a univariate AR(7) model.

Try using an AR(7) or ARIMA(7,0,0) model; you will use the same lag values for consistency. Recall that the `unrate` time series was stationary, so there is no need for differencing:

```
from statsmodels.tsa.arima.model import ARIMA
model = ARIMA(train_sc['unrate'],
              order=(lag_order,0,0)).fit()
```

You can review the ARIMA model's summary with `model.summary()`. Inspect the model's performance by placing diagnostic plots on the residuals:

```
fig = model.plot_diagnostics(figsize=(12,8));
fig.tight_layout();plt.show()
```

This should produce four diagnostic subplots, like so:

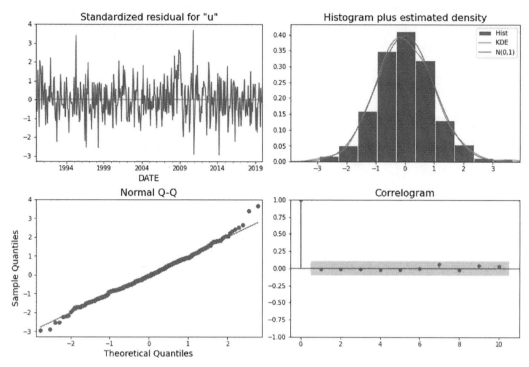

Figure 11.15 – AR(7) or ARIMA(7, 0, 0) diagnostic plots

Overall, the AR model captured the necessary information based on the autocorrelation plot.

Create a forecast using the AR model and compare the **root-mean-square error (RMSE)** scores for both models (VAR and AR):

```
from statsmodels.tools.eval_measures import mse
np.sqrt(mse(test['unrate'], forecast[:, 1]))
>> 8.070406992273286
np.sqrt(mse(test['unrate'], model.forecast(n)))
>> 8.055331303489288
```

Both models performed similarly. An AR model would be preferred over a VAR model in this case since it's a much simpler model. In the Jupyter Notebook, we plotted the forecast against the actual data for both AR and VAR, and the overall forecasts look very similar as well.

See also...

To learn more about the VAR class in statsmodels, please visit the official documentation at `https://www.statsmodels.org/dev/generated/statsmodels.tsa.vector_ar.var_model.VAR.html`.

Evaluating vector autoregressive (VAR) models

An important step when building a VAR model is to understand the model in terms of the interactions between the different endogenous variables. The statsmodels VAR implementation provides key plots to help you analyze the complex dynamic relationship between these endogenous variables (multiple time series).

In this recipe, you will continue where you left off from the previous recipe, *Forecasting multivariate time series data using VAR*, and explore different diagnostic plots, such as the **Residual Autocorrelation Function (ACF)**, **Impulse Response Function (IRF)**, and **Forecast Error Variance Decomposition (FEVD)**.

How to do it...

The following steps continue from the previous recipe. If you have not performed these steps, you can run the code from the accompanied Jupyter Notebook to follow along.

You will focus on diagnosing the VAR model that we created using the available methods:

1. The `results` object is of the `VARResultsWrapper` type, which is the same as the `VARResults` class and has access to the same methods and attributes. Start with the ACF plot of the residuals using the `plot_acorr` method:

    ```
    results.plot_acorr(); plt.show()
    ```

This should produce four plots for autocorrelation and cross-correlation of the residuals due to the `resid` parameter, which is set to `True` by default – that is, `results.plot_acorr(resid=True)`:

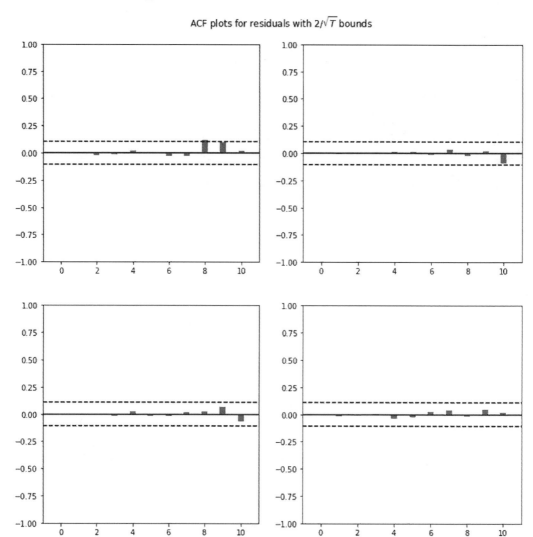

Figure 11.16 – Residual autocorrelation and cross-correlation plots

Unfortunately, the plots in *Figure 11.16* do not have proper labels. The first row of plots is based on the first variable in the DataFrame (FEDFUNDS), while the second row is based on the second variable in the DataFrame (unrate). Recall from *Figure 11.9* that for two variables, you will have two functions or models, and this translates into 2x2 residual subplots, as shown in *Figure 11.16*. If you had three variables, you would have a 3x3 subplot.

You do not want the residuals to show any significance across the lags, which is the case in *Figure 11.15*. This indicates that the model captured all the necessary information. In other words, there are no signs of any autocorrelation, which is what we would hope for.

2. You can also extract the residuals with the `resid` attribute, which would return a DataFrame with the residuals for each variable. You can use the standard `plot_acf` function as well:

```
for col in results.resid.columns:
    fig, ax = plt.subplots(1,1, figsize=(10,2))
    plot_acf(results.resid[col], zero=False,
            lags=10, ax=ax, title=f'ACF - {col}')
```

This should produce two ACF plots – one for FEDFUNDS and another for unrate. This will confirm the same finding – that there is no autocorrelation in the residuals.

3. Analyze the impulse response to shocks in the system using the `irf` method:

```
irf = results.irf()
irf.plot();plt.show()
```

The `irf` object is of the `IRAnalysis` type and has access to the `plot()` function:

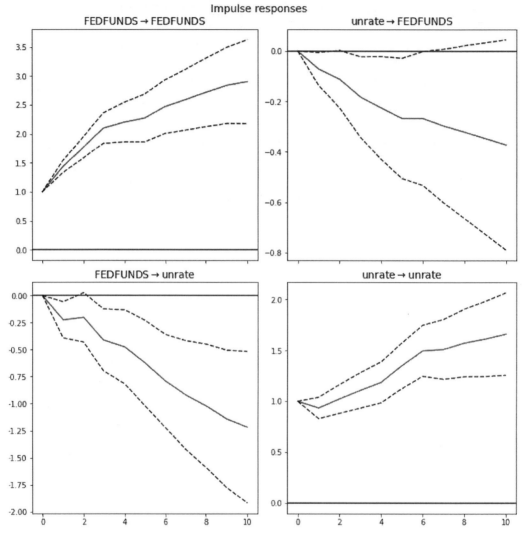

Figure 11.17 – Impulse response showing the effect of one unit change in one variable against another

The IRF analysis computes the dynamic impulse responses and the approximated standard errors, and also displays the relevant plots. The idea here is that in VAR, all the variables influence each other, and the **impulse response (IR)** traces the effect of a change (impulse) in one variable and the response from another variable (for each variable available) over each lag. The default is the first 10 lags. This technique is used to understand the dynamics of the relationship.

For example, the plot that shows **FEDFUNDS → unrate** in *Figure 11.17* illustrates how `unrate` responds to a one-point increase in FEDFUNDS across the 10 lags. More specifically, at lag 1, as FEDFUNDS increases, a negative reaction in `unrate` occurs (lower unemployment). Then, between periods 1 and 2, it looks like it is steady while FEDFUNDS increases, indicating a delayed shock or reaction (response), which is expected. A similar reaction is seen in period 3 in which a negative reaction (drop) in `unrate` is seen but then a short delay between periods 3 and 4, which drops further in period 5, can also be seen. In other words, increasing the federal funds effective rate (FEDFUNDS) did lower the unemployment rate, but the response is slower in the early periods before the full effect is shown.

If you do not want to see all four subplots, you can specify which plot you want to see by providing an `impulse` variable and a `response` variable:

```
fig = irf.plot(impulse='FEDFUNDS', response='unrate',
figsize=(5, 5))
```

4. Plot the cumulative response effect:

```
irf.plot_cum_effects();plt.show()
```

5. You can get the FEVD using the `fevd` method:

```
fv = results.fevd()
```

You can use two methods here: `fv.summary()` and `fv.plot()`. Both provide similar information:

```
fv.plot(); plt.show()
```

This will produce two FEVD plots – one for each variable. The x-axis will show the number of periods (0 to 9), while the y-axis will represent the percent (0 to 100%) that each shock contributed. Visually, this is represented as a portion of the total bar at every period. This contribution is the error variance:

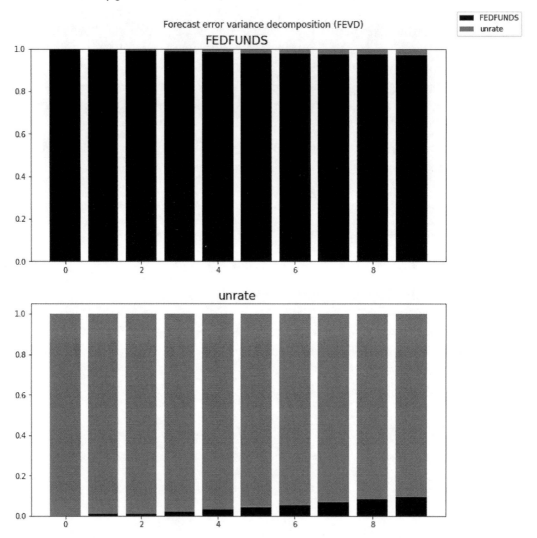

Figure 11.18 – FEVD plot for the FEDFUNDS and unrate variables

The second subplot shows the marginal contribution from FEDFUNFS in initial lags. In other words, lags 0 to 1.99% of the variation in unrate is from shocks from unrate itself. This is confirmed in the unrate -> unrate plot in *Figure 11.17*. The contribution of FEDFUNDs slowly increases but becomes more apparent around lags 8 and 9.

How it works...

The VAR implementation from statsmodels offers several options to help you understand the dynamics between the different time series (or endogenous variables). Similarly, it offers diagnostic tools to help you determine what adjustments need to be made to your original hypothesis.

There's more...

Earlier, in the *Forecasting multivariate time series data using VAR* recipe, you created a forecast plot. The results object – that is, the VARResults class – offers a convenient way for you to plot your forecasts quickly:

```
results.plot_forecast(n, plot_stderr=True);
```

Here, n is the number of future steps. This should produce two subplots, with one forecast for each variable, as shown in the following diagram:

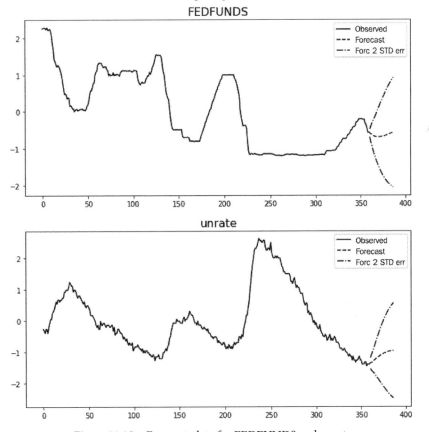

Figure 11.19 – Forecast plots for FEDFUNDS and unrate

Compare the second plot (unrate forecast) with the one shown in *Figure 11.14*. The results are the same.

See also...

To learn more about the `VARResults` class and all the available methods and attributes, visit the official documentation at `https://www.statsmodels.org/dev/generated/statsmodels.tsa.vector_ar.var_model.VARResults.html`.

Forecasting volatility in financial time series data with GARCH

When working with financial time series data, a common task is measuring **volatility** to represent uncertainty in future returns. Generally, volatility measures the spread of the probability distribution of returns and is calculated as the variance (or standard deviation) and used as a proxy for quantifying volatility or risk. In other words, it measures the dispersion of financial asset returns around an expected value. Higher volatility indicates higher risks. This helps investors, for example, understand the level of return they can expect to get and how often their returns will differ from an expected value of the return.

Most of the models we discussed previously (for example, ARIMA, SARIMA, and Prophet) focused on forecasting an observed variable based on past versions of itself. These models lack modeling changes in variance over time (heteroskedasticity).

In this recipe, you will work with a different kind of forecasting: forecasting and modeling changes in variance over time. This is known as volatility. In general, volatility is an important measure of risk when there is uncertainty and it is an important concept when working with financial data.

For this reason, you will be introduced to a new family of algorithms related to **Autoregressive Conditional Heteroskedasticity** (**ARCH**). The ARCH algorithm models the change in variance over time as a function of squared error terms (innovations) of a time series. An extension of ARCH is the **GARCH** model, which stands for **Generalized Autoregressive Conditional Heteroskedasticity**. It extends ARCH by adding a moving average component.

GARCH is popular in econometrics and is used by financial institutes that assess investments and financial markets. Predicting turbulence and volatility is as important as trying to predict a future price, and several trading strategies utilize volatility, such as the mean reversion strategy.

Before moving on, let's define the components of a general ARCH model:

- *Autoregressive*, a concept we explored in *Chapter 10, Building Univariate Time Series Models Using Statistical Methods,* means that the current value of a variable is influenced by past values of itself at different periods.

- *Heteroskedasticity* means that the model may have different magnitudes or variability at different time points (variance changes over time).

- *Conditional*, since volatility is not fixed, the reference here is on the constant that we place in the model to limit heteroskedasticity and make it conditionally dependent on the previous value or values of the variable.

In this recipe, you will create a GARCH model of order (p, q), also known as lags. q is the number of past (lag) squared residual errors ϵ^2, while q is the number of past (lag) variances σ^2 since variance is the square of standard deviation.

> **GARCH Orders**
>
> It can sometimes be confusing when talking about the p and q orders. In literature, q is usually the ARCH order, while p is the GARCH order, as described earlier. In the `arch` Python library, they are switched. In the `arch` package, p is described as the lag order of the symmetric innovation, while q is described as the lag order of lagged volatility.

From `arch`, you will use the `arch_model` function. The parameters can be broken down into three main components based on the GARCH model's assumptions: a *distribution* that's controlled by the `dist` parameter that defaults to `normal`, a *mean* model that's controlled by the `mean` parameter that defaults to `Constant`, and a *volatility* process that's controlled by the `vol` parameter that defaults to `GARCH`.

Getting ready

In this recipe, you will be using the `arch` library, which contains several volatility models, as well as financial econometrics tools. The library produces similar output to those from the statsmodels library. At the time of writing, the latest version is `5.1.0`.

To install `arch` using `pip`, use the following command:

```
pip install arch
```

To install `arch` using `conda`, use the following command:

```
conda install arch-py -c conda-forge
```

How to do it...

When using the `arch_model` function from the `arch` library to build the GARCH model, there are a few parameters that need to be examined: whether the distribution is normal with `dist='normal'` by default, whether the mean is constant with `mean='Constant'` by default, and the volatility type with `vol='GARCH'` by default.

You will be using the Microsoft daily closing price dataset for this recipe. Follow these steps:

1. Start by loading the necessary libraries for this recipe:

```
from arch import arch_model
```

2. Load the `msft.csv` dataset:

```
msft = pd.read_csv('../../datasets/Ch11/msft.csv',
                   index_col='Date',
                   parse_dates=True)
```

3. You will need to convert the daily stock price into a daily stock return. This can be calculated as $R = \dfrac{P_t - P_{t-1}}{P_{t-1}}$, where P_t is the price at time t and P_{t-1} is the previous price (1 day prior). This can easily be done in pandas using the `DataFrame.pct_change()` function. `.pct_change()` has a `periods` parameter that defaults to 1. If you want to calculate a 30-day return, then you must change the value to 30:

```
msft['returns'] = 100 * msft.pct_change()
msft.dropna(inplace=True, how='any')
```

Plot both the daily stock price and daily return:

```
msft.plot(subplots=True,
          title='Microsoft Daily Closing Price and Daily
Returns')
```

This will produce the following plot:

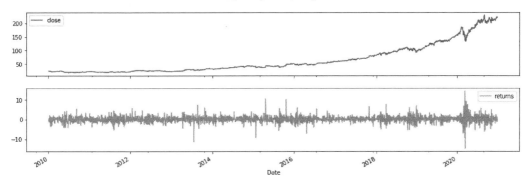

Figure 11.20 – Microsoft daily closing price and daily returns

4. Split the data into 90% train and 10% test sets:

```
idx = round(len(msft) * 0.90)
train = msft.returns[:idx]
test = msft.returns[idx:]
print(f'Train: {train.shape}')
print(f'Test: {test.shape}')
>>
Train: (2491,)
Test: (277,)
```

5. Now, fit the GARCH(p, q) model. Start with the simple GARCH(1,1) model with all the default options – that is, mean='Constant', distribution as dist='normal', volatility as vol='GARCH', p=1, and q=1:

```
model = arch_model(train,
                   p=1, q=1,
                   mean='Constant',
                   vol='GARCH',
                   dist='normal')
results = model.fit(update_freq=5)
>>
Iteration:       5,   Func. Count:      36,   Neg. LLF:
4374.845453710037
Iteration:      10,   Func. Count:      62,   Neg. LLF:
4361.891627557763
```

```
Optimization terminated successfully    (Exit mode 0)
        Current function value: 4361.891627557763
        Iterations: 11
        Function evaluations: 66
        Gradient evaluations: 11
```

Using `update_freq=5` affects the output's frequency. The default is 1, which updates on every iteration. To print the summary, use the `.summary()` method:

```
results.summary()
```

This will produce the following output:

Constant Mean - GARCH Model Results

Dep. Variable:	returns	**R-squared:**	0.000
Mean Model:	Constant Mean	**Adj. R-squared:**	0.000
Vol Model:	GARCH	**Log-Likelihood:**	-4361.89
Distribution:	Normal	**AIC:**	8731.78
Method:	Maximum Likelihood	**BIC:**	8755.07
		No. Observations:	2491
Date:	Mon, Mar 28 2022	**Df Residuals:**	2490
Time:	03:49:12	**Df Model:**	1

Mean Model

	coef	std err	t	P>|t|	95.0% Conf. Int.
mu	0.1156	2.702e-02	4.279	1.877e-05	[6.266e-02, 0.169]

Volatility Model

	coef	std err	t	P>|t|	95.0% Conf. Int.
omega	0.3594	0.127	2.836	4.574e-03	[0.111, 0.608]
alpha[1]	0.1458	4.424e-02	3.294	9.861e-04	[5.904e-02, 0.232]
beta[1]	0.6912	8.177e-02	8.454	2.821e-17	[0.531, 0.852]

Covariance estimator: robust

ω, α and β are estimated by Maximum Likelihood Method

Figure 11.21 – GARCH model summary

The *omega*, *alpha*, and *beta* parameters (the $\omega, \alpha,$ and β symbols) of the GARCH model are estimated using the maximum likelihood method. Notice that the *p-value* for the coefficients indicates they are significant.

You can access several of the components that you can see in the summary table by calling the appropriate attribute from the `results` object – for example, `results.pvalues`, `results.tvalues`, `results.std_err`, or `results.params`.

6. Next, you must evaluate the model's performance. Start by plotting the standardized residuals and conditional volatility using the `plot` method:

```
results.plot(); plt.show()
```

We get the plot as follows:

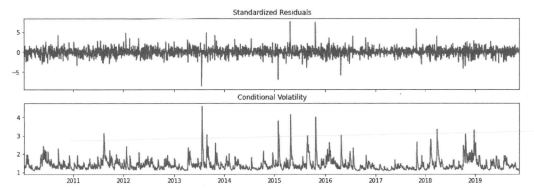

Figure 11.22 – Model diagnostics for the GARCH model

Plot a histogram for the standardized residuals. You can obtain this using the `std_resid` attribute:

```
results.std_resid.hist(bins=20)
plt.title('Standardized Residuals')
```

Examine whether the standardized residuals are normally distributed:

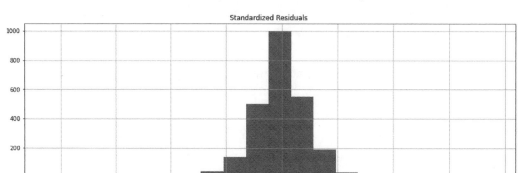

Figure 11.23 – Model diagnostics for the GARCH model

The histogram shows the standardized residuals being normal. Another test you can perform to check for the existence of autocorrelation is the *Ljung-Box* test. Test for autocorrelation for the first 10 lags by using `acorr_ljungbox` from the statsmodels library:

```
from statsmodels.stats.diagnostic import acorr_ljungbox
from statsmodels.stats.diagnostic import acorr_ljungbox
acorr_ljungbox(results.std_resid,
               lags=10,
               return_df=True)['lb_pvalue']
```

The null hypothesis assumes no autocorrelation. We reject the null hypothesis if the p-value is less than 0.05. At lags 1 to 7, we cannot reject the null hypothesis and there is *no* autocorrelation. Things change starting from lag 8 onward and we can reject the null hypothesis.

7. To make a prediction, use the `.forecast()` method. The default is to produce a 1 step ahead forecast. To get n number of steps ahead, you will need to update the `horizon` parameter:

```
msft_forecast = results.forecast(horizon=test.shape[0])
```

8. To access the predicted future variance (or volatility), use the `.variance` property from the `msft_forecast` object:

```
forecast = msft_forecast.variance[-1:]
```

You can also evaluate the predicted mean. Recall that when you fit the model, you indicated that the mean is Constant. This is further validated if you examine the mean:

```
msft_forecast.mean[-1:]
```

This will show a constant value of 0.115615 across all horizons.

How it works...

GARCH (p,q) can be written as follows:

$$\sigma_t^2 = \omega + \sum_{i=1}^{q} \alpha_i \epsilon_{t-i}^2 + \sum_{j=1}^{p} \beta_j \sigma_{t-j}^2$$

Omega, alpha, and beta (ω, α, β) are parameters here. The p order is commonly referred to as the GARCH order, while q is referred to as the ARCH order. The GARCH(1,1) that you implemented can be written as follows:

$$\sigma_t^2 = \omega + \alpha \epsilon_{t-1}^2 + \beta \sigma_{t-1}^2$$

Innovations versus Errors in Time Series

In literature, and specific to time series, you will come across the term *innovations*. For example, the ARCH order q may be referred to as lagged square innovations as opposed to lagged residual errors. To make things simple, you can think of innovations similar to how you may think of prediction errors, a common term that's used in machine learning. To learn more about innovations, please visit the following Wikipedia page: https://en.wikipedia.org/wiki/Innovation_(signal_processing).

There's more...

Previously, when implementing the GARCH model, the mean was set to Constant. Let's explore the impact of changing it to Zero.

Let's start with mean='Zero':

```
model = arch_model(train,
                   p=1, q=1,
                   mean='Zero',
```

```
                      vol='GARCH',
                      dist='normal')
  results = model.fit(disp=False)
```

This should produce the GARCH summary in a tabular format:

Zero Mean - GARCH Model Results

Dep. Variable:	returns	R-squared:	0.000
Mean Model:	Zero Mean	Adj. R-squared:	0.000
Vol Model:	GARCH	Log-Likelihood:	-4371.30
Distribution:	Normal	AIC:	8748.59
Method:	Maximum Likelihood	BIC:	8766.06
		No. Observations:	2491
Date:	Mon, Mar 28 2022	Df Residuals:	2491
Time:	04:37:36	Df Model:	0

Volatility Model

	coef	std err	t	P>|t|	95.0% Conf. Int.
omega	0.3455	0.127	2.717	6.594e-03	[9.624e-02, 0.595]
alpha[1]	0.1306	3.998e-02	3.266	1.091e-03	[5.220e-02, 0.209]
beta[1]	0.7113	8.038e-02	8.850	8.787e-19	[0.554, 0.869]

Figure 11.24 – GARCH(1, 1) with a zero mean

Notice that in *Figure 11.23*, there is no mean model like the one shown in *Figure 11.20*. It is common to use a Zero Mean when you want to model the two separately: a Volatility Model and a Mean Model.

See also

To learn more about the arch library, please visit the official documentation at https://arch.readthedocs.io/en/latest/univariate/introduction.html.

12

Forecasting Using Supervised Machine Learning

In this chapter, you will explore different **machine learning** (**ML**) algorithms for time series forecasting. Machine learning algorithms can be grouped into **supervised** learning, **unsupervised** learning, and reinforcement learning. This chapter will focus on supervised machine learning. Preparing time series for supervised machine learning is an important phase that you will be introduced to in the first recipe.

Furthermore, you will explore two machine learning libraries: **scikit-Learn** and **sktime**. scikit-learn is a popular machine learning library in Python that offers a wide range of algorithms for supervised and unsupervised learning and a plethora of tools for data preprocessing, model evaluation, and selection. Keep in mind that scikit-learn, or `sklearn`, is a generic ML library and not specific to time series data. On the other hand, the `sktime` library, from the Alan Turing Institute, is a dedicated machine learning library for time series data.

In this chapter, we will cover the following recipes:

- Preparing time series data for supervised learning
- One-step forecasting using linear regression models with scikit-learn
- Multi-step forecasting using linear regression models with scikit-learn
- Forecasting using non-linear models with sktime
- Optimizing a forecasting model with hyperparameter tuning
- Forecasting with exogenous variables and ensemble learning

Technical requirements

You will be working with the **sktime** library, described as *"a unified framework for machine learning with time series"*. Behind the scenes, sktime is a wrapper to other popular ML and time series libraries, including scikit-learn. It is recommended to create a new virtual environment for Python so that you can install all the required dependencies without any conflicts or issues with your current environment.

If you need a quick refresher on creating a virtual Python environment, check out the *Development environment setup* recipe, from *Chapter 1, Getting Started with Time Series Analysis*. The chapter covers two methods: using conda and venv.

The following instructions will show how to create a virtual environment using conda. You can call the environment any name you like. For the following example, we will name the environment sktime:

```
>> conda create -n sktime python=3.9 -y
>> conda activate sktime
>> conda install -c conda-forge sktime-all-extras
```

To make the new sktime environment visible within Jupyter, you can run the following code:

```
python -m ipykernel install —user —name sktime —display-name
"sktime"
```

To install using pip, run the following command:

```
pip install "sktime[all_extras]"
```

You will be working with three CSV files in this chapter: Monthly Air Passenger, Monthly Energy Consumption, and Daily Temperature data. Start by importing the common libraries:

```
import pandas as pd
import matplotlib.pyplot as plt
import numpy as np
from pathlib import Path

import warnings
warnings.filterwarnings('ignore')
```

Load air_passenger.csv, energy_consumption.csv, and daily_weather. csv as pandas DataFrames:

```
path = Path('../../datasets/Ch12/')
daily_temp = pd.read_csv(path.joinpath('daily_weather.csv'),
                    index_col='DateTime',
                    parse_dates=True)
daily_temp.columns = ['y']

energy = pd.read_csv(path.joinpath('energy_consumption.csv'),
                    index_col='Month',
                    parse_dates=True)
energy.columns = ['y']

air = pd.read_csv(path.joinpath('air_passenger.csv'),
                    index_col='date',
                    parse_dates=True)
air.columns = ['y']
```

Then, add the proper frequency for each DataFrame:

```
daily_temp.index.freq = 'D'
energy.index.freq = 'MS'
air.index.freq = 'M'
```

You can plot the three DataFrames to gain an understanding of how they differ:

```
daily_temp.plot(title='Avg Daily Weather Temperature in C')
energy.plot(title='Monthly Energy Consumption')
air.plot(title='Monthly Passengers')
```

When plotting the datasets, observe how each time series exhibits different characteristics. This initial insight will be helpful as you as proceed with the recipes in the chapter. In addition, you will realize how an algorithm's performance will vary when applied to different time series data.

You can download the Jupyter notebooks and requisite datasets from the GitHub repository:

- Jupyter notebook: https://github.com/PacktPublishing/Time-Series-Analysis-with-Python-Cookbook./blob/main/code/Ch12/Chapter%2012.ipynb.

- Datasets: https://github.com/PacktPublishing/Time-Series-Analysis-with-Python-Cookbook./tree/main/datasets/Ch12.

Understanding supervised machine learning

In supervised machine learning, the data used for training contains known past outcomes, referred to as dependent or target variable(s). These are the variables you want your machine learning (ML) model to predict. The ML algorithm learns from the data using all other variables, known as independent or predictor variables, to determine how they are used to estimate the target variable. For example, the target variable is the house price in the house pricing prediction problem. The other variables, such as the number of bedrooms, number of bathrooms, total square footage, and city, are the independent variables used to train the model. You can think of the ML model as a mathematical model for making predictions on unobserved outcomes.

On the other hand, in unsupervised machine learning, the data contains no labels or outcomes to train on (unknown or unobserved). Unsupervised algorithms are used to find patterns in the data, such as the case with clustering, for example, customer segmentation, anomaly detection, or recommender systems.

Generally, there are two types of supervised machine learning: **classification** and **regression**. In classification, the goal is to predict which class (or label) a particular observation belongs to. In other words, you are predicting a discrete value, for example, whether an email is spam or not spam or whether a transaction is fraudulent or not. The two examples represent a binary classification problem, but you can have a multi-class classification problem, such as the case with image classification. Some popular classification algorithms include Logistic Regression, Random Forests, K-Nearest Neighbors, and Support Vector Machines, to name a few.

In regression, you predict a continuous variable, such as the price of a house or a person's height. In regression, you can have a simple linear regression problem with one independent variable and one target variable, a multiple regression problem with more than one independent variable and one target variable, or a multivariate multiple regression problem with more than one independent variable and more than one dependent variable. Some popular linear regression algorithms include Linear Regression, Lasso Regression, and Elastic Net Regression. These examples are considered linear algorithms that assume a linear relationship between the variables.

Interestingly, several of the classification algorithms mentioned earlier can be used for regression; for example, you can have a Random Forest Regression, K-Nearest Neighbors Regression, and Support Vector Machines Regression. These regressors can capture non-linear relationships and produce more complex models.

Preparing time series data for supervised learning

In supervised ML, you must specify the *independent* variables (predictor variables) and the dependent variable (target variable). For example, in scikit-learn, you will use the fit(X, y) method for fitting a model, where X refers to the independent variable and y to the target variable.

Generally, preparing the time series data is similar to what you have done in previous chapters. However, additional steps will be specific to supervised ML, which is what this recipe is about. The following highlights the overall steps:

1. Inspect your time series data to ensure there are no significant gaps, such as missing data, in your time series. If there are gaps, evaluate the impact and consider some of the imputation and interpolation techniques discussed in *Chapter 7, Handling Missing Data.*

2. Understand any stationarity assumptions in the algorithm before fitting the model. If stationarity is an assumption before training, then transform the time series using the techniques discussed in the *Detecting time series stationarity* section in *Chapter 9, Exploratory Data Analysis and Diagnosis*.

3. Transform your time series to contain independent and dependent variables. To do this, you will define a sliding window to convert the data into a window of inputs. For example, if you decide that the past five periods (lags) should be used to predict the current period (the sixth), then you will create a sliding window of five periods. This will transform a univariate time series into a tabular format. A univariate time series has only one dependent variable and no independent variables. For example, a five-period sliding window will produce five independent variables x_1, x_2, x_3, x_4, x_5, which are lagged versions of the dependent variable. This representation of multiple inputs (a sequence) to one output is referred to as a one-step forecast. This will be the focus of this recipe. *Figure 12.1* illustrates this concept.

4. Before training a model, split that data into training and test sets. Sometimes, you may need to split it into training, validation, and test sets, as you will explore in *Chapter 13, Deep Learning for Time Series Forecasting*.

5. Depending on the algorithm, you may need to scale your data; for example, in scikit-learn, you can leverage the `StandardScaler` or the `MinMaxScaler` class When making your predictions, you will need to *inverse* the transform to restore the results to their original scale, for example, you can use the `inverse_transform` method from scikit-learn.

How to do it...

In this recipe, you will prepare time series data for supervised learning by creating independent variables from a univariate time series. The following illustrates how a sliding window of five periods creates the dependent (target) variable at a time (t) and five independent variables $(x_1, x_2, x_3, x_4, x_5)$. In the daily temperature data, this means a five-day sliding window.

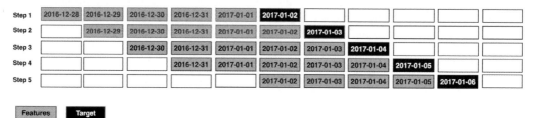

Figure 12.1 – Example of a five-day sliding window for daily temperature data

Since you will be transforming all three DataFrames, you will create functions to sin the process:

1. Inspect for missing data in the DataFrames. If there is missing data, then perform a simple fill forward imputation. First, make a copy so you do not change the original DataFrames:

```
air_copy = air.copy()
energy_copy = energy.copy()
daily_temp_copy = daily_temp.copy()
```

Create the handle_missing_data function:

```
def handle_missing_data(df):
    n = int(df.isna().sum())
    if n > 0:
        print(f'found {n} missing observations...')
        df.ffill(inplace=True)
```

Pass each DataFrame to the handle_missing_data function:

```
for df in [air_copy, energy_copy, daily_temp_copy]:
    handle_missing_data(df)
```

Only the daily_weather DataFrame had two NaN (missing values).

2. Create the one_step_forecast function, which returns a DataFrame with a specified number of independent variables (columns) and a target variable (column). The total number of columns returned is based on the sliding window parameter (number of columns = sliding window + 1). This is illustrated in Figure 12.2. This technique was described in *Machine Learning Strategies for Time Series Forecasting*, Lecture Notes in Business Information Processing. Berlin, Heidelberg: Springer Berlin Heidelberg (https://doi.org/10.1007/978-3-642-36318-4_3). Create the function using the following:

```
def one_step_forecast(df, window):
    d = df.values
    x = []
    n = len(df)
    idx = df.index[:-window]
    for start in range(n-window):
        end = start + window
        x.append(d[start:end])
```

```
cols = [f'x_{i}' for i in range(1, window+1)]
x = np.array(x).reshape(n-window, -1)
y = df.iloc[window:].values
df_xs = pd.DataFrame(x, columns=cols, index=idx)
df_y = pd.DataFrame(y.reshape(-1), columns=['y'],
    index=idx)
return pd.concat([df_y, df_xs], axis=1).dropna()
```

The `one_step_forecast` function will transform a time series with a specified number of steps (the sliding window size).

For simplicity, transform all three DataFrames with the same sliding window size of five periods, `window=5`. Recall, the weather data is daily, so one period represents one day, while for the air passenger and energy consumption datasets, a period is equivalent to one month:

```
air_os = one_step_forecast(air_copy, 5)
energy_os = one_step_forecast(energy_copy, 5)
daily_temp_os = one_step_forecast(daily_temp_copy, 5)
```

3. You will need to split the data into training and test sets. You could use the `train_test_split` function from scikit-learn with `shuffle=False`. An alternative is to create the `split_data` function to split the data:

```
def split_data(df, test_split=0.15):
    n = int(len(df) * test_split)
    train, test = df[:-n], df[-n:]
    return train, test
```

The following shows how to use the `split_data` function:

```
train, test = split_data(air_os)
print(f'Train: {len(train)} Test: {len(test)}')
>> Train: 119 Test: 20
```

4. Certain algorithms benefit from scaling the data. You can use the StandardScaler class from scikit-learn. In this recipe, you will create the Standardize class with three methods: the fit_transform method, will fit on the training set and then transforms both the training and test sets, the inverse method is used to return a DataFrame to its original scale and the inverse_y method to inverse the target variable (or a specific column and not the entire DataFrame):

```python
class Standardize:
    def __init__(self, split=0.15):
        self.split = split

    def _transform(self, df):
        return (df - self.mu)/self.sigma

    def split_data(self, df):
        n = int(len(df) * test_split)
        train, test = df[:-n], df[-n:]
        return train, test

    def fit_transform(self, train, test):
        self.mu = train.mean()
        self.sigma = train.std()
        train_s = self._transform(train)
        test_s =  self._transform(test)
        return train_s, test_s

    def transform(self, df):
        return self._transform(df)

    def inverse(self, df):
        return (df * self.sigma)+self.mu

    def inverse_y(self, df):
        return (df * self.sigma[0])+self.mu[0]
```

The following shows how you can use the `Standardize` class:

```
scaler = Standardize()
train_s, test_s = scaler.fit_transform(train, test)
train_original = scaler.inverse(train_s)
y_train_original = scaler.inverse_y(train_s['y'])
```

The `Standardize` class also has additional methods, such as `split_data` for convenience.

You will be leveraging these functions in the recipes of this chapter for data preparation.

How it works...

Preparing time series data for supervised learning is summarized in *Figure 12.1* and *Figure 12.2*. For example, in a regression problem, you are essentially transforming a univariate time series into a multiple regression problem. You will explore this concept further in the following *One-step forecasting using linear regression models with scikit-learn* recipe.

The window size parameter can be adjusted to fit your need. In the recipe, we used a split window of five (5) periods, and you should experiment with different window sizes.

There's more...

In the previous section, with the `one_step_forecast` function, you produced additional columns to represent independent variables used in model training. The new columns are referred to as features. The process of engineering these new features, as you did earlier, is called **feature engineering**. In this, you create new features (columns) that were not part of the original data to improve your model's performance.

The sliding window is one technique to create new features based on past observations. Other techniques can be used to extract features from time series data to prepare it for supervised machine learning. For example, you could create new columns based on the date column, such as day of the week, year, month, quarter, season, and other date-time features.

The following is an example of engineering date time related features using pandas:

```
df['day_of_week'] = df.index.dayofweek
df['days_in_month'] = df.index.days_in_month
df['month_end'] = df.index.is_month_end.astype(int)
df['is_leap'] = df.index.is_leap_year.astype(int)
```

```
df['month'] = df.index.month
df.head()
```

Even though you will be using the `one_step_forecast` function throughout the chapter, you should explore other feature engineering techniques and experiment with the different algorithms introduced in this chapter.

See also

To learn more about the `StandardScaler` class from `sklearn`, you can read the official documentation here: https://scikit-learn.org/stable/modules/generated/sklearn.preprocessing.StandardScaler.html.

To learn more about the `train_test_split` function from `sklearn`, you can read the official documentation here: https://scikit-learn.org/stable/modules/generated/sklearn.model_selection.train_test_split.html.

In the next recipe, you will build regression models using `sklearn`.

One-step forecasting using linear regression models with scikit-learn

In *Chapter 10, Building Univariate Time Series Models Using Statistical Methods*, you were introduced to statistical models such as **autoregressive (AR)** type models. These statistical models are considered *linear models*, where the independent variable(s) are lagged versions of the target (dependent) variable. In other words, the variable you want to predict is based on past values of itself at some lag.

In this recipe, you will move from statistical models into ML models. More specifically, you will be training different linear models, such as Linear Regression, Elastic Net Regression, Ridge Regression, Huber Regression, and Lasso Regression. These are considered *linear regression models* and assume a linear relationship between the variables.

In the previous recipe, you transformed a univariate time series into a multiple regression problem with five independent variables and one dependent variable (a total of six columns), as shown in the following diagram:

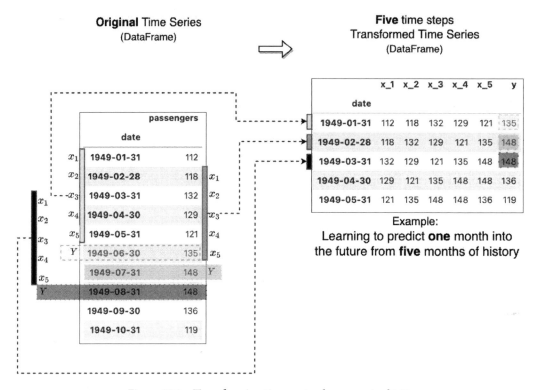

Figure 12.2 – Transforming time series for supervised ML

For the representation in *Figure 12.2*, the multiple linear regression equation would be as follows:

$$\hat{y} = \beta_0 + \beta_1 X_1 + \beta_2 X_2 \dots + \beta_5 X_5 + \epsilon$$

Where $\hat{y}$ is the estimated (predicted) value, $(\beta_1, \beta_2, \dots, \beta_5)$ are the coefficients for each independent variable $(X_1, X_2, \dots, X_5)$, β_0 is the intercept, and ϵ is the residual or error term. Remember, the independent variables that were created $(X_1, X_2, \dots, X_5)$ are lagged versions of the dependent variable (Y) created using a sliding window. You can simplify the equation in matrix notation by adding an X_0 term, which is a constant value of one ($X_0 = 1$). This will give us the following equation:

$$\hat{y} = \beta X + \epsilon$$

In linear regression, you want to minimize the errors (loss), which is the difference between the actual value, Y_i, and the estimated value, $\hat{y}_i$. More specifically, it is the square loss at each data point. If we take the sum of these squared losses or errors, you get the **residual sum of square (RSS)**. The cost function (RSS) is what you want to minimize. This results in our **objective function** being written as follows:

$$min \sum_{i=1}^{n} \left(Y_i - \sum_{j=0}^{m} \beta_j X_{ij} \right)^2$$

Sometimes, you will see the objective function as minimizing the **mean squared error (MSE)**, which is obtained by dividing the RSS by the degrees of freedom (for simplicity, you can think of it as the number of observations).

You will train different types of linear regression models and, in the *How it works...* section, you will explore what makes them different.

How to do it...

In this recipe, you will continue using the three DataFrames you loaded from the *Technical requirements* section of this chapter. You will leverage the functions and classes created in the previous *Preparing time series data for supervised learning* recipe.

Start by loading the necessary classes and functions for this recipe. Make a copy of the DataFrames to ensure they do not get overwritten:

```
from sklearn.linear_model import (LinearRegression,
                                  ElasticNet,
                                  Ridge,
                                  Lasso,
                                  HuberRegressor)
air_cp = air.copy()
en_cp = energy.copy()
dw_cp = daily_temp.copy()
```

The following steps will use the energy consumption data for demonstration. You should use the same steps on all three DataFrames, as shown in the accompanying *Jupyter notebook*:

1. Use the `handle_missing_data` function to ensure there are no missing values:

```
handle_missing_data(en_cp)
```

2. Use `one_step_forecast` to convert the time series DataFrames into a supervised learning problem with 10 steps (windows):

```
en_reg = one_step_forecast(en_cp, 10)
```

Feel free to change the window size.

3. Split and scale the data using the `split_data` function and the `Standardize` class. Later, you can use the class instance to inverse the scaling:

```
train_en, test_en = split_data(en_reg,
        test_split=0.10)
scaler_en = Standardize()
train_en_s, test_en_s =
        scaler_en.fit_transform(train_en,test_en)
```

Common error metrics used in regression are **Mean Squared Error(MSE)** or **Root Mean Squared Error(RMSE)**. These are scale-dependent, so if you experiment with different model configurations, for example, scale your data using the `Standardize` class function, this will impact the scores and make it difficult to compare. Another popular error metric in forecasting is **Mean Absolute Percentage Error(MAPE)**, which is more intuitive to interpret since it is expressed as a percentage and is scale-independent. For certain problems, MAPE may not be suitable. For example, with the daily temperature data, MAPE puts a heavier penalty on negative errors (you can have negative Celsius). With MAPE, you cannot divide by zero (Celsius at zero can be problematic). Additionally, measuring temperature as a percentage may not make sense in this case.

It's a good practice to capture different metrics, and in this case, you will capture both RMSE and MAPE by importing them from `sktime`. Note that `sklearn` does support both MSE and MAPE. The third metric, which has been proposed as an alternative to the shortcoming of MAPE, is the **Mean Absolute Scaled Error (MASE)** metric. You will use MASE from the `sktime` library as well:

```
from sktime.performance_metrics.forecasting import(
MeanAbsolutePercentageError,
```

```
MeanSquaredError,

MeanAbsoluteScaledError)
```

Create an instance of each of the classes to use later in the recipe:

```
mse = MeanSquaredError()
mape = MeanAbsolutePercentageError()
mase = MeanAbsoluteScaledError()
```

Note, you will be calculating RMSE as the square root of MSE, for example, using `np.sqrt(mse(y_actual - y_hat))`.

4. Create the `train_model` function that takes the training and test sets, then fits the model on the train set and evaluates the model using the test set using MAPE, MASE, and RMSE. The function will return a dictionary with additional model information:

```
def train_model(train, test, regressor, reg_name):
    X_train, y_train  = train.drop(columns=['y']),
train['y']
    X_test, y_test  = test.drop(columns=['y']), test['y']
    print(f'training {reg_name} ...')

    regressor.fit(X_train, y_train)

    yhat = regressor.predict(X_test)
    rmse_test = np.sqrt(mse(y_test, yhat))
    mape_test = mape(y_test, yhat)
    mase_test = mase(y_true=y_test, y_pred=yhat, y_
train=y_train)
    residuals = y_tes—.values - yhat

    model_metadata = {
        'Model Name': reg_name, 'Model': regressor,
        'RMSE': rmse_test, 'MAPE': mape_test,
        'MASE': mase_test,
        'yhat': yhat, 'resid': residuals,
        'actual': y_test.values}

    return model_metadata
```

The function returns the model and evaluation metrics against the test data, the forecast, and the residuals.

5. Create a dictionary that contains the regression algorithms and their names (keys) to use in a loop. This makes it easier later to update the dictionary with additional regressors:

```
regressors = {
    'Linear Regression': LinearRegression(),
    'Elastic Net': ElasticNet(0.5),
    'Ridge Regression': Ridge(0.5),
    'Lasso Regression': Lasso(0.5),
    'Huber Regression': HuberRegressor()}
```

The three regressors, *Ridge*, *Lasso*, and *ElasticNet*, add a regularization (penalization) term to the objective function. All three take an alpha (α) parameter, which determines the penalization factor for the coefficients. This is a hyperparameter you can experiment with; for now, you will use the value (0.5).

6. The train_model function fits and evaluates one model at a time. Create another function, train_different_models, which can loop through the dictionary of regressors and calls the train_model function. The function will return the results from each regressor as a list:

```
def train_different_models(train, test, regressors):
    results = []
    train, test = split_data(data, test_split=0.10)
    for reg_name, regressor in regressors.items():
        results.append(train_model(train,
                                    test,
                                    regressor,
                                    reg_name))
    return results
```

Pass the dictionary of regressors along with the training and test sets to the train_different_models function and store the results:

```
en_results = train_different_models(train_en_s,
             test_en_s, regressors)
```

7. You can convert the results into a DataFrame to view the scores and model name:

```
cols = ['Model Name', 'RMSE', 'MAPE', 'MASE']
en_results = pd.DataFrame(en_results)
en_results[cols].sort_values('MASE')
```

The preceding code should produce the following results:

	Model Name	RMSE	MAPE	MASE
4	Huber Regression	0.433456	0.722893	0.524400
2	Ridge Regression	0.431843	0.823255	0.559494
0	Linear Regression	0.433747	0.818459	0.560989
1	Elastic Net	0.986061	2.000000	1.274611
3	Lasso Regression	0.986061	2.000000	1.274611

Figure 12.3 – Results of all five regression models on the energy consumption data

You can update the sort_values method to use RMSE or MAPE and observe any changes in the ranking. Note that you did not reset the index since the order (row ID) is aligned with the order from the regressors dictionary.

8. The en_results list contains the actual test results (actual), the forecast value (yhat), and the residuals (resid). You can use these to visualize the model's performance. Create a plot_results function to help diagnose the models:

```
from statsmodels.graphics.tsaplots import plot_acf
def plot_results(cols, results, data_name):
    for row in results[cols].iterrows():
        yhat, resid, actual, name = row[1]
        plt.title(f'{da—a_name} - {name}')
        plt.plot(a—ual, 'k--', alpha=0.5)
        plt.plot(yhat, 'k')
        plt.legend(['actual', 'forecast'])
        plot_acf(resid, zero=False,
                title=f'{da—a_name} -
                Autocorrelation')
        plt.show()
```

Notice the use of the `plot_acf` function from `statsmodels` to evaluate the residuals. The following is an example of using the `plot_results` function on the energy consumption data:

```
cols = ['yhat', 'resid', 'actual', 'Model Name']
plot_results(cols, en_results, 'Energy Consumption')
```

The preceding code should produce *two* plots for each of the *five* models (a total of 10 plots for the energy consumption data). For each model, the function will output a line plot comparing out-of-sample data (*test* data) against the forecast (*predicted* values) and a residual autocorrelation plot. The following shows the two plots for the Hubber Regression model:

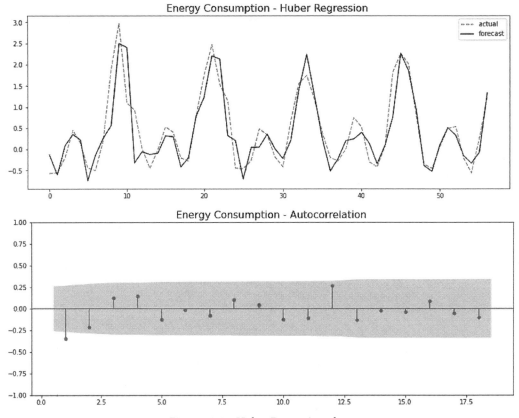

Figure 12.4 – Huber Regression plots

The accompanying Jupyter notebook shows all 10 plots for each dataset. Observe from the notebook how the models rank and behave differently on different time series processes.

From *Figure 12.4*, the Hubber Regression model seems to perform well with a potential for further tuning. Later in this chapter, you will explore hyperparameter tuning in the *Optimizing a forecasting model with hyperparameter tuning* recipe.

How it works...

Once a time series is prepared for supervised ML, you can use any regression algorithm to train a model. This is summarized in *Figure 12.2*. The function for transforming the time series is called `one_step_forecast`, to remind you that we are preparing the data so that a *sequence* of inputs is given (the independent variables) to produce a *single* output (*one-step forecast*).

Later, in the *Forecasting using non-linear models with sktime* recipe, you will explore more regressors (linear and non-linear) and how to deal with trend and seasonality.

There's more...

The three regression models, *ElasticNet*, *Lasso*, and *Ridge*, add a **regularization** (penalization) term to the objective function that we want to minimize. In *Lasso Regression*, the regularization term can reduce the coefficient (the βs in the objective function) of the least important features (independent variables) to *zero*, and thus eliminating them. This added penalization term is called **L1 regularization**. In *Ridge Regression*, the regularization term is referred to as **L2 regularization** and can shrink the coefficients of the least important features but *does not eliminate* them (no zero coefficients). *ElasticNet Regression*, on the other hand, is a hybrid between the two by combining L1 and L2 regularization terms.

Regularization helps avoid overfitting during training and allows the model to better generalize. Additionally, L1 regularization can be used for *feature selection*.

You can inspect the coefficients to observe the effects, as shown in the following code block:

```
cols = ['Model Name', 'Model']
en_models = en_results.iloc[0:4][cols]

for row in en_models.iterrows():
    print(row[1][0])
    print(row[1][1].coef_)
```

This should produce the following:

```
Linear Regression
[ 0.02739136  0.02052173  0.03768302  0.06630472  0.01417452
-0.08727704
   0.02856578 -0.13640839  0.14165493  0.70683461]
Elastic Net
[0.          0.          0.          0.          0.          0.
   0.          0.          0.04077799 0.37835549]
Ridge Regression
[ 0.0273999   0.02054709  0.0377177   0.06625515  0.01414968
-0.08721396
   0.02844889 -0.13622568  0.14175768  0.7065417 ]
Lasso Regression
[0.          0.          0.          0.          0.          0.          0.
   0.          0.          0.2536153]
```

The energy consumption data has 10 *features*. Observe how the *Linear Regression* model estimated higher coefficient values (*weights*) for the last two features. On the other hand, the *ElasticNet Regression* model eliminated the first 8 features by estimating the coefficients at zero. The *Ridge Regression* model produced similar results as the Linear Regression model, reducing the weights of the least significant features (thus shrinking their effect). Lastly, the *Lasso Regression* model only deemed the last feature as significant by eliminating the rest (with zero coefficients).

Recall that these features were engineered and represent lags or the past values of the dependent variable (y). The coefficients from the four models suggest that the 10th feature (or lag) is alone significant in making a future prediction.

Let's examine this concept and see whether one feature is sufficient for the energy consumption dataset. Retrain the models using only the *10th* feature, as in the following:

```
en_10 = en_reg[['y', 'x_10']]
train_en10, test_en10 = split_data(en_10, test_split=0.10)
scaler_en10 = Standardize()
train_en10_s, test_en10_s =
        scaler_en.fit_transform(train_en10, test_en10)
en_10_results = train_different_models(train_en10_s,
        test_en10_s, regressors)
cols = ['Model Name', 'RMSE', 'MAPE', 'MASE']
```

```
en_10_results = pd.DataFrame(en_results)
en_10_results[cols].sort_values('MASE')
```

If you rank the models by the scores and plot the results, you will notice that the performance from using just *one* feature (X_{10}) produces similar results obtained from using all 10 features ($X_1, X_2, ..., X_{10}$).

See also

To learn more about the different regression models available in the scikit-learn library, visit the main regression documentation here: `https://scikit-learn.org/stable/supervised_learning.html#supervised-learning`.

To learn more about how different ML algorithms for time series forecasting compare, you can reference the following research paper:

Ahmed, Nesreen K., Amir F. Atiya, Neamat El Gayar, and Hisham El-Shishiny. *An Empirical Comparison of Machine Learning Models for Time Series Forecasting.* Econometric Reviews 29, no. 5–6 (August 30, 2010): 594–621. `https://doi.org/10.1080/07474938.2010.481556`.

In the next recipe, you will explore **multi-step forecasting** techniques.

Multi-step forecasting using linear regression models with scikit-learn

In the *One-step forecasting using linear regression models with scikit-learn* recipe, you implemented a one-step forecast; you provide a sequence of values for the past 10 periods ($X_1, X_2, ..., X_{10}$) and the linear model will forecast the next period (X_{11}), which is referred to as Y. This is called **one-step forecasting**.

For example, in the case of energy consumption, to get a forecast for December 2021 you need to provide data for the past 10 months (February to November). This can be reasonable for monthly data, or quarterly data, but what about daily or hourly? In the daily temperature data, the current setup means you need to provide temperature values for the past 10 days to obtain a one-day forecast (just one day ahead). This may not be an efficient approach since you have to wait until the next day to observe a new value to feed to the model to get another one-day forecast.

What if you want to predict more than one future step? For example, you want three months into the future (X_{11}, X_{12}, X_{13}) based on a sequence of 10 months ($X_1, ..., X_{10}$). This concept is called a *multi-step forecast*. In the *Preparing time series data for supervised learning* recipe, we referenced the paper *Machine Learning Strategies for Time Series Forecasting* for preparing time series data for supervised ML. The paper also discusses *four strategies* for multi-step forecasting, such as the *Recursive* strategy, the *Direct* strategy, **DirRec (Direct-Recursive)** strategy, and *Multiple Output* strategies.

In this recipe, you will implement a *Recursive* forecasting strategy. This will help you gain an idea of what a multi-step forecasting is all about. This is useful when you want to forecast further into the future beyond the out-of-sample (test) data that you have at hand.

The following illustrates the idea behind the recursive strategy. It is still based on one-step forecasts that are reused (recursively) to make the next one-step prediction, and the process continues (think of a loop) until you get all the future steps, known as future horizons, produced.

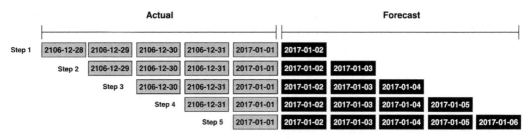

Figure 12.5 – Sliding window (five periods) with multi-step forecasts of daily temperature

At each step in *Figure 12.5*, you are still performing a one-step forecast. The gray boxes represent the actual *observed* values, and the black boxes represent estimated or forecasted values. If you want to forecast into the future, let's say five periods ahead, and your actual observed data ends on 2017-01-01, you will need to provide five past periods from 2016-12-28 to 2017-01-01 to get a one-step forecast for 2017-01-02. The estimated value on 2017-01-02 is used as an input to estimate the next one-step to forecast for 2017-01-03. This recursive behavior continues until all five future steps (horizons) are estimated.

How to do it...

In this recipe, you will be using the models obtained from the previous *One-step forecasting using linear regression models with scikit-learn* recipe. A recursive multi-step strategy is used in the forecasting (prediction) phase:

1. From the previous recipe, you should have three DataFrames (`air_results`, `dw_results`, and `en_results`) that contain the results from the trained models. The following steps will use `dw_results` for demonstration (daily weather), you should be able to apply the same process on the remaining DataFrames (as demonstrated in the accompanying Jupyter Notebook).

    Extract the model and the model's name. Recall that there are five trained models:

    ```
    models = dw_results[['Model Name','Model']]
    ```

2. Create the `multi_step_forecast` function, which consists of a `for` loop that makes a one-step future forecast (estimate) using the model's `predict` method. On each iteration or step, the estimated value is used as input to produce the next one-step estimate for another future step:

    ```
    def multi_step_forecast(data, model, steps=10):
        forecast = []
        for i in range(steps):
            one_step_pred = model.predict(np.array(data).
    reshape(1,-1))[0]
            forecast.append(one_step_pred)
            _ = data.pop(0)
            data.append(one_step_pred)
        return np.array(forecast)
    ```

    In the Jupyter notebook, there is another version of the `multi_step_forecast` function that takes a *NumPy* array instead of a Python list. In NumPy, you can use the `roll` function as opposed to the `pop` and `append` methods used here. Both implementations work the same way.

3. Capture the last row from `test_dw_s` DataFrame. This represents the last 10 observations. Recall that the DataFrame was created using a 10-period sliding window, and the last row represents observations from 2016-12-22 to 2016-21-31:

    ```
    dw_ms = test_dw_s.drop(columns = ['y']).iloc[-1].tolist()
    ```

4. Loop through the models and pass the `dw_ms` list, the model, and the number of future steps (for example, 10 future steps) to the `multi_step_forecast` function:

```
frcst_dw = {}
models = dw_results[['Model Name','Model']]
for i in models.iterrows():
    pred = multi_step_forecast(dw_ms, steps=10,
        model=i[1]['Model'])
    pred = scaler_dw.inverse_y(pred)
    frcst_dw[i[1]['Model Name']] = pred
```

The predicted values are stored in the `frcst_dw` dictionary. The values have been inversely scaled to their original scale using the `inverse_y` method.

5. Create a plot to compare actuals versus predicted for the daily temperature data:

```
for name, pred in frcst_dw.items():
    actual = dw_cp.iloc[-10:]
    ax = actual.plot(style='k-.')
    pd.Series(pred, index=dw_cp.index[-10:]).plo—
style='k--o', ax=ax)
    plt.title(f'Multi-Step Forecasting with {name}')
    plt.legend(['actual', 'forecast'])
    plt.show()
```

The preceding code should produce five plots; a plot for each model. The following shows the output from the first model: Linear Regression.

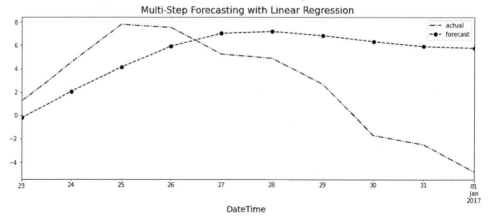

Figure 12.6 – 10-day forecast using a recursive multi-step forecast

One problem with the recursive strategy is that as you go further into the future, you are exclusively relying on the estimated values and any associated estimation errors. This can cause an accumulated effect of these errors as you progress further into the future, making the forecast highly biased.

How it works...

Multi-step forecasting is useful in situations that require more than one step forecast into the future. You implemented a recursive strategy to produce a multi-step forecast, which is essentially a one-step forecast repeated as many times as the number of future steps required. At each iteration, the prediction from one step is used as an input in the next step to make another one-step prediction. One of the drawbacks is that the model is using estimated values that can contain prediction errors to make more predictions.

To illustrate this, the following shows an example of extending the forecast to 20 steps (beyond the actual observations available) and you can observe how these errors accumulate.

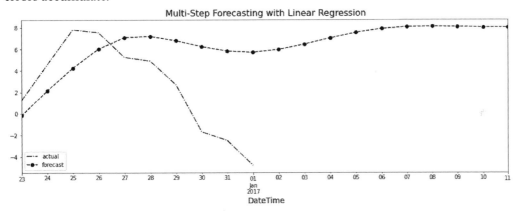

Figure 12.7 – Example of using a recursive strategy for a longer future horizon

A second approach is the *direct strategy*, which creates multiple models for each future step. Each model produces a one-step forecast, but they act independently. This can cause a maintenance issue; for example, to produce a 10-day forecast, you will have 10 models. Additionally, this independence is a lost opportunity to capture dependencies that would occur from one prediction to another. The direct strategy can suffer from high variance.

The third approach, the *DirRec strategy*, is a hybrid of *direct* and *recursive* and a way to mitigate their individual shortcomings. In the next section, you will see a fourth approach, the *multiple output strategy*.

In the *Forecasting using non-linear models with sktime* recipe, you will explore a simpler approach to implementing different multi-step strategies.

There's more...

In the *Multiple output* strategy, you will create a similar sliding window function as you did with the one_step_forecast function. However, the new function will also take an output window. For example, you will provide a 10-sliding window for input and a 10-sliding window for output and the resulting DataFrame will contain $(X_1, X_2, ..., X_{10})$ for the independent variables (features) and $(Y_1, Y_2, ..., Y_{10})$ for the target variables. This is a **one-shot** approach in which you provide a *sequence* as input and get a *sequence* as output.

The multiple_output function takes a window_in parameter for the number of features to be generated, and a window_out parameter for the number of target variables to be generated:

```python
def multiple_output(df, window_in, window_out):
    d = df.values
    x = []
    y = []
    n = len(df)
    idx = df.index[:-window_in]
    print(len(idx))
    for start in range(n-window_in):
        end = start + window_in
        out = end + window_out
        x.append(d[start:end].ravel())
        y.append(d[end:out].ravel())

    cols_x = [f'x_{i}' for i in range(1, window_in+1)]
    cols_y = [f'y_{i}' for i in range(1, window_out+1)]

    df_xs = pd.DataFrame(x,  index=idx, columns=cols_x)
    df_y = pd.DataFrame(y, index=idx, columns=cols_y)
    return pd.concat([df_xs, df_y], axis=1).dropna()
```

The following is an example of using the multiple_output function to produce a sequence of 10 as input features and a sequence of 10 as target variables:

```python
win_in, win_out = 10, 10
dw_mo = multiple_output(dw_cp, win_in, win_out)
dw_mo.columns
>> Index(['x_1', 'x_2', 'x_3', 'x_4', 'x_5', 'x_6', 'x_7',
```

```
'x_8', 'x_9', 'x_10',
        'y_1', 'y_2', 'y_3', 'y_4', 'y_5', 'y_6', 'y_7', 'y_8',
'y_9', 'y_10'],
      dtype='object')
```

Train a *linear regression* model on this new dataset. Follow a similar process for splitting and scaling the data as in the previous recipe:

```
train_dw, test_dw = split_data(dw_mo, test_split=0.10)
scaler_dw = Standardize()
train_dw_s, test_dw_s =
      scaler_dw.fit_transform(train_dw,test_dw)
X_train, y_train = train_dw_s.iloc[: , :win_in],
      train_dw_s.iloc[:, win_out:]
X_test, y_test = test_dw_s.iloc[: , :win_in],
      test_dw_s.iloc[:, win_out:]
```

Now, you can fit the model and then make a prediction:

```
lr = LinearRegression()
lr.fit(X_train, y_train)
mo_pred = lr.predict(X_test)[-1]
```

Create a plot to compare the forecast against the out-of-sample or test data:

```
mo_pred = scaler_dw.inverse_y(lr.predict(X_test)[-1])
dates = pd.date_range('2016-12-13', freq='D', periods=20)
inputs, outputs = dates[:win_in], dates[win_out:]
pd.Series(test_dw.iloc[-1].values, index=dates).plo—
style='k--', alpha=0.5)
pd.Series(mo_pred, index=outputs).plot(style='k-o')
plt.title('Multiple Output for Multi-Step Forecasting with
Linear Regression')
plt.legend(['Actual', 'Forecast'])
```

This should produce the following time series plot:

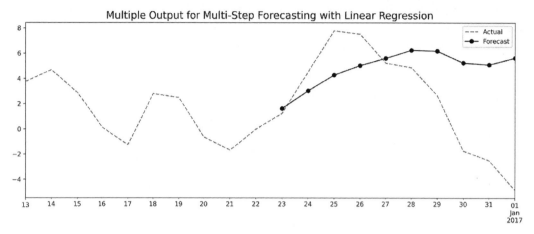

Figure 12.8 – Daily temperature 10-day forecast using the multiple output strategy

Compare the performance in *Figure 12.8* with *Figure 12.6*.

See also

To learn more about multi-step forecasting, you can refer to *Machine Learning Strategies for Time Series Forecasting*. Lecture Notes in Business Information Processing. Berlin, Heidelberg: Springer Berlin Heidelberg. https://doi.org/10.1007/978-3-642-36318-4_3.

Forecasting using non-linear models with sktime

In the previous recipes, you had to prepare the time series data to make it suitable for supervised ML. This is because scikit-learn (sklearn) is a general ML library and not specific for time series forecasting. This is where *sktime* is positioned to fill in the gap as a unified machine learning framework for time series. In this recipe, you will explore how to create a ML pipeline that prepares any time series data and can use algorithms from a standard ML library such as sklearn.

In *Chapter 13, Deep Learning for Time Series Forecasting*, you will explore other non-linear models, such as Recurrent Neural Networks. In this recipe, you will explore different algorithms that can capture non-linear relationships such as K-Nearest Neighbors Regression.

How to do it...

You will train multiple regressors (linear and non-linear) from `sklearn`. The recipe will cover data preparation, model training, forecasting, and comparing performance between the models. You will create a pipeline using the `TransforemdTargetForecaster` class from `sktime`.

You will be working with the energy consumption dataset that was loaded earlier in the *Technical requirements* section.

Before starting with the recipe, make sure to import all the required libraries upfront:

```
from sklearn.ensemble import (RandomForestRegressor,
                              GradientBoostingRegressor,
                              ExtraTreesRegressor)
from sklearn.linear_model import LinearRegression
from sklearn.neighbors import KneighborsRegressor
from sktime.forecasting.all import (
        Deseasonalizer, Detrender,
        temporal_train_test_split,
        mean_absolute_percentage_error as mape,
        mean_squared_percentage_error as mspe,
        mean_squared_error as mse,
        ForecastingHorizon,
        NaiveForecaster,
        TransformedTargetForecaster,
        PolynomialTrendForecaster)
from sktime.forecasting.compose import make_reduction
```

With all the required classes and functions loaded, you can start with the first step. Note in the following the *energy consumption* data is used for demonstration. You should be able to apply the same process on the other two datasets:

1. Make a copy of the `energy` DataFrame for this recipe:

    ```
    df = energy.copy()
    ```

2. You will need to split the data into training and test sets using the `split_data` function created earlier:

    ```
    train, test = split_data(df)
    ```

3. The `sktime` library uses a similar ML framework as scikit-learn, such as the use of the `fit` method for training a model and the `predict` method to make predictions. You will explore five different regressors from sklearn: *Linear Regression, Random Forest Regressor, Gradient Boosting Regressor, Extra Tree Regressor*, and *KNN Regressor*. You will include a *Naive Forecaster* with a `mean` strategy. The Naive Forecaster will be the baseline model to compare how the other regressors perform.

Since the process for training the models is similar on all regressors, you will create a function, `make_forecast`, that takes in the training dataset, a regressor, the number of future horizons (steps), and a window size. The function returns a pandas `Series` of the predicted values.

In the `make_forecast` function, you will create a *pipeline* using the `TransformedTargetForecaster` class to apply a set of transformations, for example, removing *trend* and *seasonality* using the `Detrender` and `Deseasonalizer` classes, respectively. You have performed these tasks individually in *Chapter 10, Building Univariate Time Series Models Using Statistical Methods*. Here you will leverage the `TransformedTargetForecaster` class to chain these steps:

```
def make_forecast(data, n, regressor, window=12):
    fh = ForecastingHorizon(np.arange(n) + 1, is_
relative=True)
    forecaster = [
            ("", Deseasonalizer(sp=12,
model="additive")),
            ("detrebd", Detrender(forecaster=Polynomial
TrendForecaster(degree=1)))]
    if not isinstance(regressor, NaiveForecaster):
        reg = ("forecaster", make_reduction(
            regressor,
            strategy='recursive',
            window_length=window,
            scitype='tabular-regressor'))
        forecaster.append(reg)
        model = TransformedTargetForecaster(forecaster).
fit(data.values)

    else:
        model = regressor.fit(data.values)

    predicted = pd.Series(
            model.predict(fh=fh).reshape(-1),
```

```
            index= test.index
                )
    return predicted
```

Notice the use of the make_reduction function in the pipeline before fitting (training) the model. This will create a reduced regression for the time series data. You will learn more on the concept of a reduced form in the *How it works...* section. For now, realize that make_reduction will return a RecursiveTabularRegressionForecaster class, and the default strategy parameter is recursive.

4. Create a Python dictionary for the different regressors so you can loop through and pass each one to the make_forecast function. You will append the returned predictions as a new column to the test DataFrame for easier comparison:

```
regressors = {
            'Naive Forecaster' :
NaiveForecaster(strategy='mean', sp=12),
            'Linear Regression': LinearRegression(),
            'K-Nn Regressor': KneighborsRegressor(n_
neighbors=5),
            'Extra Tree Regressor':
ExtraTreesRegressor(),
            'Random Forest Regressor':
RandomForestRegressor(),
            'Gradient Boosting Regressor':
GradientBoostingRegressor()
            }

for k, reg in regressors.items():
    print(f'training {reg} ...')
    test[k] = make_forecast(train, len(test),
regressor=reg , window=15)
```

Once execution is completed, the test DataFrame should have a shape of (88, 7), indicating 88 rows and 7 columns. The last *6 columns* are based on each model.

5. Plot the predictions from each regressor against the test data. To do so, loop through the results in the test DataFrame and keep in mind that the observed out-of-sample (test data) values are in the first column:

```
for i in test.iloc[: , 1:]:
    ax = df[-2*len(te-):].plot(style='k-', alpha=0.45,
```

```
title=i)
    test[i].plot(ax=ax)
    plt.legend(['Actual', i])
    plt.show()
```

The preceding code should produce five total plots. The following figure displays the results from three models: *Naive Forecaster, Linear Regression, and K-NN Regressor:*

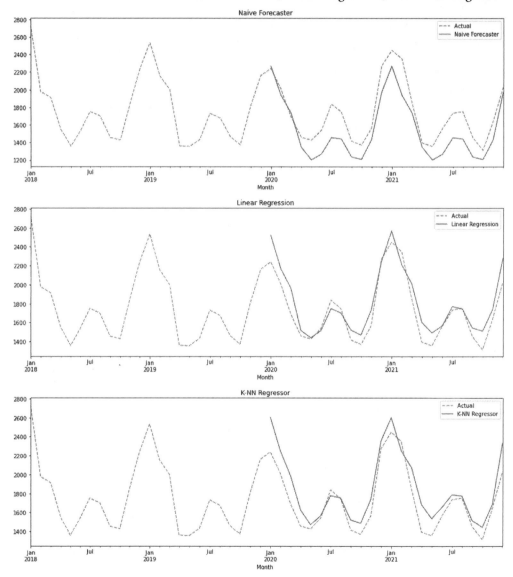

Figure 12.9 – Example of plotting each regressor's prediction against the actual data

Visually, aside from the Naive Forecaster, all the models seem to perform well. Using performance metrics is a much better approach to evaluate the models numerically; for example, using *MASE, sMAPE, MAPE*, and *RMSE*, to name a few. Recall that Naive Forecaster is a baseline model from which we want to achieve better results.

Create the `evaluate` function that will evaluate all the models:

```
def evaluate(df, train, sort_by='MASE'):
    evals = pd.DataFrame(index=['sMAPE', 'MAPE', 'RMSE'])
    y_truth = df['y']
    y_predicted = df.drop(columns=['y'])
    for p in y_predicted:
        evals.loc['sMAPE', p] = mape(y_truth, y_
predicted[p], symmetric=True)
        evals.loc['MAPE', p] = mape(y_truth, y_
predicted[p], symmetric=False)
        evals.loc['RMSE', p] = np.sqrt(mse(y_truth, y_
predicted[p]))
        evals.loc['MASE', p] = mase(y_truth, y_
predicted[p], y_train=train)
    return evals.T.sort_values(by=sort_by)
```

The function will return a sorted DataFrame by `MASE` (default) which can be updated to one of `MAPE`, `RMSE`, `MASE`, or `sMAPE`.

6. Call the function and pass the `test` and `train` sets:

```
evaluate(test, train)
```

	sMAPE	MAPE	RMSE	MASE
K-NN Regressor	0.088718	0.095485	192.449319	0.685551
Random Forest Regressor	0.099764	0.107576	211.802685	0.783351
Extra Tree Regressor	0.101279	0.109252	213.193772	0.794356
Linear Regression	0.105661	0.114187	219.063673	0.828132
Gradient Boosting Regressor	0.109251	0.118294	226.483574	0.860031
Naive Forecaster	0.133619	0.123643	242.222293	0.957688

Figure 12.10 – Comparing the different regressor models

It looks like the *KNN-Regressor* model performed best, followed by the *Random Forest* model. Both models can handle non-linearity. Overall, all regressors did outperform the Naive Forecaster model.

How it works...

In this recipe, you were able to use multiple regressors from the `sklearn` library by leveraging `sktime`. This was made possible using the `TransformedTargetForecaster` class and the `make_reduction` function. `TransformedTargetForecaster` allowed you to create a chain of steps, a **pipeline**, to transform the time series. For example, three transformations were used: the `Deseasonalizer` class, the `Detrender` class, and the `make_reduction` function.

You can think of the `make_reduction` function (from sktime) as comparable to the `one_step_forecast` and the `multi_step_forecast` functions you created in earlier recipes. For example, the `make_reduction` function was used to prepare the time series allowing you to use any regressor from the scikit-learn library.

Let's examine the `make_reduction` parameters:

```
make_reduction(estimator,
               strategy='recursive',
               window_length=10,
               scitype='infer')
```

There are four parameters:

- `estimator`: The ML estimator in this recipe was the regressor (for example, `LinearRegression`) that is being passed.

- `strategy`: There are three strategies: `direct` (*default*), `recursive`, or `multioutput`. These strategies are intended for multi-step time series forecasting, similar to what is proposed and discussed in the *Multi-step forecasting using linear regression models with scikit-learn* recipe of this chapter. The `make_reduction` function makes it easy for you to explore and experiment with the different strategies. This is similar to the `multi_step_forecast` you created earlier.

- `window_length`: The length of the sliding window. The default value is `10`. This is similar to the `one_step_forecast` you created earlier.

- `scitype`: This stands for *scientific type* and can be either `infer` (default), `tabular-regressor`, or `time-series-regressor`. For the data you are using, a DataFrame, the `tabular-regressor`, is selected (inferred).

There's more...

Let's see how the ML models (regressors) compare against an ARIMA model using `auto_arima` from the `pmdarima` library. You explored `auto_arima` in the *Forecasting time series data using auto_arima* recipe from *Chapter 11, Additional Statistical Modeling Techniques for Time Series*.

You will use `auto_arima` to determine the best *(p, d, q)* orders for the non-seasonal components, and the *(P, D, Q)* orders for the seasonal components:

```
from pmdarima import auto_arima
n = len(test)
fh = ForecastingHorizon(np.arange(n) + 1)
arima = auto_arima(y=train, seasonal=True, m=12, suppress_
warnings=True)
```

Once completed, you can examine the results with `arima.summary()`. The best model is `SARIMAX(1, 1, 1)x(1, 0, 1, 12)`.

Add the output predictions to the `test` DataFrame and run the `evaluate` function again:

```
test['ARIMA'] = arima.predict(n)
evaluate(test)
```

This should produce a DataFrame with sorted models based on the *MASE* score:

	sMAPE	MAPE	RMSE	MASE
K-NN Regressor	0.088718	0.095485	192.449319	0.685551
ARIMA	0.098918	0.093266	184.699337	0.705350
Random Forest Regressor	0.099764	0.107576	211.802685	0.783351
Extra Tree Regressor	0.101279	0.109252	213.193772	0.794356
Linear Regression	0.105661	0.114187	219.063673	0.828132
Gradient Boosting Regressor	0.109251	0.118294	226.483574	0.860031
Naive Forecaster	0.133619	0.123643	242.222293	0.957688

Figure 12.11 – Comparing the different ML models with ARIMA

You can plot the two best models to see how they compare visually:

```
ax = train.1—['2011':].plot(style='—', alpha=0.35)
test['ARIMA'].plot(ax=ax, style='k-.')
test['K-NN Regressor'].plot(ax=ax, style='k-o')
plt.legend(['train', 'ARIMA', 'KNN'])
```

This should produce a time series plot showing the training data from January 2011 to August 2014, and the estimated forecasts from both the ARIMA model and the K-NN regression model from September 2014 to December 2021.

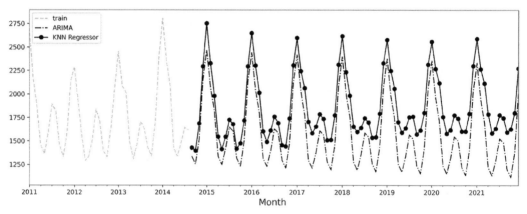

Figure 12.12 – Comparing K-NN regression with an ARIMA model

The ARIMA model did a decent job overall compared to more advanced ML regressors. This is sometimes the case with smaller univariate time series. Keep in mind that the ML models (regressors) are not optimized yet (via hyperparameter tuning) while the ARIMA model was optimized by `auto_arima` to find the best hyperparameters (the seasonal and non-seasonal orders). ML algorithms are great for working with more complex multivariate time series data, as you will explore in the *Forecasting with exogenous variables and ensemble learning* recipe.

ML optimization with hyperparameter tuning is an essential step to ensure you are getting the best configuration and performance for the model of choice.

See also

In this recipe, you used sklearn for running different regression models. What made this possible was using sktime's `TransformedTargetForecaster` class and the `make_reduction` function:

- To learn more about sktime's `TransformedTargetForecaster` for creating a pipeline, you can visit the documentation page here: `https://www.sktime.org/en/stable/api_reference/auto_generated/sktime.forecasting.compose.TransformedTargetForecaster.html`.

- To learn more about the `make_reduction` function, you can visit the documentation page here: `https://www.sktime.org/en/stable/api_reference/auto_generated/sktime.forecasting.compose.make_reduction.html`.

In the next recipe, you will explore how you can optimize an ML model.

Optimizing a forecasting model with hyperparameter tuning

You trained different regression models using default parameter values in the previous recipe. A common term for such parameters is **hyperparameters**, as these are not learned by the model but instead supplied by the user, influencing the model's architecture and behavior.

In this recipe, you will examine how you can find optimal hyperparameter values for the KNN Regresssor (from the previous recipe). You will perform a cross-validated grid search using sktime's *ForecastingGridSearchCV*.

You have performed a grid search in the *Forecasting univariate time series data with non-seasonal ARIMA* recipe from *Chapter 10, Building Univariate Time Series Models Using Statistical Methods*. Similarly, you were introduced to different automated methods for finding optimal hyperparameters in `auto_arima` under the *Forecasting time series data using auto_arima* recipe in *Chapter 11, Additional Statistical Modeling Techniques for Time Series*.

Getting ready

You will load the same libraries from the previous recipe, *Multi-step forecasting using linear regression models with scikit-learn*. The following are the additional classes and functions you will need for this recipe.

You will import the three classes, `ForecastingGridSearchCV`, `SlidingWindowSplitter`, and `MeanAbsolutePercentageError`. The metric class will be used in the cross-validated grid search for evaluating the different models, but you could use any other metric:

```
from sktime.forecasting.all import (
        ForecastingGridSearchCV,
        SlidingWindowSplitter,
        MeanAbsolutePercentageError)
```

How to do it...

You will build a K-NN regression model based on the results from the previous recipe, , and then work on optimizing the model with hyperparameter tuning. The following steps will use the energy DataFrame, but you should be able to apply the same steps on the other two datasets:

1. Make a copy of the energy DataFrame and split the data into training and test sets:

    ```
    df = energy.copy()
    train, test = split_data(df)
    ```

2. You will use the `TransformedTargetForecaster` class to create a pipeline for transforming the time series:

    ```
    n = len(test)
    fh = ForecastingHorizon(np.arange(n) + 1, is_
    relative=True)
    forecaster = TransformedTargetForecaster(
        [("deseasonalize",
    Deseasonalizer(model="multiplicative", sp=12)),
        ("detrend", Detrender(forecaster=PolynomialTrendFore
    caster(degree=1))),
        ("forecast",
            make_reduction(
                KNeighborsRegressor(),
    ```

```
                    scitype="tabular-regressor",
                    window_length=12,
                    strategy="recursive",
            ), ),  ])
```

Train the model using the `fit` method:

```
forecaster.fit(train.values)
```

Store the predictions as a new column in the test DataFrame using the `predict` method:

```
test['KNN-Regressor'] = forecaster.predict(fh)
```

3. You will use the `evaluate` function created in the preceding *Multi-step forecasting using linear regression models with scikit-learn* recipe to evaluate the model:

```
evaluate(test, train)
>>
sMAPE     MAPE     RMSE     MASE
0.090378  0.097746  225.568315  0.751772
```

4. Inspect the parameters available from the forecaster object with the `get_params` method. The following shows a small subset of the output:

```
'forecast__estimator__metric': 'minkowski',
 'forecast__estimator__metric_params': None,
 'forecast__estimator__n_jobs': None,
 'forecast__estimator__n_neighbors': 5,
 ....
```

The output shows the available hyperparameters that you can control.

5. Create a Python dictionary to define the hyperparameters you want to optimize against. The following is an example:

```
hyperparams_grid = {
    "forecast__estimator__n_neighbors": [i for i in
range(3,11)],
    "deseasonalize__model": ['multiplicative',
'additive'],
    "forecast__estimator__p": [1,2]}
```

In the preceding code, there are three hyperparameters with a range of values to evaluate against. In grid search, at every iteration, a model is trained and evaluated using a different combination of values until all combinations have been evaluated. When using `ForecastingGridSearchCV`, you can specify a metric to use for evaluating the models, for example, `scoring=smape`.

6. To perform **cross-validation** on time series, you will use the `SlidingWindowSplitter` class and define a sliding window at 80% of the `df` DataFrame (notice you are not using the `train` DataFrame). This means that 80% of the data will be allocated for the training fold and while the testing fold based on `fh`, or forecast horizon. Create the grid search object `grid_csv` using the `ForecastingGridSearchCV` class:

```
cv = SlidingWindowSplitter(window_length=int(len(train) *
0.80), fh=fh)
smape = MeanAbsolutePercentageError(symmetric=True)
grid_csv = ForecastingGridSearchCV(
    forecaster,
    strategy="refit",
    cv=cv,
    param_grid=hyperparams_grid,
    scoring=smape,
    return_n_best_forecasters=1,
    verbose=1)
```

Currently, *sktime* only supports *grid search* and *random search*.

Notice that `verbose` is set to `1` to print a summary for the number of computations. The default is `verbose=0`, which will not print anything.

7. To initiate the process and train the different models, use the `fit` method:

```
grid_csv.fit(train.values, fh=fh)
```

The following output is based on the 8 hyperparameters listed earlier:

```
Fitting 2 folds for each of 32 candidates, totalling 64
fits
```

The total number of models to be evaluated is `64`.

The cross-validated process produced 2 folds. There are 32 total combinations (`n_neighbors(8)` X `seasonality(2)` X `P(2)` = 32). The total number of models that will be trained (`fit`) is 2 x 32 = 64. Alternatively, you could use `ForecastingRandomizedSearchCV`, which performs a randomized cross-validated grid search to find optimal hyperparameters and is generally faster, but there is still a random component to the process.

8. Once the grid search process is completed, you can access the list of optimal hyperparameters using the `best_params` attribute.:

```
grid_csv.best_params_
>>
{'deseasonalize__model': 'additive',
 'forecast__estimator__n_neighbors': 7,
 'forecast__estimator__p': 2}
```

9. You can use the `predict` method from the `grid_csv` object to produce a forecast. Store the results as a new column in the `test` DataFrame to compare the results from the optimized hyperparameters against the default values used earlier in the recipe:

```
test['KNN_optimized'] = grid_csv.predict(fh)
```

Use the `evaluate` function to compare the two results:

```
evaluate(test, train)
```

This should produce a DataFrame comparing the two models, `RandomForestRegressor` and `RandomForestRegressor_optim`, that looks like this:

	sMAPE	MAPE	RMSE	MASE
KNN_optimized	0.088823	0.095325	188.102334	0.684741
KNN-Regressor	0.090378	0.097746	225.568315	0.751772

Figure 12.13 – Scores of an optimized KNN regressor and standard KNN regressor

Overall, the optimized K-NN regression did outperform the standard model with default values.

How it works...

Changing the number of folds can be controlled using `window_length` from the `SlidingWindowSplitter` class, which was set at 80% of the data.

The *sktime* library provides three splitting options for *cross-validation*: `SingleWindowSplitter`, `SlidingWindowSplitter`, and `ExpandingWindowSplitter`. The `SingleWindowSplitter` class splits the data into training and test sets only once.

The difference between the sliding and expanding splitters is how the training fold size changes. This is better explained through the following diagram:

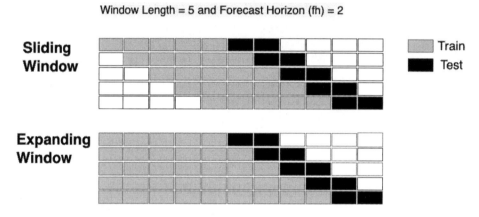

Figure 12.14 – Difference between SlidingWindowSplitter and ExpandingWindowSplitter

Notice from *Figure 12.14* that `SlidingWindowSplitter`, as the name implies, just *slides* over one step at each iteration, keeping the training and test fold sizes constant. In the `ExpandingWindowSplitter`, the training fold *expands* by one step at each iteration. The step size behavior can be adjusted using the `step_length` parameter (default is 1). Each row in *Figure 12.14* represents a model that is being trained (fitted) on the designated training fold and evaluated against the designated testing fold. After the entire run is complete the mean score is calculated.

There's more...

To get more insight into the performance at each fold, you can use the `cv_results_` attribute. This should produce a DataFrame of 32 rows, one row for each of the 32 combinations, and the mean scores are for the 2 folds:

```
grid_csv.cv_results_
```

The preceding code will return a DataFrame showing the average scores of all the folds for each combination (model).

And if you want to store the model or see the full list of parameters, you can use the `best_forecaster_` attribute:

```
model = grid_csv.best_forecaster_
model.get_params()
```

This should list all the parameters available and their values.

See also

You can learn more about the `ForecastingGridSearchCV` class from the official documentation at `https://www.sktime.org/en/v0.11.1/api_reference/auto_generated/sktime.forecasting.model_selection.ForecastingGridSearchCV.html`.

Forecasting with exogenous variables and ensemble learning

This recipe will allow you to explore two different techniques: working with multivariate time series and using ensemble forecasters. For example, the `EnsembleForecaster` class takes in a list of multiple regressors, each regressor gets trained, and collectively contribute in making a prediction. This is accomplished by taking the average of the individual predictions from each regressor. Think of this as the power of the collective. You will use the same regressors you used earlier: *Linear Regression*, *Random Forest Regressor*, *Gradient Boosting Regressor*, and *Support Vector Machines Regressor*.

You will use a Naive Regressor as the baseline to compare with `EnsembleForecaster`. Additionally, you will use *exogenous* variables with the *Ensemble Forecaster* to model a multivariate time series. You can use any regressor that accepts *exogenous* variables.

Getting ready

You will load the same modules and libraries from the previous recipe, *Multi-step forecasting using linear regression models with scikit-learn*. The following are the additional classes and functions you will need for this recipe:

```
from sktime.forecasting.all import EnsembleForecaster
from sklearn.svm import SVR
```

```
from sktime.transformations.series.detrend import
ConditionalDeseasonalizer
from sktime.datasets import load_macroeconomic
```

How to do it...

1. Load the macroeconomic data, which contains 12 features:

```
econ = load_macroeconomic()
cols = ['realgdp','realdpi','tbilrate', 'unemp', 'infl']
econ_df = econ[cols]
econ_df.shape
>> (203, 5)
```

You want to predict the unemployment rate (unemp) using exogenous variables. The exogenous variables include real gross domestic product (realgpd), real disposable personal income (realdpi), the Treasury bill rate (tbilrate), and inflation (infl). This is similar to univariate time series forecasting with exogenous variables. This is different from the VAR model which is used with multivariate time series and treats the variables as endogenous variables.

2. The reference for the *endogenous*, or univariate, variable in sktime is y and X for the *exogenous* variables. Split the data into y_train, y_test, exog_train, and exog_test:

```
y = econ_df['unemp']
exog = econ_df.drop(columns=['unemp'])
test_size = 0.1
y_train, y_test = split_data(y, test_split=test_size)
exog_train, exog_test = split_data(exog, test_split=test_
size)
```

3. Create a list of the regressors to be used with EnsembleForecaster:

```
regressors = [
    ("LinearRegression", make_
reduction(LinearRegression())),
    ("RandomForest", make_
reduction(RandomForestRegressor())),
    ("SupportVectorRegressor", make_reduction(SVR())),
    ("GradientBoosting", make_
reduction(GradientBoostingRegressor()))]
```

4. Create an instance of the `EnsembleForecaster` class and the `NaiveForecaster()` class with default hyperparameter values:

```
ensemble = EnsembleForecaster(regressors)
naive= NaiveForecaster()
```

5. Train both forecasters on the training set with the `fit` method. You will supply the univariate time series (y) along with the exogenous variables (X):

```
ensemble.fit(y=y_train, X=exog_train)
naive.fit(y=y_train, X=exog_train)
```

6. Once training is complete, you can use the `predict` method, supplying the forecast horizon and the test exogenous variables. This will be the unseen `exog_test` set:

```
fh = ForecastingHorizon(y_test.index, is_relative=None)
y_hat = pd.DataFrame(y_test).rename(columns={'unemp':
'test'})
y_hat['EnsembleForecaster'] = ensemble.predict(fh=fh,
X=exog_test)
y_hat['RandomForest'] = naive.predict(fh=fh, X=exog_test)
```

7. Use the `evaluate` function that you created earlier in the *Forecasting using non-linear models with sktime* recipe:

```
y_hat.rename(columns={'test':'y'}, inplace=True)
evaluate(y_hat)
```

This should produce a DataFrame comparing the two forecasters:

	sMAPE	MAPE	RMSE	MASE
EnsembleForecaster	1.211790	1.000520	1.338320	4.454848
NaiveForecaster	0.946033	2.490779	1.537844	4.522654

Figure 12.15 – Evaluation of NaiveForecaster and EnsembleForecaster

Overall, `EnsembleForecaster` did better than `NaiveForecaster`.

You can plot both forecasters for a visual comparison as well:

```
styles = ['k--','rx-','yv-']
for col, s in zip(y_hat, styles):
    y_hat[col].plot(style=s, label=col,
                    title='EnsembleForecaster vs
```

```
NaiveForecaster' )
plt.legend();plt.show()
```

The preceding code should produce a plot showing all three time series for EnsembleForecaster, NaiveForecaster, and the test dataset.

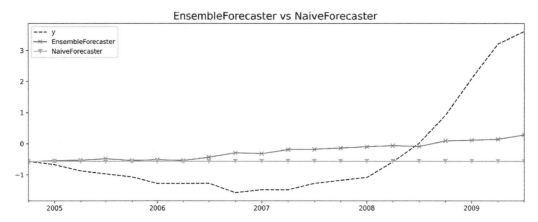

Figure 12.16 – Plotting the three forecasters against the test data

Remember that neither of the models was optimized. Ideally, you can use k-fold cross-validation when training or a cross-validated grid search, as shown in the *Optimizing a forecasting model with hyperparameter tuning* recipe.

How it works...

The EnsembleForecaster class from sktime is similar to the VotingRegressor class in sklearn. Both are ensemble estimators that fit (train) several regressors and collectively, they produce a prediction through an aggregate function. Unlike VotingRegressor in sklearn, EnsembleForecaster allows you to change the aggfunc parameter to either *mean* (default), *median, min,* or *max.* When making a prediction with the predict method, only one prediction per one-step forecast horizon is produced. In other words, you will not get multiple predictions from each base regressor, but rather the aggregated value (for example, the *mean*) from all the base regressors.

Using a multivariate time series is made simple by using exogenous variables. Similarly, in statsmodels, an ARIMA or SARIMA model has an exog parameter. An ARIMA with exogenous variables is referred to as ARIMAX. Similarly, a seasonal ARIMA with exogenous variables is referred to as SARIMAX. To learn more about exogenous variables in statsmodels, you can refer to the documentation here: https://www.statsmodels.org/stable/endog_exog.html.

There's more...

The `AutoEnsembleForecaster` class in sktime behaves similar to the `EnsembleForecaster` class you used earlier. The difference is that the `AutoEnsembleForecaster` class will calculate the optimal weights for each of the regressors passed. The `AutoEnsembleForecaster` class has a regressor parameter that takes a list of regressors and estimates a weight for each class. In other words, not all regressors are treated equal. If none are provided, then the `GradientBoostingRegressor` class is used instead, with a default `max_depth=5`.

Using the same list of regressors, you will use `AutoEnsembleForecaster` and compare the results with `RandomForest` and `EnsembleForecaster`:

```
from sktime.forecasting.compose import AutoEnsembleForecaster
auto = AutoEnsembleForecaster(forecasters=regressors,
                        method='feature-importance')
auto.fit(y=y_train, X=exog_train)
auto.weights_
>>
[0.1239225131192647,
 0.2634642533645639,
 0.2731867227890818,
 0.3394265107270897]
```

The order of the weights listed are based on the order from the regressor list provided. The highest weight was given to `GradientBoostingRegressor` at 34% followed by `SupportVectorRegressor` at 27%.

Using the `predict` method, let's compare the results:

```
y_hat['AutoEnsembleForecaster'] = auto.predict(fh=fh, X=exog_
test)
evaluate(y_hat, y_train)
```

This should produce a DataFrame comparing all three forecasters:

	sMAPE	MAPE	RMSE	MASE
EnsembleForecaster	1.211790	1.000520	1.338320	4.454848
NaiveForecaster	0.946033	2.490779	1.537844	4.522654
AutoEnsembleForecaster	1.351585	0.795818	1.423364	4.876082

Figure 12.17 – Evaluation of RandomForest, EnsembleForecaster, and AutoEnsembleForecaster

Keep in mind that the number and type of regressors (or forecasters) used in both `EnsembleForecaster` and `AutoEnsembleForecaster` will have a significant impact on the overall quality. Keep in mind that none of these models have been optimized and are based on default hyperparameter values.

See also

To learn more about the `AutoEnsembleForecaster` class, you can read the official documentation here: `https://www.sktime.org/en/stable/ api_reference/auto_generated/sktime.forecasting.compose. AutoEnsembleForecaster.html`.

To learn more about the `EnsembleForecaster` class, you can read the official documentation here: `https://www.sktime.org/en/stable/api_reference/ auto_generated/sktime.forecasting.compose.EnsembleForecaster. html`.

13
Deep Learning for Time Series Forecasting

If you have been searching the web for topics on data science, artificial intelligence, or **machine learning**, it is hard to escape headlines on **deep learning**. Deep learning is a subset of machine learning and excels when dealing with large and complex data, as it can extract complex features with minimal human involvement. Deep learning works well with structured and unstructured data and can be used in supervised, unsupervised, and semi-supervised learning. Several innovations have contributed to its wide adoption, such as the **transfer learning** technique allowing data scientists to leverage existing pre-trained models, saving a significant development and training time. Transfer learning, the ability to extend a pre-trained model, helped accelerate the adoption of deep learning, which is known to require massive amounts of data, specialized hardware, and longer times to train.

This chapter focuses on using deep learning for time series forecasting – more specifically, using different deep learning architectures suitable for sequential data such as time series data. There are different deep learning architectures for solving various problems. For example, **Recurrent Neural Networks (RNNs)** and their two variants, the **Long-Short Term Memory (LSTM)** and **Gated Recurrent Unit (GRU)**, **Convolutional Neural Networks (CNNs)**, **Autoencoders**, and **Generative Adversarial Networks (GANs)** and its extensions, such as **Deep Boltzmann Machines (DBM)** and **Deep Belief Network (DBN)**, to name a few.

There are many popular open source libraries and frameworks in Python for deep learning, such as TensorFlow (Google), PyTorch (Facebook), Microsoft **Cognitive Toolkit** or **CNTK** (Microsoft), MXNet (Apache), Chainer (Preferred Networks), and PaddlePaddle (Baidu), to name a few. This chapter will focus on two main libraries – **Keras (TensorFlow)** and **PyTorch**.

In this chapter, you will see the following recipes:

- Forecasting with an RNN using Keras
- Forecasting with LSTM using Keras
- Forecasting with a GRU using Keras
- Forecasting with an RNN using PyTorch
- Forecasting with LSTM using PyTorch
- Forecasting with a GRU using PyTorch

In *Chapter 12, Forecasting Using Supervised Machine Learning*, you learned how to prepare time series data for machine learning in the *Preparing time series data for supervised learning* recipe. The process and steps are the same for this chapter since you will be training deep learning models in a supervised learning manner. In addition, you will be reusing many of the functions from *Chapter 12, Forecasting Using Supervised Machine Learning*.

Technical requirements

Throughout this chapter, you will be using the same datasets and functions used in *Chapter 12, Forecasting Using Supervised Machine Learning*. The `handle_missing_data` and `one_step_forecast` functions will remain the same.

The Standardize class will be modified slightly to include a split_data method that splits a dataset into **train**, **validation**, and **test** sets. The validation set is used to evaluate the model's performance at each epoch. The following is the updated code for the Standardize class that you will be using throughout this chapter:

1. Start by loading the datasets and preprocessing the time series to be suitable for supervised learning. These are the same steps you followed in *Chapter 12, Forecasting Using Supervised Machine Learning*:

```
Class Standardize:
    def __init__(self, df, split=0.10):
        self.data = df
        self.split = split

    def split_data(self):
        n = int(len(self.data) * self.split)
        train, test = self.data.iloc[:-n], self.data.
iloc[-n:]
        n = int(len(train) * self.split)
        train, val = train.iloc[:-n], train.iloc[-n:]
        assert len(test) + len(train) + len(val) ==
len(self.data)
        return train, test, val

    def _transform(self, data):
        data_s = (data - self.mu)/self.sigma
        return data_s

    def fit_transform(self):
        train, test, val = self.split_data()
        self.mu, self.sigma = train.mean(), train.std()
        train_s = self._transform(train)
        test_s = self._transform(test)
        val_s = self._transform(val)
        return train_s, test_s, val_s

    def inverse(self, data):
```

```
            return (data * self.sigma)+self.mu

    def inverse_y(self, data):
        return (data * self.sigma[-1])+self.mu[-1]
```

2. The following shows an example using energy consumption data. The Jupyter notebook covers all three datasets for your reference:

```
import pandas as pd
import matplotlib.pyplot as plt
import numpy as np
from pathlib import Path
import warnings
warnings.filterwarnings('ignore')
path = Path('../../datasets/Ch13/')
energy = pd.read_csv(path.
joinpath(                       'energy_consumption.csv'),
                    index_col='Month',
                    parse_dates=True)
energy.columns = ['y']
energy.index.freq = 'MS'
en_df = one_step_forecast(energy, 10)
```

3. Scale the data using the updated `Standardize` class:

```
scale_en = Standardize(en_df)
train_en, test_en, val_en = scale_en.fit_transform()
```

You should now have three DataFrames for each dataset – for example, from the preceding code, you have `train_en`, `test_en`, and `val_en`, which will be referenced throughout the chapter.

Installing the deep learning libraries

All the datasets used in this chapter are available in the GitHub repository: `https://github.com/PacktPublishing/Time-Series-Analysis-with-Python-Cookbook./tree/main/datasets/Ch13`.

There are two Jupyter notebooks that contain additional content for your reference:

- A TensorFlow/Keras version: `https://github.com/PacktPublishing/Time-Series-Analysis-with-Python-Cookbook./blob/main/code/Ch13/Chapter%2013%20-%20tensorflow.ipynb`

- A PyTorch version: `https://github.com/PacktPublishing/Time-Series-Analysis-with-Python-Cookbook./blob/main/code/Ch13/Chapter%2013%20-%20pytorch.ipynb`

Deep learning libraries can be broken down into either **low-level**, **high-level**, or both. High-level libraries allow for quick prototyping and experimentation when testing various architectures, such as the case with Keras. On the other hand, a low-level library gives you more flexibility and control, but you will have to define more aspects of a model's architecture – PyTorch and Tensorflow are examples of low-level libraries.

It is recommended that you create two separate virtual Python environments – one for *TensorFlow/Keras* and one for *PyTorch*. You can install all the required dependencies and their specific versions without causing conflicts in other environments. If you prefer, you can still try and install them together in a new virtual environment.

If you need a quick refresher on creating a virtual Python environment, check out the *Development environment setup* recipe from *Chapter 1*, *Getting Started with Time Series Analysis*. The chapter covers two methods – using `conda` and `venv`.

The following instructions will create two virtual environments using `conda`. You can call the environments any name you like.

Installing TensorFlow

The following example will name the environment `TensorFlow`:

```
>> conda create -n tensorflow python=3.9 -y
>> conda activate tensorflow
>> pip install tensorflow
```

For the latest instructions or troubleshooting, please visit the main page here: `https://www.tensorflow.org/install`.

To make the new `tensorflow` environment visible within Jupyter, you can run the following code:

```
python -m ipykernel install --user --name tensorflow --display-name "tensorflow"
```

Installing PyTorch

The following example will name the environment `pytorch`. This will install CPU-only support:

```
>> conda create -n pytorch python=3.9 -y
>> conda activate pytorch
>> conda install pytorch torchvision torchaudio cpuonly -c
pytorch
```

For GPU instructions, the latest information, or troubleshooting, please visit the documentation here: `https://pytorch.org/`.

To make the new `pytorch` environment visible within Jupyter, you can run the following code:

```
python -m ipykernel install --user --name pytorch --display-
name "pytorch"
```

Understanding artificial neural networks

Deep learning utilizes artificial neural networks that consist of connected neurons or nodes. The following diagram represents a shallow neural network (single layer) to highlight the different components:

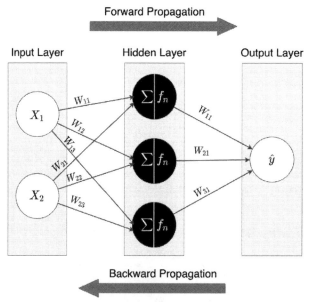

Figure 13.1 – A single-layer neural network

A network with more than one hidden layer is considered a *deep neural network*. In *Figure 13.1*, there are three layers – an **input layer**, a **hidden layer**, and an **output layer**.

The hidden layer represents a layer of connected neurons that perform a mathematical function. In its basic form, a neuron performs a linear function. For example, the first neuron in the hidden layer will perform a simple **linear transformation** – $X_1 \times W_{11} + X_2 \times W_{21}$. Improving how neurons pass information from one layer to another is done by adding an **activation function**. For example, common activation functions for the *hidden* layer nodes include *Sigmoid*, *ReLU*, or *Tanh*, which are non-linear functions. This allows the neurons to determine what information gets passed to the next connected neuron or layer in a deep neural network with multiple hidden layers. When the neuron applies a ReLU activation function after the linear transformation, you get $ReLU(X_1 \times W_{11} + X_2 \times W_{21})$. This is what allows neural networks the ability to capture *non-linear relationships*. Generally, you will have different activation functions for the hidden and the output layers.

The choice of activation functions for the *output* layer will depend on the type of problem you are solving – for example, using a *sigmoid* activation for binary or multilabel classifications, a *softmax* activation for multiclass classification, or *linear* activation for regression.

When an entire dataset passes through all the layers in a forward direction (**forward propagation**) and then again in a reverse backward direction (**backward propagation**), this cycle is what we call an **epoch** (one complete pass).

Once the data goes through forward propagation to compute the output from the input (training) data, the estimated value(s) are compared with the actual known observations. The weights ($W_{11}, W_{12}, ...$) are the parameters that the model estimates (learns) through the fitting or training process. Initially, when the training starts, the weights are initialized with some random values. The weights then get adjusted through the backward propagation process, based on some *loss function* that the network wants to minimize. This is essentially the process of learning from mistakes. There is also a bias term and an associated weight that is being learned by the model, which is usually denoted as W_0.

When training a deep learning network, you will need to provide values for several **hyperparameters**. These hyperparameters influence how the network learns and how fast it can converge to find the best parameter values (weights).

In this chapter, as you build different artificial neural network architectures for time series forecasting, you will learn about some of these hyperparameters and how they are used – for example, the *learning rate*, the number of *epochs*, the *batch size*, the *number of layers*, *nodes*, the *loss function*, and *activation functions*.

The following represents different neural network architectures for sequential data that you will build in this chapter:

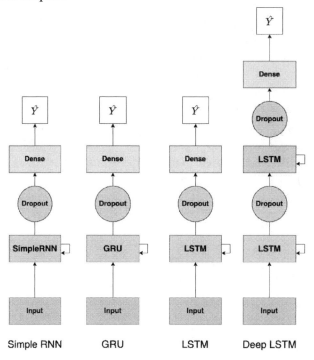

Figure 13.2 – Different neural network architectures for working with sequential data

Let's get started with the recipes.

Forecasting with an RNN using Keras

RNNs initially entered the spotlight with **Natural Language Processing** (**NLP**), as they were designed for sequential data, where past observations, such as words, have a strong influence on determining the next word in a sentence. This need for the artificial neural network to retain memory (*hidden state*) inspired the RNN architecture. Similarly, time series data is also sequential, and since past observations influence future observations, it also needs a network with memory. For example, an artificial neural network like the one in *Figure 13.1* is considered a **Feed-Forward Artificial Neural Network** (**FFN**), as depicted by the arrows pointing from nodes in one layer to the next in one direction; each node has one input and one output. In RNNs, there is a feedback loop where the output of one node or neuron is fed back (the recursive part) as input, allowing the network to learn from a prior time step acting as a memory. *Figure 13.3* shows a recurrent cell being unfolded to illustrate how the network passes output recursively at each time step (five in this example):

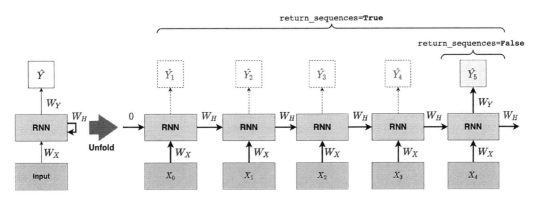

Figure 13.3 – Unfolding an RNN

Unlike an FFN, in an RNN, we have two outputs and two sets of weights – W_X for the input and W_H for the hidden state or memory.

How to do it...

Keras offers two methods for creating your models, either by using the `Model` class or the `Sequential` class. You will start with the `Sequential` API first, and in the *There's more...* section, you will be introduced to the `Model` class, also referred to as the *Functional API*:

1. Start by loading the needed classes, specifically the `Sequential` class:

```
from tensorflow.keras import Sequential
from tensorflow import keras
from tensorflow.keras.metrics import
RootMeanSquaredError, MeanAbsoluteError
from keras.layers import Dense, SimpleRNN, Dropout
```

2. Create the `features_target_ts` function that takes a dataset and returns an `x` split (independent variables or features) and `y` split (dependent or target variables):

```
def features_target_ts(*args):
    y = [col.pop('y').values.reshape(-1, 1) for col in
args]
    x = [col.values.reshape(*col.shape, 1)
                for col in args]
    return *y, *x
```

3. You can pass the train, test, and validation sets to the `features_target_ts` function, and it will return six splits:

```
(y_train_en, y_val_en,
 y_test_en, x_train_en,
 x_val_en, x_test_en) = features_target_ts(train_en,
                                           val_en,
                                           test_en)
```

4. Create the `create_model` function, which is used to construct the network's architecture. The `Sequential` class will sequentially add or stack the different layers in the order added, hence the name. You will implement the `SimpleRNN` architecture shown in *Figure 13.2*:

```
def create_model(train, units, dropout=0.2):
    model = keras.Sequential()
    model.add(SimpleRNN(units=units,
                        return_sequences=False,
                        input_shape=(train.shape[1],
                                     train.shape[2])))
    model.add(Dropout(dropout))
    model.add(Dense(1))

    return model
```

The `create_model` function will return a `Sequential` object which contains the architecture (the layers and their configuration). You are adding a dropout layer that randomly drops some of the units by setting them to zero. The frequency is set at `0.2` (20%), indicating the fraction of the input units to drop. `return_sequence` is set to `False`, indicating that only the last output is returned, as shown in *Figure 13.3*.

5. Create the `train_model_ts` function, which takes as input the returned `Sequential` object (which we are calling `model`), and the training and validation sets. The function will compile and train the model on the training sets and use the validation sets for evaluation at each epoch. During the training process, it will print output at each epoch, displaying the scores against the training and validation sets:

```
def train_model_ts(model,
                   x_train, y_train, x_val, y_val,
                   epochs=500,
```

```
                    patience=12,
                    batch_size=32):

    model.compile(optimizer='adam',
                  loss='mean_squared_error',
                  metrics=[RootMeanSquaredError(),
                           MeanAbsoluteError()])

    es = keras.callbacks.EarlyStopping(
                  monitor="val_loss",
                  min_delta=0,
                  patience=patience)

    history = model.fit(x_train,y_train,
            shuffle=False, epochs=epochs,
            batch_size=batch_size,
            validation_data=(x_val, y_val),
            callbacks=[es], verbose=1)
    return history
```

The function will return the `history` object, which is a Python dictionary that includes all the scores captured at each epoch for the training and validation sets.

6. Create the `plot_forecast` function, which will take the `model` object to make a prediction (forecast) and print out the predicted values against the actual values (out-of-sample) in the test set. Additionally, the function takes the `history` dictionary to plot the model's performance during training, so you can visually evaluate the model for any signs of overfitting:

```
def plot_forecast(model, x_test, y_test, index, history):
    fig, ax = plt.subplots(2, 1)
    (pd.Series(history.history['loss'])
                    .plot(style='k',alpha=0.50,
title='Loss by Epoch',
                          ax = ax[0], label='loss'))
    (pd.Series(history.history['val_loss'])
                    .plot(style='k',ax=ax[0],label='val_
loss'))
    ax[0].legend()
```

```
    predicted = model.predict(x_test)
    pd.Series(y_test.reshape(-1),
            index=index).plot(style='k--', alpha=0.5,
ax=ax[1],
                                    title='Forecast vs
Actual',
                                    label='actual')
    pd.Series(predicted.reshape(-1),
            index=index).plot(
        style='k',label='Forecast', ax=ax[1])
    fig.tight_layout()
    ax[1].legend();plt.show()
```

The function displays two subplots – the first plot will contain the performance during training (training and validation loss) and the bottom chart will compare the forecast. Note that there is another version of this function in the Jupyter notebook that produces three subplots – loss (mae), rmse, and the forecast.

7. Use the create_model function to create the Sequential object:

```
model_en_simpleRNN = create_model(x_train_en, units=32)
```

You can print out the model's summary using the summary method:

```
model_en_simpleRNN.summary()
```

The code will produce the summary of the model, as follows:

```
Model: "sequential"
```

Layer (type)	Output Shape	Param #
simple_rnn (SimpleRNN)	(None, 32)	1088
dropout (Dropout)	(None, 32)	0
dense (Dense)	(None, 1)	33

```
Total params: 1,121
Trainable params: 1,121
Non-trainable params: 0
```

Figure 13.4 – The SimpleRNN architecture summary

8. Train the model using the `train_model` function:

```
history_en_simpleRNN = train_model(model_en_simpleRNN, x_
train_en, y_train_en, x_val_en, y_val_en, batch_size=64)
```

Once the preceding line is executed, you will see a printout summary at each epoch. The following shows the results of the last two epochs:

```
Epoch 144/500
8/8 [==============================] – 0s 6ms/step – loss: 0.0761 – root_m
ean_squared_error: 0.2759 – mean_absolute_error: 0.2130 – val_loss: 0.1445
– val_root_mean_squared_error: 0.3802 – val_mean_absolute_error: 0.2916
Epoch 145/500
8/8 [==============================] – 0s 7ms/step – loss: 0.0844 – root_m
ean_squared_error: 0.2906 – mean_absolute_error: 0.2206 – val_loss: 0.1421
– val_root_mean_squared_error: 0.3769 – val_mean_absolute_error: 0.2940
```

Figure 13.5 – RMSE and MAE for the training and validation sets at each epoch

Note that the training ended at epoch `145` (not `500`). There will be more on that in the *How it works...* section.

9. Evaluate the model using the `plot_forecast` function:

```
plot_forecast(model_a_simpleRNN, x_test_air, y_test_air,
test_air.index, history_a_simpleRNN)
```

This should produce two subplots:

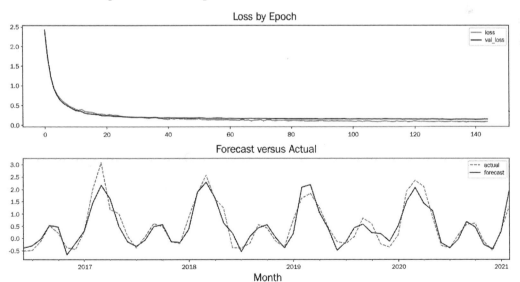

Figure 13.6 – A SimpleRNN model performance on the energy consumption data

The top plot, **Loss by Epoch**, helps you evaluate the overall training process. The goal is to minimize the loss function, and both curves (training loss and validation loss) are going down smoothly and not departing from each other, which can be a sign of overfitting.

You can continue the same process on the other datasets. The Jupyter notebook will include the results for the *energy consumption*, *air passengers*, and *daily temperature* datasets.

How it works...

In *Figure 13.3*, in an RNN, there are two coefficients that are being estimated by the model – W_x and W_h. The illustration is a simplification to help you understand how an RNN layer unfolds. In other words, the unfolding representation is just one cell being reused recursively where the output is fed back as input, thus carrying past information (memory) to the next computation.

An RNN unit performs the following computation:

$$h_t = \tanh\left(W_{ih}x_t + b_{ih} + W_{hh}h_{(t-1)} + b_{hh}\right)$$

It is a linear equation followed by a non-linear activation function —the hyperbolic tangent function (or *tanh*). The h_t is the hidden state at the current time t, h_{t-1} is the previous hidden state at time $t-1$, x_t is the input at the time t, and $W_{ih}, W_{hh}, b_{ih},$ and b_{hh} are the coefficients. The following figure illustrates this computation inside an RNN unit.

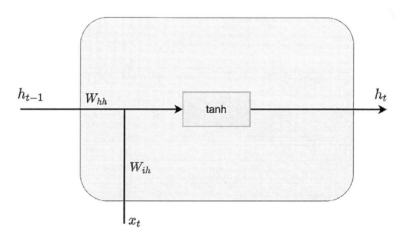

Figure 13.7 – RNN

The hidden state, what we call the memory, is being passed as output from one step to another recursively, as shown in the unfolded diagram in *Figure 13.3*.

In *Figure 13.6*, note that at some point, the loss stops dropping, hits a plateau, and does not improve. The training ended at epoch `145` and did not continue for all 500 epochs. This was due to the `EarlyStopping` class. You passed the following as a callback in the model's `fit` method:

```
es = keras.callbacks.EarlyStopping(monitor="val_loss",
  patience=patience)
```

This saves unnecessary compute time if the model is not improving. The `patience`, an integer, is a threshold representing the number of epochs with no improvements before stopping the training. In this example, you used `patience=12` against the validation loss.

The `SimpleRNN` class uses `tanh` as the activation function by default, which is a popular choice for RNNs, LSTMs, and GRUs. Since the final output is a continuous numeric value, a Dense layer was used. The activation function for the `Dense` layer is `None` (default) which results in a linear transformation. *Figure 13.1* shows how a linear transformation is followed by an activation function, so when it is set to `None` it reduces to just a linear transformation.

There's more...

You will create the same RNN architecture that you created earlier but this time using the *functional API* (the `Model` class):

1. Start by importing the needed classes:

   ```
   from tensorflow.keras import Model
   from keras.layers import (Dense,
                   SimpleRNN, Dropout,
                   Input)
   ```

2. Create a new `create_model` function:

   ```
   def create_model(train, units, dropout=0.2):

       input_data = Input(shape=(10,1))
       rnn = SimpleRNN(units, return_sequences=True)(input_
   data)
       dropout = Dropout(dropout)(rnn)
   ```

```
output = Dense(1)(dropout)
model = Model(inputs=input_data, outputs=output)
return model
```

Note how each layer references the previous layer, which is different than the `Sequential` approach used earlier.

You can continue with the training and evaluation following the same steps.

See also

To learn more about the `SimpleRNN` class, you can review the documentation here: `https://keras.io/api/layers/recurrent_layers/simple_rnn/`.

Forecasting with LSTM using Keras

There are a few shortcomings in using RNNs – for example, an RNN's memory is short term and does not do well when persisting a longer-term memory.

In the previous recipe, you trained a small RNN architecture with one hidden layer. In a deep RNN, with multiple hidden layers, the network will suffer from the **vanishing gradient** problem – that is, during backpropagation, as the weights get adjusted, it will be unable to change the weights of much earlier layers, reducing its ability to learn. Because of this, the output becomes influenced by the closer layers (nodes).

In other words, any memory of earlier layers decays through time, hence the term **vanishing**. This is an issue if you have a very long sequence – for example, a long paragraph or long sentence – and you want to predict the next word. In time series data, how problematic the lack of long-term memory is will vary, depending on your goal and the data you are working with. More specifically, your domain knowledge about the time series process comes into play. If long-term memory is needed, then LSTM offers a more robust solution to RNNs. Another alternative is the GRU, which you will explore in the following recipe.

How to do it...

In this recipe, you will continue from the previous recipe. All the time series preprocessing steps and functions will be the same. The following steps will highlight any necessary changes needed. The energy consumption data is used in the following steps. The Jupyter notebook will include the steps and output for other datasets – *air passengers* and *daily temperature*:

1. Create another `create_model` function that is similar to the one you used in the previous recipe. The only difference will involve replacing the RNN layer with the LSTM layer. You will use the `Sequential` class and follow the LSTM architecture in *Figure 13.2*:

```
def create_model(train, units, dropout=0.2):
    model = keras.Sequential()
    model.add(LSTM(units=units,
                    input_shape=(train.shape[1],
                                  train.shape[2])))
    model.add(Dropout(dropout))
    model.add(Dense(1))

    return model
```

Use the `create_model` function to create a sequential object:

```
model_en_lstm = create_model(train=x_train_en, units=32)
model_en_lstm.summary()
```

This should print out the summary of the network, as shown in *Figure 13.4*.

2. Use the `train_model_ts` function to train the model and store the returned dictionary as `history_en_lstm`:

```
history_en_lstm = train_model_ts(model_en_lstm, x_train_
en, y_train_en, x_val_en, y_val_en, batch_size=64)
```

This will print output at each epoch, similar to that in *Figure 13.5*.

3. Use the `plot_forecast` to evaluate the LSTM model:

```
plot_forecast(model_en_lstm, x_test_en, y_test_en, test_
en.index, history_en_lstm)
```

The preceding code should produce two subplots, one for the training process (training loss and validation loss) and another comparing the forecast against out-of-sample (test) data.

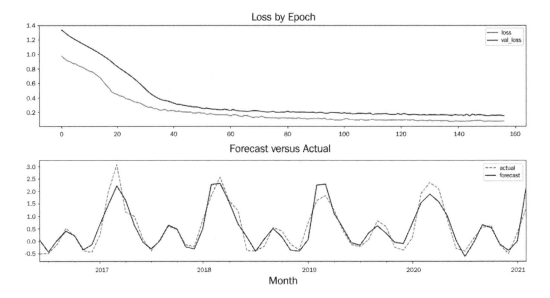

Figure 13.8 – LSTM model performance on the energy consumption data

Note that the training ended at 157. Initially, the validation loss was lagging behind the training loss but then got reduced to an acceptable level.

How it works...

An LSTM unit is very similar to an RNN but with additional enhancements. An RNN only has a hidden state (h), while an LSTM adds another state – the **cell state** (C).

In an LSTM unit, there are *four* main gates (the *input, input modulation, forget,* and *output* gates) that determine how the cell state gets updated. The following diagram shows how the cell and hidden state from a previous node (C_{t-1}, h_{t-1}) gets fed with the input (x_t) to produce a new cell state and hidden state (C_t, h_t).

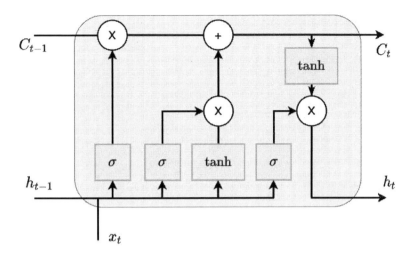

Figure 13.9 – An LSTM cell

Gates are mathematical computations:

- $i_t = \sigma(W_{ii}x_t + b_{ii} + W_{hi}h_{t-1} + b_{hi})$

- $f_t = \sigma(W_{if}x_t + b_{if} + W_{hf}h_{t-1} + b_{hf})$

- $g_t = \tanh(W_{ig}x_t + b_{ig} + W_{hg}h_{t-1} + b_{hg})$

- $o_t = \sigma(W_{io}x_t + b_{io} + W_{ho}h_{t-1} + b_{ho})$

- $c_t = f_t \odot c_{t-1} + i_t \odot g_t$

- $h_t = o_t \odot \tanh(c_t)$

Where g_t is the input modulation gate, i_t is the *input gate*, f_t is the *forget gate*, c_t is the *cell state*, and both h_t and o_t represent the *output gate*, which determines the value of the hidden state that gets passed on. Finally, σ is the sigmoid activation function. In many works of literature, i_t and g_t are referred to as input gates (thus describing an LSTM with three gates and not four).

There's more...

Using the functional API (the `Model` class), you can create a deep LSTM with two hidden layers (two LSTM layers):

```
from tensorflow.keras import Model
from keras.layers import (Dense,
                SimpleRNN, Dropout,
                Input
def create_model(train, units, dropout=0.2):

    input_data = Input(shape=(10,1))
    lstm_1 = LSTM(units, return_sequences=True)(input_data)
    dropout_1 = Dropout(dropout)(lstm_1)
    lstm_2 = LSTM(units)(dropout_1)
    dropout_2 = Dropout(dropout)(lstm_2)
    output = Dense(1)(dropout_2)
    model = Model(inputs=input_data, outputs=output)

    return model
```

Note that when stacking multiple RNN, GRU, or LSTM layers, you need to set `return_sequences` to `True`. The last LSTM layers in the preceding code are set to `False`, the default parameter value.

See also

To learn more about the LSTM class, you can review the documentation here: `https://keras.io/api/layers/recurrent_layers/lstm/`.

Forecasting with a GRU using Keras

The GRU was proposed as an alternative to the RNN to combat the vanishing gradient problem by introducing the gates concept. As with an LSTM, the gates are used to regulate what and how the data flows. These gates are mathematical functions that act as filters to ensure only significant pieces of information are being retained.

How to do it...

In this recipe, you will continue from the *Forecasting with an RNN using Keras* recipe. All the time series preprocessing steps and the functions will be the same. The following steps will highlight any necessary changes needed. The energy consumption data is used in the following steps. The Jupyter notebook will include the steps and outputs for other datasets – *air passengers* and *daily temperature*:

1. Create another `create_model` function that is similar to the one you used in the previous recipe. The only difference will involve replacing the RNN layer with the GRU layer. You will use the `Sequential` class and follow the GRU architecture in *Figure 13.2*:

```python
def create_model(train, units, dropout=0.2):
    model = keras.Sequential()
    model.add(GRU(units=units,
                  input_shape=(train.shape[1],
                               train.shape[2])))
    model.add(Dropout(dropout))
    model.add(Dense(1))
    return model

    return model
```

Use the `create_model` function to create a sequential object:

```python
model_en_gru = create_model(x_train_en, units=32)
model_en_gru.summary()
```

This should print out a summary of the network, as shown in *Figure 13.4*.

2. Use the `train_model_ts` function to train the model and store the returned dictionary as `history_en_gru`:

```python
history_en_gru = train_model_ts(model_en_gru, x_train_en,
y_train_en, x_val_en, y_val_en, batch_size=64)
```

This will print output at each epoch, similar to that in *Figure 13.5*.

3. Use the `plot_forecast` to evaluate the LSTM model:

```python
plot_forecast(model_en_gru, x_test_en, y_test_en, test_
en.index, history_en_gru)
```

The preceding code should produce two subplots, one for the training process (training loss and validation loss), and another comparing forecast against out-of-sample (test) data:

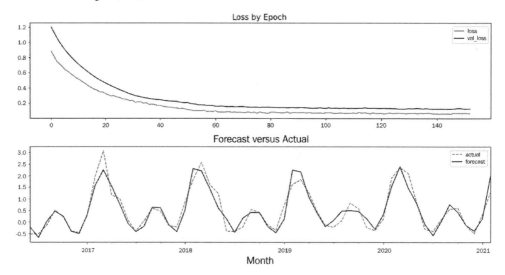

Figure 13.10 – GRU model performance on the energy consumption data

Note that the training ended at `153`. Initially, the validation loss was lagging behind the training loss but then got reduced to an acceptable level.

How it works...

The GRU is a simplified version of the LSTM with only two gates (the *update* and *reset* gates) and one state – the hidden state (h_t).

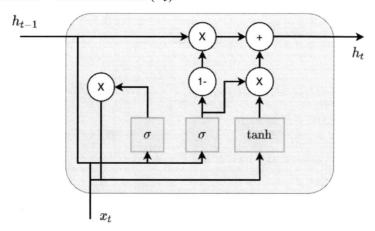

Figure 13.11 – A GRU cell

Compare *Figure 13.11* with *Figure 13.9*; note that an LSTM unit has two states (a cell state and hidden state) while a GRU only has one state.

The GRU unit performs the following computations:

- $r_t = \sigma\left(W_{ir}x_t + b_{ir} + W_{hr}h_{(t-1)} + b_{hr}\right)$
- $z_t = \sigma\left(W_{iz}x_t + b_{iz} + W_{hz}h_{(t-1)} + b_{hz}\right)$
- $n_t = tanh\left(W_{in}x_t + b_{in} + r_t * \left(W_{hn}h_{(t-1)} + b_{hn}\right)\right)$
- $h_t = (1 - z_t) * n_t + z_t * h_{(t-1)}$

Where h_t is the new hidden state, h_{t-1} is the previous hidden state, r_t is the *reset gate*, and z_t is the *update gate*. Both reset and update gates use the input data and apply a linear transformation, followed by a sigmoid function. σ is the sigmoid activation function used in the reset and update gates.

There's more...

If you have been following along, you should have four models – an RNN, LSTM, deep LSTM, and a GRU – for each of the datasets. In the Jupyter notebook, there are two additional architectures being added – bidirectional LSTM and LSTM with a `TimeDistributed` layer.

Toward the end of the notebook, the models are compared for each dataset – *air passengers*, *energy consumption*, and *daily temperature*. This is done using the model's `evaluate` method, using the test sets. The models were sorted using the **RMSE** score:

- The following is the output for the air passenger data:

	MSE	RMSE	MAE
GRU	0.724080	0.850929	0.703160
SimpleRNN	1.206688	1.098493	0.974018
Bidirectional	1.208408	1.099276	0.805906
LSTM	1.229816	1.108971	0.811656
Deep LSTM	1.352662	1.163040	0.843578
TimeDistributed	2.704924	1.644665	1.474382

Figure 13.12 – Models ranked by RMSE for air passenger data

- Note that the GRU was the winner on the air passenger data. The following is the output for the daily temperature data:

	MSE	RMSE	MAE
Deep LSTM	0.667481	0.816995	0.601264
GRU	0.721008	0.849122	0.719908
LSTM	0.734652	0.857119	0.694010
SimpleRNN	0.831809	0.912036	0.759248
Bidirectional	1.032825	1.016280	0.842255
TimeDistributed	3.058280	1.748794	1.531964

Figure 13.13 – Models ranked by RMSE for daily temperature data

- Note that for the daily temperature data, the deep LSTM was the winner. Finally, the following is the output for the energy consumption data:

	MSE	RMSE	MAE
SimpleRNN	1.081594	1.039997	0.911351
GRU	1.515763	1.231163	1.072095
LSTM	3.644953	1.909176	1.806012
Deep LSTM	4.054580	2.013599	1.903199
Bidirectional	5.531262	2.351863	2.222646
TimeDistributed	5.575944	2.361344	2.197815

Figure 13.14 – Models ranked by RMSE for energy consumption data

Note that **SimpleRNN** was the winner for the energy consumption data.

The point here is that how the model behaves depends on many factors, including the type of data you are dealing with.

See also

To learn more about the GRU class, you can review the documentation here: `https://keras.io/api/layers/recurrent_layers/gru/`.

Forecasting with an RNN using PyTorch

In the previous recipes, you used Keras to build different deep learning architectures with minimal changes to code. This is one of the advantages of a high-level API – it allows you to explore and experiment with different architectures very easily.

In this recipe, you will build a simple RNN architecture using PyTorch, a low-level API.

Getting ready

You will be using the functions and steps used to prepare the time series for supervised learning. The one exception is with the `features_target_ts` function, it will be modified to return a PyTorch **Tensor** object as opposed to a NumPy ndarray object. In PyTorch, `tensor` is a data structure similar to NumPy's ndarray object but optimized to work with **Graphical Processing Units (GPUs)**.

You can convert a NumPy ndarray to a PyTorch Tensor object using the `torch.from_numpy()` method and convert a PyTorch Tensor object to a NumPy ndarray object using the `detach.numpy()` method:

```
numpy_array = train_air.values
type(numpy_array)
>> numpy.ndarray
torch_tensor = torch.from_numpy(numpy_array)
type(torch_tensor)
>> torch.Tensor
from_torch_to_numpy = torch_tensor.detach().numpy()
type(from_torch_to_numpy)
>> numpy.ndarray
```

It is not necessary in the previous example to use the `detach` method; you could have just used the `numpy()` method only. However, as you proceed with the recipes, it is a good practice to detach a tensor with a gradient from the computational graph.

Create the `features_target_pt` function to return a PyTorch Tensor object:

```
def features_target_pt(*args):
    y = [torch.from_numpy(col.pop('y').values.reshape(-1,1)).
float() for col in args]
    x = [torch.from_numpy(col.values.reshape(*col.shape, 1)).
```

```
float()
                    for col in args]
    return *y, *x
```

With this change, you should be able to continue with the remaining steps to create your `x_train`, `x_val`, `x_test`, `y_train`, `y_val`, and `y_test` Tensor objects from each of the three datasets.

How to do it...

The following steps will use the energy consumption data. You can follow the same steps with the other datasets. The Jupyter notebook will include the steps and outputs for other datasets – *air passengers* and *daily temperature*:

1. Split the train, validate, and test sets into x (features or independent variables) and y (dependent or target variables) using the `features_target_ps` function:

    ```
    (y_train_en, y_val_en,
    y_test_en, x_train_en,
    x_val_en, x_test_en) = features_target_pt(train_en,
                                    val_en,
                                    test_en)
    ```

2. Create an RNN class that will inherit from the `Module` class (RNN is a subclass of `Module`). The `Module` class is the base class for all neural network modules in PyTorch. You will also need to define many aspects of the implementation using a low-level framework. This includes defining the `forward` method and `init_hidden` method:

    ```
    class RNN(nn.Module):
        def __init__(self, input_size, output_size, n_
    features, n_layers):
            super(RNN, self).__init__()
            self.n_layers = n_layers
            self.hidden_dim = n_features
            self.rnn = nn.RNN(input_size, n_features, n_
    layers, batch_first=True)
            self.dropout = nn.Dropout(0.2)
            self.fc = nn.Linear(n_features, output_size)

        def forward(self, x, hn):
    ```

```
           # batch_first=True -> (batch_size, seq_length,
    input_size)
           x = x.view(1, x.shape[0], x.shape[1])
           rnn_o, hn = self.rnn(x, hn)
           rnn_o = self.dropout(rnn_o)
           # reshape
           rnn_o = rnn_o.view(-1, self.hidden_dim)
           output = self.fc(rnn_o)
           return output, hn
        def init_hidden(self):
           weight = next(self.parameters()).data
           hidden = weight.new(self.n_layers, 1, self.
    hidden_dim).zero_()
           return hidden
```

If you run the following, you will confirm that RNN is now a subclass of the Module class:

```
issubclass(RNN, nn.Module)
>> True
```

The architecture for this RNN class is like SimpleRNN in *Figure 13.6*. The output layer uses the nn.Linear class, which is equivalent to the Dense class in Keras without an activation function (activation=None).

3. You will need to create the train_model_pt function. The goal is to create a generalized train_model_pt function to be used throughout any of the PyTorch recipes, using different datasets and different architectures such as an RNN, a GRU, or LSTM. The code is pretty long, and you can see the full implementation in the Jupyter notebook. In the following steps, the code is broken down, but keep in mind that everything presented is inside the train_model_pt function.

    The first step in the train_model_pt function is to create an instance of the RNN model (or any other model) and pass the necessary parameters needed to instantiate the model class:

```
def train(model_type='RNN', **kwargs):
    if model_type=='RNN':
        model = RNN(kwargs['input_size'],
                    kwargs['output_size'],
                    kwargs['units'],
                    kwargs['n_layers'])
```

To make the function flexible, you will use `**kwargs`, allowing you to pass
a dictionary for the hyperparameters. The `model` object is an instance of the RNN
class you created earlier.

4. Next, in the `train_model_pt` function, you will define the model's criterion for
   training. This is the **loss function** that the model will improve against. Recall that in
   Keras, inside `model.compile`, you used `loss='mean_squared_error'` and
   `optimizer='adam'`. Similarly, the criterion here will use the `nn.MSELoss` class,
   and the optimizer will be the `torch.optim.Adam` class:

```python
criterion = nn.MSELoss()
optimizer = torch.optim.Adam(model.parameters(),
lr=kwargs['lr'])
```

5. Extract the training, testing, and validation sets from `**kwargs`:

```python
x_train, y_train = kwargs['train_data']
x_val, y_val   = kwargs['val_data']
x_test, y_test = kwargs['test_data']
```

Define a `history` object to keep track of the training and validation loss:

```python
history = {'loss': [], 'val_loss': []}
```

6. In PyTorch, when training a model, you will use the `model.train()` method,
   which signals training mode (the default behavior), thus keeping track of the
   gradient, and utilizes the dropout layers. When switching to evaluation mode,
   you will use `model.eval()` with `torch.no_grad()`:

```python
model.train()
epochs = kwargs['epochs']
print_every = kwargs['print_every']

for batch_i, epoch in enumerate(range(epochs)):
    h = model.init_hidden()
    optimizer.zero_grad()
    pred, h = model(x_train, h) #model(x_train)
        #hidden = hidden.data
    loss = criterion(pred, y_train)
    loss.backward()
    optimizer.step()
    if batch_i % print_every == 0:
```

```
        model.eval()
        with torch.no_grad():
            val_h = model.init_hidden()
            val_p, val_h = model(x_val, val_h)
            val_loss = criterion(val_p, y_val)
            history['val_loss'].append(val_loss.item())
        model.train()
        history['loss'].append(loss.item())
        print(f'{batch_i}/{epochs} - Loss:   {loss.
item()}, val_loss: {val_loss.item()}')
```

In the preceding code, you are looping through each epoch, initializing the hidden state (W_{hh}). On each iteration, you will evaluate on the validation set and store both results from training and validation (`loss` and `val_loss`).

7. Once the training and validation cycles are completed, you can use the trained model to make predictions:

```
## Prediction
model.eval()
with torch.no_grad():
    h0 = model.init_hidden()
    y_hat = model(x_test, h0)
y_hat, _ = y_hat
mse_loss_air = criterion(y_hat, y_test)
print(f'Test MSE Loss: {mse_loss_air.item():.4f}')
```

Note that in the prediction section of the `train_model_pt` function, you are using the testing set.

8. In the `train_model_pt` function, you will also produce some plots to help understand the model's performance:

```
## Plotting
fig, ax = plt.subplots(2, 1)
ax[0].set_title(f'{model_type}: Loss and Validation Loss
per epoch')
ax[0].plot(history['loss'], 'k--', label='loss')
ax[0].plot(history['val_loss'], 'k', label='val_loss')
ax[0].legend()
ax[1].set_title(f"{model_type} TEST MSE = {mse_loss_air.
```

```
item():.4f}: Forecast vs Actual (Out-of-Sample data)")
scale = kwargs['scale']
actual = scale.inverse_y(y_test.detach().numpy().ravel())
pred = scale.inverse_y(y_hat.detach().numpy().ravel())
idx = kwargs['idx']
pd.Series(actual, index=idx).plot(style='k--',
label='actual', alpha=0.65)
pd.Series(pred, index=idx).plot(style='k',
label='forecast')
fig.tight_layout()
ax[1].legend(); plt.show()
```

9. Finally, the `train_model_pt` function will return the two objects, `model` and `history`:

```
return model, history
```

The train function will return the trained model and the history, which contains the training and validation loss on each epoch. To avoid having to print output at each epoch, the `print_every` parameter was added. For example, if `print_every` was set to 50, then it will print the scores at every 50 epochs.

10. To use the `train_model_pt` function, define your parameters for the energy consumption data:

```
params_en = {'input_size':x_train_air.shape[1],
'output_size':1,
'units':32,
'n_layers':1,
'epochs': 500,
'print_every': 20,
'lr': 0.01,
'train_data': (x_train_en, y_train_en),
'val_data': (x_val_en, y_val_en),
'test_data': (x_test_en, y_test_en),
'idx': test_en.index,
'scale': scale_en}
```

11. You will pass `params_en` to the `train_model_pt` function to start training the model:

```
en_rnn, history_en_rnn = train_model_pt('RNN', **params_
en)
```

The preceding code will print an output similar to that in *Figure 13.5* but every 20 epochs. Once training is done, two subplots will be displayed. The first plot shows the training process (loss and validation loss), and the second one compares the forecast against the test data.

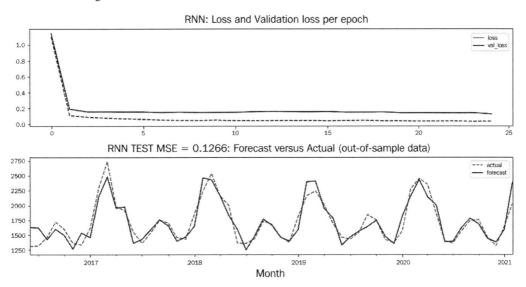

Figure 13.15 – RNN performance on energy consumption data

Overall, there is no sign of overfitting, and the overall results look promising.

How it works...

In PyTorch, you had to define more aspects of the model and architecture than with a lower-level framework such as Keras. The advantage here is that you gain more flexibility and can create complex solutions and architectures, but the process may be more time-consuming.

Tensors are the core building blocks in PyTorch and are very similar to NumPy's ndarrays. When building the RNN, you had to inherit from the nn.Module class. This will be the case when you build any neural network model in PyTorch, since nn.Module is the base class.

There's more...

PyTorch offers a `Sequential` class that allows you to define your model architecture quickly.

The following defines an RNN architecture with a dropout:

```
n_hidden = 32
input_size = x_train_en.shape[1]
n_layers = 1
output = 1
model = torch.nn.Sequential(
    torch.nn.RNN(input_size, n_hidden, n_layers),
    torch.nn.Dropout(0.5),
    torch.nn.Linear(n_hidden, output)
)
```

See also

To learn more about the RNN class, you can review the documentation here: https://pytorch.org/docs/stable/generated/torch.nn.RNN.html.

Forecasting with LSTM using PyTorch

In this recipe, you will use the same `train_model_pt` function from the previous *Forecasting with an RNN using PyTorch* recipe. The function trains the model, captures loss function scores, evaluates the model, makes a forecast using the test set, and finally, produces plots for further evaluation.

You will still need to define a new class for the LSTM model.

How to do it...

The following steps will use the energy consumption data. You can follow the same steps with the other datasets. The Jupyter notebook will include the steps and outputs for other datasets – *air passengers* and *daily temperature*:

1. Create an LSTM class that will inherit from the `Module` class. The setup will be similar to the RNN class created earlier, but now you have two states (the cell state and the hidden state) and not just one:

    ```
    class LSTM(nn.Module):
        def __init__(self, input_size, output_size, n_
    ```

```
features, n_layers):
        super(LSTM, self).__init__()
        self.n_layers = n_layers
        self.hidden_dim = n_features
        self.lstm = nn.LSTM(input_size, n_features, n_
layers, batch_first=True)
        self.dropout = nn.Dropout(0.2)
        self.fc = nn.Linear(n_features, output_size)


    def forward(self, x, hn):
        # batch_first=True -> (batch_size, seq_length,
input_size)
        x = x.view(1, x.shape[0], x.shape[1])
        lstm_o, hn = self.lstm(x, hn)
        lstm_o = self.dropout(lstm_o)
        # reshape
        lstm_o = lstm_o.view(-1, self.hidden_dim)
        output = self.fc(lstm_o)
        return output, hn
    def init_hidden(self):
        weight = next(self.parameters()).data
        hidden = (weight.new(self.n_layers, 1, self.
hidden_dim).zero_(),
                    weight.new(self.n_layers, 1, self.
hidden_dim).zero_())
        return hidden
```

2. Modify the `train_model_pt` function by adding another `elif` statement to handle when `model_type=='LSTM'`:

```
elif model_type=='LSTM':
        model = LSTM(kwargs['input_size'],
                    kwargs['output_size'],
                    kwargs['units'],
                    kwargs['n_layers'])
```

3. Use the `params_en` dictionary you defined earlier and pass it to the `train_model_pt` function:

```
en_lstm, history_en_lstm = train_model_pt('LSTM',
**params_en)
```

The preceding code will print an output every 20 epochs, similar to *Figure 13.5*. Once training is done, two subplots will be displayed. The first plot shows the training process (loss and validation loss), and the second one compares the forecast against the test data.

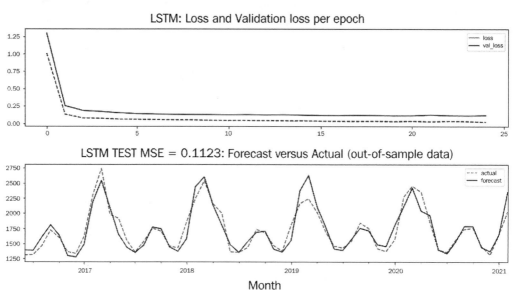

Figure 13.16 – LSTM performance on energy consumption data

Overall, from the loss per epoch plot, there is no sign of overfitting, and the MSE on the test set is lower than the RNN model (see *Figure 13.15*).

How it works...

The implementation of the `LSTM` class is very similar to the RNN, except for the number of states. Notice that in the `init_hidden` method, the hidden object, which is a tuple, contains two sets of weights — cell state and hidden state.

```
Hidden = (weight.new(self.n_layers, 1, self.hidden_dim).zero_
(),

                 weight.new(self.n_layers, 1, self.hidden_
dim).zero_())
```

Compare this to the RNN class, which only has one state:

```
hidden = weight.new(self.n_layers, 1, self.hidden_dim).zero_()
```

There's more...

You added a dropout layer for the `SimpleRNN`, `LSTM`, and `GRU` models in the Keras recipes. Similarly, in our PyTorch recipes, the `nn.Dropout` class is added.

Alternatively, in PyTorch, the RNN, LSTM, and GRU classes have a `dropout` parameter that is set to zero by default. You can change this value by providing a probability (values from 0 to 1). This will introduce a dropout on the output of each layer (RNN, LSTM, or GRU), except the last layer.

For example, in the LSTM class, you can update the dropout parameter in the nn.LSTM class, as shown in the following:

```
self.lstm = nn.LSTM(input_size, n_features, n_layers, batch_
first=True, dropout=0.40)
```

As with the previous recipe using PyTorch for RNN, you can use the `Sequential` class for the LSTM architecture.

The following defines an LSTM architecture with a dropout:

```
n_hidden = 32
input_size = x_train_en.shape[1]
n_layers = 1
output = 1
model = torch.nn.Sequential(
    torch.nn.LSTM(input_size, n_hidden, n_layers),
    torch.nn.Dropout(0.5),
    torch.nn.Linear(n_hidden, output)
)
```

See also

To learn more about the LSTM class, you can review the documentation here: `https://pytorch.org/docs/stable/generated/torch.nn.LSTM.html`.

Forecasting with a GRU using PyTorch

In this recipe, you will use the same `train_model_pt` function from the previous *Forecasting with an RNN using PyTorch* recipe. The function trains the model, captures loss function scores, evaluates the model, makes a forecast using the test set, and finally, produces plots for further evaluation.

You will still need to define a new class for the GRU model.

How to do it...

1. Create a GRU class that will inherit from `Module` class. The setup will be similar to the `RNN` class, but unlike the `LSTM` class, you only handle one state (the hidden state):

```python
class GRU(nn.Module):
    def __init__(self, input_size, output_size, n_
features, n_layers):
        super(GRU, self).__init__()
        self.n_layers = n_layers
        self.hidden_dim = n_features
        self.gru = nn.GRU(input_size, n_features, n_
layers, batch_first=True)
        self.dropout = nn.Dropout(0.2)
        self.fc = nn.Linear(n_features, output_size)

    def forward(self, x, hn):
        # batch_first=True -> (batch_size, seq_length,
input_size)
        x = x.view(1, x.shape[0], x.shape[1])
        gru_o, hn = self.gru(x, hn)
        gru_o = self.dropout(gru_o)
        # reshape
        gru_o = gru_o.view(-1, self.hidden_dim)
        output = self.fc(gru_o)
        return output, hn
    def init_hidden(self):
        weight = next(self.parameters()).data
        hidden = weight.new(self.n_layers, 1, self.
```

```
hidden_dim).zero_()
        return hidden
```

2. Modify the `train_model_pt` function by adding another `elif` statement to handle when `model_type=='GRU'`:

```
elif model_type=='GRU':
        model = LSTM(kwargs['input_size'],
                    kwargs['output_size'],
                    kwargs['units'],
                    kwargs['n_layers'])
                    kwargs['n_layers'])
```

3. Use the `params_en` dictionary you defined earlier and pass it to the `train_model_pt` function:

```
en_gru, history_en_gru = train_model_pt('GRU', **params_
en)
```

The preceding code will print output every 20 epochs, similar to that shown in *Figure 13.5*. Once training is done, two subplots will be displayed. The first plot shows the training process (loss and validation loss), and the second one compares the forecast against the test data.

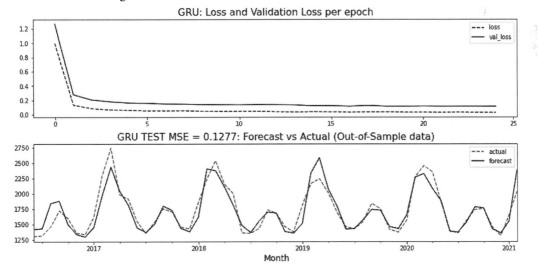

Figure 13.17 – GRU performance on energy consumption data

Overall, from the loss per epoch plot, there is no sign of overfitting, and the MSE on the test set is slightly higher than the RNN model (see *Figure 13.15*).

How it works...

Overall, the GRU implementation is very similar to the RNN class. The `init_hidden` method in both classes is the same, since they only manage one hidden state.

There's more...

As with the previous recipe using PyTorch for RNN, you can use the `Sequential` class for the GRU architecture.

The following defines the GRU architecture with a dropout:

```
n_hidden = 32
input_size = x_train_en.shape[1]
n_layers = 1
output = 1
model = torch.nn.Sequential(
    torch.nn.GRU(input_size, n_hidden, n_layers),
    torch.nn.Dropout(0.5),
    torch.nn.Linear
```

See also

To learn more about the GRU class, you can review the documentation here: `https://pytorch.org/docs/stable/generated/torch.nn.GRU.html`.

14

Outlier Detection Using Unsupervised Machine Learning

In *Chapter 8, Outlier Detection Using Statistical Methods*, you explored parametric and non-parametric statistical techniques to spot potential outliers. The methods were simple, interpretable, and yet quite effective.

Outlier detection is not straightforward, mainly due to the ambiguity surrounding the definition of what an outlier is specific to your data or the problem that you are trying to solve. For example, though common, some of the thresholds used in *Chapter 8, Outlier Detection Using Statistical Methods*, are still arbitrary and not a rule that you should follow. Therefore, having domain knowledge is vital to making the proper judgment when spotting outliers.

In this chapter, you will be introduced to a handful of machine learning-based methods for outlier detection. Most of the machine learning techniques for outlier detection are considered *unsupervised* outlier detection methods, such as **Isolation Forests (iForest)**, unsupervised **K-Nearest Neighbors (KNN)**, **Local Outlier Factor (LOF)**, and **Copula-Based Outlier Detection (COPOD)**, to name a few.

Generally, outliers (or anomalies) are considered a rare occurrence (later in the chapter, you will see this referenced as the contamination percentage). In other words, you would assume a small fraction of your data are outliers in a large data set. For example, 1% of the data may be potential outliers. However, this complexity requires methods designed to find patterns in the data. Unsupervised outlier detection techniques are great at finding patterns in rare occurrences.

After investigating outliers, you will have a historical set of labeled data, allowing you to leverage semi-supervised outlier detection techniques. This chapter focuses on unsupervised outlier detection.

In this chapter, you will be introduced to the **PyOD** library, described as *"a comprehensive and scalable Python toolkit for detecting outlying objects in multivariate data."* The library offers an extensive collection of implementations for popular and emerging algorithms in the field of outlier detection, which you can read about here: `https://github.com/yzhao062/pyod`.

You will be using the same New York taxi dataset to make it easier to compare the results between the different machine learning methods in this chapter and the statistical methods from *Chapter 8, Outlier Detection Using Statistical Methods*.

The recipes that you will encounter in this chapter are as follows:

- Detecting outliers using KNN
- Detecting outliers using LOF
- Detecting outliers using iForest
- Detecting outliers using **One-Class Support Vector Machine (OCSVM)**
- Detecting outliers using COPOD
- Detecting outliers with PyCaret

Technical requirements

You can download the Jupyter notebooks and datasets required from the
GitHub repository:

- Jupyter notebooks: `https://github.com/PacktPublishing/Time-Series-Analysis-with-Python-Cookbook./blob/main/code/Ch14/Chapter%2014.ipynb`

- Datasets: `https://github.com/PacktPublishing/Time-Series-Analysis-with-Python-Cookbook./tree/main/datasets/Ch14`

You can install PyOD with either `pip` or Conda. For a `pip` install, run the
following command:

```
pip install pyod
```

For a Conda install, run the following command:

```
conda install -c conda-forge pyod
```

To prepare for the outlier detection recipes, start by loading the libraries that you will be
using throughout the chapter:

```
import pandas as pd
import numpy as np
import matplotlib.pyplot as plt
from pathlib import Path
import warnings
warnings.filterwarnings('ignore')
plt.rcParams["figure.figsize"] = [16, 3]
```

Load the `nyc_taxi.csv` data into a pandas DataFrame as it will be used throughout
the chapter:

```
file = Path("../../datasets/Ch8/nyc_taxi.csv")
nyc_taxi = pd.read_csv(folder / file,
                       index_col='timestamp',
                       parse_dates=True)
nyc_taxi.index.freq = '30T'
```

You can store the known dates containing outliers, also known as ground truth labels:

```
nyc_dates =  [
        "2014-11-01",
        "2014-11-27",
        "2014-12-25",
        "2015-01-01",
        "2015-01-27"]
```

Create the `plot_outliers` function that you will use throughout the recipes:

```
def plot_outliers(outliers, data, method='KNN',
                  halignment = 'right',
                  valignment = 'top',
                  labels=False):

    ax = data.plot(alpha=0.6)

    if labels:
        for i in outliers['value'].items():
            plt.plot(i[0], i[1], 'v', markersize=8,
markerfacecolor='none', markeredgecolor='k')
            plt.text(i[0], i[1]-(i[1]*0.04), f'{i[0].
strftime("%m/%d")}',
                        horizontalalignment=halignment,
                        verticalalignment=valignment)
    else:
        data.loc[outliers.index].plot(ax=ax, style='rX',
markersize=9)
    plt.title(f'NYC Taxi - {method}')
    plt.xlabel('date'); plt.ylabel('# of passengers')
    plt.legend(['nyc taxi','outliers'])
    plt.show()
```

As you proceed with the outlier detection recipes, the goal is to see how the different techniques capture outliers and compare them to the ground truth labels, as follows:

```
tx = nyc_taxi.resample('D').mean()
known_outliers = tx.loc[nyc_dates]
plot_outliers(known_outliers, tx, 'Known Outliers')
```

The preceding code should produce a time series plot with X markers for the known outliers:

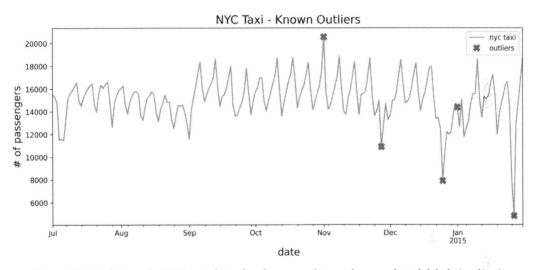

Figure 14.1 – Plotting the NYC taxi data after downsampling with ground truth labels (outliers)

> **PyOD's Methods for Training and Making Predictions**
>
> Like scikit-learn, PyOD offers familiar methods for training your model and making predictions by providing three methods: `model.fit()`, `model.predict()`, and `model.fit_predict()`.
>
> In the recipes, we will break down the process into two steps by first fitting the model (training) using `.fit()` and then making a prediction using `.predict()`.

In addition to the `predict` method, PyOD provides two additional methods: `predict_proba` and `predict_confidence`.

In the first recipe, you will explore how PyOD works behind the scenes and introduce fundamental concepts, for example, the concept of `contamination` and how `threshold_` and `decision_scores_` are used to generate the binary labels (*abnormal* or *normal*). These concepts will be covered in more depth in the following recipe.

Detecting outliers using KNN

The KNN algorithm is typically used in a supervised learning setting where prior results or outcomes (labels) are known.

It can be used to solve classification or regression problems. The idea is simple; for example, you can classify a new data point, Y, based on its nearest neighbors. For instance, if k=5, the algorithm will find the five nearest data points (neighbors) by distance to the point Y and determine its class based on the majority. If there are three blue and two red nearest neighbors, Y is classified as blue. The K in KNN is a parameter you can modify to find the optimal value.

In the case of outlier detection, the algorithm is used differently. Since we do not know the outliers (labels) in advance, KNN is used in an *unsupervised* learning manner. In this scenario, the algorithm finds the closest *K* nearest neighbors for every data point and measures the average distance. The points with the most significant distance from the population will be considered outliers, and more specifically, they are considered global outliers. In this case, the distance becomes the score to determine which points are outliers among the population, and hence KNN is a *proximity-based algorithm*.

Generally, proximity-based algorithms rely on the distance or proximity between an outlier point and its nearest neighbors. In KNN, the number of nearest neighbors, *k*, is a parameter you need to determine. There are other variants of the KNN algorithm supported by PyOD, for example, **Average KNN (AvgKNN)**, which uses the average distance to the KNN for scoring, and **Median KNN (MedKNN)**, which uses the median distance for scoring.

How to do it...

In this recipe, you will continue to work with the `tx` DataFrame, created in the *Technical requirements* section, to detect outliers using the KNN class from PyOD:

1. Start by loading the KNN class:

```
from pyod.models.knn import KNN
```

2. You should be familiar with a few parameters to control the algorithm's behavior. The first parameter is `contamination`, a numeric (float) value representing the dataset's fraction of outliers. This is a common parameter across all the different classes (algorithms) in PyOD. For example, a `contamination` value of `0.1` indicates that you expect 10% of the data to be outliers. The default value is `contamination=0.1`. The contamination value can range from `0` to `0.5` (or 50%). You will need to experiment with the contamination value, since the value influences the scoring threshold used to determine potential outliers, and how many of these potential outliers are to be returned. You will learn more about this in the *How it works...* section of this chapter.

   For example, if you suspect the proportion of outliers in your data at 3%, then you can use that as the contamination value. You could experiment with different contamination values, inspect the results, and determine how to adjust the contamination level. We already know that there are 5 known outliers out of the 215 observations (around 2.3%), and in this recipe, you will use 0.03 (or 3%).

   The second parameter, specific to KNN, is `method`, which defaults to `method='largest'`. In this recipe, you will change it to the `mean` (the average of all *k* neighbor distances). The third parameter, also specific to KNN, is `metric`, which tells the algorithm how to compute the distances. The default is the `minkowski` distance but it can take any distance metrics from scikit-learn or the SciPy library. Finally, you need to provide the number of neighbors, which defaults to `n_neighbors=5`. Ideally, you will want to run for different KNN models with varying values of *k* and compare the results to determine the optimal number of neighbors.

3. Instantiate KNN with the updated parameters and then train (fit) the model:

```
knn = KNN(contamination=0.03,
            method='mean',
            n_neighbors=5)
knn.fit(tx)
>>
KNN(algorithm='auto', contamination=0.05, leaf_size=30,
method='mean',
    metric='minkowski', metric_params=None, n_jobs=1, n_
neighbors=5, p=2,
    radius=1.0)
```

4. The `predict` method will generate binary labels, either 1 or 0, for each data point. A value of 1 indicates an outlier. Store the results in a pandas Series:

```
predicted = pd.Series(knn.predict(tx),
                        index=tx.index)
print('Number of outliers = ', predicted.sum())
>>
Number of outliers =   6
```

5. Filter the `predicted` Series to only show the outlier values:

```
outliers = predicted[predicted == 1]
outliers = tx.loc[outliers.index]
outliers
>>
Timestamp   value
2014-11-01   20553.500000
2014-11-27   10899.666667
2014-12-25   7902.125000
2014-12-26   10397.958333
2015-01-26   7818.979167
2015-01-27   4834.541667
```

Overall, the results look promising; four out of the five known dates have been identified. Additionally, the algorithm identified the day after Christmas as well as January 26, 2015, which was when all vehicles were ordered off the street due to the North American blizzard.

6. Use the `plot_outliers` function created in the *Technical requirements* section to visualize the output to gain better insight:

```
plot_outliers(outliers, tx, 'KNN')
```

The preceding code should produce a plot similar to that in *Figure 14.1*, except the x markers are based on the outliers identified using the KNN algorithm:

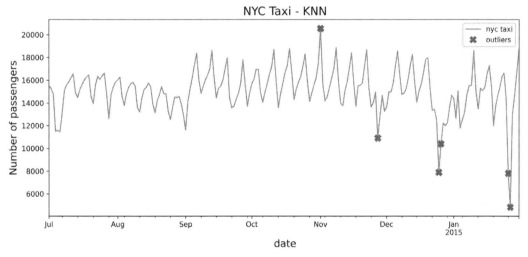

Figure 14.2 – Markers showing the identified potential outliers using the KNN algorithm

To print the labels (dates) along with the markers, just call the `plot_outliers` function again, but this time with `labels=True`:

```
plot_outliers(outliers, tx, 'KNN', labels=True)
```

The preceding code should produce a similar plot to the one in *Figure 14.2* with the addition of text labels.

How it works...

The unsupervised approach to the KNN algorithm calculates the distance of an observation to other neighboring observations. The default distance used in PyOD for KNN is the Minkowski distance (the p-norm distance). You can change to different distance measures, such as the Euclidean distance with `euclidean` or `l2` or the Manhattan distance with `manhattan` or `l1`. This can be accomplished using the `metric` parameter, which can take a string value, for example, `metric='l2'` or `metric='euclidean'`, or a callable function from scikit-learn or SciPy. This is a parameter that you experiment with as it influences how the distance is calculated, which is what the outlier scores are based on.

Traditionally, when people hear KNN, they immediately assume it is only a supervised learning algorithm. For unsupervised KNN, there are three popular algorithms: ball tree, KD tree, and brute-force search. The PyOD library supports all three as `ball_tree`, `kd_tree`, and `brute`, respectively. The default value is set to `algorithm="auto"`.

PyOD uses an internal score specific to each algorithm, scoring each observation in the training set. The `decision_scores_` attribute will show these scores for each observation. Higher scores indicate a higher potential of being an abnormal observation:

```
knn_scores = knn.decision_scores_
```

You can convert this into a DataFrame:

```
knn_scores_df = (pd.DataFrame(scores,
            index=tx.index,
            columns=['score']))
knn_scores_df
```

Since all the data points are scored, PyOD will determine a threshold to limit the number of outliers returned. The threshold value depends on the *contamination* value you provided earlier (the proportion of outliers you suspect). The higher the contamination value, the lower the threshold, and hence more outliers are returned. A lower contamination value will increase the threshold.

You can get the threshold value using the `threshold_` attribute from the model after fitting it to the training data. Here is the threshold for KNN based on a 3% contamination rate:

```
knn.threshold_
>> 225.0179166666657
```

This is the value used to filter out the significant outliers. Here is an example of how you reproduce that:

```
knn_scores_df[knn_scores_df['score'] >= knn.threshold_].sort_
values('score', ascending=False)
```

The output is as follows:

timestamp	score
2015-01-27	4862.058333
2015-01-26	2474.508333
2014-12-25	2441.250000
2014-11-01	1806.850000
2014-12-26	1009.616667
2014-11-27	608.250000
2014-09-27	225.604167

Figure 14.3 – Showing the decision scores from PyOD

Notice the last observation on `2014-09-27` is slightly above the threshold, but it was not returned when you used the `predict` method. If you use the contamination threshold, you can get a better cutoff:

```
n = int(len(tx)*0.03)
knn_scores_df.nlargest(n, 'score')
```

Another helpful method is `predict_proba`, which returns the probability of being normal and the probability of being abnormal for each observation. PyOD provides two methods for determining these percentages: `linear` or `unify`. The two methods scale the outlier scores before calculating the probabilities. For example, in the case of `linear`, the implementation uses `MinMaxScaler` from scikit-learn to scale the scores before calculating the probabilities. The `unify` method uses the z-score (standardization) and the Gaussian error function (`erf`) from the SciPy library (`scipy.special.erf`).

You can compare the two approaches. First, start using the `linear` method to calculate the prediction probability, you can use the following:

```
knn_proba = knn.predict_proba(tx, method='linear')
knn_proba_df = (pd.DataFrame(np.round(knn_proba * 100, 3),
        index=tx.index,
        columns=['Proba_Normal', 'Proba_Anomaly']))
knn_proba_df.nlargest(n, 'Proba_Anomaly')
```

For the `unify` method, you can just update `method='unify'`.

To save any PyOD model, you can use the `joblib` Python library:

```
from joblib import dump, load
# save the knn model
dump(knn, 'knn_outliers.joblib')
# load the knn model
knn = load('knn_outliers.joblib')
```

There's more...

Earlier in the recipe, when instantiating the KNN class, you changed the value of `method` for calculating the outlier *score* to be `mean`:

```
knn = KNN(contamination=0.03,
        method='mean',
        n_neighbors=5)
```

Let's create a function for the KNN algorithm to train the model on different scoring methods by updating the method parameter to either mean, median, or largest to examine the impact on the decision scores:

- largest uses the largest distance to the *k*th neighbor as the outlier score.

- mean uses the average of the distances to the *k* neighbors as the outlier score.

- median uses the median of the distances to the *k* neighbors as the outlier score.

Create the knn_anomaly function with the following parameters: data, method, contamination, and k:

```
def knn_anomaly(df, method='mean', contamination=0.05, k=5):
    knn = KNN(contamination=contamination,
            method=method,
            n_neighbors=5)
    knn.fit(df)
    decision_score = pd.DataFrame(knn.decision_scores_,
                        index=df.index, columns=['score'])
    n = int(len(df)*contamination)
    outliers = decision_score.nlargest(n, 'score')
    return outliers, knn.threshold_
```

You can run the function using different methods, contamination, and *k* values to experiment.

Explore how the different methods produce a different threshold, which impacts the outliers being detected:

```
for method in ['mean', 'median', 'largest']:
    o, t = knn_anomaly(tx, method=method)
    print(f'Method= {method}, Threshold= {t}')
    print(o)
```

The preceding code should print out the top 10 outliers for each method (with contamination at 5%):

```
Method= mean, Threshold= 220.32916666666603
                score
timestamp
2015-01-27  4862.058333
2015-01-26  2474.508333
2014-12-25  2441.250000
2014-11-01  1806.850000
2014-12-26  1009.616667
2014-11-27   608.250000
2014-09-27   225.604167
2014-07-06   224.208333
2014-12-28   223.562500
2015-01-19   223.562500
Method= median, Threshold= 211.64999999999995
                score
timestamp
2015-01-27  5563.416667
2014-12-25  2997.541667
2015-01-26  2984.437500
2014-11-01  1847.083333
2014-12-26  1113.812500
2014-11-27   612.104167
2014-12-29   251.520833
2014-12-27   238.062500
2015-01-19   238.062500
2014-12-28   219.145833
Method= largest, Threshold= 411.85624999999993
                score
timestamp
2015-01-27  6629.729167
2015-01-26  3645.291667
2014-12-25  3562.145833
2014-11-01  1865.437500
2014-12-26  1191.916667
2014-11-27   690.208333
2014-07-06   518.583333
2014-07-04   471.083333
2014-12-19   436.604167
2014-09-27   431.750000
```

Figure 14.4 – Comparing decision scores using different KNN distance metrics

Notice the top six (represent the 3% contamination) are identical for all three methods. The order may vary and the decision scores are different between the methods. Do notice the difference between the methods is more apparent beyond the top six, as shown in *Figure 14.4*.

See also

Check out the following resources:

- To learn more about unsupervised KNN, the scikit-learn library has a great explanation about its implementation: `https://scikit-learn.org/ stable/modules/neighbors.html#unsupervised-nearest- neighbors`.

- To learn more about PyOD KNN and the different parameters, visit the official documentation here: `https://pyod.readthedocs.io/en/latest/pyod. models.html?highlight=knn#module-pyod.models.knn`.

Detecting outliers using LOF

In the previous recipe, *Detecting outliers using KNN*, in the KNN algorithm, the decision scoring for detecting outliers was based on the distance between observations. A data point far from its KNN can be considered an outlier. Overall, the algorithm does a good job of capturing global outliers, but those far from the surrounding points may not do well with identifying local outliers.

This is where the LOF comes in to solve this limitation. Instead of using the distance between neighboring points, it uses density as a basis for scoring data points and detecting outliers. The LOF is considered a **density-based algorithm**. The idea behind the LOF is that outliers will be further from other data points and more isolated, and thus will be in low-density regions.

It is easier to illustrate this with an example: imagine a person standing in line in a small but busy Starbucks, and everyone is pretty much close to each other; then, we can say the person is in a high-density area and, more specifically, **high local density**. If the person decides to wait in their car in the parking lot until the line eases up, they are isolated and in a low-density area, thus being considered an outlier. From the perspective of the people standing in line, who are probably not aware of the person in the car, that person is considered not reachable even though that person in the vehicle can see all of the individuals standing in line. So we say that the person in the car is not reachable from their perspective. Hence, we sometimes refer to this as **inverse reachability** (how far you are from the neighbors' perspective, not just yours).

Like KNN, you still need to define the *k* parameter for the number of nearest neighbors. The nearest neighbors are identified based on the distance measured between the observations (think KNN), then the **Local Reachability Density** (**LRD** or **local density** for short) is measured for each neighboring point. This local density is the score used to compare the *k*th neighboring observations and those with lower local densities than their *k*th neighbors are considered outliers (they are further from the reach of their neighbors).

How to do it...

In this recipe, you will continue to work with the `tx` DataFrame, created in the *Technical requirements* section, to detect outliers using the LOF class from PyOD:

1. Start by loading the `LOF` class:

    ```
    from pyod.models.lof import LOF
    ```

2. You should be familiar with a few parameters to control the algorithm's behavior. The first parameter is `contamination`, a numeric (float) value representing the dataset's fraction of outliers. For example, a value of `0.1` indicates that you expect 10% of the data to be outliers. The default value is `contamination=0.1`. In this recipe, you will use `0.03` (3%).

    The second parameter is the number of neighbors, which defaults to `n_neighbors=5`, similar to the KNN algorithm. Ideally, you will want to run different models with varying values of *k* (`n_neighbors`) and compare the results to determine the optimal number of neighbors. Lastly, the `metric` parameter specifies which metric to use to calculate the distance. This can be any distance metrics from the scikit-learn or SciPy libraries (for example, Euclidean or Manhattan distance). The default value is the Minkowski distance with `metric='minkowski'`. Since the Minkowski distance is a generalization for both the Euclidean ($l2$) and Manhattan distances ($l1$), you will notice a p parameter. By default, p=2 indicates Euclidean distance, while a value of p=1 indicates Manhattan distance.

3. Instantiate LOF by updating `n_neighbors=5` and `contamination=0.03` while keeping the rest of the parameters with the default values. Then, train (fit) the model:

    ```
    lof = LOF(contamination=0.03, n_neighbors=5)
    lof.fit(tx)
    >>
    LOF(algorithm='auto', contamination=0.03, leaf_size=30,
    ```

```
metric='minkowski',
   metric_params=None, n_jobs=1, n_neighbors=5,
novelty=True, p=2)
```

4. The `predict` method will output either 1 or 0 for each data point. A value of 1 indicates an outlier. Store the results in a pandas Series:

```
predicted = pd.Series(lof.predict(tx),
                          index=tx.index)
print('Number of outliers = ', predicted.sum())
>>
Number of outliers =  6
```

5. Filter the predicted Series to only show the outlier values:

```
outliers = predicted[predicted == 1]
outliers = tx.loc[outliers.index]
outliers
>>
Timestamp      value
2014-10-31   17473.354167
2014-11-01   20553.500000
2014-12-25   7902.125000
2014-12-26   10397.958333
2015-01-26   7818.979167
2015-01-27   4834.541667
```

Interestingly, it captured three out of the five known dates but managed to identify the day after Thanksgiving and the day after Christmas as outliers. Additionally, October 31 was on a Friday, and it was Halloween night.

6. Use the `plot_outliers` function created in the *Technical requirements* section to visualize the output to gain better insight:

```
plot_outliers(outliers, tx, 'LOF')
```

The preceding code should produce a plot similar to that in *Figure 14.1*, except the x markers are based on the outliers identified using the LOF algorithm:

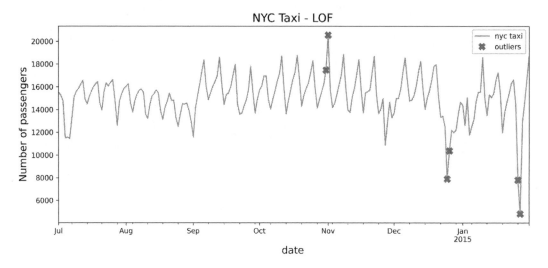

Figure 14.5 – Markers showing the identified potential outliers using the LOF algorithm

To print the labels (dates) with the markers, just call the `plot_outliers` function again but this time with `labels=True`:

```
plot_outliers(outliers, tx, 'LOF', labels=True)
```

The preceding code should produce a similar plot to the one in *Figure 14.5* with the addition of text labels.

How it works...

The LOF is a density-based algorithm that assumes that outlier points are more isolated and have lower local density scores compared to their neighbors.

LOF is like KNN in that we measure the distances between the neighbors before calculating the local density. The local density is the basis of the decision scores, which you can view using the `decision_scores_` attribute:

```
timestamp    score
2014-11-01   14.254309
2015-01-27   5.270860
2015-01-26   3.988552
```

```
2014-12-25   3.952827
2014-12-26   2.295987
2014-10-31   2.158571
```

The scores are very different from those in *Figure 14.3* for KNN.

For more insight into `decision_scores_`, `threshold_`, or `predict_proba`, please review the first recipe of this chapter, *Detecting outliers using KNN*.

There's more...

Like the LOF, another extension of the algorithm is the **Cluster-Based Local Outlier Factor** (**CBLOF**). The CBLOF is similar to LOF in concept as it relies on cluster size and distance when calculating the scores to determine outliers. So, instead of the number of neighbors (`n_neighbors` like in LOF), we now have a new parameter, which is the number of clusters (`n_clusters`).

The default clustering estimator, `clustering_estimator`, in PyOD is the k-means clustering algorithm.

You will use the CBLOF class from PyOD and keep most parameters at the default values. Change the `n_clusters=8` and `contamination=0.03` parameters:

```
from pyod.models.cblof import CBLOF
cblof = CBLOF(n_clusters=4, contamination=0.03)
cblof.fit(tx)
predicted = pd.Series(lof.predict(tx),
                      index=tx.index)
outliers = predicted[predicted == 1]
outliers = tx.loc[outliers.index]
plot_outliers(outliers, tx, 'CBLOF')
```

The preceding code should produce a plot similar to that in *Figure 14.1* except the x markers are based on the outliers identified using the CBLOF algorithm:

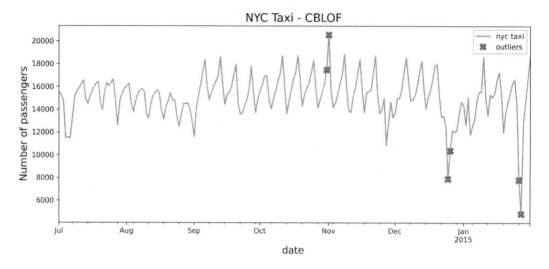

Figure 14.6 – Markers showing the identified potential outliers using the CBLOF algorithm

Compare *Figure 14.6* with *Figure 14.5* (LOF) and notice the similarity.

See also

To learn more about the LOF and CBLOF algorithms, you can visit the PyOD documentation:

- LOF: `https://pyod.readthedocs.io/en/latest/pyod.models.html#module-pyod.models.lof`

- CBLOF: `https://pyod.readthedocs.io/en/latest/pyod.models.html#module-pyod.models.cblof`

Detecting outliers using iForest

iForest has similarities with another popular algorithm known as Random Forests. Random Forests is a **tree-based** supervised learning algorithm. In supervised learning, you have existing labels (classification) or values (regression) representing the target variable. This is how the algorithm learns (it is supervised).

The name *forest* stems from the underlying mechanism of how the algorithm works. For example, in classification, the algorithm randomly samples the data to build multiple weak classifiers (smaller decision trees) that collectively make a prediction. In the end, you get a forest of smaller trees (models). This technique outperforms a single complex classifier that may overfit the data. Ensemble learning is the concept of multiple weak learners collaborating to produce an optimal solution.

iForest, also an *ensemble learning* method, is the unsupervised learning approach to Random Forests. The iForest algorithm isolates anomalies by randomly partitioning (splitting) a dataset into multiple partitions. This is performed recursively until all data points belong to a partition. The number of partitions required to isolate an anomaly is typically smaller than the number of partitions needed to isolate a regular point. The idea is that an anomaly data point is further from other points and thus easier to separate (isolate).

In contrast, a normal data point is probably clustered closer to the larger set and, therefore, will require more partitions (splits) to isolate that point. Hence the name, isolation forest, since it identifies outliers through isolation. Once all the points are isolated, the algorithm will create an outlier score. You can think of these splits as creating a decision tree path. The shorter the path length to a point, the higher the chances of an anomaly.

How to do it...

In this recipe, you will continue to work with the nyc_taxi DataFrame to detect outliers using the IForest class from the PyOD library:

1. Start by loading the IForest class:

```
from pyod.models.iforest import IForest
```

2. There are a few parameters that you should be familiar with to control the algorithm's behavior. The first parameter is contamination. The default value is contamination=0.1 but in this recipe, you will use 0.03 (3%).

The second parameter is n_estimators, which defaults to n_estimators=100. This is the number of random trees generated. Depending on the complexity of your data, you may want to increase this value to a higher range, such as 500 or more. Start with the default smaller value to understand how the baseline model works—finally, random_state defaults to None. Since the iForest algorithm randomly generates partitions for the data, it is good to set a value to ensure that your work is reproducible. This way, you can get consistent results back when you rerun the code. Of course, this could be any integer value.

3. Instantiate IForest and update the contamination and random_state parameters. Then, fit the new instance of the class (iforest) on the resampled data to train the model:

```
iforest = IForest(contamination=0.03,
                  n_estimators=100,
                  random_state=0)
iforest.fit(nyc_daily)
>>
IForest(behaviour='old', bootstrap=False,
contamination=0.05,
    max_features=1.0, max_samples='auto', n_
estimators=100, n_jobs=1,
    random_state=0, verbose=0)
```

4. Use the predict method to identify outliers. The method will output either 1 or 0 for each data point. For example, a value of 1 indicates an outlier.

Let's store the results in a pandas Series:

```
predicted = pd.Series(iforest.predict(tx),
                      index=tx.index)
print('Number of outliers = ', predicted.sum())
>>
Number of outliers =   7
```

Interestingly, unlike the previous recipe, *Detecting outliers using KNN*, iForest detected 7 outliers while the KNN algorithm detected 6.

5. Filter the predicted Series to only show the outlier values:

```
outliers = predicted[predicted == 1]
outliers = tx.loc[outliers.index]
outliers
```

```
>>
timestamp    value
2014-11-01   20553.500000
2014-11-08   18857.333333
2014-11-27   10899.666667
2014-12-25   7902.125000
2014-12-26   10397.958333
2015-01-26   7818.979167
2015-01-27   4834.541667
```

Overall, iForest captured four out of the five known outliers. There are additional but interesting dates identified that should trigger an investigation to determine whether these data points are outliers. For example, November 8, 2014, was detected as a potential outlier by the algorithm, which was not considered in the data.

6. Use the `plot_outliers` function created in the *Technical requirements* section to visualize the output to gain better insight:

```
plot_outliers(outliers, tx, 'IForest')
```

The preceding code should produce a plot similar to that in *Figure 14.1* except the x markers are based on the outliers identified using the iForest algorithm:

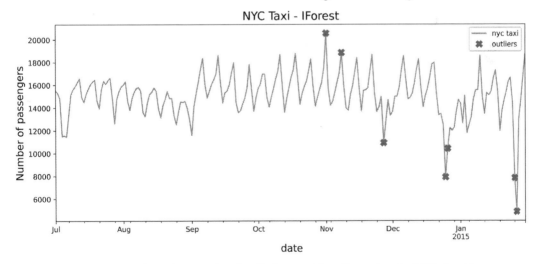

Figure 14.7 – Markers showing the identified potential outliers using the LOF algorithm

To print the labels (dates) with the markers, just call the `plot_outliers` function again but this time with `labels=True`:

```
plot_outliers(outliers, tx, 'IForest', labels=True)
```

The preceding code should produce a similar plot as the one in *Figure 14.7* with the addition of text labels.

How it works...

Since iForest is an ensemble method, you will be creating multiple models (tree learners). The default value of `n_estimators` is `100`. Increasing the number of base estimators may improve model performance up to a certain level before the computational performance takes a hit. So, for example, think of the number of estimators as trained models. For instance, for 100 estimators, you are essentially creating 100 decision tree models.

There is one more parameter worth mentioning, which is the `bootstrap` parameter. It is a Boolean set to `False` by default. Since iForest randomly samples the data, you have two options: random sampling with replacement (known as *bootstrapping*) or random sampling without replacement. The default behavior is sampling without replacement.

There's more...

The iForest algorithm from PyOD (the `IForest` class) is a wrapper to scikit-learn's `IsolationForest` class. This is also true for the KNN used in the previous recipe, *Detecting outliers using KNN*.

Let's explore this further and use scikit-learn to implement the iForest algorithm. You will use the `fit_predict()` method as a single step to train and predict, which is also available in PyOD's implementations across the various algorithms:

```
from sklearn.ensemble import IsolationForest
sk_iforest = IsolationForest(contamination=0.03)
sk_prediction = pd.Series(sk_iforest.fit_predict(tx),
                          index=tx.index)
sk_outliers = sk_prediction[sk_prediction == -1]
sk_outliers = tx.loc[sk_outliers.index]
sk_outliers
>>
timestamp    value
2014-11-01   20553.500000
```

```
2014-11-08   18857.333333
2014-11-27   10899.666667
2014-12-25   7902.125000
2014-12-26   10397.958333
2015-01-26   7818.979167
2015-01-27   4834.541667
```

The results are the same. But do notice that, unlike PyOD, the identified outliers were labeled as -1, while in PyOD, outliers were labeled with 1.

See also

The PyOD iForest implementation is actually a wrapper to the `IsolationForest` class from scikit-learn:

- To learn more about PyOD iForest and the different parameters, visit their official documentation here: `https://pyod.readthedocs.io/en/latest/pyod.models.html?highlight=knn#module-pyod.models.iforest`.

- To learn more about the `IsolationForest` class from scikit-learn, you can visit their official documentation page here: `https://scikit-learn.org/stable/modules/generated/sklearn.ensemble.IsolationForest.html#sklearn-ensemble-isolationforest`.

Detecting outliers using One-Class Support Vector Machine (OCSVM)

Support Vector Machine (SVM) is a popular supervised machine learning algorithm that is mainly known for classification but can also be used for regression. The popularity of SVM comes from the use of kernel functions (sometimes referred to as the **kernel trick**), such as linear, polynomial, **Radius-Based Function (RBF)**, and the sigmoid function.

In addition to classification and regression, SVM can also be used for outlier detection in an unsupervised manner, similar to KNN, which is mostly known as a supervised machine learning technique but was used in an unsupervised manner for outlier detection, as seen in the *Outlier detection using KNN* recipe.

How to do it...

In this recipe, you will continue to work with the `tx` DataFrame, created in the *Technical requirements* section, to detect outliers using the `ocsvm` class from PyOD:

1. Start by loading the `OCSVM` class:

   ```
   from pyod.models.ocsvm import OCSVM
   ```

2. There are a few parameters that you should be familiar with to control the algorithm's behavior. The first parameter is `contamination`. The default value is `contamination=0.1` and in this recipe, you will use `0.03` (3%).

   The second parameter is `kernel`, which is set to `rbf`, which you will keep as is.

   Instantiate OCSVM by updating `contamination=0.03` while keeping the rest of the parameters with the default values. Then, train (fit) the model:

   ```
   ocsvm = OCSVM(contamination=0.03, kernel='rbf')
   ocsvm.fit(tx)
   >>
   OCSVM(cache_size=200, coef0=0.0, contamination=0.03,
   degree=3, gamma='auto',
       kernel='rbf', max_iter=-1, nu=0.5, shrinking=True,
   tol=0.001,
       verbose=False)
   ```

3. The `predict` method will output either `1` or `0` for each data point. A value of `1` indicates an outlier. Store the results in a pandas Series:

   ```
   predicted = pd.Series(ocsvm.predict(tx),
                         index=tx.index)
   print('Number of outliers = ', predicted.sum())
   >>
   Number of outliers =  5
   ```

4. Filter the predicted Series to only show the outlier values:

   ```
   outliers = predicted[predicted == 1]
   outliers = tx.loc[outliers.index]
   outliers
   >>
   timestamp    value
   2014-08-09   15499.708333
   ```

```
2014-11-18   15499.437500
2014-11-27   10899.666667
2014-12-24   12502.000000
2015-01-05   12502.750000
```

Interestingly, it captured one out of the five known dates.

5. Use the `plot_outliers` function created in the *Technical requirements* section to visualize the output to gain better insight:

```
plot_outliers(outliers, tx, 'OCSVM')
```

The preceding code should produce a plot similar to that in *Figure 14.1* except the x markers are based on the outliers identified using the LOF algorithm:

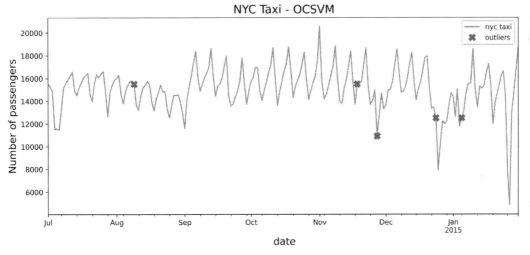

Figure 14.8 – Line plot with markers and text labels for each outlying point using OCSVM

When examining the plot in *Figure 14.8*, it is not clear why OCSVM picked up on those dates as being outliers. The RBF kernel can capture non-linear relationships, so you would expect it to be a robust kernel.

The reason for this inaccuracy is that SVM is sensitive to data scaling. To get better results, you will need to standardize (scale) your data first.

6. Let's fix this issue and standardize the data and then rerun the algorithm again:

```
from pyod.utils.utility import standardizer
scaled = standardizer(tx)
predicted = pd.Series(ocsvm.fit_predict(scaled),
                      index=tx.index)
```

```
outliers = predicted[predicted == 1]
outliers = tx.loc[outliers.index]
outliers
>>
timestamp    value
2014-07-06   11464.270833
2014-11-01   20553.500000
2014-11-27   10899.666667
2014-12-25   7902.125000
2014-12-26   10397.958333
2015-01-26   7818.979167
2015-01-27   4834.541667
```

Interestingly, now the model identified four out of the five known outlier dates.

7. Use the `plot_outliers` function on the new result set:

```
plot_outliers(outliers, tx, 'OCSVM Scaled'))
```

The preceding code should produce a more reasonable plot, as shown in the following figure:

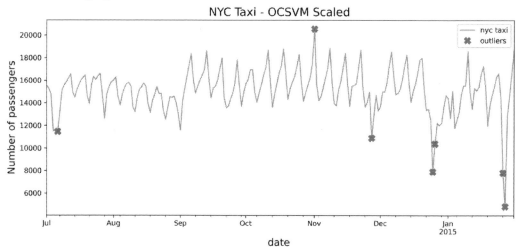

Figure 14.9 – OCSVM after scaling the data using the standardizer function

Compare the results from *Figure 14.9* and *Figure 14.8* to see how scaling made a big difference in how the OCSVM algorithm identified outliers.

How it works...

The PyOD implementation for OCSVM is a wrapper to scikit-learn's `OneClassSVM` implementation.

Similar to SVM, `OneClassSVM` is sensitive to outliers and also the scaling of the data. In order to get reasonable results, it is important to standardize (scale) your data before training your model.

There's more...

Let's explore how the different kernels perform on the same dataset. In the following code, you test four kernels: `'linear'`, `'poly'`, `'rbf'`, and `'sigmoid'`.

Recall that when working with SVM, you will need to scale your data. You will use the scaled dataset created earlier:

```
for kernel in ['linear', 'poly', 'rbf', 'sigmoid']:
    ocsvm = OCSVM(contamination=0.03, kernel=kernel)
    predict = pd.Series(ocsvm.fit_predict(scaled),
                        index=tx.index, name=kernel)
    outliers = predict[predict == 1]
    outliers = tx.loc[outliers.index]
    plot_outliers(outliers, tx, kernel, labels=True)
```

The preceding code should produce a plot for each kernel so you can visually inspect and compare the difference between them:

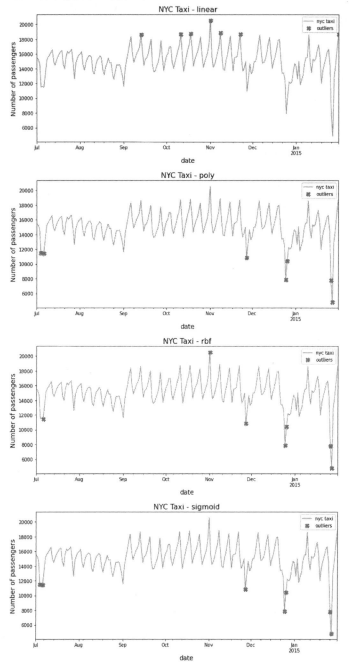

Figure 14.10 – Comparing the different kernels with OCSVM

Interestingly, each kernel method captured slightly different outliers. You can rerun the previous code to print out the labels (dates) for each marker by passing the `labels=True` parameter.

See also

To learn more about the OCSVM implementation, visit the official documentation here: `https://pyod.readthedocs.io/en/latest/pyod.models.html#module-pyod.models.ocsvm`.

Detecting outliers using COPOD

COPOD is an exciting algorithm based on a paper published in September 2020, which you can read here: `https://arxiv.org/abs/2009.09463`.

The PyOD library offers many algorithms based on the latest research papers, which can be broken down into linear models, proximity-based models, probabilistic models, ensembles, and neural networks.

COPOD falls under probabilistic models and is labeled as a *parameter-free* algorithm. The only parameter it takes is the *contamination* factor, which defaults to `0.1`. The COPOD algorithm is inspired by statistical methods, making it a fast and highly interpretable model. The algorithm is based on copula, a function generally used to model dependence between independent random variables that are not necessarily normally distributed. In time series forecasting, copulas have been used in univariate and multivariate forecasting, which is popular in financial risk modeling. The term copula stems from the copula function joining (coupling) univariate marginal distributions to form a uniform multivariate distribution function.

How to do it...

In this recipe, you will continue to work with the `tx` DataFrame to detect outliers using the `COPOD` class from the PyOD library:

1. Start by loading the `COPOD` class:

    ```
    from pyod.models.copod import COPOD
    ```

2. The only parameter you need to consider is `contamination`. Generally, think of this parameter (used in all the outlier detection implementations) as a threshold to control the model's sensitivity and minimize the false positives. Since it is a parameter you control, ideally, you want to run several models to experiment with the ideal threshold rate that works for your use cases.

For more insight into `decision_scores_`, `threshold_`, or `predict_proba`, please review the first recipe, *Detecting outliers using KNN*, of this chapter.

3. Instantiate COPOD and update `contamination` to `0.03`. Then, fit on the resampled data to train the model:

```
copod = COPOD(contamination=0.03)
copod.fit(tx)
>>
COPOD(contamination=0.5, n_jobs=1)
```

4. Use the `predict` method to identify outliers. The method will output either `1` or `0` for each data point. For example, a value of `1` indicates an outlier.

Store the results in a pandas Series:

```
predicted = pd.Series(copod.predict(tx),
                      index=tx.index)
print('Number of outliers = ', predicted.sum())
>>
Number of outliers =  7
```

The number of outliers matches the number you got using iForest.

5. Filter the predicted Series only to show the outlier values:

```
outliers = predicted[predicted == 1]
outliers = tx.loc[outliers.index]
outliers
>>
timestamp   value
2014-07-04  11511.770833
2014-07-06  11464.270833
2014-11-27  10899.666667
2014-12-25  7902.125000
2014-12-26  10397.958333
2015-01-26  7818.979167
2015-01-27  4834.541667
```

Compared with other algorithms you have explored so far, you will notice some interesting outliers captured with COPOD that were not identified before. For example, COPOD identified July 4, a national holiday in the US (Independence Day). It happens to fall on a weekend (Friday being off). The COPOD model captured anomalies throughout the weekend for July 4 and July 6. It happens that July 6 was an interesting day due to a baseball game in New York.

6. Use the `plot_outliers` function created in the *Technical requirements* section to visualize the output to gain better insights:

```
plot_outliers(outliers, tx, 'COPOD')
```

The preceding code should produce a plot similar to that in *Figure 14.1*, except the x markers are based on the outliers identified using the COPOD algorithm:

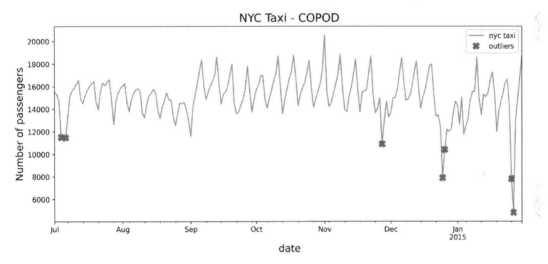

Figure 14.11 – Markers showing the identified potential outliers using the COPOD algorithm

To print the labels (dates) with the markers, just call the `plot_outliers` function again, but this time with `labels=True`:

```
plot_outliers(outliers, tx, 'COPOD', labels=True)
```

The preceding code should produce a similar plot to the one in *Figure 14.11* with the addition of text labels.

How it works...

COPOD is an advanced algorithm, but it is still based on probabilistic modeling and finding statistically significant extremes within the data. Several tests using COPOD have demonstrated its superb performance against benchmark datasets. The appeal of using COPOD is that it is parameter-free (aside from the contamination factor). So, as a user, you do not have to worry about hyperparameter tuning.

There's more...

Another simple and popular probabilistic algorithm is the **Median Absolute Deviation** (**MAD**). We explored MAD in *Chapter 8, Outlier Detection Using Statistical Methods*, in the *Outlier detection using modified z-score* recipe, in which you built the algorithm from scratch.

This is a similar implementation provided by PyOD and takes one parameter, the threshold. If you recall from *Chapter 8, Outlier Detection Using Statistical Methods*, the threshold is based on the standard deviation.

The following code shows how we can implement MAD with PyOD. You will use threshold=3 to replicate what you did in *Chapter 8, Outlier Detection Using Statistical Methods*:

```
from pyod.models.mad import MAD
mad = MAD(threshold=3)
predicted = pd.Series(mad.fit_predict(tx),
                      index=tx.index)
outliers = predicted[predicted == 1]
outliers = tx.loc[outliers.index]
outliers
>>
timestamp    value
2014-11-01   20553.500000
2014-11-27   10899.666667
2014-12-25   7902.125000
2014-12-26   10397.958333
2015-01-26   7818.979167
2015-01-27   4834.541667
```

This should match the results you obtained in *Chapter 8, Outlier Detection Using Statistical Methods*, with the modified z-score implementation.

See also

To learn more about COPOD and its implementation in PyOD, visit the official documentation here: `https://pyod.readthedocs.io/en/latest/pyod.models.html?highlight=copod#pyod.models.copod.COPOD`.

If you are interested in reading the research paper for *COPOD: Copula-Based Outlier Detection* (published in September 2020), visit the arXiv.org page here: `https://arxiv.org/abs/2009.09463`.

Detecting outliers with PyCaret

In this recipe, you will explore PyCaret for outlier detection. PyCaret (`https://pycaret.org`) is positioned as *"an open-source, low-code machine learning library in Python that automates machine learning workflows"*. PyCaret acts as a wrapper for PyOD, which you used earlier in the previous recipes for outlier detection. What PyCaret does is simplify the entire process for rapid prototyping and testing with a minimal amount of code.

You will use PyCaret to examine multiple outlier detection algorithms, similar to the ones you used in earlier recipes, and see how PyCaret simplifies the process for you.

Getting ready

The recommended way to explore PyCaret is to create a new virtual Python environment just for PyCaret so it can install all the required dependencies without any conflicts or issues with your current environment. If you need a quick refresher on how to create a virtual Python environment, check out the *Development environment setup* recipe, from *Chapter 1, Getting Started with Time Series Analysis*. The chapter covers two methods: using conda and venv.

The following instructions will show the process using conda. You can call the environment any name you like; for the following example, we will name our environment pycaret:

```
>> conda create -n pycaret python=3.8 -y
>> conda activate pycaret
>> pip install "pycaret[full]"
```

In order to make the new `pycaret` environment visible within Jupyter, you can run the following code:

```
python -m ipykernel install --user --name pycaret --display-
name "PyCaret"
```

There is a separate Jupyter notebook for this recipe, which you can download from the GitHub repository:

```
https://github.com/PacktPublishing/Time-Series-Analysis-with-
Python-Cookbook./blob/main/code/Ch14/Chapter%2014-pycaret.
ipynb
```

How to do it...

In this recipe, you will not be introduced to any new concepts. The focus is to demonstrate how PyCaret can be a great starting point when you are experimenting and want to quickly evaluate different models. You will load PyCaret and run it for different outlier detection algorithms:

1. Start by loading all the available functions from the `pycaret.anomaly` module:

    ```
    from pycaret.anomaly import *
    setup = setup(tx, session_id = 1, normalize=True)
    ```

    This should display the following:

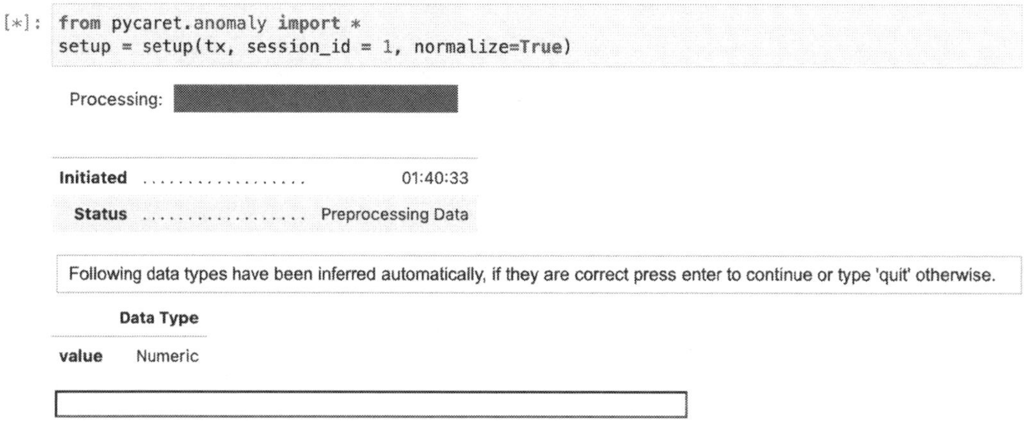

    ```
    [*]:  from pycaret.anomaly import *
          setup = setup(tx, session_id = 1, normalize=True)
    ```

    Processing: ███████████████

    Initiated 01:40:33
    Status .... Preprocessing Data

    Following data types have been inferred automatically, if they are correct press enter to continue or type 'quit' otherwise.

	Data Type
value	Numeric

    Figure 14.12 – Showing the initial screen in Jupyter Notebook/Lab pending user response

You will need to hit the *Enter* key to confirm and it will continue with the process. In the end, you see a long list of parameters (49 in total) and their default values. These parameters represent some of the preprocessing tasks that are automatically performed for you:

	Description	Value
0	session_id	1
1	Original Data	(215, 1)
2	Missing Values	0
3	Numeric Features	1
4	Categorical Features	0
5	Ordinal Features	0
6	High Cardinality Features	0
7	High Cardinality Method	None
8	Transformed Data	(215, 1)
9	CPU Jobs	-1
10	Use GPU	0
11	Log Experiment	0
12	Experiment Name	anomaly-default-name
13	USI	316f
14	Imputation Type	simple
15	Iterative Imputation Iteration	None
16	Numeric Imputer	mean
17	Iterative Imputation Numeric Model	None
18	Categorical Imputer	mode
19	Iterative Imputation Categorical Model	None
20	Unknown Categoricals Handling	least_frequent
21	Normalize	1
22	Normalize Method	zscore
23	Transformation	0
24	Transformation Method	None
25	PCA	0

Figure 14.13 – The first 25 parameters and their values

2. To print a list of available outlier detection algorithms, you can run `models()`:

```
models()
```

This should display a pandas DataFrame, as follows:

ID	Name	Reference
abod	Angle-base Outlier Detection	pyod.models.abod.ABOD
cluster	Clustering-Based Local Outlier	pyod.models.cblof.CBLOF
cof	Connectivity-Based Local Outlier	pyod.models.cof.COF
iforest	Isolation Forest	pyod.models.iforest.IForest
histogram	Histogram-based Outlier Detection	pyod.models.hbos.HBOS
knn	K-Nearest Neighbors Detector	pyod.models.knn.KNN
lof	Local Outlier Factor	pyod.models.lof.LOF
svm	One-class SVM detector	pyod.models.ocsvm.OCSVM
pca	Principal Component Analysis	pyod.models.pca.PCA
mcd	Minimum Covariance Determinant	pyod.models.mcd.MCD
sod	Subspace Outlier Detection	pyod.models.sod.SOD
sos	Stochastic Outlier Selection	pyod.models.sos.SOS

Figure 14.14 – Available outlier detection algorithms from PyCaret

Notice these are all sourced from the PyOD library. As stated earlier, PyCaret is a wrapper on top of PyOD and other libraries, such as scikit-learn.

3. Let's store the names of the first eight algorithms in a list to use later:

```
list_of_models = models().index.tolist()[0:8]
list_of_models
>>
['abod', 'cluster', 'cof', 'iforest', 'histogram', 'knn',
'lof', 'svm']
```

4. Loop through the list of algorithms and store the output in a dictionary so you can reference it later for your analysis. To create a model in PyCaret, you simply use the `create_model()` function. This is similar to the `fit()` function in scikit-learn and PyOD for training the model. Once the model is created, you can use the model to predict (identify) the outliers using the `predict_model()` function. PyCaret will produce a DataFrame with three columns: the original `value` column, a new column, `Anomaly`, which stores the outcome as either 0 or 1, where 1 indicates an outlier, and another new column, `Anomaly_Score`, which stores the score used (the higher the score, the higher the chance it is an anomaly).

You will only change the contamination parameter to match earlier recipes using PyOD. In PyCaret, the contamination parameter is called `fraction` and to be consistent, you will set that to `0.03` or 3% with `fraction=0.03`:

```
results = {}
for model in list_of_models:
    cols = ['value', 'Anomaly_Score']
    outlier_model = create_model(model, fraction=0.03)
    print(outlier_model)
    outliers = predict_model(outlier_model, data=tx)
    outliers = outliers[outliers['Anomaly'] == 1][cols]
    outliers.sort_values('Anomaly_Score',
ascending=False, inplace=True)
    results[model] = {'data': outliers, 'model': outlier_
model}
```

The `results` dictionary contains the output (a DataFrame) from each model.

5. To print out the outliers from each model, you can simply loop through the dictionary:

```
for model in results:
    print(f'Model: {model}')
    print(results[model]['data'], '\n')
```

This should print the results for each of the eight models. The following are the first two models from the list as an example:

```
Model: abod
                     value  Anomaly_Score
timestamp
2014-11-01   20553.500000      -0.002301
2015-01-27    4834.541667      -0.007914
```

```
2014-12-26    10397.958333           -3.417724
2015-01-26     7818.979167         -116.341395
2014-12-25     7902.125000         -117.582752
2014-11-27    10899.666667         -122.169590
2014-10-31    17473.354167        -2239.318906


Model: cluster
                      value    Anomaly_Score
timestamp
2015-01-27     4834.541667         3.657992
2015-01-26     7818.979167         2.113955
2014-12-25     7902.125000         2.070939
2014-11-01    20553.500000         0.998279
2014-12-26    10397.958333         0.779688
2014-11-27    10899.666667         0.520122
2014-11-28    12850.854167         0.382981
```

How it works...

PyCaret is a great library for automated machine learning, and recently they have been expanding their capabilities around time series analysis and forecasting and anomaly (outlier) detection. PyCaret is a wrapper over PyOD, the same library you used in earlier recipes of this chapter. *Figure 14.14* shows the number of PyOD algorithms supported by PyCaret, which is a subset of the more extensive list from PyOD: https://pyod. readthedocs.io/en/latest/index.html#implemented-algorithms.

See also

To learn more about PyCaret's outlier detection, please visit the official documentation here: https://pycaret.gitbook.io/docs/get-started/ quickstart#anomaly-detection.

15

Advanced Techniques for Complex Time Series

Time series data can contain complex seasonality – for example, recorded hourly data can exhibit daily, weekly, and yearly seasonal patterns. With the rise of connected devices – for example, the **Internet of Things (IoT)** and sensors – data is being recorded more frequently. For example, if you examine classical time series datasets used in many research papers, many were smaller sets and recorded less frequently, such as annually or monthly. Such data contains one seasonal pattern. More recent datasets and research now use higher frequency data, recorded in hours or minutes.

Many of the algorithms we used in earlier chapters can work with seasonal time series. Still, they assume there is only one seasonal pattern, and their accuracy and results will suffer on more complex datasets.

In this chapter, you will explore new algorithms that can model a time series with multiple seasonality for forecasting and decomposing a time series into different components.

In this chapter, you will explore the following recipes:

- Decomposing time series with multiple seasonal patterns using MSTL

- Forecasting with multiple seasonal patterns using the **Unobserved Components Model (UCM)**

- Forecasting time series with multiple seasonal patterns using Prophet

- Forecasting time series with multiple seasonal patterns using NeuralProphet

Technical requirements

In this chapter, you will be using the *Hourly Energy Consumption* data from Kaggle (`https://www.kaggle.com/datasets/robikscube/hourly-energy-consumption`). Throughout the chapter, you will be working with the same energy dataset to observe how the different techniques compare.

The ZIP folder contains 13 CSV files, which are available in this book's GitHub repository and can be found here: `https://github.com/PacktPublishing/Time-Series-Analysis-with-Python-Cookbook./tree/main/datasets/Ch15`.

The recipes of this chapter will use one of these files, but feel free to explore the other ones. The files represent hourly energy consumption measured in **megawatts (MW)**.

Start by loading the data as a pandas DataFrame and prepare the data for the recipes. You will also load the shared libraries used throughout the chapter:

```
import pandas as pd
import numpy as np
import matplotlib.pyplot as plt
from pathlib import Path
from statsmodels.tools.eval_measures import rmse, rmspe
import warnings

warnings.filterwarnings('ignore')
```

Read the `AEP_hourly.csv` file:

```
folder = Path('../../datasets/Ch15/')
file = folder.joinpath('AEP_hourly.csv')
df = pd.read_csv(file, index_col='Datetime', parse_dates=True)
```

The time series is not in order and has some duplicate entries. The following are simple steps to clean up the data:

```
df.sort_index(inplace=True)
df = df.resample('H').max()
df.ffill(inplace=True)
```

You should have a DataFrame with `121296` records of hourly energy consumption from October 2004 to August 2018 (around 15 years).

Understanding state-space models

In this chapter, you will see references to state-space models. In *Chapter 10, Building Univariate Time Series Models Using Statistical Methods*, you were introduced to exponential smoothing (Holt-Winters) and ARIMA-type models. Before defining what state-space models are, I want to point out that these models can be represented in a state-space formulation.

State-Space Models (SSM) have their roots in the field of engineering (more specifically control engineering) and offer a generic approach to modeling dynamic systems and how they evolve over time. In addition, SSMs are widely used in other fields, such as economics, neuroscience, electrical engineering, and other disciplines.

In time series data, the central idea behind SSMs is that of **latent variables**, also called **states**, which are continuous and sequential through the time-space domain. For example, in a univariate time series, we have a **response** variable at time t; this is the observed value termed Y_t, which depends on the true variable termed X_t. The X_t variable is the latent variable that we are interested in estimating – which is either **unobserved** or cannot be measured. In state space, we have an underlying state that we cannot measure directly (unobserved). An SSM provides a system of equations to estimate these unobserved states from the observed values and is represented mathematically in a vector-matrix form. In general, there are two equations – a *state equation* and an *observed equation*. One key aspect of their popularity is their flexibility and ability to work with complex time series data that can be multivariate, non-stationary, non-linear, or contain multiple seasonality, gaps, or irregularities.

In addition, SSMs can be generalized and come in various forms, several of which make use of **Kalman filters** (Kalman recursions). The benefit of using SSMs in time series data is that they are used in *filtering*, *smoothing*, or *forecasting*, as you will explore in the different recipes of this chapter.

Kalman Filters

The Kalman filter is an algorithm for extracting signals from data that is either noisy or contains incomplete measurements. The premise behind Kalman filters is that not every *state* within a system is directly observable; instead, we can estimate the state indirectly, using observations that may be contaminated, incomplete, or noisy.

For example, sensor devices produce time series data known to be incomplete due to interruptions or unreliable due to noise. Kalman filters are excellent when working with time series data containing a considerable signal-to-noise ratio, as they work on smoothing and denoising the data to make it more reliable.

Decomposing time series with multiple seasonal patterns using MSTL

The Decomposing time series data recipe in *Chapter 9, Exploratory Data Analysis and Diagnosis*, introduced the concept of time series decomposition. In those examples, the time series had one seasonal pattern, and you were able to decompose it into three main parts – trend, seasonal pattern, and residual (remainder). In the recipe, you explored the `seasonal_decompose` function and the `STL` class (**Seasonal-Trend decomposition using Loess**) from statsmodels. Recall, in an additive model, your time series is reconstructed by the following equation:

$$Y_t = S_t + T_t + R_t$$

Here, S_t, T_t, R_t represent the seasonal, trend, and remainder components at time t respectively. But what about data with higher frequency – for example, IoT devices that can record data every minute or hour? Such data may exhibit multiple seasonal patterns.

Given the limitations of traditional seasonal decomposition approaches, a new approach for decomposing time series with multiple seasonality was introduced in a paper published by Bandara, Hyndman, and Bergmeir, titled *MSTL: A Seasonal-Trend Decomposition Algorithm for Time Series with Multiple Seasonal Patterns*. The paper was published in July 2021, which you can read here: `http://arxiv.org/abs/2107.13462`.

Multiple STL Decomposition (MSTL) is an extension of the STL algorithm and similarly is an additive decomposition, but it extends the equation to include multiple seasonal components and not just one:

$$Y_t = S_t^1 + S_t^2 + \cdots + S_t^n + T_t + R_t$$

Here, n represents the number of seasonal cycles. The algorithm iteratively fits the STL decomposition for each seasonal cycle (frequency identified) to get the decomposed seasonal components – $S_t^1 + S_t^2 + \cdots + S_t^n$. Once the iterative process for each seasonal cycle is completed, the trend component is estimated. If the time series does not have any seasonal components, MSTL will only estimate the trend.

Getting ready

The authors initially implemented the paper referenced earlier in R language as the `mstl` function in the `forecast` package.

In Python, the algorithm is implemented in `statsmodel` as the `MSTL` class. At the time of writing, the `MSTL` class is only available in the *development* version of `statsmodels`, which is the `0.14.0` version. The current stable version is `0.13.2`. The following instructions will show you how to install the *development* version.

It is highly advised that you create a separate virtual environment for Python. If you need a quick refresher on creating a virtual Python environment, check out the *Development environment setup* recipe from *Chapter 1, Getting Started with Time Series Analysis*.

You can install with `pip` using the following command:

```
pip install git+https://github.com/statsmodels/statsmodels
```

How to do it...

Generally, high-frequency data exhibits multiple seasonal patterns. For example, hourly time series data can have a daily, weekly, and annual pattern. You will start by importing the `MSTL` class from statsmodels and explore how to decompose the energy consumption time series.

1. Import the `MSTL` class:

    ```
    from statsmodels.tsa.seasonal import MSTL
    plt.rcParams["figure.figsize"] = [14, 10]
    ```

2. Create four variables to hold values for day, week, month, and year calculations; this way, you can reference these variables. For example, since the data is hourly, a day is represented as 24 hours and a week as 24 X 7, or simply day X 7:

```
day = 24
week = day*7
month = round(week*4.35)
year = round(month*12)
print(f'''
day = {day} hours
week = {week} hours
month = {month} hours
year = {year} hours
''')
```

3. Start by providing the different seasonal cycles you suspect – for example, a daily and weekly seasonal pattern:

```
mstl = MSTL(df, periods=(day, week))
```

Since the data's frequency is hourly, a daily pattern is observed every 24 hours and weekly every 24 x 7 or 168 hours.

4. Use the fit method to fit the model. The algorithm will first estimate the two seasonal periods $(S^1_{\{24\}}, S^2_{\{24*7\}})$, then the trend, and finally, the remainder:

```
results = mstl.fit()
```

5. The results object is an instance of the DecomposeResult class, which gives access to the seasonal, trend, and resid attributes. The seasonal attribute will display a DataFrame with two columns labeled seasonal_24 and seasonal_168. You can plot each attribute individually or use the plot method to plot all the components:

```
ax = results.plot()
ax.tight_layout
```

The preceding code will produce five subplots for the observed trend, seasonal_24 (daily), seasonal_168 (weekly), and resid (the remainder) respectively:

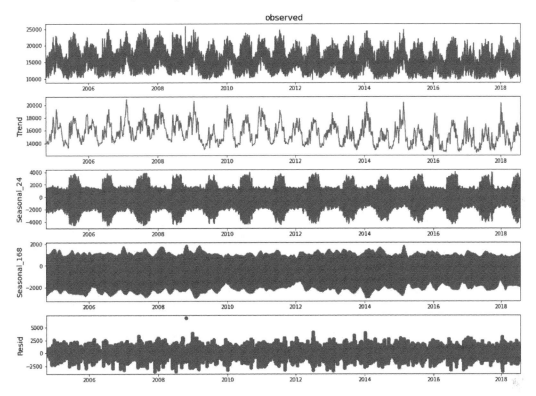

Figure 15.1 – The MSTL decomposition plot for the energy consumption data

Given the amount of data, it is hard to observe the extracted patterns. Slice the data to zoom in for a better visual perspective.

6. Generally, you would expect a daily pattern where energy consumption peaks during the day and declines at nighttime. Additionally, you would anticipate a weekly pattern where consumption is higher on weekdays compared to weekends when people travel or go outside more. An annual pattern is also expected, with higher energy consumption peaking in the summer than in other cooler months.

   Slice the data and plot the components individually. Start with the daily seasonal pattern:

```
fig, ax = plt.subplots(2, 1, figsize=(16, 6))
(results.seasonal['seasonal_24']
        .loc['2016-01-04':'2016-01-06']
```

```
            .plot(ax=ax[0],
                  title='Daily Seasonality in January'))
(results.seasonal['seasonal_24']
          .loc['2016-07-04':'2016-07-06']
          .plot(ax=ax[1],
                  title='Daily Seasonality in July'))
fig.tight_layout(); plt.show()
```

The preceding code will show two subplots – 3 days in `January` (Monday–Wednesday) and 3 days in `July` (Monday–Wednesday):

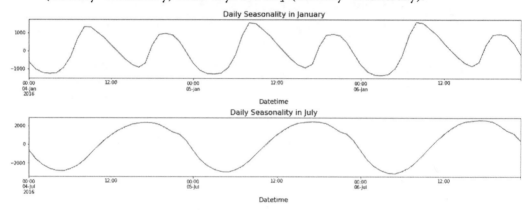

Figure 15.2 – Daily pattern in January compared to July

There is a repeating pattern of peaks during the day, which declines as it gets closer to the evening. Note that in the summertime, the daily pattern changes. For example, the daily pattern is similar in July, except the peak during the day is extended longer into later in the evening, possibly due to air conditioners being used at night before the weather cools down a little.

7. Perform a similar slice for the weekly seasonal pattern:

```
# mask = results.seasonal.index.month==7
fig, ax = plt.subplots(2, 1, figsize=(16, 6))
(results.seasonal['seasonal_168']
          .loc['2016-01-04':'2016-01-10']
          .plot(ax=ax[0],
                  title='Weekly Seasonality in January'))
(results.seasonal['seasonal_168']
          .loc['2016-07-04':'2016-07-10']
          .plot(ax=ax[1],
```

```
                  title='Weekly Seasonality in July'))
    fig.tight_layout(); plt.show()
```

The preceding code should produce a similar plot to Figure 15.2, displaying the entire first week in January 2016 (Monday–Sunday) and July 2016 (Monday–Sunday). There is a noticeable pattern of highs during weekdays that slowly decays during the weekend. During July, the sharper drop in the weekend is possibly due to people enjoying outdoor activities. You can review the plots in the accompanying Jupyter Notebook.

Overall, the results (from daily and weekly) suggest an annual influence indicative of an annual seasonal pattern. In the There's more section, you will explore how you can expose this annual pattern (to capture repeating patterns every July as an example).

How it works...

MSTL is a simple and intuitive algorithm for decomposing time series data with multiple seasonal patterns.

The parameter `iterate` in MSTL defaults to `iterate=2`, which is the number of iterations the algorithm uses to estimate the seasonal components. At each iteration, the algorithm applies the STL algorithm to estimate the seasonal component for each seasonal period identified.

There's more...

You will update windows to `[121, 121]` for each seasonal component in the following code. The default values for `windows` are `[11, 15]`. The default value for `iterate` is 2, and you will update it to 5.

```
mstl = MSTL(df, periods=(24, 24*7), iterate=4, windows=[121,
121])
results = mstl.fit()
```

You can use the same code from previous section to plot the daily and weekly components. You will notice that the output is smoother due to the `windows` parameter (increased). The `windows` parameter accepts integer values to represent the length of the seasonal smoothers for each component. The values must be odd integers. The `iterate` determines the number of iterations to improve on the seasonal components.

See also

To learn more about the MSTL implementation, you can visit the official documentation here: `https://www.statsmodels.org/devel/generated/statsmodels.tsa.seasonal.MSTL.html`.

Forecasting with multiple seasonal patterns using the Unobserved Components Model (UCM)

In the previous recipe, you were introduced to MSTL to decompose a time series with multiple seasonality. Similarly, the **Unobserved Components Model (UCM)** is a technique that decomposes a time series (with multiple seasonal patterns), but unlike MSTL, the UCM is also a forecasting model. Initially, the UCM was proposed as an alternative to the ARIMA model and introduced by Harvey in the book *Forecasting, structural time series models and the Kalman filter,* first published in 1989.

Unlike an ARIMA model, the UCM decomposes a time series process by *estimating* its components and does not make assumptions regarding stationarity or distribution. Recall, an ARIMA model uses differencing (the d order) to make a time series stationary.

There are situations where making a time series stationary – for example, through differencing – is not achievable. The time series can also contain irregularities and other complexities. This is where the UCM comes in as a more flexible and interpretable model.

The UCM is based on the idea of latent variables or unobserved components of a time series, such as level, trend, and seasonality. These can be estimated from the observed variable.

In statsmodels, the `UnobservedComponents` class decomposes a time series into a trend component, a seasonal component, a cyclical component, and an irregular component or error term. The equation can be generalized as the following:

$$y_t = \mu_t + \gamma_t + c_t + \epsilon_t$$

Here, y_t is the observed variable at time t, and u_t, γ_t, c_t represent the trend, seasonal, and cyclical components. The ϵ_t term is the irregular component (or disturbance). You can have multiple seasons as well. The main idea in the UCM is that each component, called **state**, is modeled in a probabilistic manner, since they are unobserved. The UCM can also contain autoregressive and regression components to capture their effects.

How to do it...

In this recipe, you will use the UCM implementation in statsmodels. You will use the same energy dataset loaded in the *Technical requirements* section. In the *Decomposing time series with multiple seasonal patterns using MSTL* recipe, you were able to decompose the seasonal pattern into daily, weekly, and yearly components. You will use this knowledge in this recipe:

1. Start by importing the `UnobservedComponents` class:

    ```
    from statsmodels.tsa.statespace.structural import
    UnobservedComponents
    ```

2. You will use the UCM model to forecast one month ahead. You will hold out one month to validate the model, and you will split the data to train and test sets accordingly:

    ```
    train = df.iloc[:-month]
    test = df.iloc[-month:]
    ```

3. You can plot the data to see the train and test splits:

    ```
    ax = train.iloc[-year:].plot(style='k-', alpha=0.45)
    test.plot(ax=ax, style='k')
    ```

    The preceding code will display a time series split, one year's worth of hourly energy usage data from the train set, followed by one month of usage from the test set.

4. `UnobservedComponents` takes several parameters. Of interest is `freq_seasonal`, which takes a dictionary for each frequency-domain seasonal component – for example, daily, weekly, and annually. You will pass a list of key-value pairs for each period. Optionally, within each dictionary, you can also pass a key-value pair for harmonics. If no harmonic values are passed, then the default would be the `np.floor(period/2)`:

    ```
    params = {'level':'dtrend',
              'irregular':True,
              'freq_seasonal':[{'period': day},
                              {'period': week},
                              {'period': year}],
              'stochastic_freq_seasonal':[False, False, False]}
    model = UnobservedComponents(train, **params)
    ```

You can now fit the model on the training data using the `fit` method:

```
results = model.fit()
```

By default, the `fit` method uses the `lbfgs` solver.

5. Once training is complete, you can view the model's summary using the `summary` method:

```
results.summary()
```

The `results` objects is of type `UnobservedComponentsResultsWrapper`, which gives access to several properties and methods, such as `plot_components` and `plot_diagnostics`, to name a few.

6. `plot_diagnostics` is used to diagnose the model's overall performance against the residuals:

```
fig = results.plot_diagnostics(figsize=(14, 6))
fig.tight_layout()
```

The preceding code should produce 2 x 2 subplots:

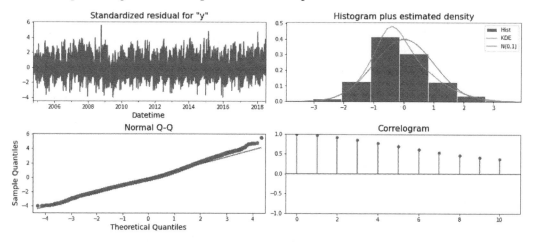

Figure 15.3 – Residual diagnostics plots

7. You can plot the components, which will produce six subplots using the smoothed results – predicted versus observed, the level component, the trend component, seasonal (24), seasonal (168), and seasonal (8772). The plots for freq_ seasonal are too condensed (given the number of observations) to visibly see any pattern for the daily and weekly seasonal components. Instead, you will plot each component individually by slicing the data. For now, use plot_components, but disable the freq_seasonal output, as shown in the following:

```
fig = results.plot_components(figsize=(15, 6),
                              freq_seasonal=False,
                              which='smoothed')
fig.tight_layout()
```

By default, the value for the which parameter is smoothed. This should produce three subplots (excluding the three frequency domains for the seasonal periods, which you will plot in the next step):

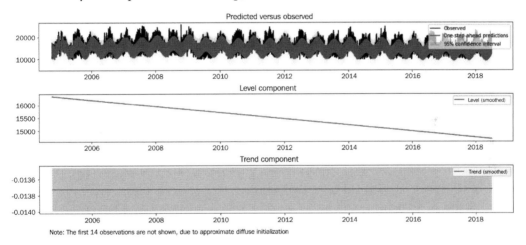

Figure 15.4 – Plot for three components from the UCM model

8. You can access the data behind each component from the results object. For example, you can access freq_seasonal, which should contain a list of three dictionaries, one for each seasonal period, daily, weekly, and yearly, based on what you provided in the key-value pair when you initialized the model (see *Step 4*). Each dictionary contains six outputs or keys, as shown in the following:

```
len(results.freq_seasonal)
>> 3
results.freq_seasonal[1].keys()
```

```
>>
dict_keys(['filtered', 'filtered_cov', 'smoothed',
'smoothed_cov', 'offset', 'pretty_name'])
```

You will plot using the smoothed results for each period, starting with daily.

9. Plot the daily seasonal component. For easier interpretation, slice the data to show 24 hours (1 day):

```
daily = pd.DataFrame(results.freq_seasonal[0]
['smoothed'],
                            index=train.index,
columns=['y']).iloc[:day]
daily['hour_of_day'] = daily.index.strftime(date_format =
'%I:%M:%S %p')
daily.plot(y='y', x='hour_of_day', title='Daily
Seasonality')
```

The preceding code should show a plot representing 24 hours (zoomed in) to focus on the daily pattern. The x-axis ticker labels are formatted to display the time (and **AM/PM**):

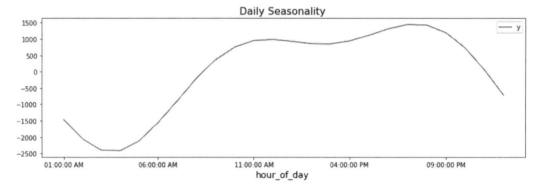

Figure 15.5 – Plotting the daily seasonal component

Note that the spike in energy consumption starts around 11:00 AM, peaking at around 9:00 PM, and then declines during the sleeping time until the following day. We had a similar observation in the previous recipe using MSTL.

10. Plot the weekly component. Similarly, slice the data (zoom in) to show only one week – ideally, Sunday to Sunday – as shown in the following:

```
weekly = pd.DataFrame(results.freq_seasonal[1]
['smoothed'],
                            index=train.index,
```

```
columns=['y']).loc['2004-10-03': '2004-10-10']
weekly['day_name'] = weekly.index.strftime(date_format =
'%A')
weekly.plot(y='y', x='day_name', title='Weekly
Seasonality')
```

The preceding code should produce a plot showing a whole week to observe the weekly seasonal component. The *x*-axis ticker labels will display the day's name to make it easier to compare weekends and weekdays:

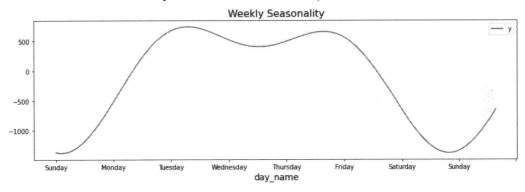

Figure 15.6 – Plotting the weekly seasonal component

Notice the spikes during the weekdays (Monday to Friday), which later dip during the weekend. We had a similar observation in the previous recipe using `MSTL`.

11. Plot the `annual` seasonal component. Similarly, slice the data to show a full year (January to December):

```
annual = pd.DataFrame(results.freq_seasonal[2]
['smoothed'],
                                index=train.index,
columns=['y']).loc['2005']
annual['month'] = annual.index.strftime(date_format =
'%B')
ax = annual.plot(y='y', x='month', title='Annual
Seasonality')
```

The preceding code should produce a plot 1 full year from the yearly seasonal component. The *x*-axis ticker labels will display the month name:

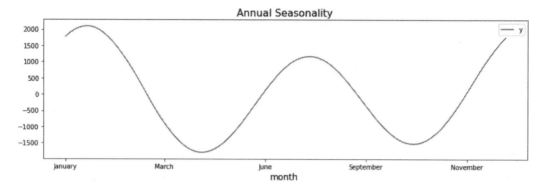

Figure 15.7 – Plotting the yearly seasonal component

Notice the spike in January and another spike from July to August.

12. Finally, use the model to make a prediction and compare it against the out-of-sample set (test data):

```
prediction = results.predict(start=test.index.min(),
                end=test.index.max())
test.plot(style='k--', alpha=0.5)
prediction.plot(style='k')
plt.legend(['Actual', 'Predicted'])
plt.title('Out-of-Sample Forecast: Actual vs Predicted')
```

The preceding code should produce a plot that compares the `test` (actual) values against the predicted:

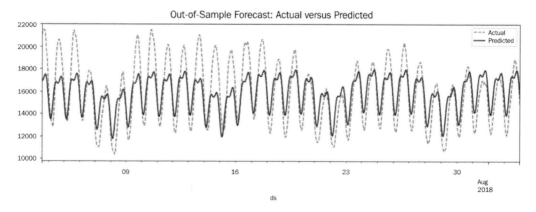

Figure 15.8 – Actual versus predicted using the UCM

13. Calculate the RMSE and RMSPE using the functions imported from statsmodels earlier in the *Technical requirements* section. You will use the scores to compare with other methods:

```
rmspe(test['y'], prediction)
>> 1.0676342700345198
rmse(test['y'], prediction)
>> 1716.1196099493693
```

How it works...

The UCM is a very flexible algorithm that allows for the inclusion of additional models. For example, in the previous recipe, you used 'level':'dtrend', which specifies the use of a *deterministic trend* model, adding the following equations:

$$y_t = \mu_t + \epsilon_t$$

$$\mu_t = \mu_{t-1} + \beta$$

You can specify other model to use either by passing the full name, 'level': 'deterministic trend', or the abbreviated name, 'dtrend'. The statsmodels library provides an extensive list of models that you can specify – for example, 'local linear deterministic trend' or 'lldtrend', 'smooth trend' or 'strend', and 'local linear trend' or 'ltrend'.

For a complete list of all the available models and the associated equations, you can visit the documentation here: https://www.statsmodels.org/dev/generated/statsmodels.tsa.statespace.structural.UnobservedComponents.html#r0058a7c6fc36-1.

Keep in mind that when you provide key-value pairs to the 'freq_seasonal' parameter, each seasonal component is modeled separately.

There's more...

Rerun the same UCM model, but this time, reduce the harmonics to one (1):

```
params = {'level':'dtrend',
          'irregular':True,
          'freq_seasonal':[{'period': day, 'harmonics':1},
                           {'period': week, 'harmonics':1},
                           {'period': year, 'harmonics':1}],
```

```
        'stochastic_freq_seasonal':[False, False, False]}

model = UnobservedComponents(train, **params)
results = model.fit()
```

If you run the component plots, you will notice that all the plots are overly smoothed. This is even more obvious if you plot the predicted values against the test data (the full code is available in the accompanying Jupyter Notebook):

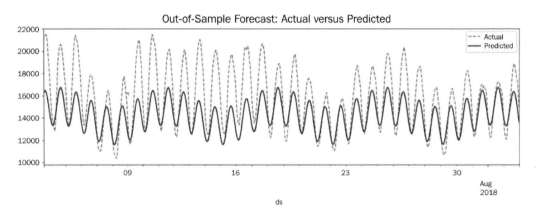

Figure 15.9 – The UCM forecast versus the actual with lower harmonic values

Calculate RMSE and RMSPE and compare against the first UMC model:

```
rmspe(test['y'], prediction)
>> 1.271709112104233
rmse(test['y'], prediction)
>> 2336.3055139809103
```

This model overly generalizes, producing overly smoothed results, making it perform much worse than the first model.

See also

To learn more about the UCM implementation in statsmodels, you can visit the official documentation here:

https://www.statsmodels.org/dev/generated/statsmodels.tsa.statespace.structural.UnobservedComponents.html

Forecasting time series with multiple seasonal patterns using Prophet

You were introduced to Prophet in *Chapter 11, Additional Statistical Modeling Techniques for Time Series*, under the *Forecasting time series data using Facebook Prophet* recipe, using the milk production dataset. The milk production dataset is a monthly dataset with a trend and one seasonal pattern.

The goal of this recipe is to show how you can use Prophet to solve a more complex dataset with multiple seasonal patterns. Preparing time series data for supervised learning is an important step, as shown in *Chapter 12, Forecasting Using Supervised Machine Learning*, and *Chapter 13, Deep Learning for Time Series Forecasting*. Similarly, the feature engineering technique for creating additional features is an important topic when training and improving machine learning and deep learning models. One benefit of using algorithms such as the *UCM* (introduced in the previous recipe) or *Prophet* is that they require little to no data preparation, can work with noisy data, and are easy to interpret. Another advantage is their ability to decompose a time series into its components (`trend` and multiple `seasonal` components).

How to do it...

In this recipe, you will continue using the same energy consumption dataset (the `df` DataFrame) and perform a similar split for the train and test sets. If you recall, in Prophet, you had to reset the index and rename the index and the observed column as `ds` and `y` respectively:

1. Start by importing the `Prophet` library:

    ```
    from prophet import Prophet
    from prophet.plot import add_changepoints_to_plot
    ```

2. You already loaded the dataset into a pandas DataFrame (as `df`) in the *Technical requirements* section. You will need to reset the index and rename the columns to use in *Prophet*. Start by making a copy of the original DataFrame, since you will be using it for other recipes:

    ```
    energy = df.copy()
    energy.reset_index(inplace=True)
    energy.columns = ['ds', 'y']
    ```

3. Split the data into train and test sets using the same split from the previous recipe:

```
train = energy.iloc[:-month]
test = energy.iloc[-month:]
```

4. Fit the model using all default options and have Prophet automatically detect the seasonal components. If you recall, the `train` DataFrame is already set to the `H` frequency:

```
model = Prophet().fit(train)
```

In *Chapter 11, Additional Statistical Modeling Techniques for Time Series*, when you fit the model on the milk data, you got these two messages:

```
INFO:prophet:Disabling weekly seasonality. Run prophet
with weekly_seasonality=True to override this.
INFO:prophet:Disabling daily seasonality. Run prophet
with daily_seasonality=True to override this.
```

The messages indicate that Prophet did not detect weekly or daily seasonal patterns and turned them off. But now, using the energy consumption data, you should not see any message. This indicates Prophet has already identified all three – the daily, weekly, and yearly seasonal patterns.

5. Use the `make_future_dataframe` method to extend the `train` DataFrame forward for a specific number of periods and at a specified frequency. In this case, it will be the number of `test` observations:

```
n = len(test)
future = model.make_future_dataframe(n, freq='H')
```

The frequency is indicated as hourly with `freq='H'`.

6. Use the `predict` method, which takes the `future` DataFrame for making predictions. If you recall, Prophet will make in-sample predictions to cover the entire period from the train set and then extend to future predictions (this will be compared to the out-of-sample test dataset):

```
forecast = model.predict(future)
```

7. Inspect the components using the `plot_components` method:

```
model.plot_components(forecast); plt.show()
```

The preceding code should produce four subplots, representing the trend, weekly, yearly, and daily seasonal trends. The following only shows the `seasonal` components:

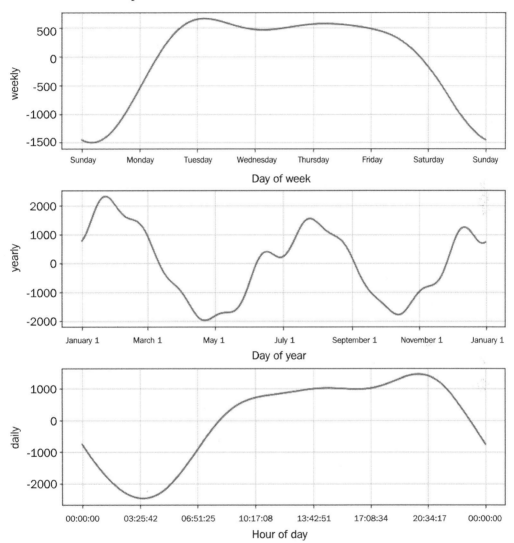

Figure 15.10 – Time series seasonal components automatically detected by Prophet

Compare the seasonal components from Prophet in *Figure 15.10* with those obtained from the UMC (*Figure 15.5*, *Figure 15.6*, and *Figure 15.7*). Overall, the daily and weekly components in *Figure 15.10* look identical to those from the UMC. The difference is in the yearly component; there are more wiggles in *Figure 15.10* when compared to a smoother plot in *Figure 15.7*.

8. The forecast DataFrame contains the predicted values for in-sample and out-of-sample under the `yhat` column. Slice the forecast DataFrame to show only the out-of-sample predictions and compare them with the test set.

    ```
    prediction = forecast.iloc[test.index[0]:].set_
    index('ds')['yhat']
    ```

    You can now use this sliced DataFrames for plotting, similar to the plot created in *Figure 15.8*:

    ```
    test.set_index('ds').plot(style='k--', alpha=0.5)
    prediction.plot(style='k')
    plt.legend(['Actual', 'Predicted'])
    plt.title('Out-of-Sample Forecast: Actual vs Predicted')
    ```

    The preceding code should produce a time series plot showing the actual (test) data against the predicted values from Prophet:

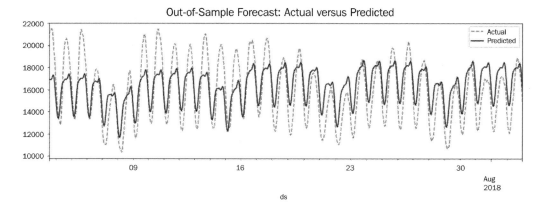

Figure 15.11 – Actual versus Predicted with Prophet

9. Calculate the `RMSE` and `RMSPE` values:

    ```
    rmspe(test['y'].values, prediction.values)
    >> 1.2587190915113151
    rmse(test['y'].values, prediction.values)
    >> 1885.143242946697
    ```

Based on RMSE and RMSPE, the UMC model in *Figure 15.8* performed better than the Prophet model. The UMC scores were `1.0676342700345198` and `1716.1196099493693` for RMSE and RMSPE respectively.

How it works...

Prophet automated many aspects of building and optimizing the model because `yearly_seasonality`, `weekly_seasonality`, and `daily_seasonality` parameters were set to `auto` by default, allowing Prophet to determine which ones to turn on or off based on the data.

So far, you have used Prophet on time series with single seasonality and now again on a time series with multiple seasonality. The process for training a model and making predictions is the same, making Prophet a very appealing option due to its consistent framework.

There's more...

One of the nice things about Prophet is that the algorithm uses *changepoint* detection, and you can display the significant changepoints using the `add_changepoints_to_plot` function. If you recall from *Chapter 11*, *Additional Statistical Modeling Techniques for Time Series*, Prophet initially starts with 25 changepoints, using 80% of the training data:

```
fig = model.plot(forecast, ylabel='Energy Consumption')
add_changepoints_to_plot(fig.gca(), model, forecast,
threshold=0.01)
plt.show()
```

This will show the forecast plot from Prophet with added indicators for the significant changepoints:

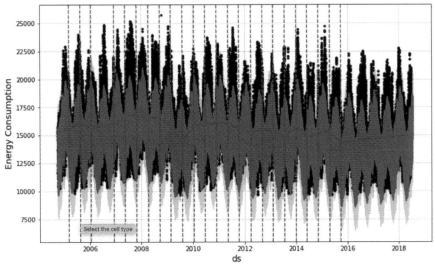

Figure 15.12 – Using Prophet to display the significant changepoints and the forecast

In the `add_changepoints_to_plot` function, the threshold parameter is set to 0.01 (default), and increasing the value will reduce the number of changepoints displayed. Compare the trend line in *Figure 15.12* to the trend component obtained from step 7 (using plot_components)

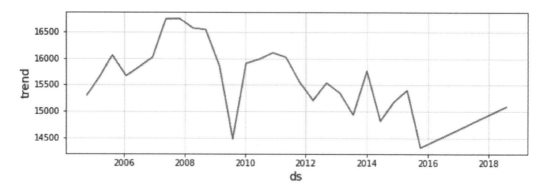

Figure 15.13 – The trend component from Prophet

This aligns with how the piece-wise regression was determined based on the detected changepoints. The inflection points in the trend are based on those changepoints.

See also

Prophet supports both Python and R. For more information on the Python API, visit the documentation here: `https://facebook.github.io/prophet/docs/quick_start.html#python-api`.

Forecasting time series with multiple seasonal patterns using NeuralProphet

NeuralProphet was inspired by the Prophet library and **Autoregressive Neural Network (AR-Net)** to bring a new implementation, leveraging deep neural networks to provide a more scalable solution.

Prophet was built on top of PyStan, a Bayesian inference library, and is one of the main dependencies when installing Prophet. Conversely, NeuralProphet is based on PyTorch and is as used as the deep learning framework. This allows NeuralProphet to scale to larger datasets and generally provides better accuracy than Prophet. Like Prophet's method, NeuralProphet performs hyperparameter tuning and fully automates many aspects of time series forecasting.

In this recipe, you will compare the results using NeuralProphet against Prophet.

Getting ready

It is recommended to create a new virtual Python environment this way, you can install all the required dependencies without any conflicts or issues with your current environment.

If you need a quick refresher on creating a virtual Python environment, check out the *Development environment setup* recipe from *Chapter 1, Getting Started with Time Series Analysis*. The chapter covers two methods – using conda and venv.

The following instructions will show how to create a virtual environment using conda. You can call the environment any name you like – in the following example, we will name our environment neuralprophet:

```
>> conda create -n neuralprophet python=3.9 -y
>> conda activate neuralprophet
>> pip install "neuralprophet[live]"
```

To make the new neuralprophet environment visible within Jupyter, you can run the following code:

```
python -m ipykernel install --user --name neuralprophet
--display-name "NeuralProphet"
```

If you need additional libraries to install – for example, statsmodels – you can use pip:

```
>> pip install statsmodels
```

How to do it...

NeuralProphet makes it easy to transition from Prophet, as they follow a very similar framework for training the model:

1. Start by importing the library:

    ```
    from neuralprophet import NeuralProphet
    ```

2. You will use the same `energy` dataset created in the *Forecasting time series with multiple seasonal patterns using Prophet* recipe. Instead of splitting the dataset into train and test sets, you will split into train, validation, and test sets. The validation set will be used during the training process to evaluate at every epoch:

```
energy = df.copy()
energy.reset_index(inplace=True)
energy.columns = ['ds', 'y']
train = energy.iloc[:-month*2]
val = energy.iloc[-month*2:-month]
test = energy.iloc[-month:]
```

This is a similar approach taken in *Chapter 13, Deep Learning for Time Series Forecasting*.

3. You will create an instance of the NeuralProphet class with default parameters. You will use the `fit` method, passing both the `train` and `val` sets:

```
m = NeuralProphet()
metrics = m.fit(train, validation_df=val)
```

4. Similar to Prophet, you will use the `make_future_dataframe` method to extend the `train` DataFrame forward for a specific number of periods and at a specified frequency. In this case, it will be the total number of `test` and `val` observations:

```
n = len(test)+len(val)
future = m.make_future_dataframe(df=train, periods=n)
forecast = m.predict(df=future)
```

5. You plot the components using the `plot_components` method:

```
fig = m.plot_components(forecast)
```

This should produce four subplots for trend and one for each seasonal pattern (daily, weekly, and yearly). The following only shows the seasonal components:

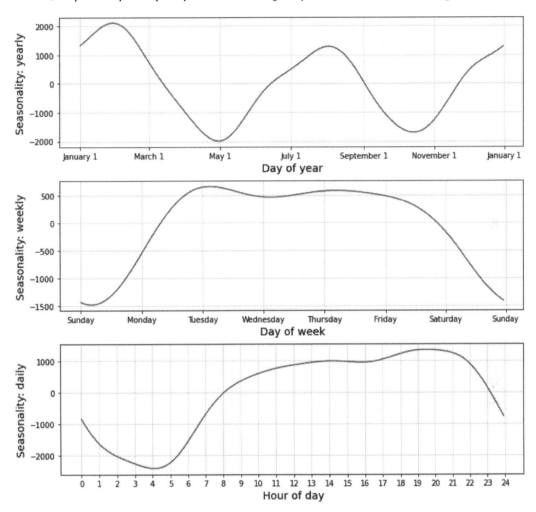

Figure 15.14 – The time series seasonal components automatically detected by NeuralProphet

6. NeuralProphet provides the `plot_parameters` method, which gives more insight into the individual coefficients for the significant changepoints – for example, trend changepoints:

```
fig = m.plot_parameters()
```

This should display a similar plot to *Figure 15.14* but with more insight into the trend behavior. The following only shows the trend component:

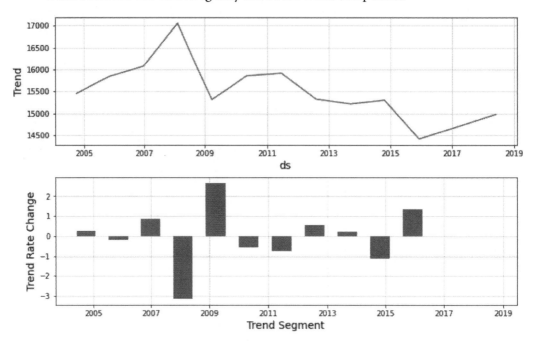

Figure 15.15 – Trend changepoints affecting the overall trend

7. Compare the out-of-sample prediction values with the test dataset:

```
prediction = forecast.set_index('ds').loc['2018-07-03
14:00:00':]['yhat1']
test.set_index('ds').plot(style='k--', alpha=0.5)
prediction.plot(style='k')
plt.legend(['Actual', 'Predicted'])
plt.title('Out-of-Sample Forecast: Actual vs Predicted')
```

This should produce a plot similar to *Figure 15.11*:

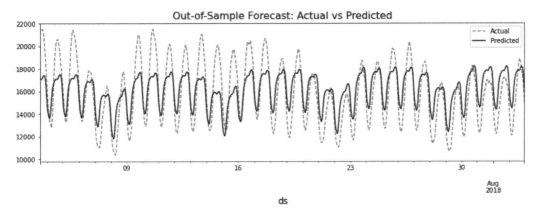

Figure 15.16 – Actual versus Predicted with NeuralProphet

Compare *Figure 15.16* with *Figure 15.11*. They look similar, which is why you will need to capture some metrics to quantify the performance and make it easier to compare the two models.

8. Calculate both RMSE and RMSPE:

```
from statsmodels.tools.eval_measures import rmse, rmspe
rmspe(test['y'].values, prediction.values)
>> 1.1729025662066894
rmse(test['y'].values, prediction.values)
>> 1796.2832495706689
```

Overall, both RMSE and RMSPE for NeuralProphet indicate that the model outperforms Prophet.

How it works...

Similar to Prophet, NeuralProphet also decomposes a time series into its components. NeuralProphet can include different terms such as **trend**, **seasonality**, **autoregression** (the n_lags parameter), **special events** (the add_events method), **future regressors** (exogenous variables with the add_future_regressor method), and **lagged regressors** (the add_lagged_regressor method). The autoregression piece is based on AR-Net, an autoregressive neural network. NeuralProphet allows you to add recurring special events – for example, a Superbowl game or a birthday. The time series modeling process is similar to that in Prophet, which was made by design. Keep in mind that NeuralProphet was built from the ground up, leveraging PyTorch, and is not a wrapper to Prophet.

There's more...

NeuralProphet offers flexibility and extensibility (and is very modular for anyone that wants to extend its capabilities). The library also provides additional features tailored to working with deep neural networks, such as logging performance, cross-validation, spitting data, benchmarking, and experimentation.

Let's explore some of these features.

You can change the learning rate when you first initialize the model, and use the `split_df` method to split data into train and test sets. You can also specify a holdout portion (a percentage from the train set) to be used for validation on each epoch:

```
m = NeuralProphet(learning_rate = 0.1)
train, test = m.split_df(df=energy, freq="H", valid_p=0.2)
train_results = m.fit(df=train, freq="H")
```

The validation is set at 20% (`0.2`) of the training set. Using the `test` method, you can get the scores against the test set:

```
test_results = m.test(df=test)
print(test_results)
>>

SmoothL1Loss        MAE           RMSE
0       0.013963   1375.211322   1707.669455
```

`train_results` contains the scores for each epoch. You can instruct `NeuralProphet` to plot these:

```
m = NeuralProphet(learning_rate = 0.1)
train, test = m.split_df(df=energy, freq="H", valid_p=0.2)
metrics = m.fit(df=train, freq="H", validation_df=test,
progress="plot")
```

This will refresh the plot on each iteration so that you can see how the model is learning during the fitting (training) process. This way, you do not have to wait until the training is complete. The following is a snapshot during training:

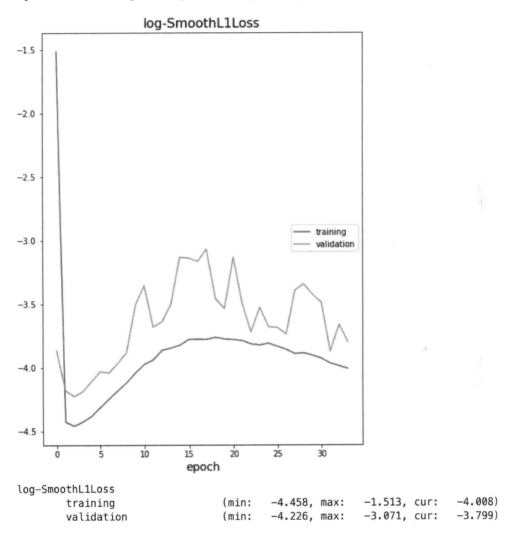

```
log-SmoothL1Loss
        training            (min:   -4.458, max:   -1.513, cur:   -4.008)
        validation          (min:   -4.226, max:   -3.071, cur:   -3.799)
```

Figure 15.17 – NeuralProphet allows you to visualize performance while training

Once training is complete (in this case, at the 57 epoch), the plot will show the final output at all epochs. You can print the last row, as shown in the following code block:

```
metrics.tail(1)
>>
SmoothL1Loss             MAE        RMSE  RegLoss  SmoothL1Loss_
val  \
57      0.010846  1198.940338  1553.954677       0.0
0.013929


         MAE_val      RMSE_val
57   1372.159271  1705.552796
```

See also

To learn more about NeuralProphet, you can reference the official documentation here: https://neuralprophet.com/html/contents.html.

Index

W

Y

Z

Packt.com

Subscribe to our online digital library for full access to over 7,000 books and videos, as well as industry leading tools to help you plan your personal development and advance your career. For more information, please visit our website.

Why subscribe?

- Spend less time learning and more time coding with practical eBooks and Videos from over 4,000 industry professionals

- Improve your learning with Skill Plans built especially for you

- Get a free eBook or video every month

- Fully searchable for easy access to vital information

- Copy and paste, print, and bookmark content

Did you know that Packt offers eBook versions of every book published, with PDF and ePub files available? You can upgrade to the eBook version at packt.com and as a print book customer, you are entitled to a discount on the eBook copy. Get in touch with us at customercare@packtpub.com for more details.

At www.packt.com, you can also read a collection of free technical articles, sign up for a range of free newsletters, and receive exclusive discounts and offers on Packt books and eBooks.

Other Books You May Enjoy

If you enjoyed this book, you may be interested in these other books by Packt:

Time Series Analysis on AWS

Michaël Hoarau

ISBN: 9781801816847

- Understand how time series data differs from other types of data
- Explore the key challenges that can be solved using time series data
- Forecast future values of business metrics using Amazon Forecast
- Detect anomalies and deliver forewarnings using Lookout for Equipment
- Detect anomalies in business metrics using Amazon Lookout for Metrics
- Visualize your predictions to reduce the time to extract insights

Hands-On Data Preprocessing in Python

Roy Jafari

ISBN: 9781801072137

- Use Python to perform analytics functions on your data
- Understand the role of databases and how to effectively pull data from databases
- Perform data preprocessing steps defined by your analytics goals
- Recognize and resolve data integration challenges
- Identify the need for data reduction and execute it
- Detect opportunities to improve analytics with data transformation

Packt is searching for authors like you

If you're interested in becoming an author for Packt, please visit `authors.packtpub.com` and apply today. We have worked with thousands of developers and tech professionals, just like you, to help them share their insight with the global tech community. You can make a general application, apply for a specific hot topic that we are recruiting an author for, or submit your own idea.

Share Your Thoughts

Now you've finished *Time Series Analysis with Python Cookbook*, we'd love to hear your thoughts! Scan the QR code below to go straight to the Amazon review page for this book and share your feedback or leave a review on the site that you purchased it from.

https://packt.link/r/1-801-07554-9

Your review is important to us and the tech community and will help us make sure we're delivering excellent quality content.

Made in the USA
Las Vegas, NV
19 September 2022

55575187R00345